❊ by David T. Bazelon

THE PAPER ECONOMY
POWER IN AMERICA: The Politics of the New Class
NOTHING BUT A FINE TOOTH COMB

NOTHING BUT A FINE TOOTH COMB

❊ Essays in
Social Criticism,
1944–1969

by David T. Bazelon

SIMON AND SCHUSTER   *New York*

FIRST PRINTING

SBN 671–20467–X Clarion
SBN 671–20335–5 Trade
Library of Congress Catalog Card Number: 74–84116
Designed by Irving Perkins
Manufactured in the United States of America

ACKNOWLEDGMENTS

Many of the articles and essays in this book originally appeared in magazines or other media. Permission to reprint the following pieces is gratefully acknowledged.

"Rediscovery of America: *America and Cosmic Man*, by Wyndham Lewis," reprinted courtesy of *Partisan Review*; copyright 1949 by *Partisan Review*.
"It's All There: *Statistical Abstract of the United States: 1959*," reprinted courtesy of *The Reporter*; copyright © 1959 by *The Reporter*.
"Financial Parochialism: *The National Wealth of the United States in the Postwar Period*, by Raymond Goldsmith," reprinted from *Commentary* by permission; copyright © 1963 by the American Jewish Committee.
"Non-Rule in America," reprinted from *Commentary* by permission; copyright © 1963 by the American Jewish Committee.
"Kennedy and After," reprinted with permission from *The New York Review of Books*; copyright © 1963 by *The New York Review*.
"Eleanor Roosevelt, 1884–1962," reprinted courtesy of Columbia Records; originally appeared as album copy for the Columbia Records production of "Eleanor Roosevelt: My Husband and I."
"Evolution of a Leviathan: *Behemoth: The Structure and Practice of National Socialism, 1933–1944*, by Franz Neumann" originally appeared in *Contemporary Jewish Record*; copyright 1945 by the American Jewish Committee.
"The Efficacy of Madness: *The Goebbels Diaries, 1942–1943*, edited by Louis P. Lochner," reprinted from *The New Leader* by permission; copyright 1948 by The American Labor Conference on International Affairs, Inc.
"Trotsky: The Hero as Symbol," reprinted from *Dissent* by permission; copyright © 1959 by *Dissent*.
"The Kids and the Cockers," reprinted from *Dissent* by permission; copyright © 1965 by *Dissent*.
"It Don't Pay to Kill the Ruling Class," reprinted from *Review of Existential Psychology and Psychiatry*; copyright © 1968 by *Review of Existential Psychology and Psychiatry*.

❊ DEDICATION

*To the past-memory of my father;
and the future-memory of my son.*

CONTENTS

❊ Bill Bailey, Won't You Please Come Home?

It was on one Monday morning,
The sun was shining fine,
The lady love of old Bill Bailey
Was hanging clothes on the line
In her back yard, and crying hard;

She'd married a B&O brakeman
Who'd up'd and throwed her down,
Bellering like a prune-fed calf,
With the freight-gang hanging around,
And to this crowd, she cried out loud:

Won't you come home, Bill Bailey,
Won't you come home?
She cried the whole night long.
I'll do the cooking, honey,
I'll pay the rent:
I know I've done you wrong.

Remember that rainy evening
I throwed you out,
With nothing but a fine tooth comb?
I know I'm to blame; well, ain't that a shame?
Bill Bailey, won't you please come home?

—HUGHIE CANNON (1902)

PREFACE

THIS COLLECTION is a kind of autobiography. There is no good reason to indulge autobiography except on the conviction that one's personal events stand for something that is, or should be, of general interest. I do have this conviction; but my having it cannot make it true or useful for others. My life as presented in my writing stands for something only if you agree that it does.

I take this risk because I am now old enough to be especially concerned about the generational passage. In fact, it is lately always in my thoughts. A few years after I became the father of a son, my own father died; and youth around the world began their newest moves. I found that I was unable to give all the loving care to my son that I had never forgiven my father for not giving me. Him dead and me a father, I forgave him. But that was a bare beginning, since now I know that fathers are only people like me. So I believe in the importance of personal history in this country where so often it substitutes for tradition—and I have not yet forgiven my father for sharing so little of his with me. He had only patches of traditional heritage to offer; and I fear that I have none for my son, except what may be implicit in my literary career.

It is my view, of course, that there is value in the writing collected here. But there is something more, I feel, than the quality or remaining utility of any individual piece of writing. There is the quarter-century example of a particular intellectual and literary effort, in the time and manner in which it occurred—an example that is now a fatherhood fact of sorts for the new generation, if it chooses to accept it as such. So, short of writing a real autobiography, I have attempted here and there in this book to indicate the character of my career, as a setting for the presentation of my work.

America is an eccentric country—and I claim appropriateness for the eccentricity of my career, and its use in presenting this collection of my work. There are no traditions in this country so good that everyone must submit to one or another of them. Many of us are unavoidably self-created. I have participated in several intellectual traditions, have benefited from each, and have felt finally at home in none. So I was never an authoritative writer in the sense that the source or certification added much to any sentence of mine—including the times when I might reasonably have posed as one. Always my effort has been speculative and suggestive—even if speaking, occasionally, in a loud firm voice.

In *The Tradition of the New*, Harold Rosenberg most effectively characterizes the weird role of our traditions. After quoting Crèvecoeur—"The American is a new man," etc.—he recalls an image of Braddock's defeat: "the Redcoats marching abreast through the woods, while from behind trees and rocks naked Indians and coonskinned trappers pick them off with musket balls." The Redcoats were defeated in the New World, he suggests, by their superior knowledge of warfare. "The difficulty of the Redcoats was that they were in the wrong place. . . . In honor of the dream-defeated Braddock, I call the hallucination of the displaced terrain, originating in style, Redcoatism." Then he suggests that Crèvecoeur was too sanguine in his discovery of the American's newness: "To be a new man is not a condition but an effort. . . ." He completes his image by saying, "In honor of Braddock's foes I call this anti-formal or trans-formal effort Coonskinism. . . . Coonskinism is the search for the principle that applies, even if it applies only once. For it, each situation has its own exclusive key." Thus, Coonskinism is the self-contradictory "tradition of the new."

I was a self-conscious Coonskinner from the beginning, as were many others like me but who gave up writing, never got down to it, or died young. Maybe with this book I can exemplify us, not exactly to excuse, explain, or try to make lovable, but just to put it on the record (as we used to say in one of my other professions). It might be salutary for the New Youth to know that this kind of cultural freebooting—as well as traditional Ph.D.-ism at the university and mindless anti-intellectuality back home—is part of their fatherhood heritage. (*But beware:* a new man is a new man, not someone who imitates a used-to-be new man.)

I'll go a little further: It might be salutary, for everyone concerned, to remind even those of my own generation who marched in Redcoat file that there were Coonskinners behind the library stacks —and *bang!* you're dead.

Washington, D.C.   D.T.B.
February 1969

INTRODUCTION

A Writer Between Generations

I CAME to New York in the fall of 1943 to make my way as a writer. A couple of years later, I thought I had. After that, doubts as to the whole endeavor accumulated; but so did the writing. Now, a quarter of a century has passed, and I have published a half-million words "in the best places"—which is what I like to tell people who seem to be questioning my existence. But whatever I tell people, the fact is that I, too, question my existence; and, for me, the half-million words are no answer.

Anyway, here is a representative selection of them.

But I am plagued by the question of what they are no answer to. Stated differently, why did I do with my life what I did by bothering to write them—why did it seem so compellingly important at the time? Thus, my purpose in publishing this collection is not merely to create another one-volume calling card; rather, to confront the essential fact of having been the particular kind of writing intellectual I have been ever since that early September day when I was twenty and walked out of Grand Central Station into all my now-known tomorrows.

I was met by my college pal, Calder Willingham, who has since gotten rich writing good movies and better novels. In those days, Calder was just poor and eager and wild and daring—as, come to think of it, who was not? We had planned to leave school and meet in New York, thus to repeat the proven career-pattern of James T. Farrell, with whom we were both corresponding (I suspect that Farrell has written millions of words of advice to young writers over the years, including—as with me—which of the forty-odd volumes of

Balzac's *La Comédie Humaine* to read first). I was on that classic thin gold-thread from home, after my getaway money ran out; but Calder scrounged and bellhopped and borrowed. I think I was envious, in a way: the list of odd jobs on the dust jacket of your first novel was, in those days, the equivalent of a graduate degree.

Calder and I had some excitement setting out in life and discovering New York and so on—we lived in a rooming house on 58th Street near Sixth Avenue, a cultural beginner's neighborhood, and luckily stumbled upon a nest of female dance students—before he left town for jobs like putting out a camp newspaper in Georgia and bellhopping in Beverly Hills. But mostly what happened to me in New York was that I looked up Isaac Rosenfeld a few days after I arrived. Like me (and Farrell), Isaac was from Chicago. Young men from the provinces; as I recall, there was a lot of that in Balzac.

In many ways, Isaac was a very exceptional person. Exceptionally talented as a literary stylist and talker and performer (his imitations of friends were hilarious) and scene-maker and general doer. But, most exceptional of all, with him you could take your own life seriously, any part of it you wanted, and he would really help—he really wanted to help. That was the great novelist in him that never got squared away, never got down to writing novels. (He died young, after writing a pretty good standard Ph.D.-type family background novel and, for No. 2, a wild one called *The General*, written at the height of the Kafka wave and, in its ebb, not published.) All of Isaac's good friends, including myself, believed that he could and would one day write a great comic novel—maybe like Gogol—about Village intellectual life. That is, about us. With hindsight, I see now that we believed this so deeply not simply because of his unquestioned talent, but also because he had done so much, as a novelist merely marking time, to create the serio-comic scene he would one day memorialize. (We were all so devoted to The Word that each of us was willing to take his lumps, personally, in the course of its grand realization—unlike the inhabitants of some other Peyton Places.)

Anyway, Isaac introduced me to people—indeed, through him I met most of the population of my future life in New York, both the famous and the merely significant. He was a *center*; and his utterly undistinguished apartment on Barrow Street was a *meeting-place*. Isaac had come to New York—perhaps in 1940—to study philosophy with Sidney Hook (I think); anyway, the Chicago Writers'

Project of the WPA had folded, spreading unemployed talent, including his, in all directions. By that time, however, there were nearly jobs (that brief hiatus after WPA released, and before OWI saved, an important segment of mankind) and Isaac had occupied one on the trade journal *Ice Cream World*. When I got to New York, he had already advanced in his editing-for-eating career to an Editorial Position with the *New Republic*. It was still a shame and a disgrace to work for the *New Republic*—because they had defended the Moscow Trials, and hadn't exactly done everything else right either—but what the hell, a job was a job, even if it was high class.

But, more important, Isaac was writing for *Partisan Review*—and only a year or two away from becoming their *shoyne boychick* of the newer generation. *Partisan Review*, originally the literary/political magazine of the New York John Reed Club (stolen from that Communist party front-organization at the time and because of the Moscow Trials), was then vitally engaged in becoming the major cultural influence it intended to become (and used to be).

To characterize as much history as the PR Grouping represented, in one or two sentences, is at least impossible; so I will take three or four. First of all, the unplaced talent that for a while found a place there: it would take too long to mention all the important names, but just a few years ago the two current major novels were written by graduates, Mary McCarthy and Saul Bellow (each of whom was firmly identified with the Grouping, from the beginning of his and her career, not merely passing through). Besides people, there was The Issue: to integrate literary modernism and the best in Marxist thought, thus to build yet another immigrant beachhead on the American shore. And The Method: *chutzpah*—directed against the established academy, on both Marxist and modernist grounds. And, finally, The Ethnic: everybody was Jewish, or acting that way—especially including Mary McCarthy and Dwight Macdonald, our most distinguished *goyim*. (It was a necessary badge of dishonor.) The PR Grouping served for its time as a great market-place of sensibility; a highly significant *ad hoc* or street university; and, all in all, one of our better European imports.

Isaac's gang—especially his boyhood pals, Oscar Tarcov and Saul Bellow, as well as some University of Chicago classmates—were known as the Chicago Dostoyevskians. Through them, an important provincial connection with the metropolitan center was established. I guess I was the last of the travelers from Chicago to join in. Anyway, I was always The Kid, the youngest by five years and more. And Isaac Rosenfeld, perhaps the brightest burned-out star of them all, provided me with a whole new life in the literary capital. He had me writing a book review for the *New Republic* within a few days of my arrival in New York and not much later sent me around to see Dwight Macdonald who, in a breakaway from the reduced political emphasis of *Partisan Review*, was then getting ready to publish *Politics*—which became the only high-level critical voice during the remainder of the War.

The Big What that Isaac was connected with in New York was— to The Kid from Chicago—an astoundingly bright new world, filled with Jews of marvelous variety: like a supermarket kind of candy-store, with versions of heritage, row-upon-row, freely to be chosen from: candy-daddies in shapes and sizes only later to be reckoned with. Yes, I was looking for a father—and I found them.

I was second-generation; they were not. It took me nearly twenty years to come to terms with the fact: to have elaborated it at the time would have been substantially inauthentic. (It still is.) I know a great deal about light mulattoes calling themselves "black."

A couple of years ago I ran into a woman I had known in those early days—an authentic Bronx intellectual who in fact has since become something of a Jewish scholar. We had barely exchanged pleasantries when a special greedy smile appeared (after long study, I now know what this bit of intellectual femininity means: *I am going to eat you alive—wait a minute, as soon as I find the horseradish*), and she remarked, "For crissake, when did you become so Jewish?" I tried to explain how it happened, but she wasn't having any. "Come on, you had a clear midwestern accent; you didn't know a word of Yiddish; you can't fool me—I remember it." See? Already I was "fooling" her. So, before she had a chance to explain my anti-Semitism to me, I smiled sheepishly, etc. (which, after equally long study, means: *Lady, you'll never find the horseradish*).

I am a self-created, phony Jew. I admit it—that is, I am willing and I still try, occasionally, to admit it. No-go: the best I get is a forgiving glance. Gentiles think I am trying to "pass" in an unacceptably primitive fashion; Jews with genuine ethnicity in their upbringing are nonplused, and simply deal with my implausible chatter as best they can. The only ones who understand and sympathize are the two or three second-generation Jews who have done what I did

—and the numerous intellectual Gentiles who were tempted to do it.

It took years of effort to create this absurd condition. When it finally began to bore me a while back, however, I found that it was ineradicable. The me-inside-me I talk to all day long no longer had the youthful daring to learn to speak naked American (and, being a writer, I certainly could not fetter or forego that essential me-to-me conversation). Also, thinking further about the matter, I realized that my artificial and amateurish *Yiddishkeit* was only one of many similar efforts I have made on my father's behalf. He was so busy being an American, don't blame him. *He knew! What did he know?* (As his own father might have said.)

What led me into this endeavor, apart from my own ambition and the loud voices of my friends, was my startled reading of Sartre's *Qu'est-ce que le juif?* when I was too young and too logical to resist it. Such a brilliant *goy!* He convinced me that I faced the iron choice of existing as an authentic or as an inauthentic Jew. Loaded at the time with *chutzpah*, I went for the jugular. And that's how I became such a fraud.

I try on occasion to admit that I am a phony Jew; but I refuse to apologize for it. The reason is that I have been living out this special life of mine in America, and here the Jew-as-metaphor—born, created, or merely borrowed—is peculiarly appropriate. Jews everywhere have always been Somebody Else: that was the Big Thing that God laid on them. And since (*really*) so many people in America were almost Somebody Else, anyone trained to the role was clearly starting ahead of the crowd—even if type-cast. There is no question: When the Jew and America came together, something very special happened.

The Jews were *it*—rather than some other ethnic grouping—because something weird in that multi-millennial training stint of theirs set them up superbly for the mad American dash for Success. Unfortunately, it also set them up for the three other recent forms of their self-destruction (as an historical entity): the special European death, which will haunt humanity forevermore; the equally modern transformation in Israel where all-of-a-sudden a Jew is known and identified by his nationalistic love of shovels and test-tubes; and the rather more traditional social death in the Soviet Union (which happened before in Spain). But in America they were massacred by Success: what money-making missed, the culture-business got. My father, who failed, died of bitter embarrassment. In fact and finally, however, he spanned the generations: having flopped in plastic novelties and music boxes, at death's door he had a hit in modern educational materials.

The Jews were it, but not just the Jews: it has been reported on good authority that Mike Quill's brogue was well rehearsed and retained. The talented Mario Puzo, I am certain, will one day write a whole book illustrating the over-all point with an Italian accent. Why not? It's an *American* story. With the Jews, however, there was more new-identity eagerness and capacity: after all, we had Al Jolson, Hollywood, sociology, General Sarnoff, and a substantial hunk of middle-management advertising—and that's leaving out the Sephardim and the fancy Germans from before the Civil War. Who else from steerage can claim that good? It all began with Show Biz-out-of-Seventh-Ave.; and went from there to the Intellectual sons. And, as I indicated, so quick in some instances—and the fathers so preoccupied—that the sons had to concoct traditions the same way sexual knowledge was gained: on the street. We made do with a "sense of being Jewish"—basic training in ferocious effort, which of course required an underlying literacy in the traditional language of that people's disaster (even if taught in English). The point is that America called forth that effort; which effort could well utilize the contradictions and complexities of that supporting "language of the Jews."

So, to begin with, I became a *Jewish* intellectual—even if I had to scramble some to get there.

Here is my big point, merely introduced by the foregoing *Yiddish-keit* story: we are a communityless nation. For almost all Americans, *community is either a current principle frantically held, or an ethnic memory similarly treasured* (or, in my case, manufactured). The factual America, now, is a mess of job-oriented consumers—who hardly know what they are doing, much less remember where they came from—enjoying merely spatial contiguity. (For national modern use, the WASP small town—our only home-grown whisper of community—is an ethnic memory just like Minsk: in fact, a museum-piece.) Community here is even less traditional than marriage, which indeed has been recruited, in a burst of hysteria, to substitute for same: wherever and however, community is for us an act of will and imagination; and, after that, mere fashion and bad habit and TV. *So little of substance outside the media* (and other similarity of life based on product-use) *and the job* (and other shared formative experiences like college, the army, the gang) *is given to us that all of it can be classed as debris more or less useful in our determined and forward-looking community-creation.* The only American community we really believe in and accept is that of The Successful. This belief works, however, only for those who persist in seeing themselves as failures. For the anointed ones, this Believed Community is a grisly parody of the real, friendly thing. In the end, our community of the Successful is merely a further invitation to greater consumption and accompanying self-celebration—the really American way, the power to command the celebrity-goodies of life (as if that were the whole story), and the powerlessness to deal with life effectively in any other way.

Community according to shared principle is the coming thing, as ethnic memories fade. We are now experiencing a runaway politicalizing of that trend. This kind of sloganeering effort at community is so utterly American—deriving so obviously from the slogan-culture of media advertising—that the blatant anti-Americanism of those leading the parade seems weirdly similar to Jewish or other ethnic self-hatred. It is almost as if we had decided that the only way to stick together was to enforce small-town or ethnic conformism on a national scale—naturally using the only natural materials available, namely, simple moralistic ideas. Another New Beginning in the revivalist nation (this time managed by Ph.D. rednecks). E.g.: the best-educated people in the United States were not able to disavow the Vietnam war policy without attacking historical blood-letting in general. A technological advance over thermite called "napalm" (thermite was widely used in World War II), providing for limited rather than uncontrolled burning, became the ferociously moral symbol for the resistance to the war itself, the policy leading to it, and the refusal to discuss any other discussable issue conceivably related thereto. This willful emphasis on one means of horror out of scores of possible ones was exquisitely American in forcing a single aspect of technology to represent Everything.

On the right wing, community-by-shared-principle has surfaced in even purer form: whatever we want to say is true, is thereby true, if we want to say it strongly enough. All history, past and future, is what we will it, if only we will it enough. The difference between the left wing and the right wing in America is that the former takes its cues for True Posture from the national popular-culture reports of history, and the latter does not feel that need (remembering something rocklike and less current). The latter, therefore, has only the standard national dream-like nonsense, and somewhat more dearly held money, with which to deny the obvious dynamisms of American life—the frantic pace of change accompanied by overadvertised affluence. The left wing is devoted to a more current, fashionable misrepresentation of American life and its apparent options. Only when fear is about to reduce us to the power of money itself and traditional frontier mindlessness, pure and simple, does it look like the right wing will establish its own version of national order. In fact, of course, neither wing ever really settles anything finally. The greatest achievement of the migrant and ostrich-like American people is that, generation after generation, they have triumphed over their own lack of history and culture or other connection. This kind of victory as a way of life is a problem mostly for intellectuals, who require a higher degree of order. (Strange, isn't it, that this requirement now produces such clever self-destructiveness among our more civilized citizens?)

Consumerism—grabbing all those goodies, with the media pistol-whipping us from the home to the shopping center and back again—is our basic national community (or, according to one's image of human connection, our substitute for it). I have lived in this absurd community, as weakness dictated, with the status of an ungrateful visitor (more than that as for movie-going, however). I never made very much money, so never really got caught up in the buying game; nor was I much interested. My father was like that, too: he never spent on anything except grabbing dinner-checks to which he was not entitled, and my education. (I'm not certain, but for the latter I think he actually stole a little.) For him, money-making was mostly a box-score kept by the natives.

Instead of the usual Consumerism and money-making, my life has been based on a magnificent effort to confuse ideas and community, mind and body, conversation and life. The energy and talent I have devoted to this absurd project! My excuse—no, my explanation (or the beginning of it)—is that this dominating impulse had very deep roots. My life as I know it began with a certain problem of the body, coming to awareness at age three or four or five. I had an accident and lost an arm. This problem stimulated my mind ahead of time, or out of sequence, and this led almost immediately, I think, to two different but simultaneous distortions of emphasis: (1) I sought too much outside my own physical being for compensatory jurisdiction (control in fact and by right) of my own body; and (2) I became both internally and externally imperialist as to the jurisdiction of the mind—my own and others. (Please excuse this manner of stating the matter: as one consequence of what I am trying to describe, many people told me I should become a lawyer and, helplessly, I finally did. So now I talk like one.)

These two distortions came together, and set the pattern of my life, when I was seven. This did not happen inevitably, out of some merely self-generated dynamic. Its occurrence had to do with my family circumstance (the obvious hothouse of hot ideas about community). My parents screamed at each other—frequently, devotedly, as if the realest thing of all was then happening. I got the message; but I couldn't accept it. Instead, I mobilized my distortions, or they were mobilized for me (at that age, the difference is not important), to recreate the basic family community by digging into the source of the difficulty with the tin shovel of my own reason and need. (My older sister regularly slammed the door of her private room: what she did inside, no one ever knew.) For the next five or six years, until the advent of puberty, I refereed all quarrels between my mother and father: significantly, these were also the worst years of the Depression, and the family was on the road most of the time. Anyway, I was the youngest and most devoted marriage counselor in the history of our nation. Shortly after I retired, battle-worn and utterly defeated, Mayor Edward J. Kelly himself personally pinned the Eagle Scout medal on my deserving chest—right there in the actual Chamber of Thieves of the City of Chicago.

Veterans of Waterloo and Gettysburg lived out their lives recounting the glories of That Defeat. Not less have I. This experience of the inner battleground has served as my basic training in community-building; the compulsive use of intellect in that process (I have not lost an argument or won anything important in my family since the age of seven); and the various techniques of controlling the terror and other emotions consequent upon having to be where one is in a community-less place like America, with whatever one has to make do with.

What was I, what would I have been, apart from these distortions, and their particular mobilization? I don't know (and imagining is no fun). I guess I was or would have been gorgeous and perfect, like my father and my son before they, too, became somewhat overinvolved in willful community-mending here in America.

When I gave up on marriage counseling as a way of family life—following one last grand confrontation, which my sister sabotaged—the consequences, or at least the rapidly succeeding events, were extreme and fateful and seem to me to presage all the warring elements of my life-long personality. The major happenings were these:

1. The choo-choo train that was to carry me from home was on the tracks and rolling. Many times I looked back, but never for a true return. Any salvation of mine could thereafter be initiated only by further escape. All this was accomplished more by instinct than reflection (although I was already an intellectual, lacking only the confirming experience of reading my first book as one).

2. As if from nowhere, I suddenly discovered a comic talent. I became an appreciated performer, a leader in schoolroom hijinx, and shortly abandoned actual fist-fighting forever. Previously, my greatest social success had been in fighting; thereafter, it was all to be in word-performance—mostly comic—and the verbal fist-fighting kind.

3. I made an initial effort at praying, waited the better part of a week for results, and have never again spoken seriously to any but an imagined God.

4. After long reflection, I made the toughest judgment of my life. I closed out the counseling file by deciding that my ferocious father —who, in the absence of calculated self-interest, could speak reasonably to no one but me—had to bear the major responsibility for the interminable screaming and unlivable emotionality of the home; that I didn't love my mother as much after the counseling years as I had when they began, and that her mind and soul were unforgivably less available than my father's; and finally that, however much it shamed me, I preferred my father as a person and a presence, for his charm, quickness, ferocity, tobacco smell, and even (much later) his intelligence—all in all, for his magnificence as a life-performer, even though he never took the immediate family seriously as an audience and would come home only to sulk and glower. In short, whatever its provocation, I despised my mother's martyrdom.

5. Also, to speak quickly, I embarked on a course of ritual self-

containment by collecting, trading, and stealing stamps; got a dumb answer from a teacher and never trusted one again; joined the Boy Scouts as if it were the Foreign Legion and ended my career several years later as a decorated cashiered colonel; agreed with The Powers to become a lawyer on the single condition that I be allowed to survive the public school system without adopting the hideous notion that I in any way belonged there; and of course suffered the eternal earthquake of puberty—with its marvel of masturbation and the overwhelming dream of redemption through love of a female stranger.

But mainly I stumbled into the public library. Or, more exactly, I finished the last of their Tom Swift books and, for the first time, stayed on to look at the other shelves. I haven't any genuine recollection why I chose two yellow books both with the title *Boston*! The reason could have been the redundancy, or a desire to travel; it couldn't, then, have been emerging snobbery. I do recollect, however, that the reading was very much different from what I expected —whatever that was. The two volumes were first a fictional and then a factual recounting of the Sacco-Vanzetti story by Upton Sinclair. So, at an appropriate moment, I had stumbled upon a perfect metaphor of injustice. (I must have been somewhere between eleven and thirteen at the time.)

Then I read other political books—Stuart Chase, and George Soule's *The Coming American Revolution*; and I even took out a subscription to the *New Republic*. Until I finally escaped to the University of Illinois at seventeen, I argued New Deal economics with my father and his friends. What a wonderful way of bitching him: You're in business, you believe in justice, well then, etc., etc. After my initial effort in counseling, my second intellectual career was as a political streetfighter in the home. It served to fill time, but in the end was strangely as frustrating as my first effort. My father, however, did end up switching party allegiance and voting for Roosevelt, because of the Nazis; my New Deal arguments mostly helped him to justify that changeover. My mother always responded by affirming that she had always been a Southern Democrat. So, to fill my time with her, and for my own convenience, I taught her to listen to radio reports of baseball games. I succeeded marvelously ("I don't care what happened, they're *my* Cubbies!") and she has ever since been addicted to radio baseball—even after television arrived.

People have called me "brilliant," in order to dismiss me, since I was a boy. My mother created the pattern. Mostly, she wanted me to be somebody else; so did a lot of other people important in my life. It has taken me a lifetime of intellectuality to get the best of all of them by becoming truly me. But did I? They made me an intellectual, and I don't really like it.

What they did was to con me into taking on the toughest jobs at the lowest pay. In basic American terms, they threw me out of Boston and told me to go make another settlement in Ohio, because I was so brilliant and unwelcome. But, it must be admitted, all basic American effort is frontier effort of this kind. And, increasingly during my lifetime certainly, the American frontier is a mental and spiritual one. All the Conestoga wagons roll west, today, in libraries and laboratories and other quiet rooms.

The reason I don't much care for the life and work that was thus "chosen" for me—being an intellectual—is simply that it is too strenuously lonely on this frontier. The United States is a very lonely place in any event. Given our "thin" communal beginnings, and the generational transfer of these inadequate "traditions" occurring at a nearly unbearable pace, we are all excessively self-created: so many Americans live their lives as if they were mostly writing a novel about it. So it seems an untoward exaggeration of this dangerous national condition that one's own circumstance be endlessly elaborated in image and idea—as a matter of daily work. Thinking in America should perhaps be a part-time occupation for everyone. Thinking in general, I mean: the usual conniving and brokerage and other immediately expedient thought ought, if anything, to be multiplied. It constitutes the essential twine and glue that holds our flimsy social forms together, and is much to be preferred to the numerous revivalist ideologies and enthusiasms and other bursts of fashion that typically compete with our despicable practicality in this national adhesive function.

Thick communal beginnings and a tight generational passage are the required conditions of happy intellectuality. Along with most Americans, I can only imagine these. Even a rich world of symbol-reference, in the absence of such conditions, is inadequate: no language or other art form can make up for the absence. But the burden to do so nevertheless has fallen traditionally upon the communicator; and the modern attempt of the artist to make his language account for the absent conditions is killing. It is only the devilish temptation to satisfy oneself with an artificially trained elite audience that has kept us in business at all during the endless decades since the eighteenth century introduced our modern complexity—and traduced the ultimate problem of human communication.

Thus the modern power of critics, who create audiences for favored communicators. What Mencken alone did for Dreiser in establishing the latter's reputation, teams of scholars were later recruited to accomplish for Eliot, Joyce, Pound, etc. Out of my own historical moment, I remember a writer who had been so completely prepared for by highbrow critics that the reading was quite superfluous: she wrote and wrote and rewrote a silly butch novel that, if it had not derived from Flaubert and had not been sentimentally ugly throughout, would have been studied by scholars only. In the 1940's, we were properly prepared as an audience, so we read it avidly. This is not a period of great expression: it is a period of exceptionally shrewd workmanship—and occasional genius-thrusts (e.g., Norman Mailer) in the transcendent business of discovering or creating audiences.

Without tradition or common experience, there is no language. That is the awful truth too long ignored. There is no final magic in words. The occasional *zoom* is in meaning unexpectedly come alive —and that has reference to commonality of experience, condition, fantasy, identification: *reference*, newly recognized. Words are just words: they are the instruments of meaning, not the thing itself. Also with other symbols—and paint, and sound, and so on. There is a forgotten reality of the relation between artist and audience that has now been fudged-over with high-class conversation for nearly two centuries. Enough. Unless we get back in touch with the reality of communicator/audience, the entire intellectual endeavor is in basic jeopardy. We could end up talking nonsense to each other, in highly fashionable terms.

A pause is indicated here, to connect up some of the strands that have been and will be—and can only be—adumbrated in this brief essay about my experience of having been an intellectual in this eccentric country during the recent very busy and noisy quarter-century. I choose the theme of "community" as primary because, despite its difficulty, it is. Primary for understanding this country, modern life, and the potentials of intellectuals in relation thereto. Please note the similarity of root—"community" and "communication." Community is *assumed* for purposes of language. This assumption is no longer justified—not for all language, not for any particular meaning to be conveyed by language. Please note, also, the current incredible use of the word "meaningful"—revoltingly recurrent in the usage of our people, all the way from President to recently reformed dropouts. One says "meaningful" when one does not know or does not dare to say what one means—as in "Meaningful program for the cities," etc. So this non-word has now become one of the more meaningful ones in our current language: because of the lack of tradition and other commonality of experience that underlies the so-called community that might create or constitute audiences to embrace the language of a communicator, i.e., an intellectual. (Get the point?)

Perhaps the biggest burden in being an intellectual is that you are called upon to direct and delimit your own thoughts—to keep them from running away with you—without enough help from the outside. Some measure of thought-control of this kind is of course essential to existence: the utterly examined life is unlivable. But the presumption of high-flown intellectuality is that we all think fully and freely about everything and anything; our thought is also supposed to be intensely individualistic—hardly even borrowed at all. The fancy working-out of these presumptions provides the key to how it was and is to be an intellectual in this country, where there is no given community to save us from the infinitude of our own potential absurdity.

If I said that all reasonably successful intellectuals detest the American circumstance, neglecting few opportunities to revile it, while all reasonably successful businessmen adore and constantly celebrate it, I would certainly be overstating the matter. But by how much? Think of confirming examples in your acquaintance: each, you will note, is lying. The business of celebration is strained and unbelievable; and the intellectual's catalog of detestation is not only monotonous, but also omits mention of considerable gratification (much of it even machine-fed).

Why these heady distortions?

I think we are simply confronted with two different forms of American thought-control—and no American life without one or another. Style is of the essence. That of the businessman derives from boosterism (a special form of "nationalism" invented for the non-nation)—the religious belief in rising land values, along with other imperatives of salesmanship; and the proper care and feeding of profit-and-loss statements. I have always been fascinated by the fact that business borrowed the language of psychology in naming economic conditions—most notably in calling an economic downturn a "depression," and terming the insistence on immediate payment in gold a "panic" (not to mention a windfall as a "killing"). But the decisive psychological word in business has always been "confidence"—a thought-control category clear-and-simple. A businessman/salesman has confidence when he cons himself into the rosy view—that is, strictly limits his thought to the perspective of clearing inventory at the named price.

So also the intellectual, except that his inventory is ideational, of course; and he never really gets around to naming his price. He ought to, but he just doesn't. The reason, I think, is that the intellectual is our current frontiersman—the new frontier of American endeavor being spiritual Nightmare and no longer materialistic Dream. And *frontier* pricing—of either variety—partakes more greedily of far-horizon perspective (being, by definition, the measure of exchange in a not-yet-organized market). The world of ideas is underdeveloped, much less well organized than that of the distribution of goods; and its importance only recently recognized.

To be an intellectual nowadays is not at all what it used to be: today, it involves one in a form of class struggle.* Intellectuality is now an *economic* fact, in addition to (instead of?) whatever else it used to be. College degrees are important pieces of paper—some even as valuable as 1,000 shares of IBM, maybe (with the advantage over the latter that they are inalienable; you can't lose them as you can lose other "property," through bad judgment or lousy luck or excessive daring). But the newly affluent intellectual in America, trading upon his academic qualification and organizational position, has only now reached a stage of development comparable to the loud grabbiness of businessmen in the post–Civil War period; next, I fear, comes the pious rapacity of the Twenties.

•

* For elaboration of my views of the working intellectual as constituting a New Class, see especially the pieces collected in Section 9 of this book.

In my quarter-century view, the intellectual is now the purest expression and profoundest victim of "Americanism"—if the term is properly conceived as the ideology of the "thin" society abjectly dependent, for lack of anything more substantial, on moralistic symbols. So, just as those earlier Foreigners, rushing blindly off the boat to embrace their own frontier infinity, readily became the most fully realized victims of capitalist metaphysics, our intellectuals are "doing their own thing" as just about the same American thing as their forebears.

The quintessential Americanism of the New Class intellectual is identified by his tropistic negativism—an inverted boosterism derived from Good Guy/Bad Guy moralism. This folk material taken from frontier Protestantism has now, moreover, been made widely available on network television—that baby-sitting sur-reality of the postwar generations. Just as the rosy view can be a terrible tyranny, so also this *Hey-another-boil!* outlook. But it is a drag to have to detest everything irrespective of race, creed, or color. Especially as one becomes aware that the underlying point of this greedy general disparagement is that the New Class is not yet in control of the country: they are knocking the other guy's real estate, and will boost it better than he did—be assured—once it is theirs. (So many intellectuals, after all, earn their livings in advertising and related booster-industries.) So, Che Guevara replaces Adam Smith as a primary irrelevance: what else is new?

What else is that intellectuals undo themselves when they adopt simple measures of thought-control. To be short about it, certified conformity as to opinion and language is regularly chosen by intellectuals as the favored means of community-building. But this kind of coercive equality, among individuals ostensibly striving for uniqueness and excellence, is disastrous: indeed, an absolute contradiction in terms. Intellectuals absolutely require community not only allowing for, but based on, difference and variety; yet they are impelled to sustain their fragile community by ideational conformity —coerced similarity of opinion.

From the outside, intellectuals seem to be freer than other groups —exactly because they are pointedly disengaged from those very groups observing them. But from the inside, exactly the same freedoms can be tyrannous. For example, at Village parties in the past there was always one intellectual girl escorted by a businessman she might have to marry to support her artistic endeavors. The poor bastard never had anybody to talk to—except me. Others would come over only to favor him with a few moments of benign contempt. I, of course, suffered demerits for low taste in thus revealing my interest in money-making and job-holding (which for me have always been exotic objects of study).

So I suggest that the intellectual life in the United States, unfortunately, must be understood as a desperate effort *not* to think any more—certainly any more individually—than may be necessary at the time to qualify as an intellectual.

To base community on conformity of consciousness is a very dangerous ploy, as the history of any orthodoxy will attest. If indulged (it will be: it seems irresistible to communityless intellectuals hellbent on community-building), its extreme daring should be acknowledged, and the whole endeavor subjected to continuous criticism of a sharply self-conscious kind. Since we are nearly communityless, it may be that we must be daring in just this way. But in this dangerous effort to create community, even with slogans and ideological prescriptions and other mood-medicine, we should retain perspective. Mine is this: *Community is the home the body finds.* The mind does not, deeply, need a home (except to justify its own limitations, which should instead be acknowledged without justification). That is, the mind does not need a home *if the body has one.* If it does not, then inevitably the mind is conscripted to provide a make-believe one. My point is that this inevitable conscription must be submitted to with cunning, candor, and contempt—toward self and others. (One way or another, the body's home will certainly give the mind much to think about.)

I make no brief here for the non-intellectual who, to ensure his own community, is able and willing to dispense with mind altogether. He merely finds, too late, that it is indispensable; and that his body, certainly as it ages, is equally unhomed with all the other bodies—and with no adequate mind left as guide through that special purgatory.

An intellectual is someone who emphasizes and exaggerates intellect and ideas—*for whatever reason, and with whatever result, and wherever in his life.*

Any such emphasis and exaggeration will consequentially create difficulties in any of the many non-intellectual areas of the intellectual's existence. This is the *lock* of the problem of intellectuality:

the *key* is a fancy piece of metal called body/mind dualism. Or, more simply (I do not intend a technical philosophical argument), the great contradiction between idea and emotion.

We want to, we must control our thoughts so that they will not, uncontrolled, lead our emotions astray, and all else in life that follows upon emotion, including basic bodily being. The outer-reach of necessary thought-control is belief in one or two simple ideas to control all other (and complicatedly dangerous) ones. This outer-reach method is too costly in terms of will: single simple ideas control all others as a good machine-gun emplacement controls an approaching squad—they do not control, they slaughter, ideas. But the need for control that is not slaughter is perhaps the deepest human need of all. This was the burden of historical religion, only occasionally borne with success; and where persisting need for such control strikes, there we feel the loss of traditional religion most deeply in that there, also, we now actually experience the wildest exfoliation of uprooted religious emotion fastening upon moments and objects of daily life—especially those of media culture. (But how far can one go to cooperate with the cultural amateurs of the media in conning oneself? They need so much assistance.)

The contradiction and conflict between idea and emotion—this *ground* of necessary thought-control—finds its deepest beginning in the residual sexuality of the modern body. Later, oral chemical-intake, elaborate anal imagination, enforced movement or quiescence, and other physiological inventions—these mechanisms and devices of the socially oriented mind invade what remains of the "natural" animal we used to be (and never really get over having been). The point is that the body's free and independent existence is mostly an illusion and certainly a wasting asset, as one ages in the modern urban organizational environment—which we created, and the youth were born into. In my generation, we believed in some kind of higher sexuality to preserve the animal fundament against aging existence. The youth, with no memories uncorrupted by television, believe only in immediate physical movement—whether or not sexual and even as the idiot Pepsi Generation—or the farthest fantasies of such physicalism, when the actual thing is impossible: i.e., violence. The violence of affluent radicals (the spearhead of concern, at this point) is not traditional violence, however: it is immediate physical action *merely accompanied by* fantasies of violence—done by or to be done upon them—and this is the source of the new politics of escalated disruption.

It is this existential difference in body knowledge and direction that creates and constitutes the now-notorious Generation Gap. This is what it means, specifically, to say that they are younger: they believe in *their* immediate possibilities of action rather than *our* ideas of possible action now-and-later. We need their action, they need our ideas. But the lines of communication are down. So, age-old issues in the life of awareness now center on this particular body-difference. Opposite categories like romanticism/classicism, radical/conservative, content/form, new/old were always, at bottom, various ways of stating one's personal perspective on the Grand Problem of conflicted emotion and intellect. Now these, too, are conscripted to war upon or make peace with this great generational thing.

We can see farther than we can feel. Also, with age, the emphasis naturally and inevitably shifts from feeling to seeing. All men die; good ideas, never. The body, and whatever relies upon the body, must lose. But not ahead of time; and no loss to dying ideas is justified. That is the ideal. D. H. Lawrence, our last great romantic Christian, could not accept this fact. He aged badly; luckily, he died young. And he hated Jews for their prior sense of age. He knew, and was willing to learn, nothing about age. I say *that* is as foolish as never having been young. All men are both—except those who are more symbol than man, like a Kennedy brother or a G. B. Shaw. (The farthest importance of the Kennedys is that they represent the early demise of eternal youth, like Keats.)

Now that I feel old, I believe in the rights of age. And I speak for them. And I fight for space of my own on this basis, just as I did when I was different kinds of kid. So to the youth: If you are an age autocrat, I am your enemy. You want to make a deal? Good enough. But I have bad news for you: you are not in my class when it comes to deal-making knowledge. Sorry, I'm on top of that: I've been around longer.

We live by seeing *and* feeling: by being both young *and* old. But the need for animal/human connection, for modes of feeling, is deeper—deep enough to drown our best-aged ideas: nearly lemming-like. This conflict is not to be resolved (nor are any great ones). It is to be endured and expressed, at higher and higher levels; and—eventually and hopefully—with growing mutual appreciation of either generation's good work well done. The battle between youth and age is a misdirected war against death which neither can win. The war against death can be "won" only by living-together.*

I was in my own youth a Lawrencian—sex was everything to me, to whom everything was intellectual. Physical embrace was the sacrament of my existence, which was and remained (with ultimate will) intellectual. It has been a very strenuous and dangerous form of life. Please understand me: I was not playing a chaser's game—*I needed those girls*. And not as an end, but as a means. Because I could not readily control my body on my own; and I was not suited to controlling it with the machine-gun assistance of One or Two Simple Ideas. So after puberty my life was an absolute contradiction, which I handled as best I could with the meager resources of deception (self- and otherwise) at my disposal. Only recently have I come to understand just what a destructive contradiction this has been on which to try to base an entire life.

I can state this clearly: I always wanted conversation with women, primarily with women, and then to bed. Since women always take conversation as a form of weakness on the man's part—and, this weakness coming from a "him," therefore status on their part—I was early in life called upon, painfully, to interrupt my own most desired conversation with women in a brutal manner, in order to get laid at all. (It was so easy for me to talk myself out of initial good luck.) This was then held against me as exhibiting excessive carnal appetite and untoward disinterest in Them-As-People. Once—one time only—this was not a problem. The experience, coming too late in life, turned me upside down. I began to imagine What It Would Have Been Like If—and my life is now forever corrupted by regret. Apparently there are a few women who like both activities equally, and need misuse neither; and I just never met them. That is my idea of really lousy luck.

It seems an irresistible conclusion that, for intellectual men, the practical "resolution" of body/mind dualism—an essential for continued fruitful existence as an intellectual—is in the utterly historical keeping of willing women (that's a *double entendre*). To have to have something like a real conversation before you can safely get an

* Unfortunately, this is also true of the still unresolved war between the sexes.

erection is a spiritual tyranny beyond description, and *vice versa*. If you are serious about both. It is set up here, in the United States, that to want either is to lack seriousness about the other. Heterosexuality will not survive this challenge. (Sometimes I worry about conversation itself.) There will be homosexuals and talkers here like England only had nightmares about. Unless some shrewd women decide to put an end to the awful drift by encouraging an easy flow, back and forth, between carnal and verbal conversation.

Without being so sexily autobiographical, let's discuss intellectual method. Whether or not, when, and the way in which you get laid, if you are an intellectual, is frightfully important; but how you think —painful as it is to say this—is even more so.

To be succinct, any way at all that one can manage to bring off the mutual interpenetration of ideas and experience is good method. We should be willing to pay high prices for this, even including distortions of experience and inadequate scholarship. Personally, I have always preferred to talk about abstract ideas with businessmen and about money with highbrow intellectuals. But I am extreme. (I am told that in France they have a category for me—*primitif*. I wish to hell they had it here: I think we need it more.) I didn't start out intending any such daring perverseness, I can assure you. I read footnotes so long and so devotedly that to this day I have to put my hand over my eyes to interrupt operation of the tropism. But it's not so much of a problem because I don't read so much any more. (Twenty-five years ago, however, I dropped out of the University of Chicago because attendance there was interfering with my studies.) I have ended up with this rather unlivable method for simple but compelling reasons: I can't stop thinking speculatively and in general, or else I would have submerged myself in American experience by becoming a businessman long ago; and I cannot abide the standard graduate student game of accumulating books-read, and using ideas and other culture mostly for adornment of self and disparagement of others. I believe in using big critical notions to analyze one's *own* nest and neighborhood.

There was a very nice professor of sociology at the University of Virginia, where I happened to be stopping in 1941. He offered to take care of me if and while I became a sociologist (which I rather wanted, then). To this day, I do not know why I went to Jefferson's university in the first place or, in the second, did not accept the professor's kind offer. He said I wouldn't have to bother with classes, or pay any more money for the privilege of not going to them. That was one of the best offers I ever had from anyone. Naturally I am compelled to speculate why I was merely complimented, but not really interested. I couldn't, then, merely have been prescient about the future of sociology: my instinct must have run more deeply. I think I knew that I needed the opportunity of non-definition. That was a big thing in my day; not having a career or much of a job, as the Depression ended, was a marvelous way of getting down to growing up.

I am now forty-five, still non-defined—that is, defined by nothing more exact than the concatenation of my particular events. And I have had so many opportunities to come out otherwise! Not that I haven't tried. Once I tried very hard, and became a fancy lawyer. At the height of my conformist endeavor, I worked on Madison Avenue for an elite firm. I used to have the strongest sensation—walking firmly from the subway to the office—that the past was all gone and the future was all there, and I qualified in that hurrying crowd. It was one of the richest experiences of my life, the only time I really felt I belonged to anything. (I was submerged in American experience, not then merely an intellectual.) It was damn good fun while it lasted. But I couldn't figure out what to do with the money I was making; inadvertently I allowed it to accumulate in the bank; in 1958 the federal government generously added thirteen weeks to the state's twenty-six weeks of unemployment compensation; and my seal of acceptance was doomed. A year without working—financed on my own!

My extended vacation started out deliciously. I would get up in the morning, look out the window at everyone going to work, and get back in bed. Then I filed everything in sight. Then I had a fight with my girl-friend. Then I began to revise and retype my poetry (a deadly sign, I have since discovered); why not write a book review or two; some notes on a few essays I might get around to after I retired on social security and other winnings; and I was off again, all unknowingly, on my one and only Everything-and-Nothing career. Today, ten years later, I sit alone in a lower-middle-class dump, as it ever was, still trying to get myself organized by the strenuous use of language. My father's son.*

* Whenever one of his millionairing projects flopped, he would go nervous all over, and stay that way until his one-shot-item gun was re-

We were talking about intellectual method. If I had possessed the good sense to accept the Kind Professor's offer at the University of Virginia, I would have become a scholar, reading endlessly in libraries. When history finally caught up with me after Sputnik, I would have experienced money, status, and the same delicious sensations I tasted briefly on Madison Avenue. Scholars live good now: you don't have to go out into the brothels of lawyering anymore. But—and I say this in all seriousness—so what? Traditional academic scholarship is no longer an adequate way of conducting man's primary intellectual business.

For one thing, the scholarly mode is accumulative, and in no hurry to get back into the flux of life. For another, it assumes that the truly useful books have already been written and need only to be discovered, read, and understood. And it confuses data and quotation collection with important ideas. It is possible to repeat every idea Freud had without having one of your own. Summarizing Freud and making his thought more readily available than he did, may well be significant work. But it must not be misunderstood as the most central intellectual work (that it has often been in the past). Take the characteristic yes-I-read-it-carefully function away from scholarship, and you will have some difficulty defining (and glorifying) what remains.

There are now so many books, and so much data, and so many educated people—too many, for the present level of organization. It is impossible to grasp it all. It is so horribly misorganized; that is, not genuinely available for use in true work or real living.

But I don't want to persist in belaboring the greatly reduced significance of traditional scholarship. The tragic truth is that there are no adequate intellectual traditions for our time—no clearly effective and comprehensive modes of finding and using ideas, and the presentation of ideas, and relating this basic intellectual work to feasible action: what John Dewey called "solving problems." The closest approach to such a modality would be that of the White House staff, if

---

loaded. His phrase for this state of non-being was perfect: He would later say that he had had "a breakdown standing up." Me, too. I wouldn't know what to do with a normal life if it walked up to me on the street, wiggled its ass, and begged me to go home with it. No more than him. (My mother did not with him and will not with me find such reflections in the slightest amusing.)

the President is interested; or all the training-and-staff of a wealthy man like a Kennedy or a Rockefeller, especially if that man is interested in being President. After these, we have some pretty good institute and faculty-department and high-power magazine arrangements. *Division of labor has arrived on the intellectual scene**—displacing the grandiose one-man scholarship of the past—and very few practicing intellectuals are ready to acknowledge, much less deal imaginatively with, the fact. In short, we were trained in handicraft and are now called upon to manage the Chevrolet Division of General Motors.

In the meantime, fashion and mere style have replaced weightier traditions and modes of procedure. It is a revolting period for the old-timers. One only hopes that a new tradition is being born, in that messy way most births occur.

Perhaps the single most certain source of the modern "method" (if there is any) is literary criticism—the analysis of language-idea-image, all in close combination, all as standing for some kind of current essence of life itself. So many people started out as literary critics: for one thing, book reviews are the Catskills of literary journalism. For another, we still hankered after the great catharsis of One Big Novel, even after that impulse to tell one perfect story of the times had been transformed into the shrewd revivalism of psychoanalysis—everyone telling his own imperfect story. Like so many others, I started out writing book reviews and autobiographical fiction. But with my lawyer/accountant's mind, I soon became bogged down in self-accusatory detail—from which I have never recovered. So I began to write about other people and other things, somewhat novelistically. There is just too much fiction in life for us to write novels in the grand old manner—or try to see life without novelistic understanding.

As to method, intellectuality has become groupish, institutionally activist, devoted to the present although slanted toward the future,

---

* Quite different from merely dividing the labor of tending the Flame of Truth, long practiced by academic departments, in which the product remains as divided as the labor that produced it: inadequate assembly, where any one fact/truth is equal to any other. There is literally no department in a university devoted to using or integrating the selected best of what the other departments produce: science dismissed theology— a previous integrative department—and philosophy, another one, decided to become technical.

and all-in-all quite different from the scholarly mode of long ago when a few people learned Greek and Latin in order to read, during a leisured lifetime, *all* of the really important books.

The literary intellectual I am describing and became is only the most extreme (and extremely self-conscious) example of the metropolitan professional: the biting edge of the New Class. He is by no means the king-pin of New Class position. More like an historian to an audience actively interested in everything but. Slowly, however, the New Class (despite its greedy devotion to the future) is discovering that what-is-to-come is equally as much a creation of history as the let's-forget-it past—and, as it edges closer, not so easily overcome by the usual arbitrary effort of will. For me, the imagined future is a mere abstract exercise in logic; whereas the past has a tangled texture supporting much richer speculation. Imagining the past tends toward dialogue; the future is more readily an egocentric creation for rationalists: the difference in difficulty, let us say, of talking *in absentia* to one's father or to one's son. (To the end of high school, history and recess were the only subjects I felt They had included for my benefit.)

This New Class—any new class—is abjectly dependent upon history for its models; and for all the other stray materials out of which the newness of the future is constructed. The literary intellectual has a special part to play in the New Class drama of institutionalizing intellect—not in the old manner of putting it away in an institution, but in the new mode of giving it institutional power with which to intervene in the historical process. *Some* intellectuals must provide disinterested analysis in the service of class interest. That has been my purpose, I now see. And I now accept it, seeing that man's great enterprise in reflective consciousness will hardly survive its recent technological triumphs, except on the victor's terms—without some sharp help from general-purpose intellectuals.

The question of New Class style is critical. Here, it may be worthwhile to compare the intellectual's pursuit of purity when I was young and today. At twenty-one, I possessed the sappiest super-ego ever. I was so pure that I took a job in a factory just to be near the Working Class (one week) and refused to see a very kind and helpful friend because he accepted the Brooks-MacLeish thesis and supported the War (several months). Mostly, we pursued *doctrinal* purity—Marxist, Freudian, or whatever—while emotionally we encouraged each other to anguish out loud. We suffered competitively in identifying with the victims and heroes of Spain, the Soviet purges, the Nazi camps, the Warsaw fighters, the French Resistance, and all the mounds of corpses and the millions of DP's.

The New Youth seem even more simple-minded to me—more convinced in their anti-intellectualism even than the middlebrow Stalinoids of my day—and absurdly devoted to primitive moral categories (which facilitate activism). Most of all, I don't see them yearning. We were soreheads, too; but filled with ambition and yearning. How are the new kids going to make it without that?

Their main purpose, apparently, is to rock the boat. Within limits, I welcome this (but I cannot find it appealing—maybe for reasons of taste, perhaps because my own impulse to do so is much depleted). If this activity startles some captain somewhere to get with it—which would certainly include foreclosing any further rocking of the boat—well and good. But Luddite rebellion, even if useful, is an act of helplessness. These kids, however, horrify me (and many others in my generation fairly well disposed toward them) mostly for two factors: (1) their mindless, willful moralism; and (2) their foolish misunderstanding of the reasons for the absence of severe coercion in the society generally and (as yet) against them specifically, which makes their disruptionist tactics feasible. So often—from the sit-ins on—they have used as-if power just as if it were real power. They should be honored for their daring and inventiveness, and then treated as the political infants they are by serious men who take politics as something more than testing the limits of authority. (Mayor Daley is not the only vicious father in our midst.)

Whatever finally comes of the recent inter-generational *shock of misrecognition*—and whether much or little is achieved in starting up the conversation with our sons once more on some more feasible and better basis—two things are very clear to me: (1) however we did it, we created them; and (2) apologetic pandering on our part will only compound the original (and still unknown) felony. Fatherhood is tragic, particularly ours. Especially in America.

For here, it is not merely our inadequate creation of the new technological order—and our even more inept, nearly filiocidal directions to our sons for living in it—but also because fatherhood never got a very firm footing on these shores. And now, confronted with an established matriarchy affecting everything except big-organization hierarchy, it is more badly situated than ever before.

The current generational passage is not the first seriously difficult one in this country's history; it is only the most surprising one. (We thought that with affluence everything would be hunky-dory.) The passage from immigrant father to first-generation son—decade after decade for the better part of a hundred years—has always been portrayed as one of tragic fulfilment, at best (the son's domestic growth upended the foreign father spiritually as well as biologically). I can personally speak for the decisive frustration of a second-generation intellectual son succeeding a first-generation businessman father. And then there is the legendary drama of the farmboy who survives the merciless exploitation of dirt-farm life to the physical maturity of late adolescence, bestows a farewell beating on his father, and is never heard from again; or the more ordinary rural-urban transition getting tangled up in the generational succession. No, this is not the first time; by no means.

Still, the Atlantic voyage—or the train ride from an Iowa cornfield to Chicago—was never so far as that from the Depression to the postwar world (no matter where you started, so long as you ended up in a suburb). The transformation has been astounding. Go back home sometime and take a look—a real look. Most of the buildings are gone, almost all of the homes have been gutted—and then refurbished with the contemporary paraphernalia of Consumerism. Most striking of all, this is a *national* fact. North, South, East, and West —inside the home and on the street—all the same. The fact of the matter is that several hundred national corporations have remade this nation physically since the War, and on standard patterns. With their advertising culture, especially as purveyed through billboards and television, they have gone far to re-make us spiritually as well. Imagine a human being who never knew anything *but* this perfected order of life; imagine your son.

Technology does not change society; it destroys it. We didn't know this; we were determined to ignore it so as to enjoy our affluence; and we had our memories to help us distort unwelcome perception. None of this suffices for the youth as it did for us. Indeed, they take our "show" of a way-of-life as a big put-on. My friend Leslie Farber suggests that they have seen the inner despair we were trying to hide even from ourselves—certainly from our sons. So the con game is over: we played hard, but we lost for lack of confidence. (If only the youth were real winners, and possessed the amount of it that, finally, we lacked!) We built a magnificent technological order —and strained ourselves ultimately to make believe it was also a society. The youth inherited the unbearable strain along with the new wealth.

We should have challenged them more with the work ahead of them, that of reconstituting a destroyed social order. Probably the Spock-fed women wouldn't let us; perhaps we didn't dare. Now they are going about just this job—but without most of what we could have given them in preparation. And, from the reservoir of fatherly despair, they draw much reason for destructiveness. Moreover, they presume to imagine that we destroyed a full, rich society actually worth preserving.

They are groupish, that's the main thing. There is not one old-fashioned headstrong individualist in the whole lot. In order to create some kind of community for themselves, the hippies are willing to get stoned and stay stoned. Just so they can cohabit, even as somnambules. What an incredible price to pay! (And what a lesson for us that they pay it.) This hunger for community—the basic human/animal connection—that we neglected to build into our shiny new world of rationalized home-and-office life, this need is now unleashed upon our barren productivity. We must make room for it; it is here to stay. The building of community—that connection for the sake of connection—is a fundamental item on the order of the day for all of us. No livability, no health, no relief from willful productivity—nor from the malaise of affluence which is its real result—without new beginnings in community-making. That is the lesson the New Youth are teaching us.

I cannot abide their groupishness—I am an old-fashioned headstrong individualist, I am sorry to say—but I have no doubt whatsoever that, as for basic social agenda, they are right in that and I am wrong. So I will Moses it along, only offering, in my cantankerous way, special observations on the putative nature of their Promised Land—and which step first, which step second, if we really do expect ever to get out of this goddamn desert.

I will even admit that the reason I cannot abide their groupishness is that I am a sorehead. I am still sore, thirty years later, about what happened and what didn't happen to me when I went to Senn High School in Chicago.

Let me explain myself to the youth: There used to be a thing, long ago, called "the rumble seat." In red leather, with long blonde hair flying out of one side of it, zipping along at thirty-five or even forty miles an hour, it was one of the most gorgeous bits of social landscape ever invented. Actually to be seen in one was the apex of the social order of high school. Much desired, seldom achieved: I was a social flop. (My darling sister, however, dated the only Jewish halfback on the high school team.) An entire evening could be turned wistful if I happened to see a rumble seat sweep by . . . and on into the fading perspective of a twilight street. (*Goddamn them!*)

Experiencing the social system of high school turned out to be an eternal shock to my spirit. Nothing I had known was any preparation for this marvelous mystery of the wider world: *it was community beyond family and gang.* That's the size of the shock it was. The rumble-seat society seemed all so gorgeous and distant: a superordinate fact of life. The truth, now I know, is that it was the most intimate fantasy, more in me (much more) than out there. If only that had made it less important! But no, this was—unmistakably and once-and-for-all—the transcendent order of existence. Everything led into the wider world: each thought, and every hunger, only another rung on the ladder to intimacy with *that* infinity—just a half block away. I have not solved this problem; nor have I betrayed it. (I may never find out which side my bread is buttered on; but I know what buttered bread is.) Although subject to the widest interpretation, this problem would never change; and it has not. *The inner life of the wider world is where Americans must live.* One becomes an American simply by discovering this; for me, it is a dashing rumble seat, with long blonde hair flying out of one side of it.

This high school thing was particularly shocking because I thought I had already discovered the truth about Social Life. At the end of grade school, with puberty immediate and graduation imminent, all of a sudden there were kissing parties one after another, week after week. This posed some problems, but nothing so difficult as touch football; and by the time graduation occurred, I felt expert enough to get by forever. During the long summer before entering high school, I went to Boy Scout camp for a couple of weeks, was elected to the Order of the Arrow, got Bird Study merit badge and tied the Carrick bend (thus assuring I would become an Eagle Scout), and even saw my way to making Senior Patrol Leader. Everything was going well.

What a delusion! There were four thousand students in that high school, hardly one of whom would admit that he had been a Boy Scout. It was scramble, scramble, scramble—not just to win the game but, even more, to discover the rules. You had to learn to dance, get an athletic letter, walk up to pretty girls and ask them for a date, pass but not excel in classwork, and join a clique. *Join a clique!* I couldn't even find one. And for four years, month after month, getting more and more hard-up. (I was a sophomore before I stumbled on a coherent definition of screwing.)

I became a socialist because the bourgeoisie invented American adolescence in order to make us all miserable enough to work for them. It was all quite clear. Still, being a socialist—while it felt good on occasion—didn't really solve anything. The real problem was how to get into a rumble seat and stop being so hard-up.

I have never forgotten the ineluctable tyranny of high school social life; nor have I ever overcome the rigid definition of self-and-group that it imposed on my later life. Yes, I have seen it repeated again and again and again. But I cannot accept it. Apparently, there was a profound lesson of group life to be learned there in high school—and everyone else learned it, while I just never got the deeper point.

So I'm a loner, despite my life-long interest in this question of community (which, as you will have noticed, I identify centrally with the whole matter of being an intellectual). My immediate family failed of being a community; so also, later, did the wider blood connection, although I gave it a run for its money (that's all it had). Mostly, I made do with gangs and pals. I have always had a close pal—too close, really, with the relation always strained by a surfeit of expectation. (This was also my problem with women.) Gangs are the best—the richest American mode—especially gangs with a purpose, like some literary or political or university ones I have known: that is, even *after* the first street gang of adolescence, devoted to sex and prowess. But I always felt like a hanger-on, and could never with certainty discover the *center* of the gang. This was especially the fact when the gang turned out to be, or threatened to become, a clique genuinely connected with the wider world—the kind I could never discover in high school.

My early experience of Social Life, just before high school, when I thought I had found the handle, was—I now see—nothing but an extension of the street gang to include some girls. Not yet, truly, the wider world. But still I know that the gang, when it retains the animal virtues of the first street gang while rising to the social connection of the later clique, is the one most creative form of community in America (and, I imagine, places like it, if there are any). But this realest gang of my dreams must account for income, sex, and purpose—all necessary support and direction. This is the *Apostolic Gang*, which can both change the world and fulfill the individual. Here is where I sign on with the New Youth—to the extent that this is their interest—even though I can never belong. And the failure of the apostolic gangs of my youth . . . well, that might have been my fault. Or we might have been ahead of our times, which were still devoted to lower-middle-class ambition.

Here, we mostly discover or create gangs, or exchange one for another: there is, as yet, no wider world. Not out there in America. Pals are a lead-in to gangs; wives and other women, a lead-out; families of the newly arrived are irrelevant in dealing with images of the wider world. But, in my generation, no one knew this—deeply enough, or in time. We kept trying all the closed-up avenues. The new kids know better: they are devoted, in their seriousness, solely to experimenting with apostolic gangs—even the Squares, who concentrate their search throughout the length of bureaucratic corridors.

Anyway, from the outset I had bone-knowledge that America Was Different. It is merely my personal story that I was not able to capsulate the differences of significance to me except by writing about general matters for twenty-five years. I believe this knowledge helps to make my past writing relevant, especially when set in the context of the life from which it emerged. That's why I now publish this collection, with accompanying indications of that context. And I do so with no authority whatsoever that is not purely and simply existential. Whatever it is, it was all done with nothing but a fine tooth comb.

> *Remember that rainy evening*
> *I throwed you out,*
> *With nothing but a fine tooth comb?*
> *I know I'm to blame; well, ain't that a shame?*
> *Bill Bailey, won't you please come home?*

I remember, honey. But that was never my home.

1

THIS ECCENTRIC COUNTRY

❀ REDISCOVERY OF AMERICA

PARTISAN REVIEW, 1949

Review of *America and Cosmic Man,*
by Wyndham Lewis

*The American experience has been eccentric enough so that
the direct application of European culture has resulted in some
weird distortions. What is required of us is, instead, to afford
greater stature to the indigenous experience as it confronts the
great European traditions, and to use these imported prisms
more flexibly, in better balanced encounters, so that they will
reveal our experience rather than afford us a mannered substitute for it. The encounter between culture and experience
in this country can occur as a lifelong conflict between mental
activity and social relevance. (Often enough, we nominate
ourselves for a serious intellectual career only after and as a
result of a negative encounter with too many of those who
could not.) So the American intellectual tends to be a hater—
of American life. But that is obviously what he is supposed to
be intellectual about. This self-defeating approach accounts
for much of our eccentricity: indeed, it ends up augmenting
the rich complexity of our national life—exactly what so repels
the American intellectual. Thus, we take a strange embarkation
point for the interior journey of the spirit (often elaborated in
New York City, the original physical port of entry).*

❀   THE USUAL attitude of intellectuals toward America is that it
is a dark (not deep: one never says America is deep in anything)—a
dark pit of capitalism, bureaucracy and other monsters of mecha-

49

nism; a slough of vulgar bourgeois values, small town narrowness, big city isolation, and grotesqueries of commercial culture; the feeding-ground of stupid, piggish politicians; and more. In a sense, of course, all of this is true. But America in the minds of American highbrows is very often little more than a nightmarish cartoon. There are a number of reasons for this. First: it is unfortunately true that the present nature of our society occasions a great deal of personal suffering in the lives of intellectuals (and one naturally feels a debt to one's own suffering, a debt easily paid with the ready cash of loathing and hatred). Second: it is time we freely admitted that there is something merely about being an intellectual that makes one very unreceptive to the true, raw substance of democratic living. Third: at best, we view America with European eyes (we are all Europeans anyway, of course). European ideas are our means of understanding America because they are very often the best and very often the only ideas available. But they can also hinder our perception of what is essentially a radically new way of life, a fresh departure in the historical experience of man, because Europe's culture was the product of an entirely different set of conditions and must undergo a process of severe adaptation before it can shed American light.

We should practice the same relation between European culture and American experience as the Europeans, in creating their culture, did between their new conditions of life and the ancient cultures of Rome and Greece. To help us in this purpose, we have a new book —from the hands of an able representative of the culture of Europe —which attempts to define the unique quality of American experience. Wyndham Lewis believes that it is "the destiny of America to produce the first of a new species of man," to replace the now moribund "Western Man." This new creature he has "seen and talked with in America." He calls him "Cosmic Man," meaning internationalist or universalist, a person unrooted in class, race, nation, or any narrowly defined community. The product of the American "melting-pot," Cosmic Man—not fully "melted" into universality as yet—will be the kind of human being fit to leave our present desert and enter the Promised Land of a world socialist state.

No one to my knowledge has ever made as much out of the "melting-pot" notion of America as Mr. Lewis does. Or, for that matter, out of the "pot" itself—the American urban environment. As he says: "My remarks have had for their object the provision of a philosophic background for my running panegyric of that 'rootless Elysium' of the American city: irresponsible, dirty, corrupt, a little crazy. . . ." The core of this "philosophic background" is contained in the chapter called "The Case Against Roots," a brilliant and original defense of what we have gotten into the bad habit of calling "alienation." He calls this rootlessness, more correctly, freedom: "Freedom and irresponsibility are commutative terms." (This is certainly half-right; whether it is altogether correct is a more difficult question.) Moreover: "The United States is full of people who have escaped from their families, figuratively." This and more is all the result of the melting-pot, the fact that America is an inverse empire that takes the world into itself rather than going out and conquering it. America "can only be something more universal than the Roman Empire, because its metropolitan area is coterminous with its imperial area." We are either a "disorderly collection of people . . . a sort of wastepaper basket"; or we are "a human laboratory for the manufacture of Cosmic Man." Mr. Lewis is certain that we are the latter.

This is a very rich book. There is not only the superlative expression of a new and fundamental perspective, but also much exciting and realistic analysis of contemporary American life: for example, Mr. Lewis' appreciation of the "American Appetite for the Incongruous"; his rare understanding of the elements of criminality in American life; or his short sketch of Roosevelt's personality, which is the most penetrating that has yet appeared on that most complex and fascinating subject. And his rambling appraisal of American history and historical personalities is refreshingly unlegendary, while not sinning on the other side of militant "debunkmanship."

No doubt, there are a good number of genuine horrors in the American experience. But—and I hope this does not sound too wayward—that is not really the point. The real point is one of emphasis, and those who emphasize the frightful aspects of our life are forgetting two primary matters: (1) that European civilization as the dominant one on our planet is finished—and therefore one can no longer choose to ignore raw and vital existences like America in favor of more highly formed ones; (2) American life has not settled in its final cast, it is confused and contradictory, and so the horrors, no matter how truly they are actually "out there," are not fully real because their status is not final. In a sense, nothing in America is altogether real but its future. The stunted, nascent, bawdy, disorganized elements of the future, however, exist in the present, and we must discover and reverence them (if we are still capable of reverence). That is our function and our fulfilment as American intellectuals—the perception and expression of our uniquely democratic future as we find it in the raw present. And if we find nothing, we are either blind or doomed. There is a very good chance that we are only blind.

❀ IT'S ALL THERE

THE REPORTER, 1959

Review of *Statistical Abstract of the United States:* 1959

I got "A" in Statistics at the University of Chicago—and have enjoyed them ever since (in utter disbelief).

They used to say of Sugar Ray Robinson that he was, pound for pound, the greatest fighter of the age; page for page, the *Abstract* is the greatest research tool of them all. We have here 1,042 pages, comprising thirty-four subject sections, consisting mostly of 1,227 statistical tables and forty-four charts, containing a half million figures, referring in detail to who we are, what we did, how many and how much of this and of that. This layman's Univac will provide the discerning purchaser with many richly puzzling evenings of varied entertainment, and when used indiscriminately or malevolently is guaranteed to Irritate Friends and Confound Other People.

For instance, did you know that it took us a hundred years to move the center of population from twenty-three miles east of Baltimore, Maryland, to twenty miles east of Columbus, Indiana, and sixty years more to get it out of Indiana to eight miles north-north-west of Olney, Richland County, Illinois, where it was left in 1950? (Incidentally, "center of population" is "that point upon which the U.S. would balance, if it were a rigid plane without weight and the population distributed thereon with each individual being assumed to have equal weight and to exert an influence on a central point proportional to his distance from the point"—which is the loveliest image of democratic equality that I have come across recently.)

Did you know that white people live eight years longer than non-white people? That in my age bracket alone there are 247,000 surplus women? That the state with the highest 1958 birth rate was New Mexico, with 33.3 per thousand? (It figures, since they had exactly that same marriage rate in 1950—the highest for any state except for Nevada's indecent 311.5 per thousand.) That each person in America who didn't eat 348 eggs last year got cheated? That in 1957 only *one* girl received a doctorate in law? (Who was she?) That in the last three years 60,000 more women than men came to the United States as immigrants, and more men than women packed up and left? Somebody knows what's what.

The thirty-four subject sections begin with "Population" and end with "Comparative International Statistics." They present twenty-seven fascinating pages on "Income, Expenditures, and Wealth," an expanded post-Sputnik coverage of "Power and Scientific Development," and encompass a universe of other subjects ranging through education, labor, business, finance, agriculture, housing, etc., etc., to quantity and value of the New England herring catch (which happily doubled between 1930 and 1957). Each section is introduced by a page or so of text that outlines the coverage, indicates general sources (the specific source is stated after each of the 1,227 tables), notes deficient material, and gives warnings as to margins of error. In addition, there is a helpful table of contents, a forty-two-page index, a marvelously useful bibliography of sources, and a three-page preface which begins with a sonorous statement that the book "is the standard summary of statistics on the social, political and economic organization of the United States." The word "summary" is exquisitely well chosen, since the material included is drawn from all Federal statistical programs and all other local government and private sources deemed relevant or usable. The great beauty of the *Abstract*, at least for the serious researcher, is that it is not only a one-volume summary of everything useful or important but that it also—as if to apologize for being only one book—leads into every other major statistical source, governmental or private.

One cannot resist offering a few statistics on how this statistical Topsy grew. The first edition was published in 1878 by the Secretary of the Treasury, nobody remembers why. For twenty-five editions it stayed in Treasury, was then shunted around between Commerce and Labor from 1902 to 1937, and since 1938 has been settled comfortably with the Bureau of the Census. Until 1912, the book was a giveaway item for Congressmen, then was sold for fifty cents through 1920. Thereafter, the price rose lackadaisically to a peak of $3.75 in 1954 and 1958; it has settled back to $3.50 this year. The coverage has changed widely over the years: e.g., about half of the early volumes were devoted to foreign commerce and navigation, now down to 5 per cent and less. For the last ten years, eighty new tables have been introduced annually. In 1948, 15,000 copies of the *Abstract* were printed and distributed; last year, 23,000 copies; this year, 24,000. (My informant at the bureau looks forward to the day when distribution will reach as high as 100,000.) About 5,000 copies are giveaways to Congress, government agencies, libraries, and contributors. The overall production cost—of the *book*, not of the statistical programs (cost unknown) of the eighty-eight government agencies and fifty-nine private firms and research organizations which contribute to the contents—is about $100,000. Sales receipts cover only Printing Office overhead and distribution; printing costs alone are $40,000, and eleven bureau employees work on the project, four of them full-time. Being an old proofreader, I contemplated the proofreading job with unabashed horror, and was naturally pleased to be informed that not all the tables have to be reset each year— just "a good many of them."

To enjoy statistics, one has to know how to read them. I suggest that they are like abstract painting in that they provide the material for meaningful images, rather than being direct representations of the images themselves. I think the ordinary irritation with statistics is similar to the ordinary person's resentment of modern art—you have to work at it too hard, and after all the effort the inner pattern that finally emerges is apt to contain deeply unresolved ambiguities. But our society is so big and complex and active that statistics, which are as abstract conceptually as abstract art is emotionally, are essential to social thinking. Conveniently enough, there is a solid basis for statistical interest among the American people—e.g., the popularity of baseball, one of the dullest games ever devised, the interest in which would be inconceivable without box scores, batting averages, and the broadcasters' incredible running commentary of minuscule statistics.

Government publications, including the *Abstract*, are so cheap that commercial bookstores don't bother to stock them: no 40 per cent markup. But all you have to do is write to the Superintendent of Documents, U.S. Government Printing Office, Washington 25, D.C. You can even misdirect your letter: they've got a department for that, too.

❀ FINANCIAL PAROCHIALISM

COMMENTARY, 1963

Review of *The National Wealth of the
United States in the Postwar Period,*
by Raymond W. Goldsmith

*The subject of subjects—wealth and the United States. It is
worthwhile, every once in a while, to take a vacation from our
daily bitterness about the unspeakable distribution of wealth
and simply contemplate with awe the absolute quantity of it
all. And growing, growing, growing.*

*With the advent of established postwar affluence, the first
stage of the American experiment in society-building came to
a happy—or at least the intended—conclusion. The require-
ments of the next stage are chilling to contemplate, in view of
our certified incompetence in relation thereto: now all two
hundred million of us—acting on behalf of the future generations of mankind—must decide what to do with this unheard-
of wealth. In the beginning, the comic view shall obtain.*

Society and statistics grow together, the one in size and the other in importance. This is one of the larger meanings of living in a mass technological society. The sad fact of the matter is that we know each other by type and category, and as contributors to the figures in one column or another. The rest is for novelists and poets (who are having a great deal of trouble keeping up with the figures). Of course, the transcendence to abstraction required by this situation most of us accomplish only spottily—and without the necessary pe-riodic effort at checking our figures and categories. Still, the statisti-cal fact (for instance) that Negroes earn less than whites, when joined with the companion statistical fact that Negroes do not live as long as whites, affords the kind of argument to racists that is an inimitable achievement of abstraction, and that can be answered only by a further retreat into the dark recesses of racism. (At this point, one returns to the novelists and the poets.)

The beautiful title of Raymond W. Goldsmith's new book of statistics is, I believe, well merited. Mr. Goldsmith is associated with the National Bureau of Economic Research, a very special, high-level organization of scholars and other important people. And he is the author (perhaps a better word for work like this would be creative director of production) of some very basic studies called A *Study of Saving in the United States* and *Financial Intermediaries in the American Economy since 1900*. The current volume is exceptionally basic, too, consisting of 110 pages of text and primary tables, 112 pages of supporting tables, and 207 pages of fundamental supporting tables. The subject is how much and what kind of tangible non-financial wealth there is in America: the book is, in effect, the best or the only or the most comprehensive—or all of these—*balance sheet of the nation*.

Mr. Goldsmith's major finding is this:

> The national wealth of the United States (i.e., the aggregate value of all tangible nonmilitary assets located in the United States plus net foreign balance), measured so far as possible by the market value of the assets or the nearest approximation to it, has increased in the postwar period from about $575 billion at the end of 1945 to just over $1,700 billion at the end of 1958, or at an annual rate of fully 8½ per cent. Wealth per inhabitant thus has more than doubled from $4,100 to $9,800, a rise by almost 7 per cent per year. . . . In constant prices of 1947–49, aggregate national wealth has increased from almost $790 billion to nearly $1,250 billion, while wealth per head has risen by one-fourth from about $5,600 to $7,100. The average annual rate of growth thus amounts to about 3⅝ per cent for aggregate wealth and to 1⅜ per cent for wealth per head.

These are big figures concerning a big country in boom time (only two recessions during the period, not counting the one it closed with). But an increase in capital since 1945 of about $10 a month a head—including heads unborn and unworried in that happy year—in the end does not bowl one over; it should have been much more. Indeed, it could have been if we had wanted to be that much more interested in the world our children will live in (which suggests one of the uses, for parents, of a really good national balance sheet).

The "findings" of a work such as this are not really the author's, but more properly occur in the course of attentive study by the reader. One can't really know what they are until some good readers tell us. The author himself found the following large points in his own reading:

1. Among many long-perspective changes in the structure of our wealth, the "most marked and significant . . . are the decline in the share of nonreproducible wealth [land, etc.] and the increase within reproducible wealth of equipment, both producer and consumer durables." (The share of land in total wealth, especially for agriculture, is a measure of national backwardness—agricultural land makes up about 45 per cent of India's wealth, and only 5 per cent of ours.)

2. The share of government, even including military assets, declined from 30 per cent in 1945 to 20 per cent in 1958. (Over the period, the average value of military equipment was equal to about two-fifths of all civilian producer durables.)

3. Both our foreign holdings and the stake of foreigners in our wealth are insignificant, which is an important difference between us and most other developed countries. (Net foreign holdings never amounted to more than 5 per cent of our wealth.)

In discussing what is involved in the preparation of national accounts such as these, Mr. Goldsmith is both a little plaintive and extremely persuasive. He utters the deep-felt hope that he won't have to do it again all by himself. It seems that apart from a few areas of investigation—especially inventories and agriculture—there is no official and continuous counting of our long-term blessings. This stands in very sharp contrast to income estimation, which is a solidly and elaborately institutionalized field. In rough terms, the difference is between stock and flow, capital and income, production potential and production-consumption actuality. We are a very statistics-minded nation, and spend a great deal of talented effort collecting all desired data, both in and out of government; in our business-dominated society, business gets all the facts it wants, at whatever cost. Why, then, this difference? In this frenetically capitalist nation, why should we be quite so remiss in our measurement of the real capital?

The answer lies, I would suggest, in the problem of financial parochialism. First of all, the primary interest of business is in assets viewed financially, rather than in real terms. And, next of all, knowledge of the actual uses of things—real values—lies on the secondary, production side of an enterprise: it is the province of the engineers and other technical people to know the actual capacity of machines; the controlling financial men are not concerned until a financial issue arises, such as buying a new machine and selling a new product. (The tax system has made the real value of equipment even less significant.) Even the balance sheets of individual enterprises are mostly financial documents, designed to impress or placate the public rather than to mislead production men. The paper world of business enterprise is devoted to profit, not production, so why should businessmen keep track of their capacity to produce? (Before and briefly after World War II, the military establishment was interested in such actual capacity and did attempt to catalogue it.)

Meanwhile, we have Mr. Goldsmith's estimates of national wealth, which are presumably the best available—although, on his own statement, not nearly adequate. (The mathematics of the matter is, for this reviewer, too complicated for comment; there is a whole chapter on the algebra, which, with much else besides, I leave to the econometricians.) But some of the problems of method are quite interesting, and even comprehensible to a layman. For example, should livestock be classified as inventory or producers' durable equipment? The latter, says Mr. Goldsmith, "as the relatively long-lived dairy cattle come to account for an increasing proportion of the total value of livestock." So it is not all just a question of a million here, and a billion there. There is, as another example, a disagreement among the experts on whether we should put the value of roads and streets on the government side of the ledger, or assume their value to be included already in the market value of adjoining private structures. (The government, so used by business, is frequently ignored or downgraded in economic counting.) The primary national asset *not* included in these accounts—the one that makes all the others possible, meaningful, or worthwhile—is people and their skills. Also air, sunlight, and water. Interestingly, the most durable and the least durable commodities and objects are also not counted—e.g., works of art and food on the table.

Why count? Because we have organized our way of life around these economic proceedings, and hardly even remember any longer what we have sacrificed to them. And further because what we actually have and what actually happens in the real world of economic things is our only guidepost (or bench mark) for manipulating the world of paper. There are two problems: one is *taste* and proportion in what we produce and consume; the other, deeper and more immediate, problem is not to be so dominated by the hokum-reality of financial considerations that we forget where we misplaced the real world. A really good, flexible national balance sheet would also certainly be of assistance to us in our efforts to deal with the issue of non-market justice in an increasingly non-market society. Not even to bring justice about, of course, but just at least to initiate an intelligent discussion of it. Who has what, and why? And how come I didn't get my share?

NON-RULE IN AMERICA

COMMENTARY, 1963

Just as the 1959 Reporter *piece started me writing* The Paper Economy *(see Section 7, below), this one led me to the second book,* Power in America: The Politics of the New Class. *With somewhat different results.*

My point in this essay was to begin to edge up on the issue of power in this country. (Money alone will not explain things, especially the "new" things.) Power is money, physical strength, good looks, talent, organizational position, well-situated parents, lucky real estate, energy, and the exploitation of the weakness of others. And much more besides. But in the United States—the most powerful nation? continent? people? thing? in all human history—only by inadvertence is power itself ever mentioned: "The public be damned"—"Get this midget off my lap"—"Screw them, build it anyway"—etc. We are devoted to morality: we are especially devoted to it as a language probably capable of obscuring all issues of power if you talk the language of morality loud and fast enough. And they do. With us, this power/morality disease is structural. *(So, that's the next book I'm writing.)*

I started writing this piece late in the evening of the publishing date of my first book. Nervousness, I guess.

The first great issue in American history was whether we were to have a federal government at all; its final resolution took about a hundred years. The second great issue of American history—which remains unresolved after another hundred years—is whether the federal government, now that we have it, is ever going to be allowed to govern.

There are two major and two minor exceptions to this formula for our history. To wage war and conduct some of the other foreign relations has always been the function of the national power. Without the pressure proceeding from these imperatives, the national government, once it had completed its second major function— namely, to assist in collecting and disbursing the lands of the continent—would probably have become purely ceremonial. As for the two minor exceptions, the first has been to contribute to the managing of the liberties and welfare of the population, while the second —and potentially most important—has been the role of the national government, inherited from the bankers in the Great Depression, in averting the domestic economic disaster which lies just beyond a conventional slowdown of production.

All other purposes and non-purposes of the federal government have been converging on this last power/purpose, and around it are currently expressed, repressed, distorted, and contained the major dynamisms of our history. We now have a country and an economy neither of which works adequately without somewhat more positive central authority than we have been accustomed to. However, we long ago decided to tolerate central government only or mostly as it dispenses favors and benefits; so that has become its characteristic manner of ruling, when it rules.

I take it as absolutely self-evident that the technological society called the United States is too big and too complex, too dynamic existentially and metaphysically too desperate, to continue to exist— adequately forearmed against disaster—under the jurisdiction of the inherited principles and techniques of non-government. From this self-evident premise, I deduce a crisis. The ideological ground of the crisis is, in essence, our profoundly absurd idea that money is a thing in itself, that there is never enough of it, that it is a private matter, and that the federal government, being public, should therefore have as little to do with it as possible. This is a long subject, and I have discussed it elsewhere.* But what mainly concerns us here is

* See *The Paper Economy.*

the institutional basis of the crisis, which is located for our day in Congress. For it is here that our refusal or inability to become a coherent nation is most clearly manifested.

It is perhaps no coincidence that the blockading role of Congress has fallen primarily upon the House of Representatives, which was designed constitutionally to exercise the original jurisdiction in fiscal matters. The Senate, which was supposed to decelerate expression of the popular will, has become the more "liberal" chamber, notwithstanding the power of filibuster.* The design has thus been inverted. (According to Neil MacNeil in *Forge of Democracy*, since 1939 the Senate has increased House appropriations by close to $3 billion annually—$32 billion in the last ten years.)

But the *entire* constitutional design—not merely the relation of the House to the upper chamber—is now badly out of whack, because of the profound backwardness of the House of Representatives. The Supreme Court has been dangerously burdened with political initiatives by the necessity of taking up the Congressional slack (the alternative, however, would have been disastrous—to revise the Constitution in favor of Congressional ineptitude). And as for the Executive Branch, I would briefly describe it as alternately benumbed and hysterical. It is becoming nearly impossible to preserve even a meaningful semblance of domestic executive leadership, despite the immense energies being devoted thereto by the current administration. The country simply cannot be run by executive order and publicity—a legislature is required as well. But instead of a legislature prepared to use national power in a positive fashion to deal with existing problems, we have non-rule by Congress. We have come, in short, to a historical dead stop.

A revealing symptom of our condition is the fact that almost every political question in America is argued on metaphysical, not political, grounds—the issue is never *how* power is to be used, but *whether* it is to exist at all or its existence acknowledged when it does. Since politics is concerned entirely and exclusively with the uses of power, it is possible to say that we have not yet arrived at

* The Senate is more "liberal," because the characteristic county-type malapportionment in the House is avoided; but less "liberal" basically because New York and Nevada both have two representatives in the chamber.

politics in this country; we are still carrying on the work of the Founding Fathers—that is, creating an American system in which the uses of power may eventually be discussed and the thing itself, politics, occur.

This negative view of power is perhaps the distinctive aspect of the American character. It subsumes our notorious Puritanism, but is not limited to it. It relates to the Puritanism in that all private power—whether exercised by you in relation to your child or by the management of General Motors with respect to the structure of urban life—is so completely overjustified from a spiritual point of view that in practice it is no longer recognized as "power" at all. (The proof is in trying to use the very word in discussing any of these private relations: people respond as if they had been insulted.) But this Puritan moralism has become so hard-pressed by the challenges of modern complexity that it now requires a kind of paranoid screen on which to project a negative image of the power it fears to acknowledge. And that negative image is the federal government. (Only war, which opens up the perspective of external hostility, is exempt from this classic prescription.) The radical right-wingers are nearly as paranoid about our own government as they are about the Soviet government—and they are simply worse than the rest of us, not all that different at bottom.

The national power which our history has denied us is desperately needed today—it is quite likely a matter of life and death. On two counts, one domestic and the other worldwide. The first has been mentioned: an advancing technological society cannot exist ungoverned; without more coherent government than we have now, we will end up crushing each other—eventually physically, as now psychologically. With more and more people living together in increasingly complicated and interdependent patternings made possible and imperative by the technology and its astounding historical pace, fewer areas of social life can safely remain free of governing. Each time we wait for problems to solve themselves, we deny the palpable world around us, thus seeking a disaster we must ultimately find. Health, education, employment, the organization of our living and working areas, along with the development of the scientific technology which is the source of all our blessings and troubles—all these require some decisive support or control by the national government, some positive use of central power.

In the second, worldwide arena, the matter is obviously a daily one of life and death, and with the current primary reliance on military posture, it must remain so. In the absence of further and deeper agreements with the Soviets, the only road forward is that of non-military initiatives; also, the more agreement we achieve, the more such initiatives—based on our domestic power—will dominate the world scene. Here lies the true unilateral path. This is the only way to force the Soviets to agree, or to deal with the abiding conflict after they agree. If we were to adapt the army, say, to the purposes of massive developmental aid, or build a new technical organization to dispense and utilize $10 or $20 billion annually in this kind of "war," the Soviets would have to respond in kind. This would certainly make them more amenable to arms reduction, since they are not nearly equal to us in over-all capacity and would be hard put to find the necessary resources. We would in effect be "spending them into submission"—or, at least, reasonableness. The idea of spending them into submission is regularly advanced in support of all new or redundant armament. To spend them into submission by means of developmental aid would be infinitely more effective and desirable from all points of view. But this alternative is not available to us, we are told, because the need is not recognized, or because the power does not exist, or because it would be improper to use the power for that purpose. Or, when the argument gets hot, all three at the same time.

Note the horribly bloated role of the military motif in overcoming, for what one might call subsistence purposes, the negative view of federal power. There is hardly a problem-area where the military umbrella has not at last been raised. From the hospital system of the Veterans Administration through the maze of general spending-support to the fostering of technologocial advance itself, the force of the military excuse and distortion is omnipresent. Defense needs have been the keystone of effective national policy, both domestic and foreign, since the New Deal ended in the recession of 1937–38. In its proportionate relation to population and GNP, the non-military role of the federal government has actually declined since that time.

To this juncture has our history brought us. The issue: to be not merely a geographical federation of constituencies, but a nation—and that for more than military reasons or by military means. Reading American history with hindsight, our deepest difficulty has been the sustained positive use of national power—to an extent that nations with more duration and less land can hardly imagine.

It seems that the whole conscious segment of the country is now being shocked into awareness of the role of Congress as the torchbearer of American power-negativism. All of a sudden—perhaps because the initial verve and top-flight press releases of the Kennedy administration cruelly revived memories of the New Deal—everyone has realized that domestic amelioration and reform have been almost entirely blocked, tabled, dribbled out, and distorted for a full quarter-century. The military umbrella had previously obscured this major fact. Yet I would suggest that the fact which has been obscured is a cultural, even spiritual one, and not a matter of how the seniority system works. For Congress expresses the profounder contradictory meanings in our history. It dominates the Judiciary as statute is superior to decision; and the Executive can initiate for the most part only ideologically when it does not carry the Congress. It is easy for the Executive or the Judiciary to make believe we are a nation, but it is impossible for Congress to do so. Where Congress acts, there a nation acted. There is no distortion and no backwardness in, around, and under our nationhood which is not represented and overrepresented in Congress. Therefore Congress cannot possibly be viewed as an unfortunate collection of technical details. Congress is, indeed, the major structural problem in our history, and never more so than today. *But structural means spiritual, not technical*—although this is the hardest proposition for an American to understand, with his traditional confounding of the two categories. What is wrong with Congress is wrong with us. The crisis of this institution is a crisis of American character and personality. Congressional non-rule perfectly expresses our personal unwillingness to abandon our adored image of infinite individualism, and enter gracefully, or at least energetically, into a generous age of technological abundance.

In a practical way, the indictment of Congress reads as follows: in the first place, not every citizen has an equal chance to achieve representation; and in the second place, even if he did, Congress is not adequately organized to create or effectuate the majority will of such properly selected representatives. The first is an ancient but worsening scandal; we soften the point of it by imagining ourselves to be more homogeneous than we are—but the Negroes have lately been making our heterogeneity harder to deny. So far as the second consideration is concerned, it may be a decade or more before we mature to a cultural-political level at which it could frustrate us in its own right.

The unrepresentative quality of our system of representation derives from direct and total, as well as partial and indirect, disenfranchisement. Briefly, the de facto system favors whites over Negroes, rural over urban, permanent residents over mobile types (especially permanent residents of sparsely populated areas), and, of course, the wealthy over the poor. Clearly, it favors the more conservative groups. So much so that, with their vested attachment to the present imbalance, the belief and willingness of conservatives to participate in the formal democratic system are being or have been undermined. That is most obviously the tragedy of the South—but it is not limited to that area. Southerners are not the only Americans to have become so accustomed to unfair advantages that they can no longer bear to contemplate the possibility of fair disadvantages—which is, of course, an essential of a democratic order.

The worst of the whole matter is the coerced denial of the right of Negroes to vote in the South. This aspect of the de facto system does not exist even under an excuse of law. White voting registrars simply refuse to register Negroes: when the point needs to be driven home, the lawlessness of the white community—working through the police or through volunteers—accomplishes whatever may be needed. Jobs are lost, loans are called, arrests are made, shots are fired. Whatever may be needed. The result is an *ad hoc* apartheid shaped in a deadly social battle by the Southern activists against both the conscience of the nation and the legal/police power of the federal government. In a way, it is worse than South Africa—worse for the whites, I mean. Because the black-and-white spiritual triumph of the white, which is the whole point of the absurd effort, is ever-beckoning, ever-denied. The entire purpose of racialism is to simplify life, but the white Southerners have in fact complicated everything almost beyond bearing. After a while, all that is left to them in this impossible situation is to wallow in the process of losing —and, by their own unspeakable definition, losing *everything*, not merely the pleasures of racialism. (Meanwhile, the Negroes go to pieces in the process of winning, because they also foolishly defined their victory as "everything.")

The struggle of the Negroes is the most exhilarating since the labor push of the Thirties. It is also much more extensive than many of us have realized. For example, the issue of poverty—the deeply disgusting issue of poverty in this wealthy nation—is a live one politically almost only as it is a subsumed part of the general Negro movement. Likewise, the massive and mounting issue of technological unemployment. Moreover, the positive bid of one-tenth of the population to overcome deprivation which ranges from the most brutal material factors to the spiritual heights of misidentity with a white God, must inevitably affect the whole white culture.

The Negroes, with their black skin as a battle-flag, may save this nation yet (I say "nation" because they insist on it). It is they who suffer most from the American dream—they are the only true believers left. The Negro movement is a religious movement, and it seems almost powerful enough to sweep the country along with it to a new spiritual level. It is religious because it requires for its own fulfillment that the whites become better people—the Negroes are not really interested in greasy hamburgers, white toilets, and another Ralph Bunche. This is the persuasive underlying truth that the Black Muslims (by denying the possibility) rely on, and that so agitates the immense talent of James Baldwin, who was and remains a greatly gifted preacher exquisitely poised above the emotional eddies of black and white. The Negroes are a small part of the population, however, and I feel their gift will always be primarily a cultural one. Their skin makes them spiritual witnesses to the current state of the white man's belief and practice. Their skin can change only in the white man's eye, just as it was created in the white man's eye. Being thus doomed, and carrying an incommensurate historical hatred, they can allow us peace only when we allow them to escape into middle-class comfort. Before that happens, the nation will have been transformed. The poor will have been raised, the unemployed hired, and practical justice of a kind proffered to many city and country victims.

The Negroes can be expected to provide a radical leavening for some time, until new comfort joins with old discouragement, and a generation settles. But if before they burn out they manage to register enough voters in the South, with federal assistance, they may well have given us a decisive turn in our political life. No matter how badly gerrymandered against them Congressional districts may be, and therefore how few Congressmen they actually elect, the time will come when state-wide candidates will have to deal with Negro blocs in Southern states. The cities are even more deeply at odds with rural districts in the South than elsewhere in the country; eventually, then, the urban and Negro blocs will together elect governors and senators. Moreover, as the Southern diehards are isolated by the continued application of federal pressure, the ordinary Southern whites will be freed from their extremist political tyranny, and will then have an opportunity to develop more normal brokerage-politics on the regular American model. It will be important at that time for the Negroes to have something to trade—namely registered, deliverable voters. Remember, it was Negro voting in the North, following the war migrations, which prepared the basis for the present movement.

However, the disenfranchisement which supports non-rule by Congress goes far beyond the parochial apartheid of the South. Most significantly, it concerns malapportionment of Congressional districts selectively across the land, which makes one man's vote worth a great deal more than the vote of another. The man with the more worthwhile vote always lives in a rural area. The apportionment patterns give full representation to our vanished farm population and the culture once sustained by it. They give power to place rather than persons—and "place" means the remnant ideology of a way of life that very few people any longer live. The facts are truly amazing. In fifteen states, the difference between the smallest and largest district is approximately equal to the apportionment factor itself—410,000 persons for each Representative. The difference between the smallest and largest in the whole country in the 87th Congress—1,015,460 for an urban district in California and 177,431 for a rural one in Michigan—was more than twice the factor. (In New York, this difference came to 645,952.)

The most dramatic characterization of the related situation in the state legislatures came from Professor Charles L. Black, Jr., of the Yale Law School in a recent discussion of the proposed Constitutional amendment which has already been sneaked through in twelve states and whose purpose is to return plenary power over voting to the states. (The campaign is almost as clever as it is disgusting: being based on the obvious community of interest of rural-dominated state legislatures and the traditional states-righters of the South, the amendment is being pushed through outside the South to escape the racist stigmata, while the Southern states are mostly holding their fire.) Professor Black has estimated that this amendment, if passed, would allow amendment of the Constitution with the support of only 15 per cent of the total American population (under the present provision, two-thirds of Congress must approve or provide for amendments). The figuring goes like this: the Constitution can be amended by thirty-eight states; the thirty-eight least populous states have 40 per cent of the population; on the average, 38 per cent of the voters—because of intrastate malapportionment—can select a majority of a state legislature; 38 per cent of 40 per cent is 15 per cent of the whole.*

This despicable campaign is a last-ditch counter-attack against the great decision of the Supreme Court in *Baker v. Carr*, the Tennessee reapportionment case, handed down March 26, 1962. Since that date, suits have been filed in thirty-six states, apportionment provisions determined to be invalid in nineteen states, and some reapportionment already carried out in fifteen states. Nothing like this has ever happened before. The *New York Times* calls it a revolution, and the *New York Times* is right. Pretty clearly, a house of cards is tumbling. As with the segregation decision, the Court has commanded a direction rather than having set down a prescription. It did not say, "One man, one vote," and it did not say either/or on federal reapportionment in Congressional elections. (Future-directed vagueness is not merely a judicial habit: it is an element of judicial power.) But since state legislatures malapportion Congressional districts in their own image, the tide has turned decisively (even if the Court refuses jurisdiction of a particular case, or decides adversely).†

Beyond malapportionment lies gerrymandering; beyond gerrymandering lies the character of campaign financing; beyond that and election there is the encounter with the seniority system, the Rules

---

* Being forced to choose, for the length of one essay, between factual demonstration and speculative elaboration, I have naturally gone along with the latter. The argument as to the significance of numerical malapportionment can, I am sure, become quite complicated. Let it. When the conservatives defend it (*and* the accompanying gerrymander) with less ferocity in practice, I will listen with more interest to their arguments in theory that fair numerical apportionment would not make any real difference anyway. As for theoretical arguments justifying malapportionment, they are beneath contempt.

† It has accepted two for argument at the fall term in 1963.

Committee in the House, and the filibuster in the Senate, and much more of that sort of negative power. And beyond all this is the capstone of structural issues: the business discipline and ideological coherence of the party system; for the sloppy characterlessness of our national parties derives from the underlying structural mess. Then the final issue—the relation between elected governmental power and the power of business, finance, and other private institutions. In confronting these issues and controlling the military, we can become a coherent democratic nation. And not until then.

Quite a program. It will not be pursued, if at all, in an orderly fashion: a little here, a little there, occasionally an awareness that something really significant has happened while everybody was milling around in a discouraged way; then, with the big-city breakthrough, an accelerating momentum. On the basic existential level, the cities have already "broken through," and quite dynamically— the problem being to bring these new life-conditions to political expression. It will happen. Not without further (and accelerating) degeneration and crisis—but that is already well under way.

Take, as an example of breakthrough, the big-city Reform movement in the Democratic party. It is huffing and puffing and blowing down the burned-out structures of the old neighborhood organizations based on immigrant illiteracy. It is doing this, so far, with little more than the impetuous hostility of disgruntled *arrivés:* the movement was so little prepared for its success, in an emotional or ideological or organizational sense, that it may only fly up the flue—a new version of the fate of the old municipal do-gooders and mugwumps. In New York City, for instance, the Reformers suffer from a hilarious form of purism whereby they are rent from end-to-end on issues like the support of electable candidates and the ten-foot-pole approach to patronage. They don't yet want to win; in a distorted fashion, they have their own version of the traditional American power-negativism. But the point not to be missed is that their impetuous victories came so easily. In California, they were an essential influence in the reshaping of that volatile state (including a professionally executed Democratic gerrymander). Understandably, their efforts did not result in the desired dictatorship of the educated consumer—but these efforts did make a great deal of difference. They are very important leavening: if the Reformers understood their role, they would be even more important. Being halfway people culturally, understanding dampens their enthusiasm, which is all the fun.

Despite the adolescent militancy of the Democratic Reformers, I want to suggest, again speculatively, that the right-wingers are providing the more substantial impetus toward party realignment or other political advance. In Congress, where it really counts, the parties have already been realigned de facto, thanks to the right-wingers. Even more important, they have the money—as limitless as Texas oil and local real estate. They are smarter than one might think in spending it, too: it is reported that the Birchers are concentrating on sparsely populated Western states where a dollar goes further in buying a new Senator. Also, the pressure of events—once more, with the Negro as catalyst—has been forcing the right-wingers together irrespective of formal party affiliation. They are mostly isolating themselves, however, which is the beginning of political death; for while such isolation concentrates and purifies ideologically, it exposes practical weakness at the same time. Once the country learns they are weak. . . . And remember, it happened with [Joseph] McCarthy. The bulwark against formal realignment is that it's more trouble than it's worth, since a formal party is meaningful and useful only nationally, and the right-wingers hardly think about that (outside of the "national" Congress, where party discipline is sufficiently ineffective to leave them all the scope they need). But Senator Strom Thurmond is officially for a realignment, and so, it appears, is Senator Karl Mundt. It would happen very quickly once the troglodytes lost their major party seniority in Congress; it may happen, even if slowly, by the attrition of history.

The idea that the country doesn't want the so-called "liberal" legislation which since 1938 it has been the function of Congress to frustrate, is nicely and regularly disproved by the fact that no one (apparently not even Barry Goldwater) dares to run for President—and indeed many state-wide offices—without substantially endorsing such legislation. And if the Republicans ever try, it will be the last time. It is culturally distressing to have to call this a "liberal" program in the first place. Each generation, it would seem, must fight its battles on terrain selected by the previous generation—there is no hope for it. But this is no reason not to recognize the embarrassing fact that major elements of the American Frustrated Program are being administered today by *conservatives* throughout Europe.

Because of our system of non-rule, we have in one bundle the old and new problems of Europe—many of the social-welfare issues and industry-articulation matters that Europe dealt with some time ago, plus the deeper and more difficult questions of long-term redistribution of income with which Europe is having at least as much trouble as we are. In America, all of these have come together under the primary non-rule issue of federal deficit financing, also known by the fighting slogans of a balanced budget, fiscal responsibility, and that final metaphor for the backside of the moon, a stable dollar. The cultured pearls which make up Congressional wisdom concerning deficit financing are the open-mouthed despair of the majority of economists in the country. But I want to make the heretical suggestion that this organized, purposeful stupidity is founded on genuine cunning. Reasonable fiscal policy and planning, in the conservative style of Europe, would mostly miss the American point. The owners and rulers abroad are "protected" by a lack of resources and, on the other hand, must get the most out of the system to forestall serious redistribution. Here, there is too much abundance to allow the redistribution problem to be brought clearly forward, and any increase in efficiency would create so much additional abundance that the problem would become so clear it would not have to be brought forward. To put the case another way: we have and can have so much here that simple distribution of physical product *without* the difficulties of redistribution of wealth would nearly suffice. Given federal deficit financing, enough additional product can be created so that none need be diverted from present recipients. Eventually, however, we will have to redistribute principal or capital paper in America, but mainly to account for the federal deficit which otherwise would grow endlessly and finally defeat its own purpose. The main thing about the deficit is that it takes unused money and spends it; but in the payment of interest it recreates more unused money. It is this latter effect which must be controlled, otherwise the point will be reached where the deficit reverses its intended effect. But a $20 billion annual deficit for a decade would hardly begin the process (it would hardly do the necessary spending job, either).

The acceptance of deficit financing by the federal government for non-military purposes is, in fact, the beginning of a liquidation of our traditional system—or at least of the traditional view of our system. More precisely, it would be a major step forward in a process of liquidation which is already well under way. But it is that one step which convinces you that you are really now on the road. Deficit financing goes beyond what taxes and the corporations have done to alter the property system: it confronts the major historical matter of the *rentiers*. That is why it is being fought so frantically throughout our society. Also, it is the issue par excellence for the non-rulers. They lead the fight with such desperate effectiveness because non-rulers must non-rule—they lose power decisively by joining in genuine rule. The blockade against federal spending is the common denominator of the non-rulers' frustration of the whole "liberal" program. Abhorrence of a deficit is the always available reason for saying "No!"

The largest and most enduring political/cultural question in the United States, however, is the relation between the backwardness enthroned in Congress and the basic industrial-financial power in the country. The relation of Congressmen to local business interests seems painfully clear. But what about the managers of big business? Is Congressional backwardness a social/political camouflage for big business? Or is the corporate power culturally incapable of confronting the social base of Congress? Or is it both—in that business may utilize the camouflage because it cannot overcome the backwardness? Take General Electric, and you have one answer: with IBM and Ford, perhaps another. The model may be the relation of big business to smaller firms in the NAM, where the screaming of the free enterprisers is clearly a screen of noise to obscure the bigger, surer managerial power in the background.

It is the ingrained irresponsibility of big national business that complicates the matter. They may have done nothing about what Congress is doing to the country for the simple and absurd reason that it has not occurred to enough of them that it is anything but the other fellow's problem. Irresponsibility of this high order, however, creates irrelevance, so that their dominant power ends up immobilized.

The deepest "malapportionment" of all, then, is this profound structural irresponsibility of corporate power. Power is quantitatively limited: if they have it, whether or not they use it, it means that we don't have it even if we would use it. The big corporations are exaggeratedly frightened of federal power in the abstract, but deal with it easily and well enough for their own limited purposes (*vide*, military procurement). Perhaps they are so preoccupied with their cat-and-mouse maneuvering vis-à-vis the Executive that they have not gotten around to noticing Congress as a separate problem (also, things went so "smoothly" there in the past). More likely, they are so unreasonably fearful of the potential power of the Executive in relation to their own that they have not felt able to dispense institutionally with the native troops supplied by Congressional suzerains, just as they have not been bold enough ideologically to dispense with NAM balderdash.

If we assume that big corporate power is by and large unwilling or unable to assist in breaking the Congressional blockade, we still want to know how active they would become in support of it, should an attack from other quarters approach success. I don't think they would fight too hard to protect the Thurmonds and the Mundts. If for no other reason, they just don't think big enough. That may indeed turn out to be their historical epitaph. Which would be too bad: for what else is there that can serve as a ready, rational counterweight to an inevitably oversized federal power?

I do not want to be taken as suggesting that politics is *all* structural-spiritual. By no means. My point is that we are at a peculiar and particular juncture, whereby certain rotten structural-spiritual timbers not only endanger the stability of the edifice, but also constitute an inviting pushover. The change I am talking about, moreover, is a big one only because it has been frustrated so long. A few billion dollars' worth a year of federal aid to education is not going to make all that much difference in the cultural quality of our lives; and a couple of billion a year well spent on medical training and facilities will still not cure cancer and heart disease. I am talking about *a fairly pallid majoritarianism*—just the minimal adjustment to the effects of a technological society, and particularly the urban and other quality-of-population problems created thereby. A truly intelligent and dynamic use of our abundant opportunities—the opportunities of technological abundance—is, I fear, quite beyond us. That will require a wait of at least one generation.

As Neil MacNeil advises us, the New Deal ended with the passage of the Wage and Hour Bill in 1938. That Congress also marks the beginning of the conservative coalition which has effectively non-ruled the country on domestic issues since then. In 1938, Sam Rayburn became majority leader, thus beginning his dominant historical role as the Great Broker of the Democratic party—which ended factually with his death, but even more importantly with his devoted leadership of the 1961 Rules Committee fight against "Judge" Smith. I am guessing that the brokerage system Rayburn presided over for nearly a quarter of a century was approaching its end, regardless of his personal fate, and wizard that he was. For two paramount reasons: the Negroes would not stand still for it much longer; and it was not good enough in the first place.

My point comes down to this: a shift of twenty to forty Representatives could in some degree redetermine American, and thus world, history. This is not a proposition that can be "proved" abstractly. It will have to be tested. Not that history is determined or redetermined by mechanical means; it is simply that the House of Representatives is currently the front-line of the political problem, and the problem is there susceptible to solution by a small shift. Now, "counting the House" for general purposes is a complex and perhaps hopeless task (on specific bills it is counted regularly and with great accuracy). Social forces do not express themselves neatly in the ideology and voting records of individual Representatives: I assume that there will always be a swing-group in the House, and the House will always be a brokerage agency. But again, the present structural situation is so out of whack that these obvious facts of political life do not obtrude at the threshold of the immediate problem. The House has passed or rejected President Kennedy's domestic measures with notably close margins. In the Rules Committee fight in the 87th Congress, the final vote was 217–212, the official or formal bloc membership being 174 Republicans, 162 Northern and Western Democrats, and 99 Democrats from the Southern states. When the President counted the House after his election (according to MacNeil), he found 180 for him and 180 against on his general domestic program, with seventy-odd "negotiable." The "negotiables" are mostly urban Republicans and some populist-minded rural types, both South and West.

The underlying problem, I have suggested, is that we have a negative view of power and we have not yet succeeded to our nationhood. But we may be closer than we realize to achieving a grossly realized national power capable of dealing with the Frustrated American Program. (That achievement is also the basis of a serious national culture, incidentally, as well as of serious legitimation of national corporate power.) The Negroes, the courts, and the new activity of the educated masses are enough, I hope and I believe, shortly to overcome the narrow margin remaining between us and our nationhood. The alternative would be a deadly drama indeed.

> NOTE: *We are now, of course, embarked on the deadly drama. But we came pretty close, before everything fell apart. The Supreme Court fulfilled the promise of* Baker v. Carr *in* Wesberry v. Sanders *and* Reynolds v. Sims, *both handed down in 1964. Following Lyndon Johnson's great electoral victory in that year, the 89th Congress—representing the necessary shift of seats in favor of the urban liberal majority—finally enacted the Frustrated American Program; in addition, it re-enacted the Civil War Amendments, thus freeing the slaves again— but still without forty acres and a mule; and accepted the beginnings of adequate fiscal management. They did everything except spend enough money; this was supposed to come a little later. But the increased domestic spending that was advertised to follow the post-Cuban détente was lost in the Vietnam escalation. Today, we escalate domestic destructiveness while waiting for the check-writers to take pen in hand.*

❀ KENNEDY AND AFTER

NEW YORK REVIEW OF BOOKS, 1963

> *I watched television around the clock, from Friday through Monday. Then I wrote this piece, which was published along with many others in a special issue of the* New York Review of Books. *That was an experience the generations shared. So another Kennedy will run for President, and maybe make it, and maybe survive it. I accept the Kennedys as an Inevitability. But a democracy that can be saved only by monarchy is not a democracy that knows what it is doing. After some of our current problems are solved or pushed aside, we will finally have to come to terms with the absurd image of equality on which the Republic was founded. Can this be prepared for? Only if the idea and the actuality are introduced to each other—in a freshly polite modern fashion.*

On November 22, 1963, nearly five thousand people died in the United States. It was an ordinary day in this respect. But on that particular Friday, President Kennedy was one of the five thousand. From the response of the nation, revealed through its culture, you would have thought that death had been invented on November 22, 1963. And for that culture, it indeed had.

The death was untimely and violent, and to this extent it was "senseless." But so are many, many other deaths. An old man, ful-filled, dies in his sleep—what a sweet passing. To arrive at this golden point, however, the old man had to grow old, and to con-front a hundred thousand times the unknowable fact of his own death. The President died less by dying young, and without nagging pain. But how much have living Americans died through him, in this modern revision, by the networks, of the martyrdom of Christ. It will turn out to be, I think, one of the greatest cultural events of the modern period.

Barring extraordinary disclosures, it was not a political assassina-tion. Even President Garfield was murdered by a disappointed, if deranged, office-seeker. But the assassination of President Kennedy was not a clearly purposeful political assassination. It was something larger. Oswald appears to have been a Communist-affiliated para-noid, and since the event occurred in the leading right-wing area of the country, the initial ambiguities are thus provided by the undis-charged psychotic potentialities of the day. This, and nothing else, is the basis of the great myth. Begin with these ambiguities, add the simple Christian fact that the man is dead, and it would be as astounding as the events themselves if one ambiguous symbol did not join with another in a pyramid of meaning mounting to a prom-inent place in the Valhalla of this Republic.

The martyr is not the man who suffers superlatively, but the man whose life takes on a startling meaning by virtue of a perfect death. In this sense, the President is a genuine martyr: so genuine that one is aghast at the wisdom of accidental history. As with any myth, the facts will be argued until the day after kingdom comes: the facts of Oswald's intention and culpability, of the Dallas police depart-ment's intentions and competence, of Lyndon Johnson's intentions and achievements—but, far beyond everything else, and despite everything else, there will be the "facts" of Kennedy's potentiality as of the moment preceding his death. Because what died was poten-tiality, and it was this that was martyred.

Starting from the perspective of the ward-heeling savvy of Honey Fitz, the multi-millionairing of Ambassador Joe, and the smooth, smart, ruthless capture of the crown by a superbly prepared New Man superbly joining and using his antecedents—one can trace a brief course in American history, developing, as it turned out, into Greek tragedy. What that family attempted; what that family did; what happened to that family. And how it reveals our history, ridding us at last of Abe's log cabin (invented by or for Harrison) and allowing us to enter a twentieth-century fantasy with city immigrants as heroes, instead of homesteading farmers.

President Kennedy's achievement—indeed his effort—was cultural rather than political, in life as so obviously in death. He did nothing commensurate with his pretension. Under extreme pressure from the streets, he delivered a splendid civil rights speech as Lincoln, also under great pressure and just as belatedly, delivered a dull but effective Emancipation Proclamation. But one was a speech, while the other was an act. And the President was clearly, at the time of his death, retreating carefully in the face of White reaction in the North.

Kennedy was young and well-favored, and so is his wife. But these assets could have become liabilities if they had been used differently. They were, instead, used very well indeed. He made youth stand for energy, and then he offered this energy in the support of proper principles. His exceptional quality was his educated intellect (exceptional for an American President), and so his style was not only energetic and proper but it also constituted a cultural advance. He took over Stevenson's clientele without much difficulty, and some Republicans besides. The over-all achievement was their style. During Kennedy's campaign, I had thought that he was acting on a careful critique of the Truman administration. But it turned out that he was concentrating on getting elected, not on making history as Roosevelt did, and that he was running against Eisenhower (which Nixon could not do because he had to make believe he *was* Eisenhower). He built up an image of energy and purposefulness, more narrowly managerial than ideologically liberal. Once elected, his hundred days were about as much like Roosevelt's as his civil rights speech was like Lincoln's Proclamation.

Until the Bay of Pigs, his administration was all excellent "task force" reports and satisfyingly professional messages to Congress. And Sorensen, no question, is a fine speech-writer. Then suddenly it turned out that Congress was hard to influence in any desired direction. And it was again discovered that the Presidency is a much bigger and more effective and satisfying office in questions of foreign policy than it is smack in the middle of a domestic mess. (Though in all fairness that red telephone could drive anybody crazy.) The steel encounter and stock market tumble ended the chance of any really serious economic measures. There remained only business bribery (the depreciation action of 1962) and the deviously, desperately inept tax bill of 1963—the last act, if ever there was one, of an over-all policy facing political bankruptcy. The political point is to achieve a purposeful deficit by any number of possible means. Kennedy's efforts to achieve this by throwing a comprehensive tax bill to the congressional wolves was an act of helplessness—encouraged, no doubt, on the business–Wall Street side of the administration by a certain lack of sincerity as well. When the President died, the whit-tler's knife had already begun work on the civil rights bill, the tax measure was nearly beyond liberal support, and neither was any longer promised for 1963. *This* Prince Hal died before Agincourt.

The inheritance left by President Kennedy is immense because he began so much, finished so little. Again, it was all style, all unful-filled. Even his two great achievements—surviving the Cuban con-frontation, and making a fact out of the limited test ban treaty—are potential in their nature. Both are preparatory, and both are exer-cises of the Presidency in the more traditional foreign sphere.

There remains his popularity. Kennedy not only had it, he desired it. He wanted to be liked by the whole world. Who doesn't? But he had the opportunity: the rest of us don't. The generic criticism in Washington is that he was deeply concerned about his popularity, that he hoarded it, that he took his natural friends for granted in order to pursue and convert his natural enemies. This psychological view fits neatly into the very special course of his actual economic policy (remembering all the while that he was very smart, he knew the score, his problem was not academic but political).

With his style, with his popularity—with all that fresh tone, that late harbinger of serious and responsible Establishment leadership in the United States, at last—he made love, to be succinct, to the American people. He concentrated on it, and he managed to get the people to love him (he was proud of his capacity to get elected, his know-how). So he left a nation of unfulfilled lovers behind him.

With this background, let us now recall the startling essence of the event—the televised community of death.

Death is not unknown to popular culture. In fact, as an accompaniment to violence and official morality, it is an all-too-frequent event. But this kind of death is short and silly, really a form of punctuation in the grammar of popular culture. Death is almost never the "subject" of a representation—except perhaps the sickening revulsion toward it put forward in postwar movies, the underside of the noble attitude toward death required in wartime films. Mostly, it is the death of detective stories, part of the convention, or an ancillary fact accompanying violence or official evil. It is mostly like Oswald's death, with the advantage that it is staged and photographed better, but with the disadvantage that it is not quite so "real." Oswald was tried on television and executed on television, a pattern of swift justice which had been fully developed earlier in TV westerns.

The networks stayed with the whole story practically around the clock for three and a half days, approximately eighty-two hours. The central character in the drama was the coffin. In mute splendor, it hypnotized the camera, just as the camera hypnotized us. Mrs. Kennedy had been closest to the President in life; she was an essential part of his public image; she was sitting next to him when he was shot; if he was not killed instantly, then in effect he died in her arms; she sat alone with the coffin during the return flight from Dallas; and hardly left the body until the funeral was over. In ancient lore, truly the wife of a fallen hero. The whole world remarked on the quality of her presence. Since she could not and was not called upon to speak, true to a visual art, not even Shakespeare could have improved upon it.

And the children: who, in a lesser performance, would have dared to have the little boy execute a toy salute to his father's coffin? And De Gaulle, the magnificent enemy conquered by death: all the great of our public governments (but not our private leaders—I did not see Roger Blough or David Rockefeller, Henry Ford II or the secretary of state of AT&T)—all filed past the coffin, on camera, the camera that wept over the coffin and interrupted the weeping only to return compulsively to Dallas, in its new effort to comprehend a new subject—real death.

Finally, on Sunday night, faced with the loss of the coffin on the following day, the camera turned to the audience. As the American people filed by the coffin under the camera, they revealed themselves as never before by the sameness of expression in their greatly varied faces. The mystery of death and the mystery of the living interacted upon and enlarged one another. I thought I had never seen the

American people before: Could these really be the persons one passes on the street every day? These are accidental encounters, but here the camera presumed to select and sum up for you. As befits a democratic art, the greatest moment was reached when the chorus spoke.

The subject of death is now included in our popular culture, which thus takes another long step in fulfilling its promise to provide us with a religion appropriate to passive consumers. The translation of life into the terms of this comprehensive culture thus continues.

It was as if America had just discovered the fact of death—and on television. What made death suddenly important was the unfulfillment of the dead man, which America suddenly recognized as its own unfulfillment. That is perhaps why it was taken so personally. And Oswald's death on the screen simply underlined the fact that, yes, death was at issue, yes, at issue on the television screen, yes, anyone in the audience can lunge forward and kill, yes, it is real, yes, it is us. It was awful, it was "just like" history.

❀ WHAT'S HAPPENING TO AMERICA

UNPUBLISHED, 1966

This piece has a history.

The Partisan Review *Bosses decided, during the War, to devote their publication to an expression of superior international taste, rather than to a gut-engagement with what was in front of them. It was a reasonable (if not daring) decision, at the time; and the magazine, with this policy, turned out to have a very substantial influence on the course of American elite-consciousness. But they could have done more and better: and I ruined my relation with William Phillips, Partisan's co-editor, telling him this in, probably, 1948. What I said was that we are in the absurd position of discovering, for instance, that Dashiell Hammett is a significant American by reading about it in one paragraph or so of something by André Gide. I said it was all right to publish whatever you could get of Gide, Eliot, Silone, etc.—but that our serious kind of literary/political effort, even granting the practical utility of tying a tail to the kite of available elitism, required us to get wet all over in the rawness of American experience as well. A year or so later, this obvious idea penetrated Phillips' active view of things (or he finally convinced Philip Rahv, who was the superior boss, of its practical validity) and PR put together a symposium entitled "America and the Intellectuals." I was not asked to contribute. (Who gets asked to a symposia-bash in New York is an important bit of status-stuff, not lightly to be handed out to overdue comers, which I then was.)*

Fifteen years later, there was another symposium—called "What's Happening to America"—and, happily, I was asked to contribute. Alas, my contribution was not published. Again, they were wrong; so I publish it now.

America is the first place on the planet, the first time in the history of our kind of animal, when and where there was ever enough of what it takes. We are the first wealthy nation. This fact so completely dominates all others that I am continually re-surprised at the capacity of our better minds to forget it, in their efforts to remember and elevate each his own more treasured reality. It is now the final hour in which to stop this sort of thing, and begin at the obvious beginning: *American wealth.* Our entire history concerns the triumph of wealth over everything else; and the heart of our present and soul of our future concerns only the problem of what to do with it, now that we are triumphantly stuck with it.

Basic economics thus transcended, the major primitive problem in America is political. But this political problem—broadly, to revise and refashion the inherited New Deal coalition—is dealt with no more realistically than the old economic one was. It is increasingly bypassed in favor of cultural, or at least "style," preoccupations and preferences. The Kennedy government-in-exile, within a decade and with or without the heir-apparent, will upend this nation so decisively in this matter that those of us who survive will end our days wondering how in God's name we could have wasted our time worrying about the eventuality. Indeed, the inevitable triumph of this brilliant new style grouping is now so clear that some few of us had better begin soon to understand it, and to sketch out the ideas essential to an eventual criticism of it.*

Because of our ethnic diversity, and the tragic unfulfillment of

---

* It never occurred to me that the second one would be killed, too.

WASP America (including its failure to lead), the first powerful appearance of dominant national style will revolt most of the best of the survivors (of whatever origin). And, for a subsequent decade or two, style will determine more of our history than substance can: the decisive power will be in the hands of style-mongers. For *Partisan Review* writers and readers, the critical personal issue is thus the same as it has always been—the vagaries of the relation between middlebrow and highbrow. (Properly understood, that touchy confrontation has been the experience of our special segment of this transitional generation—the American Stalinists were more middlebrow than Stalinist, if you know what I mean.)

In America, we are only now beginning to create a public reality that the American people are now beginning to live in—beyond get-off-the-ship and make some money, or make something or somebody else. The physical frontier ended in 1890; but the inner frontier of our American dreams of wide-continent Ultimatism—this may just have ceased recently. Meanwhile, highbrows along with most other Americans have been making the usual strenuous effort to substitute an overheated private reality for the eternally absent public one. This effort (we all know it) has now collapsed, with a resounding finality. Those who insist, nevertheless, have become dangerous: I predict a startling increase in intrahousehold crime, within the decade: "crime" is only a terminal point on a continuum of deteriorating behavior of much wider range. ("Crime in the streets" has been first to occur because the poorest need it more, and ordinarily come from overcrowded households, with less room to maneuver in.)

"... *there is reason to fear that America may be entering a moral and political crisis.*" We were born in one; never existed without one; and the fresh element today is merely that more people now have more time to confront it, and less reason or opportunity to avoid it. The major impulse of American history has been achieved —we have converted this beautiful continent into an unimagined machine of wealth—and are thus compelled to find something else to do with our remaining time and energy, namely, to explore the utterly original task of using wealth of such magnitude. (When the human race lacked wealth, it thought that having it would solve all problems: *on the contrary, the effort to create it was in part an escape from the human problems which having it now makes inescapable.*)

"*How serious is the problem of inflation? The problem of pov-*

erty?" The so-called problem of inflation is a vulgar political matter, soon to become a secondary problem of policing petty theft. Ideologically, however, it will entertain primitive minds for many decades. The problem of poverty—properly understood as a spiritual rather than a material issue (in America)—is the grand problem of the future: It is now at about the level of the issue of punitive drawing-and-quartering as a means of inducing eighteenth-century Englishmen to control themselves; we must soon decide whether we really require living examples of human failure in order to induce us to accept our own utterly inadequate Success.

"What is the meaning of the split between the administration and the American intellectuals?" The meaning is that the administration has some power the intellectuals intend to—and through Kennedy will—get. Vietnam is an occasion, not a cause. With that weird do, we are witnessing a classic example of what used to be understood as "class struggle." From the point of view of the intellectuals (the New Class), President Johnson's centrist coalition does not contain enough reserved seats for them and theirs: the second President Kennedy's will.

"Is white America committed to granting equality to the American Negro?" No. And it never will be. Indeed, before the majority of Negroes get their share of bogus Granted Equality, the whole national ritual concerning same may well have gone out of fashion. Still, Nice Negroes are even today a necessity in all aspects of semi-official life and, since they are in short supply, many more will be created to satisfy the demand. Residual Negroes—those who refuse to or cannot forgive history (as, let us say, the Zionists and some others could not)—will be assimilated to the brand new human category of Example Outsiders, now just beginning to be discussed inadequately as the problem of "poverty."

"Do you think any promise is to be found in the activities of young people today?" I would not dare think otherwise. Representing promise or threat, offering heroism or nonsense, "it" is to be found there if anywhere. If the question implicitly refers to youth activities regarding Vietnam, that is a national draft riot by and on behalf of young people from privileged families. Assuming the question to be more extensive, the real issue of our activated youth is when and how they will grow up, and into what. (For us older ones, the issue is what we did or didn't do about *that*.) Personally, I like them, and am prepared to see the world they will live in through

their eyes, as well as through my own dimming ones. The one fact that the world has changed so much so quickly can be taken to excuse both their nonsense and our educational ineffectiveness; but I urge each group to refrain from any easy overemphasis of this one fact. Mainly, because the education (of each) is not yet complete. . . . The infinitude of the relation between the generations: one day we will put that up front, where it has always belonged. Perhaps that will be the final spiritual effect of American wealth: that we will all become grand masters of nurture, accepting *all* of our historical impossibilities, and *none* of theirs. *What fathers our sons might be!*

2

▤ SOME EARLY CONCERNS

FDR: *The Dominant Personality*

❀ NOTES ON ROOSEVELT

UNPUBLISHED, 1947

Review of F.D.R.: *His Personal Letters—
Early Years,* edited by Elliott Roosevelt
(Foreword by Eleanor Roosevelt)

I no longer recall why this review, written for Commentary,
*was not published. Probably I was too young, in Elliot Cohen's
view, to presume upon the near-holy preserve of Roosevelt's
personality so soon after his death; perhaps there was just too
much amateur psychoanalysis to be stomached (I've cut most
of it). Those who were not there can hardly imagine how
BIG Roosevelt was: his absence was a dominant political fact
at least until 1952—a good part of Eisenhower's election was,
in my opinion, an inept effort to fill the void. Roosevelt was
big whether or not you liked him; I did and didn't; but he fascinated me. Certainly he was more than a President: his personality—what he would say, or not say, next; what he would
do; how he looked—was an institution. In effect, he refurbished
American optimism when it was on the ropes, and when the
country was not yet capable of transcending its hunger for the
booster view of life.*

❀ THIS CURRENT volume of Franklin D. Roosevelt's letters is the
first in a series of three projected ones. It extends from his first letter
(1887) to his mother at the age of five (a room-to-room communi-

cation: "Dear Sallie . . . I am very sorry you have a cold and you are in bed. . . . I am glad to say that my cold is better. . . . Franklin D. Roosevelt") through twenty-five fascinating pages of boyhood offerings, and nearly four hundred pages of the repetitious Groton correspondence, to the scanty communications concerning his life at Harvard: it takes us to the point of his graduation in 1904. The second volume will cover the period 1905 to 1928, and the third will contain the personal material of the time of his governorship and presidency. Volume I, *Early Years*, is made up almost exclusively of his letters to his mother. It is necessary to say of it, as of so many collections of letters, that its chief benefits will accrue to historians rather than to the general reader. Since the letters are extremely repetitious and, moreover, addressed chiefly to one person, it would be a serious error to consider the image of their author which may arise in the reader's mind as true, much less as good, biography. Especially is this the case with the life of Roosevelt, who existed and exists in most minds more as a divine emanation than as a natural man. The editorial work on the collection, undertaken by the late President's son Elliott, consists chiefly of notes which explain allusions in the letters. Since these mainly concern persons, the notes read very much like a society column. The book would have been much more readable if these had contained additional biographical material and less "lineage."

I

FDR's family tree has its American roots in two seventeenth-century forebears, Claes Martenszen Van Rosenvelt and Philippe De La Noye, the latter apparently having been a *Mayflower* passenger (or close to it). His father, James Roosevelt, was fifty-two when he married the beautiful Sara Delano, then twenty-six. James Roosevelt was a wealthy Hudson Valley patroon; FDR's mother came from a merchant family and spent part of her early years in China, where her father was "repairing war-damaged fortunes" by working for a large Boston trading firm. Thus, FDR was born and grew up in a flourishing aristocratic milieu. He had all of the advantages which money and social position, even as translated into terms of culture and a way of life, could afford in the America of his day. In several of the later letters, he expresses a derogatory attitude toward the aristocracy of Boston: he was not excluded from this highest of highest, but neither was he totally *of* it. At Harvard, he was often present at the most fashionable salons of the day, but he never identified with the special ways of Back Bay and Beacon Hill Boston. That he was not born to it, and did not aspire to it, I consider an extremely beneficent factor: Boston was already in its decline, was becoming faddist and overintellectualized. Roosevelt was superbly fortunate—he was as aristocratic as one could possibly be in America without thereby having himself firmly cut off from the primary national currents.

FDR was raised at Hyde Park, with all the paraphernalia of French and German governesses and numerous male tutors and frequent trips abroad, until he entered Groton at the age of fourteen. (From her disinclination to have him leave her, his mother kept him from boarding school for two years.) During this period, he was often in the company of adults and, otherwise, seems to have associated almost exclusively with those of his own class, even of his own larger family (there were scores of cousins, etc.). Groton, of course, is a very expensive and very exclusive upper-class preparatory school, and so for four more formative years his milieu was not exactly broadened. Not until he entered Harvard at the age of eighteen was he even faced with the issue of democratic social relations. And, naturally, even there he associated chiefly with those of his own class.

Perhaps the most striking characteristic of Roosevelt's life (certainly as revealed in these early letters) was his huge variety of interests; and, secondarily, their persistence throughout his life. In the first intramural letter to his mother, he enclosed several drawings of boats. The round of parties and engagements is in evidence even at the very tender age of six years. Also, at this early age, he had begun to collect bird's eggs under his father's guidance (Hyde Park is today filled with mounted specimens of *all* kinds). He began his famous stamp collection when only nine years old. (Elliott Roosevelt mentions "F.D.R.'s insatiable habit of collecting and keeping anything and everything. . . .") At Groton, he engaged in almost every variety of sport, excelling in golf; he was manager of the baseball team; an active member of the Groton Missionary Society; a soprano in the glee club; played the mandolin during the summer; was general secretary-factotum of the golf association at his family's usual summer resort; a debater; received the Latin prize upon his graduation; read current books; kept up his interest in naval history and science; was a reporter for the school paper; usually received a "B" average; etc. At Harvard, he was just as active, but in a more concentrated way. He largely confined his interest in sports to crew; and he spent a great deal of time working for the *Crimson*, of which he eventually became an editor. (This editorship was the great success of his whole school career, and his son Elliott gives it a prominent place among the important factors in his development.)

Psychologically, Roosevelt's wealth of objectified interests is surpassingly significant. He was always active, his energies continually had an outgoing direction. FDR was seldom if ever *alone* in any important sense, and he seems never to have suffered from any serious depression: his optimism was almost beyond belief. (One of the consequences of having multifold interests is that a failure or frustration in one of them will not be totally dispiriting, nor is it likely to induce withdrawal.) His variety of interests, his multiple activities, produced (or perhaps were the consequence of) what can be called a *generalized* relation to life. Roosevelt was extreme in nothing—unless it was in his love of food or his collecting mania. Yet he plunged into life seemingly with all his soul. In his almost total projection of himself—which was pronounced in childhood and became even more emphasized as he matured—we have some of the qualities of genius. But there was no outstanding devotion to principle, or to an idea—or, in fact, to any *one thing*. (Even as editor of the *Crimson*, time-consuming as that was, and although he carried a full academic program, he found time for numerous social activities—at school and at Hyde Park, New York and Boston—for sports, and for other personal pursuits.) He had a strong ego, which seems to have been well in control of his impulses and of any desire he might have had to be an angel. Being genuinely and successfully an aristocrat (in American terms), he was "classicist" in temperament and, though having quite an animated and charming personality, he appears never to have been much disturbed by romantic or rebellious impulses. (He took a very priggish tone toward a cousin who had some chorus-girl trouble while an undergraduate at Harvard.)

But, beyond all else, there is the high importance of FDR's extremely close relation with his mother—and this in no ordinary sense. She had at twenty-six married a widower just twice her age;

one is not surprised, therefore, to find her much engrossed in her beautiful male child born two years later. Such a marriage would seem to indicate an ambitious woman; whether or not this is so, she was certainly ambitious for her son. As the editor of *Early Years* says, the volume "exists at all because of the preoccupation which Sara Delano Roosevelt had for the future of her only child." She not only preserved the letters, but dated and corrected them as well. For the first fourteen years of his life, FDR was seldom if ever separated from his home and his mother at the same time. And when, after the eight-year separation necessitated by his education (and after the intervening death of her aged husband), the prospect of his return to her was shattered by his announcing an intention to marry, she went so far as to send him on a cruise—an upper-class technique normally reserved for starry-eyed debutantes in the movies—in the hope that his idea of marrying might evaporate. It did not, and after some further delays, she acquiesced, and he was married to his cousin, Anna Eleanor Roosevelt, after being graduated from Harvard.

There is no indication in his letters of a desire to escape the blanket of his mother's love—until he concluded his third year at Harvard. Then he wrote that he wanted to spend several weeks of his summer vacation on a brief European tour with a college friend; he insisted that he would go only if she assured him that she would not be made dissatisfied by his absence. She assented, since he had said the trip would do him good, and he made the quick tour with great enjoyment.

When a mother loves an only son overly much, it leaves, as nothing else can, a determining mark throughout life. While there are an infinity of resolutions of the problem of "smother-love"—and most of them are well jumbled—they nevertheless appear to fall into two general patterns: that of the individual who finally disengages himself from his mother only to fall into a lasting dependence on his wife; and that of the Lawrencian figure, who must spend his life in concentration on one form or other of protest, of grasping at masculinity. On the surface, Roosevelt would seem to belong to the former group. However, this "surface" is deceptively coherent: it is too much of one piece. And Roosevelt's personality is, if anything, excessively complex. (Also, we naturally cannot judge on the basis of the present letters, all addressed to his mother.)

(*Here I tried to make a psychoanalytic thing out of the following facts:* [1] *the letters are filled with references to food and his teeth; and* [2] *Sebastian de Grazia had documented the fact that Roosevelt was breast-fed for a year and a half.*)

II

FDR's very close relation to his mother, his great *variety* of interests, the inner homogeneity of his social relations until he entered into political activity, the great advantages of his background—all of these factors, I believe, speak for a profound and thoroughgoing *continuity* in his life. What was at the beginning, so was it at the end: he expressed with satisfaction (not as symptoms or fantasy) the same basic emotional interests, and in a similar way, throughout his life. Except for one activity: politics. Roosevelt was fulfilled in life shortly after he was born—patterns of personality were established and a milieu provided for their correct functioning, which would satisfy the Roosevelt "I" as much as could be for the rest of his days: the disruptions of biological growth and decay were set to cause an absolute minimum of dislocation of "continuity." He lacked only one not-too-important thing: to become in the eyes of others (objectively) what he was already securely to himself (subjectively)—that is, the most important individual in the world. In a difficult symbolic sense, Roosevelt had no reason but a political one to go "outdoors," no deep motivation to "leave home" except to become President. And so he was pre-eminently suited to be such at a time and in a country that needed a genuine President, but when and where politics was still based for the most part on "not leaving home"—I mean, where politics was still non-revolutionary.

When Freud said that the first years of an individual's life were the most important, that one's basic emotional patterns were established then, he did so to explain why most people are so unhappy in their maturity. But the same formulation of psychogenesis allows us to see why Roosevelt's life was as satisfactory and as successful as it was. *There are no sharp, devastating breaks in the course of Roosevelt's early life.* He had only one tendency which could have caused him to fail, and that disappeared after his attack of infantile paralysis:* this was described by a Groton classmate as his "independent,

* While Roosevelt's infirmity was very likely the favored point of speculation about his personality in the popular mind, it in no sense lay at

cocky manner," which he developed as he progressed to the higher forms at Groton. Frances Perkins refers to the same thing when she speaks of his air of aristocratic superiority, which in his early political career brought him into conflict with many Tammany politicians. This attitude, clearly, was an attempt to *assume* in public what had to be proven there, what his early life had already proven conclusively *to him*, namely, his innate superiority, his *right* to leadership —to *power*.

The dominant traits of FDR's personality, their successful expression in a milieu created for their expression—these can be observed by anyone. I have summed up their effects, and described abstractly what they produced, as *continuity*—a continuity in time above and beyond that granted to most of us. And this factor of continuity, I believe, can help greatly in explaining what was most deeply characteristic of Roosevelt as President (and what is undoubtedly the focal point of our interest in any President as a person)—the *manner* of his exercise of power. There is not space in these short notes to spell out the details; that would be the subject of a full biography. I will only suggest one rather important matter.

Roosevelt had a *generalized* relation to power—that is, power did not have to be of a particular nature for him. He had no prejudices about power's aspect: he ate hot dogs with the King of England. Which means that it was a democratic one (except in the limited but difficult sense in which "power" and "democracy" are terms which contradict one another). To speak symbolically again, the *kind* of power he had was determined by a majority vote of historical conditions. Roosevelt was as democratic as an aristocrat can be: he was as successful as he was because he translated the elements of his aristocracy into democratic terms. An aristocrat is born and trained, *exists*, to exercise power. (And there is nothing more eccentric or ridiculous than an aristocrat without power.) Now the political problem of a democracy consists entirely in the creation or ferreting out of aristocratic (genuinely excellent) elements: it presumes to construct a non-hereditary aristocracy of "talent" or "merit." Moreover, the genuine purpose of culture is to further the creation of aristocracy. And even more than the ability to wage war, the calibre

---

the *center* of his character. But very important it undoubtedly was. However, weighting such a matter is an extremely subtle endeavor, and we really require more facts than we now have at hand.

of the leaders it can find or produce is the test of a society's vitality. It is at this point that we begin to see biography as perhaps the most significant chapter in any history, certainly for the observer interested in human values. If values are created by men, and if salvation lies in the production of values in this world, then the naturalistic understanding of *men* is the core of the entire problem of history. As Marx said—and Freud has demonstrated—"the root is man."

For numerous reasons, Roosevelt's biography will be an intellectual work of primary importance in the coming years. For one thing, he was a crisis-President—and the crisis is still with us, though now running underground. Also, he is the obvious object against which to investigate a pressing methodological problem—i.e., the integration of the psychoanalytic view with the techniques of social and historical analysis. (His personal and political life are both extremely well documented, as is the history of the entire period of the New Deal and the War.) A correct understanding of FDR's career in relation to his time will besides have repercussions on the whole liberal-labor intellectual situation in America—the extreme crisis in which, I believe, is also in some sense a matter of the relation of personality to program.

This is not a new problem: William James, for instance, although he held some excellent beliefs, had to develop a special theory to show how one could believe *in* them. Roosevelt had no particularly original or important beliefs, but he did have, supremely, *the means for believing.*

✻   ELEANOR ROOSEVELT, 1884–1962

COLUMBIA RECORDS, 1965

After some urging, and with the help of a friend (who later quit), I got $150 for this piece—instead of $100—from the great CBS, Inc. The cheap bastards. This kind of writing is called "album-liner" and is considered hack-work to be paid for, if at all, by the fact that they spell your name right on all the copies of the albums containing the records that they may or may not sell. (This particular one contains Eleanor Roosevelt reminiscing about her life.) To the New Youth I speak *now firmly: Do not become a free-lance writer unless you absolutely have to. After twenty-five years of writing, I can state without any hesitation whatsoever: I have never been adequately paid for anything I have written. Sometimes I think the only honest expression worthy of a serious writer is to starve to death in public: everything else is chicken-shit, the easy way out.*

Why do I nevertheless publish this hack-work now? I can't help it, I think it's lovely.

"I know just how you feel and how hard it must be, but I do so want you to learn to love me a little. You must know that I will always try to do what you wish. . . . It is impossible for me to tell you how I feel toward Franklin. I can only say that my one great wish is always to prove worthy of him."

Thus, upon her engagement at the age of nineteen to her "fifth cousin, once removed," Anna Eleanor Roosevelt wrote to her future mother-in-law, Sara Delano Roosevelt. The widow thought so little of the match that she immediately dispatched her adored and only son on a cruise to the Caribbean.

The young couple—the painfully shy and awkward niece of the great Theodore Roosevelt and the tall, handsome young squire of Hyde Park, who was known to his classmates at Harvard as supercilious and "too" intellectual—were married two years later, in 1905. For very different reasons, each possessed great reservoirs of creative strength withdrawn behind the youthful masks then on view to the world. They must have met and married instinctually on this deeper level.

The marriage ceremony was scheduled to follow Theodore Roosevelt's Inauguration by only a few days. The new President gave away the bride and, of course, dominated the entire occasion. Endicott Peabody, the famous headmaster of Groton, performed the ceremony. It was not only an important social event but remarkably important in other ways, as it turned out in the course of time.

Eleanor Roosevelt had been prepared for her distinguished marriage by a childhood and adolescence of nearly unrelieved misery. It was a misery endured and ingested in upper-class surroundings, which to many is taken as no misery at all; but if we are willing to believe that children require more than the mere absence of hunger and squalor—that, in the beginning at least, bank accounts do not substitute for love and acceptance, among other things—her early story is very affecting.

To begin with, she was plain. At least she thought she was, and apparently enough people agreed, or failed to contradict her feeling, so that it became established. Most important, she was plain by comparison with her mother, who was a renowned beauty. Indeed, most of the women in her mother's family were known for their charm and good looks. Anna Hall Roosevelt, by all accounts, did not hide her strained feelings about Eleanor having missed this inheritance. Her nickname as a child was "Granny": she later wrote that her mother might say to a visitor in her presence, "She is such a funny child, so old-fashioned, that we always call her 'Granny.' " The distinguished woman, remembering those days, added, "I wanted to sink through the floor in shame. . . ."

Her father did not call her "Granny" but "Little Nell," after the character in Dickens. She received from her father, or determinedly imagined that she received from him, all of the affection missing elsewhere—but, or perhaps because, he was often absent. However that may be, within a year of each other and before she was ten, both parents died. She has written that the death of her father did not interrupt her deep attachment to him.

During the naturally awkward age until she was fifteen, she was raised with misguided rigidity by her maternal grandmother. Then, most fortunately, she was sent to an English school where for three years she came under the capable and liberating influence of a reportedly exceptional headmistress, Mlle. Souvestre, who took a special interest in her.

After this welcome hiatus, she was summoned back to be prepared for her New York "coming-out." Eleanor Roosevelt later wrote that she survived her year of peonage to partying only because she did not soon enough imagine "what utter agony it was going to be. . . ." More to her taste and proclivity, of the activities in the arsenal of proper young ladies, was charitable work. She engaged in much of this while she lived in New York City with an aunt. And soon she married Franklin Delano Roosevelt.

The early years of her marriage were characterized by a succession of pregnancies—six in ten years—and the successful reign of her mother-in-law (also, according to her own account, of nurses, servants, and governesses). The couple, with their growing family, lived in a house on East Sixty-fifth Street, chosen, staffed, and furnished by Sara Roosevelt. To all of this, with much helpful cajolement from her busy husband, she submitted. Indeed, she was a rather exaggerated "model" of feminine submissiveness.

But other capabilities began to appear in connection with her war work for the Navy League, and she began to assert herself as an energetic feminine counterpart to her husband's Washington career as Assistant Secretary of the Navy during the Wilson administration. Accompanying him during the campaign tours of 1920, when as the Democratic candidate for the vice-presidency he followed Cox to a smashing defeat, she took more in learning than she gave in real assistance. But then came the summer day at Campobello when Franklin Roosevelt sat in a wet bathing suit reading his mail and later, complaining of an aching back, took to his bed.

No illness has ever meant so much to this nation—unless we take Booth's or Burr's bullet as an illness. The reaction to the event at Campobello transformed two people; galvanized the basic creative resources of two exceptionally well-placed personalities; and—following inner travail they were better able to endure than we are to contemplate — produced leaps of personality for which any nation shall be indebted unto the seventh generation.

When Franklin Roosevelt was stricken, Eleanor Roosevelt had forty-one years of life left to her. This woman who undervalued herself, who had yearned to be needed since childhood, foreswore an easy feminine opportunity—that would have appeared as the grace of God to a lesser person—and entered into a final fight with the reigning tigress, Sara Roosevelt, as to whether their mutual male was to live as an invalid. It was her first and greatest political fight, so specifically feminine as to be awe-inspiring. She won it, and it foreshadowed many more—feminine and otherwise. Franklin Roosevelt died believing that, given time and opportunity, he would walk again. He didn't, but we did.

One would not want to so gild the lily as to repeat the years of triumph. He ranks with Washington and Lincoln, and she was always with him, to serve whatever purpose. Then he died, and she still served his purposes. She molded herself (the words are carefully chosen) with phenomenal energy and discipline into a major public influence, by virtue of her self-chosen devotion to what was given her of her self-chosen men or what she imagined in terms of them.

Eleanor and Franklin Roosevelt were both and equally upper-class figures. This was a matter of great importance to them—and even more so to us. The one thing democracy has required—and had been denied during most of its recent history in this country—is the devotion of its privileged persons. These were the two people who corrected that. They did it together—they were a wonderful partnership, these two democratic patricians: and once they showed the way, many of their class and character have followed.

Both of them represent in our history more a triumph of personality than of policy. Lest this seem a denigration, be assured of this writer's opinion that personality is far and away the more serious area of innovation. When, several decades later, we look to the New Deal for blueprints of a better society, we may well come away disappointed. But when we enter into the rich undergrowth of FDR's sense of the nation, his loving participation in the politics of the people, and his artist's acceptance of everything about them as working material, we linger for lesson after lesson. He more or less taught us how to toddle, politically.

When he died (". . . *I can only say that my one great wish is always to prove worthy of him*"), she continued. She was, all on her own, one of the chief consulting architects in the erection of the first universal Covenant of Human Rights. A piece of paper, alive by virtue of at least one good heart. Women begin where they happen to be situated at the moment, they ask for the moon, and they never give up. At least American women. Certainly Eleanor Roosevelt. Certainly American women *since* Eleanor Roosevelt. The life of Eleanor Roosevelt suggests that the creative female personality in America will imagine better men, will assist the existing ones to become better, will destroy no men in the process. She was "a woman for all seasons"—and such an epitaph would grace any female headstone.

Considering Eleanor Roosevelt's unarguable position as one of the great women of the modern period, the events in her life have an objective importance for the light they shed on her achievements. On the other hand, many people throughout this country and throughout the world simply loved and admired her without understanding or needing to know the personal history that shaped her career. To them, she was an historical "presence"—she stood for something. It is startling to look back and remember that this was the woman who wrote, ". . . *I do so want you to learn to love me a little.*"

Nazism: The Dominant Issue

❁ EVOLUTION OF A LEVIATHAN

CONTEMPORARY JEWISH RECORD, 1945

Review of *Behemoth: The Structure and
Practice of National Socialism, 1933–1944,*
by Franz Neumann

The Contemporary Jewish Record *was the precursor of Commentary, which was ultimately the partial successor of Partisan
Review. The connecting link, for me, was Clement Greenberg.
Along with Dwight Macdonald and Harold Rosenberg, he was
one of the leading voices The Kid listened to best of all. Him
I had to listen to: he was an editor of the magazine that paid
maybe more than 25 cents an hour. (Dwight paid $5.00 a page
in Politics—1,500 words—but him I was giving it to: I was
briefly His Protégé: today we are barely polite: such is the
literary life.) Clem was a Dutch Uncle—so good at it, and so
determined about it, that sometimes I would simply revert to
audience-status and devote myself to witnessing the astounding
glory of it all. Similarly with Harold Rosenberg's marvelous
monologues, and Dwight's incredible capacity to project the
putative centrality of American life to ambitious lower-middle-
class Jews, whether or not from Chicago: as a matter of fact, he
did pretty well with some high-class goyim from Europe.*

*As to Franz Neumann's book, it was very important in its
day. There was an overriding need, at the time, to bring the
facts of Stalinism and Nazism into some coherent relation
with the Marxist theory of history. This may seem less than
overwhelmingly necessary today; if so, that is a shallow way of
understanding your elders. One goes with the best ideas available and seriously confronts the most significant events occurring at the time: the best result of this effort is growth, not
eternal truth. History is a collection of examples of growth,
and failure of growth: just a collection of examples—nothing
like a hornbook of prescriptions. Our overly strenuous effort
to assimilate the facts of the Nazi order to the definitions of
classic Marxism still helps, when read subtly, to suggest politi-*

*cal potentialities—even as to a sophisticated corporate struc-
ture such as that in the United States today (at least to suggest
how lucky we have been, to date).*

When the first edition of *Behemoth* appeared in 1942, it was ap-
plauded all the way round the circle, from academic journals like
Studies in Philosophy and Social Science to Max Lerner and the
New York *Herald Tribune.* The book now occupies the status of the
most significant and comprehensive work on National Socialism.
This is surprising (although the book certainly deserves it), since
Neumann has a very definite viewpoint that cannot be called popular; nor is it open to misinterpretation. He employs concepts not
generally used in this country. His analysis is based on the capitalist
phenomenon of imperialism and on the class nature of modern society. Fundamentally, then, he is concerned with forms of exploitation, National Socialism being a new and singular variety. He con-
curs in the characterization of Nazism as the politics of capitalism
in extremis.

Neumann, as a matter of fact, goes far beyond the simple, familiar
statement that big capital in Germany supported the fledgling Nazi
party; he posits monopoly capital as the main prop of the National
Socialist regime, and devotes a major portion of his book to theoretical speculation and the sifting of data governing the question
whether or not Germany remains a capitalist country. But, before
taking up his discussion of this very complex problem, it will be
helpful to get an over-all view of the book and to follow in order
some of its main points.

The brief introductory chapter on "The Collapse of the Weimar
Republic" deserves special praise; it is an absolutely brilliant piece of
historical analysis. According to the author, the Social Democratic
party and the trade unions must be charged with the responsibility
for the failure of German democracy. The essence of their errors lay
in not seeing "that the central problem was the imperialism of German monopoly capital." Society was not re-created; rather it was adjusted to its own sins. And the Social Democrats were historically
foolish enough to shoulder the responsibility for this!

The first of the book's three main sections deals with the political
ideology of National Socialism. A significant paradox exists here:
Nazi theory is anti-theory. No ideological current or combination of
currents—except that combination which is pure opportunism and

therefore not theory at all—could satisfy the chief German frustration. "Traditional doctrines and values . . . are all hostile to the fundamental goal of National Socialism: the resolution by imperialistic war of the discrepancy between the potentialities of Germany's industrial apparatus and the actuality that existed and continues to exist." Imperialistic war can be carried on only if internal social conflicts are repressed and externalized; the Nazis have accomplished this with the double-edged sword of propaganda and terror. The Nazi terror system is well understood; but the main element of Nazi propaganda—the theory of social or racial imperialism—bears further discussion. "Social imperialism is the most dangerous formulation of National-Socialist ideology."

The doctrine of racial proletarian imperialism is a technique designed to secure a mass basis for imperialistic adventures. According to Neumann, in Germany it "fuses two basic elements: hatred of England and hatred of Marx." The theory is anti-capitalist: the war is posed as one between the "proletarian races" and the "plutocratic-capitalistic-Jewish democracies." Its purpose "is to entice the working classes. . . . National Socialism offers the worker everything offered by Marxism, *and without a class struggle*" (my italics). This is the essential point. International capitalism and international Marxism are set up simply as two wings of the same Jewish movement. Not classes, property and productive forms, or institutions, but Jews are the enemy. The theory, being directed against groups both high and low on the social scale, is a petty-bourgeois construction. And it is highly ironic that it is the German lower middle class that has suffered most under Nazism, its former members having by now been proletarianized or incorporated as instruments in the system of terror.

The chief beneficiaries of National Socialist rule have been the monopoly capitalists. In the second part of the book, entitled "Totalitarian Monopolistic Economy," Neumann presents this final definition: "The structure of the German economy is one of a fully monopolized and cartellized economy." Under the Nazis, small business has time and again lost out against the huge monopolies and cartels. The expropriation of the Jews not only benefited the monopolists more than any other group; it actually formed the spearhead of an attack on the entire class of middle businessmen. "Business in the occupied territory has been largely acquired by German industrialists, and . . . Germanization, like Aryanization, has accelerated the process of concentration of capital." Big industry could strengthen its position, even while the middle classes were being destroyed, only on the basis of full employment under a war economy. "National Socialism is built on full employment. That is its sole gift to the masses, and its significance must not be underestimated."

Is Germany a capitalist country? Or has a new structure been created, called either state capitalism or bureaucratic collectivism? The author is greatly concerned with this problem. His contention (and the weight of proof of his material) is that Germany remains a capitalist economy under the Nazis, with the antagonisms of capitalism operating on a higher historical level, no longer in a free or even open market but in the context of bureaucratic and political distortions. The profit motive still functions, but profit is bargained for in a new and increasingly political manner—and exclusively by the larger industrial groups, which continue to grow larger.

The third large section of *Behemoth* deals with the ruling and the ruled classes under "The New Society." Four groups constitute the ruling class: the party, the army, the bureaucracy, and industry. The ruling class is not homogeneous: "Nothing holds them together but the reign of terror and their fear lest the collapse of the regime destroy them all." Only "profits, power, prestige, and above all, fear." They are dependent on one another, since the fate of each is entirely bound up with the imperialistic effort. The role of the party is to maintain the unity of the people behind this effort; the party preserves "morale" by a system of propaganda and terror that penetrates all phases of life. Only on the supervisory board of the "Continental Oil Corporation" do the four groups form a single, integrated elite. That this corporation was organized to control conquered oil properties is a symbolically conclusive illustration of the nature of the Nazi regime.

The above picture is enlarged in the 100-page appendix to the second edition of *Behemoth*. The author records the further growth of the power of the party, especially of Himmler's police and the Speer Ministry of Armaments and War Production; the increase in the concentration of capital in big industry (or the "rationalization" of the cartel structure); and the decline of one of the four big groups, the bureaucracy, which has lost large areas of administrative control to the new party *Gau*. "The practitioners of violence tend to become businessmen, and the businessmen become practitioners of violence." Business and the party merge or mutually encroach upon one another. With the politicalization of market relations, business is compelled to translate its economic position into political power; while the party of terrorists must secure its rule with a base in the productive process. In this appendix, Neumann also elaborates his definition of anti-Semitism as "the spearhead of terror." This idea is proposed, in part, to replace the popular "scapegoat" theory. Other important additions to the text of the first edition—which remains unchanged—are included in the new appendix.

The chief criticism to be made of Neumann's method is that he perhaps overemphasizes the legal structure of society. (He was a labor lawyer before leaving Germany in 1933.) Large sections of the book are taken up with abstract constitutional theory. And it is this emphasis which may have led him to characterize Nazi society as anarchical because it lacks a coherent legal or political theory, and because the Nazi state does not fit any universalist definition of the state.

Neumann claims that in Germany there is no real center for the unification of political power; Hitler is a mere focus, and his decisions are the result of compromises between the four ruling groups. Thus, Hitler as the center of unification is "not institutionalized but only personalized." Therefore, the state, as the institutional form of power, cannot be said to exist in Germany. Power is not institutionalized—"we are confronted with a form of society in which the ruling groups control the rest of the population directly, without the mediation of that rational though coercive apparatus hitherto known as the state." By defining the state as essentially rational rather than coercive, Neumann is able to demonstrate the non-existence of a German state—which is simply verbal gymnastics. He does, however, definitely establish the particularized, non-universal, *non-rational* nature of Nazi law and administration, under which not even equality of oppression is practiced. In this sense, certainly, the use of the monster Behemoth as a symbol of chaos is apt.

❀ THE EFFICACY OF MADNESS

NEW LEADER, 1948

Review of *The Goebbels Diaries: 1942–1943*,
edited by Louis P. Lochner

Here, an early impression of one of the Fathers of modern advertising culture (not even an American).

In an exceptionally penetrating article, "The Common Man of the Nazis" (*Commentary*, December 1946), Martin Greenberg pointed out that the writers of the Stalinist-dominated "antifascist" movement had failed utterly to create any clear, unstereotyped picture of the Nazi personality. And he suggested that this failure exposed a human deadness at the center of the coalition that conducted the war against the Axis powers. This lack of human understanding was an obvious corollary of the inability of the Allied nations to comprehend and account for those factors in our historical period which prompted the response of Nazism and led it to success. And we may link this blankness-at-the-core to the fact that the resistance movements in the occupied countries seldom transcended a regressive, nationalist orientation—except where they fell under the sway of the Stalinists. The heritage of the resistance movements is Stalinism and Gaullism; and these movements were the best that "antifascism" had to offer. The failure of the West to offer any fresh or freshly-held perspective—and the criminal stupidities of "unconditional surrender" and terroristic air warfare which were put forward as substitutes—this failure was the Nazis' greatest strength. "We may certainly consider ourselves lucky not to be opposed by a front that is united ideologically," says Goebbels in his unique *Diaries*, which are so very revelatory of the Nazi mind and personality; and which offer so many fascinating details of the life of the Nazi regime in its critical days. It remains a difficult and demanding task to understand the *Nazi human being*. (We even dislike to couple these words!) But it is absolutely essential that we do so: otherwise, we will have gained nothing from this experience which has cost the human race so much, and the underworld realities to which Nazism gave successful expression will go uncontrolled and unassimilated, free to act in history again in an even more terri-

ble form. The usual response to Mr. Lochner's selections from
Goebbels' *Diaries* (the present volume contains only about one-
fourth of what remains of the original manuscript) is to sum up the
Nazi propaganda chief as being the sign of evil or as being insane
(often both). In the quotations from reviewers in the Doubleday
advertisement, he is referred to as "one of the most malignant minds
in history"; as having "a brilliant but distorted mind"; "the evil genius of the Nazi regime"; "one of the great scoundrels of our time";
"the little fiend"; etc. To call Goebbels crazy and evil is to call the
sun bright. The point is that this man wielded great power with
immense effect. He had a much greater grasp of reality—his huge
area of irrationality notwithstanding—than most sane men of good
will. And that is his secret, and the secret of Nazism: *the efficacy of
madness in the modern world.*

Not that all madness is efficacious, or that one must be mad to
have an effect on events; but these two matters used to be considered more or less totally disparate. I believe that that is no longer an
adequate concept, and I submit that the existence of the Nazi phenomenon affirms this view. (This question of the efficacy of madness
is too delicate and involved for discussion in a book review: it will be
helpful, however, to remember [1] that Freud demonstrated an *intimate* connection between insanity and "normal" life; and [2] that
acting "normally" in the face of "abnormal" events can be quite a
destructive practice.)

The Nazis did not create a new society (although there is enough
evidence in the *Diaries* that Goebbels genuinely thought of himself
as a revolutionary). What they did was to hold the old society together while it continued, and they contributed to (and battened
off) its degeneration. The two chief ingredients of the Nazi cement
were propaganda and terror. While Goebbels of course was the great
exponent of the former, he knew its limitations and was well aware
of the role of terror: "A sharp sword must always stand behind propaganda if it is to be really effective." The patterns of control that
were based on Gestapo-terror, were consolidated by Goebbels-
propaganda. Himmler shoved the German people into the Nazi theatre and used all the instruments of terror to keep them there;
Geobbels kept the stage inside filled with images, interpretations,
speeches, and even a dramatic "plot" which, as long as Himmler's
machine-guns and Allied stupidities were in evidence, made the audience half-believe that it *ought* to be in this theatre, even that it

was a good thing to be there. And in a situation pregnant with terror, half-belief is all that is required. ". . . I regard myself as responsible for the morale of the German people," said Goebbels. He did
an excellent job, since the Germans fought the last half of the war
practically on morale alone.

Two terms which Goebbels uses are saturated with ambiguous interior meaning: "psychology" and "politics." They are the key terms
of his approach. The latter derives its eccentricity from the former,
which is central, I believe. It is almost impossible to state precisely
what Goebbels means by "psychology." In some ways, it is a petty-
bourgeois vulgarization of the special meaning Nietzsche gave to the
term, but applied by Goebbels solely to the politics of power. And in
other ways it is a refinement and perfection of American advertising
usage. Whatever he precisely means, it is clear that Goebbels was a
pioneer in the exploitation of those great, rich areas of the mass
mind which have been made available through the fading away of
religious belief, the decay of traditional ideologies, and the "liberation" of emotional attachments which are consequences of modern
urban life.

❈ NOTHING BUT POWER: PORTRAIT
OF A FASCIST

UNPUBLISHED, 1946

Fascism was a real issue in the United States at one time. Now
it is not known by that name. Just as well; with that name, the
Good Guys got nowhere. It was so easy to oppose, so impos-
sible to understand. An entire epoch of Hollywood movies was
based on this particular bit of concerted ineptitude.

This is the first full-length article I ever wrote. It was re-
written a number of times—for Commentary, *shortly after the*
magazine was set up. It was accepted and paid for and not
published because—well, I really don't remember. But Dennis
fascinated me: a recognizably intellectual fascist, a real one,
sent to jail as a result of the wartime trials. Imagine that! Good
Guys and Bad Guys were to be recognized and distinguished
only after serious mental effort, not like in the movies at all.
Imagine that. (Please do.)

In the following essay you will probably notice, even without my urging, that bourgeois property and almost any kind of power have fascinated me from the very first days. I mention this so that no reader shall get the idea that I missed it. Please also note, however, that my ideas on this subject have developed considerably—particularly after lawyering. (You may also notice certain similarities between fascist emotionality, as characterized here, and the creatively degenerate hijinx of the current day.)

I

We stand at the apex of a rapidly decaying bourgeois culture. It is now easy to demonstrate the economic failure of capitalism. Nowhere in the world today does the traditional free market exist, with its corollary of deflationary crisis. The end of expanding capitalism can be dated at the beginning of the Great Depression (either 1912 or 1929, according to how one reads history), when for the first time all classes were united in their desire to halt the "natural" course of deflation. Government intervention in the economic process to save property-owners from the inevitable consequences of owning property signified the start of a paramount change in our form of life. Henceforth the state is the controlling economic factor. This means the politicalization of economic relations. (This great change in capitalism here described began, of course, with the development of monopolies, which are significant for overcoming the cruel impartiality of free markets. While monopolies always translated their economic power into political influence, they never did so as directly and efficiently as, for instance, under the Nazis in Germany.)

The bourgeois order meant, more than anything else, the growth of individualism. This development took place at the expense of both state and society: the state lost large segments of its control over affairs of property and conscience alike; society as a whole became less stable and less unified. The static feudal order that capitalism replaced took account of the inalienable dependencies which men in society have upon one another by delimiting the individual's individuality, by designating at birth a nearly irrevocable position for him in the social hierarchy. He was secure, and he was part of a unified moral order, belief in which was a function of faith rather than reason. So individualism introduced numerous tensions into social relations, making them very much more fluid and indeterminate, and eventually divorcing them in large part from the minutiae of moral restraint. The value of individualism is equivocal—that is the chief statement to make about it. While it has resulted in the increased creativity and material betterment of individuals, it has also meant insecurity, isolation—and powerlessness in emotional terms. The individual, gaining himself, lost the security of his relation to others.

In the change from the medieval society of class status to the individualistic bourgeois order, there became established, as there necessarily must have, a common denominator of status—money. Increasingly, money was power and power was money. The emphasis which individualism placed on the question of power, as a response to the situation of isolation and insecurity, eventually drove moral problems out of everyday life into Sunday morning. Money could be made, power achieved, only at the expense of others. Society came to be constructed around money, although it never led to material security for most people (it was necessary that there be a class of losers), and the few for whom it did soon discovered that the common denominator was too abstract, that it gave little real emotional security. Being abstract, it emptied life of much of its content. The need of one man for another, which is the empirical basis for moral behavior, remained largely unsatisfied.

Under the system of money, chance was elevated to the position of a principle. Factors of chance are controlled not by an individual's efficient capacities but by "luck," i.e., they are not controlled at all (as the market, when it is free, is uncontrolled). Chance-factors like death and the weather have always been surrounded by aleatory mechanisms, which serve mainly the purpose of emotional catharsis; games of chance are popular for the same reason. The important point here is that chance accentuates the actual powerlessness and insecurity of the individual: but "resolves" these magically.

Capitalism in its pure form pits man against nature and man against man more sharply than any other society. That is the basic meaning of bourgeois individualism; and the free market for labor and commodities is its focal expression. But the free market was no sooner proclaimed the arbiter of men's affairs than the circumvention of it began. Capitalism has been a process of monopolization at least as much as it has been the rule of the free market. Today, monopolies are supreme.

In personal terms, the process of monopolization was paralleled by what Erich Fromm called the escape from freedom. Bourgeois individuality has been very frustrating emotionally. The vistas it has opened have been more tempting than satisfying. Compulsive money-making was the one general "out" from this frustration. Although many values in life were dropped by the way in order to compete successfully in the money-game, still that game was predicated on a large number of failures—this beside the fact that the working class was left out entirely. The great middle groups, the penny-ante players, were frustrated as the workers were not—because they lived with impossible expectations.

In the present period, the frustrations of all but a few are greater by far than they have ever been. There are two ideological groups which make the frustrations produced by the present order the center of their orientations: the socialists and the fascists. It is a most important fact that the majority of the leadership of both groups is petty-bourgeois. The premise of each is frustration. The attitudes of the two groups differ in that the one emphasizes protest against the social system while the other stresses the achievement of power within it (whether or not that effort destroys it). Except for the Bolsheviks and a few other minor groups, all socialist movements have been predominantly moralistic. Faced with the prospect of seizing power and using it for the implementation of socialism, they have all balked and backed down. A few dates and places will suffice for reminders: Germany, 1919; Italy, 1920; England, 1926. The times that they have gained power, they have been socialists in name only. Socialists are moral, but they have not been able to make their protest real by fusing it with power. For the fascist, there is nothing but power.

The leading intellectual among American fascists, Lawrence Dennis, said of Huey Long that he would have made a great fascist leader because he was more interested in power than in protest. That is really the whole point. The question of the relation between morals and power is not equaled in magnitude of importance by any other problem. Dennis is of interest to us exactly because his entire work is an intellectually talented rationalization, in terms of vital historical factors, of frustration expressing itself as will to power. Every value except one—that of being conscious—is jettisoned in the construction of his attitude. The conflict between morals and power, which presents itself in every questionable act or idea of an act, is not a simple conflict and cannot be resolved, as Dennis attempts, by ignoring morals; neither can it be done away with—witness the socialists—by blinding oneself to the necessities of power. But by understanding Dennis, we may begin to see more clearly the consequences of believing or not believing in the adequacy of power alone. The belief in power as such, and at any price, though much more widespread than fascism, is the philosophical and emotional core of that ideology.

II

Since the premise of the fascist personality is the same as the premise of fascism itself, i.e., frustration, it will be relevant to begin with a few, brief biographical notes on Dennis. Any discussion of him, however, should be prefaced with the remark that he is first of all an intellectual and a writer. "I am much too intellectual to be a good demagogue," he said of himself. "I believe in palace revolution." Truly, his main efforts have been directed toward influencing and winning over the inhabitants of the palace; he has not consistently followed out the consequences of his ideas. The reason for this has an important place in his biography.

Dennis has lived his life on the fringes of the American upper class—close, but never quite in. Born in Atlanta, Ga., on Christmas Day, 1893, he was tutored abroad for many years and graduated from Phillips Exeter Academy, which he termed "one of the New England bulwarks of the American Anglophile snobocracy." He is today a member of the Harvard Club in New York City. During World War I, he trained at the Plattsburg camp, later writing that he was one of the only "commoners" in a tent with Quentin Roosevelt. For three months following his demobilization in Europe, he traveled around the continent playing the foreign exchange markets on a shoestring. (He retained his interest in this kind of gambling: in a political newsletter he put out years later, he interspersed political analysis and prognosis with timely market-advice.)

One of the more interesting and significant incidents of Dennis' career occurred in 1927 in Nicaragua during the development of a revolutionary situation there. He was at that time American chargé d'affaires, having entered the diplomatic service *by examination* in 1920. The story is this: First, he charged the State Department with favoritism, claiming that rich men's sons were being assigned to the "choice overstaffed European posts" while those with less means were left with the undesirable positions (like Nicaragua). Second, he accused Secretary of State Kellogg of instructing him to support Adolfo Díaz, the Conservative leader, against the head of the Liberal insurgents, Dr. Juan Sacasa. He also protested against an American officer, Colonel Carter, who was leading the Conservative army. It is all-important for our view of Dennis' character that, after acting admirably in a situation of blatant dollar diplomacy (but with very mixed motivation), he *retracted* his accusation against Kellogg— probably acquiescing to pressure—and was awarded a "choice" post in Paris. Then, a few months later while on leave, never having taken up the position in Paris, he resigned from the diplomatic service!

For the next three years, he was in Peru for a Wall Street banking firm, floating loans of the well-known South American variety. The great change took place after the Crash; he began to write, and his first book, *Is Capitalism Doomed?*, was published in 1932. This work was an attack on the economics which eventuated in the Great Depression. Norman Thomas said of it that "the convinced Socialist will find more ammunition in it than in most radical books." He also published in the early Thirties a number of articles in the liberal weekly, *The Nation*. It would appear that he had at this time become disillusioned with the prospects of significant success either in the aristocratic government service or with the "tops" in the big money racket. His frustrations in the real world of affairs led him to attack capitalism, whose faults he exposed; while becoming more and more cynical, he nevertheless in his work elevated the values of intellectual honesty and emotional sincerity. The tone was anti-business in an aristocratically intellectual vein. "Businessmen are socially the least intelligent and creative members of our ruling classes." They are helpless, he claimed, without their experts and advisers, their advertising men, etc. (Helpless without *him*, that is.)

Dennis was never much attracted to liberalism or socialism, for two reasons: he was repelled by the fanciful moralism rampant in the area left-of-center; further, to construct a realistic Left position beyond moralism would have run counter to his definite class prejudices and pretentions, and would have been largely irrelevant to his chief motivation, which was to compensate for his bitter frustration at being excluded from the higher councils and benefits of the ruling group. By the mid-Thirties, he had become an out-and-out fascist. In

1936, he published his second book, *The Coming American Fascism*, in which he attempted to describe "a desirable fascism." He later said, his words floating in bile, that this book was addressed to the ruling classes in the lost hope that they would accept the idea of fascism as inevitable and begin its introduction rationally and peacefully, to avoid its coming about later, after another war or collapse, by violent means and accompanied by mass upheaval. He would have preferred much more to work with the National Association of Manufacturers than with people like his co-defendants in the Sedition trial, whom he termed crackpots.

In a key phrase dated 1935, Dennis defined fascism "as a revolutionary formula for the frustrated elite in an extended crisis of the prevailing social system of liberal capitalism." In this definition are contained most of the significant terms in his theoretical approach. Perhaps the first among these, certainly the one most intimately connected with his basic frustration, is that of the elite. For Dennis, the elite is the prime mover in history. He defines this group roughly as the upper one-fourth to one-third of the population having an actual or potential monopoly of influence or power. The elite is divided into two main groups: the in-elite and the out-elite. When enough of the elite is "in," society is functioning satisfactorily; when too many members of the elite are "out," however, they become revolutionary because of their frustrations, and great changes are on the order of the day. "Broadly speaking, the in-elite, as a whole, can be controlled or disciplined only by forces within themselves." "Broadly speaking and as a whole," this posits the total release of drives to power.

Democratic controls do not exist for Dennis; he sees all democracy as a sham. Since the ruling economic groups corrupt democracy, democracy becomes nothing but an aspect of the hypocrisy of liberals. He can therefore blandly say—"I think all governments are democratic." Meaning that all governments must spend a certain amount of energy fooling the people in order to retain their power. Talking democracy, as the liberals do, is only *one* way of fooling the people. Talking race or nation are other ways. In his scheme, the masses are totally passive: "The elite always determine what the masses get." Logically, if the masses equal zero, so does democracy.

Although containing certain obvious truths—that talent and ambition are important historical factors, for instance—this elite theory

suffers from the fatal fault of explaining nothing. If a regime col-
lapses because too many significant individuals are frustrated, still
the frustration has to be accounted for in terms of historical blocks
and institutional decay. Then *these* factors determine history. Also,
it is not true that the masses are always passive. They become active
during the crisis of a social system, at exactly the same moment as do
the elite. And if the leaders of mass movements are included among
the elite, still these leaders are patterned under the pressure of mass
desires. Dennis' theory has the single value of placing his own personal frustration in the center of history's current. And of opening
unlimited vistas of power: as regards the ruling group or in-elite,
history is on his side, they cannot successfully ignore his frustration;
and, on the other hand, the masses are not really important at all. A
very neat rationalization, and one essential to fascist theory, which
expresses the egoistic dreams of the middle ranks, of the petty bourgeois besieged from above and from below—and the frustrated gentleman who condescends to lead these.

An interesting psychological parallel is suggested by his assertion
that "the free play of individual minority group self-interest tends to
make any community go to pieces." This is a projection of the attitude of mind of the compulsive individual who fears to allow the
"free play" of his own thoughts and emotions and feels it necessary
to repress all dissidence. Under fascism, there is no free play of interest, rather the "national will" is the supreme justification for whatever is done, but—"just as the Constitution is whatever the Supreme Court says it is, so the national will is whatever the Minister
of Propaganda says it is." This is the cynical beginning of amoralism,
which "realistically" accepts crime or sin and incorporates it into
institutions. The amoralist forgets the essential truth that whenever
a sin is committed there are also present unexpressed forces—defeated forces—opposing it. Power and amoralism go hand in hand
because power is required to maintain the continued repression of
these forces. If they are not repressed, then *moral* problems confront
the amoralist. The point is that moral problems do not cease to exist
because they are ignored; they represent conflicts which have *two*
actual, existing sides. Those conflicts can be solved only by giving
careful attention to the delicate, immediate relation between elements of power and of morality in each specific act. The question
cannot be resolved in general by being a moralist or an amoralist.

"The fascist scheme of things is an expression of human will which creates its own truths and values from day to day to suit its changing purposes."—As distinct from the "absolute" truths and principles on which liberalism and Communism are based. Such a scheme of things, destroying as it does all history and the rational continuity of culture, would be desired only by one who demanded "expression" above all else—whose blocked energies were beyond all rational control. And this is the fascist; and this is fascism. Will that has no other principle of consistency than its own expression is not will at all, but the abdication of will. Such expression is concerned only with the ability to express, that is, power. Nothing is changed by the consideration that, in a fascist society, individual members a good part of the time have a passive relation to the expression of expression, to power. Whether the involvement is masochistic or otherwise, still power is supreme. What the fascist does is to "give up" on the problems of our time. He no longer attempts to direct the aggression produced by his frustration against the responsible objects. The uncultured release of aggressive tendencies—produced by civilization, not by natural condition—can only be destructive, since it is irrationally unselective. We should notice here especially that "realism" as commonly upheld by "practical people," when carried to an extreme, is highly irrational in the same manner. Irrational in the sense that it ignores the necessary conditions—the realities— of acts. Morality, or the reasoned restraint on expression, is relevant to every act. The consequence of refusing to see this, of bypassing moral problems, is the irrationality of one's acts and ultimate destruction.

But it is not less irrational to ignore the requisites of power in constructing acts. Here the problem is how to be rational in an irrational world, one moving swiftly toward destruction. Dennis says we should accept this movement: "The intellectual problem is to understand, not contradict; the emotional problem, to feel with and not resent the rising tide of change and power." This is a strong tendency in everyone. The liberals, and the moderate socialists (especially more moderate *than* socialist) are impaled by a tragi-comic irony. (In this country, the liberals and the leadership of labor fulfill the same function, on a lower cultural level, that social democracy did in Europe.) Having a practical monopoly of humanitarian morals, and lacking the will to use the power they have and to struggle for more, they end up in practice by compromising with, and thereby *using*, the power of others. In practice they are not socialists at all, because they do not employ *socialist* power. They are the custodians of democratic values . . . night-watchmen of the temple no one enters. They have no power of their own; their values and their acts exist in separate worlds. The essential fault is that their ideology contains no aggressive formulae commensurate with the widespread frustrations which characterize our period.

Dennis' rejection of liberal capitalism and his espousal of fascism rather than a more intelligent alternative stem quite logically from a vulgar political error, which is consistent with his entire character, and from some very trenchant economic criticism. (The error will be dealt with subsequently.) The larger part of his writing, in fact, is concerned with economics. But it must suffice here to present only a brief resumé of his economic ideas.

His primary point is that the era of capitalist expansion is finished; that it was based on an historically exceptional set of circumstances, chiefly a number of frontiers offering easy exploitation and easy markets; that these frontiers have been exhausted, have disappeared once and for all. He lampoons the illusions of liberals and traditional capitalists who assume a continued expansion of this marvelous kind.* In general, he proposes as a response to this situation of contraction, the rationalization of the existing social and economic structure—much as Taylorism rationalized the individual industrial plant. In one of its aspects, this rationalization, as Dennis conceives it, would amount to a debtor's revolt against the *rentier*. The debt structure, both public and private, based on overcapitalization and on a legal system fitted to more prosperous times, must be revamped drastically. Also, profits must not be allowed to stand in the way of production and employment. The system of credit and money must be taken over entirely by the government. Anglophobic and anti–Wall Street, he heralds the end of the rule of money. "Mankind is destined to live by toil and struggle, not by absentee ownership."

What his position amounts to in essence is the proposal that *the rate of interest shall be legislated.* For capitalism, this means dumping the cargo in order to save the ship. Tight, totalitarian controls are required thus to preserve the system of private property and profit: "A regime respecting private property rights can also impose

* His thought was not modern—it did not begin with the simple fact of revolutionary technology overcoming both capitalist forms and socialist presumptions, each based on ideas of property rather than technology.

social responsibilities and discipline on property owners. . . ." The imposition of "discipline" on the working class goes without saying. Under this system of fascism, property rights in general become subject to political rather than legal control. "Law is a manifestation of political power and is as valid as that power is effective." *In extremis*, power becomes the single consideration. Property-owners will accept fascist controls, Dennis claims, because of the fear of losing their property altogether, and also because the state, while controlling production through a national plan and fixing arbitrarily the return on capital, is committed to a policy of sustaining production and employment and of enlarging the market; wages, of course, would be kept to a minimum. (The relation between war and an expansionist economic program need not be labored here: it will be enough to note that it makes war inevitable and perpetual.) Historically, capitalism was a series of inflationary and deflationary movements. Deflation is no longer practicable. This, fascism recognizes. And also the "fact" that, ultimately, only the state power, exercising total control over economic and social relations, can ward off the deflations which are of the essence of capitalism.

The "error" referred to above which Dennis commits in his political thinking is of the most banal, philistine kind—the confusion of revolution and counter-revolution. It brings into sharp relief both the force and the weakness of his work, which flow from the same source: his frustration at being denied a position of power in the ruling group. He can define revolution as "simply rapid change" because the direction of change is inconsequential to him, *any* change gives him (he thinks) the opportunity of achieving a powerful position. As with all frustrated persons, finally the one unbearable thing is the present situation. Although in *The Dynamics of War and Revolution*, published in 1940, Dennis makes a demagogic advance by equating socialism and fascism, he exposes the shallowness of his attitude by the following statement: "The new revolution is the product of necessities and frustrations rather than of opportunities and aspirations, as was so largely the revolution of capitalism." Actually, for the class which makes a revolution, it is the product of *both* frustrations and aspirations. Dennis does not represent that class.* Underlying his remark is the failure to distinguish between the revo-

* I was wrong—he did, at bottom. But sick like an unsprung tiger: now, they spring.

lution and the crisis which makes it possible; and an undialectical projection of the present into the future. Counter-revolution is called forth by the same crisis which makes revolution possible and necessary. Fascism is the counter-revolution. It does not resolve the crisis of capitalism. It represses, rationalizes, and aggressively externalizes the contradictions of capitalist society. That is why it is both unstable and destructive, and cannot be the face of the future, if there is any future at all.

Power and morals. Outside the area of rational discourse (tautologically) there is no rational discourse: things just happen—irrationally. But within discussion it is of the greatest importance and urgency that we approach moral problems scientifically, that is, *as one of the major necessary aspects of all acts*; along with other such aspects, like power. Talking of power and morals, we are, of course, talking of means and ends. *There is no such thing as an act without an end.* (Nor is there an end without an act: moralists who, through their almost exclusive concern with "ultimate" ends, have managed to relegate values to a dream world, a nether world with no clear or necessary relation to actual experience, have done very much indeed to discredit moral problems and to confuse analysis.) Discounting "luck," means merely as means must inevitably have destructive consequences. They are indiscriminate. While the Industrial Revolution and modern science have disclosed to mankind unimaginable vistas of growth, it is the machine, nevertheless, which is the symbol, the deadly symbol, of unattached (unended) means gone wild and mad. *The means of our salvation*—power, technology, the machine —*are destroying us.*

III

Shortly before the beginning of the European war and continuing until the middle of 1942, Dennis published a $24-a-year newsletter called *The Weekly Foreign Letter*. In it he practiced Machiavellian power analysis with a vengeance. After Pearl Harbor, he pledged allegiance to The United States and his writing took a more subtle and cynical turn. In one of the last issues of this publication, he very bitterly stated an ominous warning for the future. He forecast that Americans would become disillusioned with the democratic aims of the war and with the war's destructive futility. This disillusionment, together with an expected failure of the postwar economic organization, would provide the fuel with which a violent fascism might feed a social conflagration in this country.

Paradoxically, while making this prognosis, which is not at all impossible, Dennis also accused the administration of using the wartime emergency as a cover for instituting the essentials of fascist organization and control. He termed Roosevelt "the leading initiator" of fascism in America. Whether or not this is so—that will depend on one's definition of fascism—the chief premise of a future fascism will certainly be the failure of the democratic ideology connected with the New Deal and the War. It may well be that the liberals, by what they do as well as by what they do not do, are preparing their own collapse as did their counterparts of Weimar during the Twenties in Germany.

How shall we define fascism in order to discover its institutional beginnings in the present? It is not enough to look for hidden swastikas: many writers, from camps both Right and Left, have predicted that fascism in America will be called by another name. This remains a profound prognosis. If we define fascism economically—as state control over both the return on capital and the disbursement of wages—then we behold evidences of fascism in a large number of the government's war agencies: control is socialist in a system where income is determined solely by the value of labor. Defining fascism politically in terms of one group controlling state power and having a monopoly of the instruments of propaganda and terror, we find only scarce signs of it in the present. But mainly because it is unnecessary: (1) the two major parties are now, for all modern purposes, practically identical; (2) unlike the situation in Germany, where there was a large and independent labor press, money in America exercises almost absolute control over propaganda media.

Fascism has perhaps three major social aspects: (1) the growth in importance of hierarchical position as opposed to money in the determination of status; (2) racism; and (3) a "greater group" mythos which attempts to cover over the factors of alienation which are ineradicable in a class society.* As to the first, there are many wartime indications of significance, and trends which will have a permanent effect on our life, but it would be decidedly premature to hail the dethronement of the American god of money. Racism, however,

---

* As of 1969—television, my friends, television. (Right, McLuhan?)

has grown tremendously during the war: the internment of Japanese-Americans, setting an unheard-of precedent; the racial character of the war in the Pacific; liberal acquiescence in a Jim Crow army; etc. Any excessive growth of nationalism would be evidence of the third social aspect of fascism. In more explicitly human terms, fascism means deculturization, brutalization of elements of the population (especially declassed elements), and the loss of creative individuality for all but a few. Except for the reminder that our culture is becoming increasingly official and standardized, this question is too complex to enter into here.

The foregoing extremely brief survey can only indicate the problem of inquiry. What no one must be allowed to forget is that fascism is far, very far indeed, from being an issue of the past; and that it will not present itself clearly labeled. Also, it probably will not come all at once. Fascism is a response to the problems of capitalism in the latter's phase of decay. It will be an ever-present threat until those problems are solved. And it will mount to power only over the prostrate body of democratic socialism, which is represented or misrepresented in popular expression today largely by the liberals and the officialdom of labor. The best defense against fascism is a deeply honest critique of liberal and labor policy.

Marxism: The Dominant Method

❀ TROTSKY: THE HERO AS SYMBOL

DISSENT, 1959

Dissent *was an effort to continue what Dwight Macdonald had begun with* Politics, *after he abandoned it (just as he had started* Politics *because* Partisan Review *had shifted away from its original political emphasis). Irving Howe, almost as prolific as Macdonald, was a moving spirit behind the effort to start a new radical magazine—along with Lewis Coser, a refugee intel-*

lectual who was close to Macdonald in the beginning days of Politics. I first met Howe as "faction-editor"—a youth leader of the intellectual Trotskyite group—appointed by Macdonald (with great fairness) to select anti-pieces submitted in criticism of Macdonald's anti-Marxist New Roads writers in Politics (I had written one).

This particular article was a contribution to rethinking the socialist tradition—the major purpose for which Dissent was established. Its submission was the occasion of a faction fight, naturally. I don't know how I won it—I don't know that much about faction fights—but I did. Hooray. I have since lost a few. Also, hooray.

As for what Trotsky meant to me, and many like me, that is in the article. Trotsky, I may say for the benefit of those who did not read him when they were young and eager, was the most brilliant literary figure in the entire socialist tradition— from Thermidor to an ice-axe in Mexico. And just what modern social thought might be without that tradition, including its errors, is not worth thinking about.

I read three big thinkers when I was young and impression-able—Marx, Freud, Mead. (I read some others, but that's not the point.) I was a Marxist and a Freudian—and I couldn't possibly get over having read Mead the way I did, not at this late date (that was like first-love, and lifetime cohabitation: he was nearly a decade dead when I read him: I never read like that again—and wouldn't want to, even if I was still able).* Freud I mutter about in Section 6; here, I would like to insert one paragraph about My Marxist Background.

I am not now nor was I ever for very long a Deadhead Marxist. But I have no particular understanding of history or economics which could have occurred in the absence of my read-ing of Marx; I am my own special kind of heretic—as are many ex-Marxists. Organizationally, I was a member of the American Student Union at the University of Illinois in 1940–41, being recruited for the Young Communist League in that front group established for that purpose, until the Soviet Union was at-tacked—which required the scuttling, among other things, of my midwestern isolationism. I never joined anything again, but did become an intellectual Trotskyite fellow-traveler when I

---

* If this seems not enough for one intellectual career, then I may say that I also read (when I was in the mood) Dostoyevsky and Lawrence as if my life depended upon it, which it clearly did.

*came to New York. I have explained all of this in detail to the
United States government (unsuccessfully) and, I am happy to
say, to the quondam satisfaction of the Brooklyn Bar Association—my greatest popular literary triumph (with wisecracks).*

*Not to have been some kind of a Marxist when one was
young is simply a human condition too embarrassing, at this
late date, to discuss in the space allotted to me here in my
own book. Most people like that were only fit to inherit American real estate.*

I would like to suggest that what most characterizes Leon Trotsky,
and the revolutionary generation he symbolizes, are: (1) the dominance of ideas; (2) the need and willingness to act on them; and (3)
the fanatic belief in ideological purity. Any of these can be overdone
and lead to distortions. Given, however, the intensity of the first two
that one would expect in the life of a genius like Trotsky, together
with the circumstance of isolated frustration of the revolutionary,
and it seems to me that the pressure of all this on the third element
would create—and in Trotsky's case, did create—a highly distorted
revolutionary purism, which in turn contributed substantially to his
political failures.

Since I realize that tempers are quickly touched when old political
coals are raked over, let me try to avoid any unnecessary misunderstanding by stating immediately that I consider Trotsky to have
been magnificent in failure; that by and large his failure was socialism's failure; that it was a political and certainly *not* a moral or literary failure; and that, in failure, he remains one of the better reasons
yet offered by the twentieth century for maintaining one's integral
humanity. But when all that is said, it remains true—and it is about
time that we recognized it—that Trotsky was, *in his own terms,* a
political failure: he lost out in the struggle to preserve the revolution
in Russia, and he did not succeed in building an effective new International. His literary attack on the Third International and the
monster at the head of it, carried on without the aid of peers and at
the ultimate cost of his own life and the lives of most of his family,
was—again in his own terms—an intellectual and moral victory only.
There is a transcendent irony in the fact that Trotsky's intellectual
purity, which he believed in passionately as an indispensable requirement for political *action,* should have contributed to his failure
as a political activist and his success as—the phrase would have

choked him—a moral symbol. If he could speak to us now, I think he would in self-disgust insist on being swept into the dust-bin of History. In this, however, we will not oblige.

One more preliminary word: I beg the partisan reader to recognize that with such a man and such a subject, detailed argument is impossible in anything less than a fat book. I simply wish here to urge a proposition concerning revolutionary purism which, it seems to me, has some relevance to the intellectual reconstruction of socialism. I assume, moreover, that the reader has had some experience of the pull of ideological purism (and not necessarily in connection with Stalinism). Also, please realize that it is not part of my argument that ideas and ideas-in-action and clear-thinking have somehow become irrelevant or dangerous to the socialist movement.

Whatever else it is, politics is always the attempt by some people to exercise power over other people, for particular purposes or for the pure joy of it. Now let us grant the highest motives to Trotsky and the revolutionary elite of his generation; still, the issue was power over people. This elite utilized ideas as a means of control, first over themselves and then as an avenue to power over others. Their effort was to wring as much power-utility out of ideas as they could, and by sparing no one and nothing they did indeed create a new political technique. They were forced to this, most obviously, because ideas were what they had at hand, they wanted political power, and so they determined to make ideas as effective an instrument as possible in achieving power. Many important human and intellectual qualities or possibilities were lost to them as individuals through the rigor of their intellectuality, the exclusive focus of thought on action, and through the relentless devotion to ideological purity—to "right-thinking": but no sacrifice was too great for them. Under their stewardship, the mind of man had now at last been conscripted in toto to serve the socialist revolution. This process began slowly, with the choice of "scientific" Marxism rather than romantic anarchism; then picked up momentum in the violently symbolic world of the emigré; and finally became a "proven" article of faith with the collapse (or sell-out) of the Second International in 1914—which shattering event, they believed, was a direct result of the day-to-day disuse of ideas, the unwillingness to act on ideas, and the impurities introduced into the realm of ideas by reformism, all of which had preceded the debâcle.

So what began as a materialistic interpretation of life completed itself as one of the most original ideational penetrations of life in the history of man, a unique triumph of intellectually willed activity. It is almost as if the more these select revolutionaries repeated to themselves the tenets of the materialistic interpretation, the more fiercely they resolved to disprove them (*"Yes, yes, but not really me"*), until at last in the heart of their feelings that interpretation became the Great Lie and their willed activity became the Great Truth.

The first characterizing feature, the dominance of ideas in Trotsky's life, is proven once again in the recently published *Trotsky's Diary in Exile:* 1935. These brief notes begin inauspiciously with the statement: "The diary is not a literary form I am especially fond of. . . ." Trotsky then suggests that his may "take the form of a review of newspapers and periodicals." While there are many affecting and even some revealing personal references, the pages of this desultory diary do indeed consist mostly of political comment on newspaper reports; many times he merely pastes newspaper clippings, with underlinings and marginal comments, in the notebooks in which he kept the *Diary.*

Because the diary is so personal a form of expression, Trotsky's impresses us by the absence of expected elements, by revealing the extent to which his entire being had become intellectually political. He is aware of this himself, and suggests as a reason that "politics and literature constitute in essence the content of my personal life." When the *Diary* begins to serve its personal function, he inhibits the impulse and diverts it to politics: at one point, he feels his life to be like a prison, describes it as such for a few sentences, then abruptly interrupts himself: "But all this is trivial detail compared with the realization that the fascist reaction is moving closer every day."

Ideas are all. Describing a somber landscape, he reflects: "Life is not an easy matter. . . . You cannot live through it without falling into prostration and cynicism unless you have before you a great idea which raises you above personal misery, above weakness, above all kinds of perfidy and baseness." This is an eloquent statement of the almost religious utility of ideas in his life. Ideas, indeed, must be religious in function if one is to devote "everything" to them.

To assert that the human being loses something essential, even in politics, by this deadly overemphasis on ideas and the ideological is not at all to hold a brief for mindlessness. Nor does the assertion rest exclusively on a belief in spontaneity, recognition of the heterogeneous nature of man, or the waywardness of history itself, no one of which, however, is irrelevant to political ideas and action. It is more important to point out, simply, that ideas do not save one from either life or history; *only so much can be achieved by means of them, even in the hands of a master.* The modes of ultimate devotion and fanaticism, which have achieved both magnificence and horror in history, are religious, if religion is the area of the ultimate in man; and like religion they result in effects in the world of affairs that are too inward, overly symbolic, and at last grotesque. When the idea of class allegiance, for example, can so fully dominate one that a person thought to be without it is said to have entered "individualistic nonexistence," as Trotsky says of Emma Goldman, I suggest that the stage of the grotesque has been reached.

The second Trotskyan element—the need and willingness to act on ideas—also shows up in the *Diary*; but it hardly needs to be demonstrated. This was the aspect of Trotsky's personality, indeed of Marxism itself, which most appealed to intellectuals. The world was there to be changed, and only ideas-acted-on could change it. A noble, imaginative conception, which seemed to be the one idea to which all previous notions had tended (especially, it must be admitted, for young intellectuals who were just finding out how deeply troublesome it was to be such).

Trotsky was the impresario of this music of revolutionary action, the symphonic development of which occurs in his *History* as nowhere else. Even more than Lenin, he was the hero of the Bolshevik Revolution, that fabulous seizure of power which proved the efficacy of ideas—more the hero because of his superior literary ability, his intellectual arrogance, even the absence of those talents for organizational maneuvering that characterize the real politician, which Lenin certainly was and Trotsky just as certainly was not. Lenin is seen as the genuinely superior political strategist, creator, and leader of the Bolshevik group; but Trotsky appears as the dramatically superior *individual* who condescended to act with and for the Bolsheviks when, because of Lenin only, they were approximately as correct as he.

Trotsky served as a hero to intellectuals because of his capacity for action, his belief in it, and the fact (or illusion: it makes no difference) that action for him proceeded from ideas. Malraux fascinates intellectuals for the same reason, even though the connection between Malraux the intellectual and Malraux the activist is frequently obscure. But labor politicians, who also are supposed to act on "ideas," do not inspire because both their ideas and their acts are mediocre. The desire of intellectuals is for symbol, not for the "best" effectiveness (especially if it is mediocre) of idea or act.

Whatever else it achieved, Trotsky's orientation toward action is undoubtedly responsible for the magnificently vibrating sense of urgency and authority in his writing. We should recognize, however, that in the end this is not a certificate of truth but rather a literary quality. Even his famous or infamous identification of himself with History as a discrete essence is a literary or (if you prefer a term closer to politics) rhetorical creation. And, again, it is not dependent on the truth for its effectiveness.

The unique thing about Trotsky is that so profoundly literary a person ever became and remained so involved in politics. One explanation is that he never really succumbed to being a politician, in the organizational sense. He was, rather, a tribune of the people: he is reputed to have been a magnificent speaker before mass audiences. His nickname, in the early emigré days, was "The Pen"; and certainly when he was not in Russia—twenty-five of his sixty years—his chief efforts were devoted to writing. Even in the midst of the struggle with Stalin, he found time to write *Literature and Revolution*. In the *Diary* he says, ". . . I think that the work in which I am engaged now . . . is the most important work of my life—more important than 1917, more important than the period of the Civil War or any other." The commander of the military train remained a literary man; but with the emphasis on writing *directed toward action and effect,* suffused with the dream of action.

The identification with History, the use of the idea of history in such a personal fashion, typifies the worst uses and effects of ideational purity—which is the third, and most important and distinctive Trotskyan element. It is typical of this mode that his opponents —whether bourgeois reformers, labor leaders, socialists, Stalinists, or whosoever—are assigned for their wrong-thinking to the ash-heap of History or, depending on the venom of the moment, to their place beneath the wheels of the Juggernaut of History. Observing the bluff tactics of the Popular Front, he says: "In the good old days Victor Adler used to be a past master of such tactics, and where is his party now? . . . These gentlemen think they can cheat history. They will only cheat themselves." To which one cannot help but reply, perhaps softly, out of respect, And where is *your* party now? Purity is better than baseness by definition, but it is not necessarily more effective: and both compete in the same arena. We know now (or should) that one can purify oneself out of the possibility of political action, that perhaps Trotsky did just that with his attempted imitation of Lenin in the creation and management of the Fourth International.

What did revolutionary purism actually succeed in, viewed pragmatically? By means of it, Lenin was able to forge a tight-knit clique which under his brilliant leadership proved competent, using the ancient technique of a minority coup, to take power in a rapidly deteriorating situation. This was and is its chief justification or "proof." Without Lenin, however, this group revealed the ravages of his tight leadership, which relied so much on purism. The power he left them was ultimately inherited by a man under whose jurisdiction right-thinking quickly became unabashed thought-control. Trotsky was aware, and asserts it in his *History*, this *Diary*, and elsewhere, that the long years of training in right-thinking under Lenin did not make the Bolsheviks "right-thinkers" without Lenin (e.g., Stalin and Kamenev in April 1917 before Lenin arrived in Russia). And still he imitated Lenin in attempting to establish a system of right-thinking in the Fourth International. In this he achieved nothing, and in fact destroyed or ignored many possibilities which were his because of his commanding reputation and genius; he alienated one not-quite-right-thinker after another. An example of this was his mishandling of the opportunities presented to him by the Spanish situation, which was actually and not just potentially revolutionary. And all the previous struggle toward purity of idea was supposed to be justified because it was needed in actual revolutionary situations!

The revolutionary Marxists became disastrously doctrinaire because they believed that right-thinking was an important historical force, like the historical determinants identified by Marx, but differing happily from the latter in that one could by an act of will join up with Inevitability. In this system of revolutionary ideology, workers are never wrong, they are merely backward or misguided. It is only the intellectuals coming from petty-bourgeois backgrounds—which is all of them, including Lenin and Trotsky and you and me—who are ever wrong. Workers have either come to their inevitable class-consciousness (the only form of consciousness worth a damn), or they have not yet arrived there, but inevitably will. Intellectuals are the ones who have so much to gain from right-thinking, so much to lose by a fall from grace. One becomes a right-thinker by "overcoming" one's class background, and all failures in right-thinking are explained by reference to petty-bourgeois factors—the "return of the repressed," more or less. Now class background, let us remember—it used to be lost sight of—is an historical fact, not a matter of choice: it is not the same thing as class allegiance. But according to Lenin and Trotsky it is the only thing in history that, apparently, can be overcome by a pure act of will. The idea that class background, a continuing historical fact, can be transcended initially and then indefinitely by class allegiance, a continuing personal act, all accomplished by means of right-thinking, is called the "Vanguard" theory in revolutionary parlance.

A revolutionary thinker may be very correct in his analyses and still accompany the reformists, Stalinists, etc., into "the ash-can of History." But not according to Trotsky. For him, purity saves: the vanguard is the vanguard. I think Trotsky did not really comprehend what Lenin had done, which perhaps explains why he imitated him so ineptly or slavishly. For Lenin the politician, and after him Stalin the monster, used purism more or less consciously to create *a system of allegiance based on guilt*.

Freud thought that guilt had created the first brotherhood; but he also felt that it had been carried to unbearable lengths in the modern world. He identified the excess of guilt in the maintenance of social adhesion as basically bourgeois and Christian. After a point, guilt—even in the service of the vanguard of the proletariat—becomes self-defeating and thus an illegitimate means of control. It does not make any difference if the guilt is derived from a true crime—namely, a falling away from class allegiance, a dissolving into class background: a time comes when there is no longer any advantage at all in the increase of guilt even of a murderer, and especially not to the murderer himself. And, if the point is always to be right, then we are all murderers. There will be no "socialism" worth having until we learn how to be wrong, with dignity.

Can anyone who has had a good look at the middlebrow Stalinists in America really question that their group was, to invert one of their favorite phrases, an association by guilt? All that was required for membership was a sufficiently profound hatred of American life to frighten the isolated individual, and enough involvement in that life to facilitate the transposition of that hatred and fear into guilt. And, one should perhaps add, a kind of indigenous eagerness to substitute for thinking all those rituals for the alleviation of guilt which the movement provided. Stupidity was generated by the nature of the Stalinist movement where it was not given freely by the membership. That was the true donkey's end of revolutionary purism! And we are long past the time when, relying on the basically sentimental feeling that "it all could have been different," we can ignore this Stalinist caricature of revolutionary Marxism.

I do not emphasize the difference between purity by virtue of one's own thought and what might be called "delivered" purity because this is, really, only the difference between leader and led. If the genius-leader believes in purity personally, as an element of his own psychic economy, that is his concern. But when he insists that non-geniuses be pure, and defines purity for them, we are concerned with the social efficacy of purism, not the inner nature of leadership. This distinction is especially relevant to Trotsky, whose intellectual purity of character is perhaps in itself magnificent, but as an element projected by him into political action and control, I am suggesting, was disastrous. A dangerous and extreme device in any event, inducing guilt by purism is also a destructive waste of time unless you are doing so *as a means of building an organization*. Unlike Lenin, Trotsky was not politician enough to do this skillfully: his purity was personal.

Purism should be seen as an emotional, inutile factor in socialist thinking and organizational control, certainly in all but the most immediately revolutionary situations. I think this fact should be accepted as a tenet of socialist reconstruction.

The *Diary* affords us something of an opportunity to reflect on the present relevance of our dead hero. The end of a great tradition, he is, dead, a hero still. He was the last of the great revolutionary Marxists, and we may never see their like again. But great heroes remain vital as symbols—never more true than of Trotsky—if we can understand and forgive them for their errors and excesses. The hero by his very essence is a distortion; he has risen above a time and a place, a set of circumstances which put an iron limit on what one can do or be without distortion. A hero is an artist in life, his work of art is his career, and like the artist he emphasizes and selects, he distorts the material of life in favor of a fuller expression.

That is particularly the reason why we should be inspired by heroes, but never imitate them. And learn from their errors as well as their magnificence. In Trotsky's case, we should learn, make indelible in our minds, the inefficacy of purism in radical politics: in a sense, he lived and died to teach this to us.

Trotsky was so great a figure that one can say that history might have been different if he had been more of a political leader and less of a pure symbol: his was a grandiose political failure. But now we must understand what happened, that he became, contrary to his own most deeply felt design, a great *moral* symbol—one of the greatest of our century. It is the fate of many heroes.

The image of Trotsky had a great influence at one time on many young radicals. Influences of this kind, enmeshing themselves in the early emotional sources of ideals, tend to persist—no less for those who have loudly negated the ideal than for those who still harbor it quietly and tenderly. The publication of the *Diary* is a good occasion to rethink the Trotsky influence, for all the old chords are sounded in it, including what may be the chief one—that *there* was a nonpareil among men.

❊ THE KIDS AND THE COCKERS

DISSENT, 1965

The following expression of mine about the socialist tradition and This Generational Thing grew out of a specially assembled seminar at the Institute for Policy Studies. (I am generally called in when something old-hat is deemed relevant.) This particular tense do culminated in an argument between Arthur Waskow and myself which mainly involved, I recollect, the weight to be given to the brand-newness of the New Youth (his point) and the character of past radical efforts in America, with special emphasis on Stalinism, its social nature, and also whether it was indigenous enough to recreate itself without direct Soviet influence (my point). I don't remember who won. But he wrote me a long letter clarifying his position—his phone

was out of order—and I suggested it should have been ad-
dressed to Our Socialist Rethinking Forum; he so addressed it,
and Irving Howe asked me to write an answer. (Dissent was
doing a series, at the time, on "The 'New Radicalism.'")

The surviving socialist generation had no sufficient reason to expect
that the new fellows should or would follow their lead. The fact that
this may be very much to the disadvantage of the young activists,
does not alter the character of our reasonable expectations. Also, a
good part of what we would offer them they need like another hole
in the head.

The simple fact of the matter is that we ourselves made the tradition unavailable. This was accomplished through strenuous intellectual effort; which unfortunately succeeded far beyond our worst
fears. If some little smidgeon of the energy devoted to the pietistic
tending of the Eternal Flame of Doctrinal Purity had, instead, gone
into actual thought about the structure of American power (or even
compulsive precinct work)—if we had *helped* Marx a little—then
we might be in a position to complain. As it is, however, while viewing with dismay we had better include ourselves in the landscape. It
has to be in part our fault that after two thousand years their best
idea of political action is a Central High rendition of the Sermon on
the Mount.

The incredible idealism. What primitives. Etc. The *alta* Marxists
are correct, certainly: what a comedown from *The Eighteenth Bru-
maire of Louis Napoleon* and *The Civil War in France.* On the
other hand, so is *Dissent*—which is also, admit it, even a bit of a
comedown from the early *Partisan Review.* Why? We aged, and so
did the doctrine. The one event was unavoidable; the other could
have been handled somewhat better. It wasn't, because of the same
impulse toward purity (covering over analytical ineptitude) that
may be observed now. In our time, we asked the same question they
repeat endlessly today—*Mirror, mirror on the wall / Who is the
most radical of all?* It is just that the mirror has been changed. You
liked the old one better? That figures.

Idealism is a device of self-creation appropriate to young people
who are in the heat of the process of creating themselves. Piety,
however, is an ideal self-protective device for cockers who didn't
manage the self-creation of their youth as well as they intended.
(Don't worry, fellows: we may not live to see it, but these kids will

stumble into their own set of pieties, when the time comes.) But the big difference remains that we had the European tradition of social-ism—which perhaps could have been adequately modified and made relevant, instead of alternately enshrined and abandoned. We flubbed that opportunity; and these kids are, very irritatingly, the living proof of that fact.

They come from the pacifist tradition, and other remnants of Christian idealism. A lesser tradition? One that we were raised to believe Marx had laid low long ago? Yes. So weep, brother, weep.

The intellectual life of the cockers was initiated or focused by socialist writings, confirmed either by the October Revolution or by the Depression; theirs was created, however, by the Horror of The Bomb and the Shame of Segregation, and confirmed by Everything. Notice that mere moral assertiveness has been effective in fighting segregation and was inevitable in opposing The Bomb, since nothing much else was available—certainly nothing in the socialist tradition. But moralism, thus confirmed, oozes into neighboring brain-cells; so also did the virus of doctrinal distinctions work its way in our poor battered brains.

Beginning with The Bomb as the fundamental fact of life, rather than economic exploitation or other elements of Marxism (as we did), the new fellows come upon this item called "Communism" merely as a manufactured road-block: many of them heard about it first from McCarthy. What was for us a monumental historical trag-edy, is for them a rhetorical inconvenience. They are just not inter-ested in adapting our trauma to the framework of their current per-ceptions. This could be a serious loss, each in their own way, for both the kids and the cockers. I don't know what to do about it: they won't listen.

But I think they will be damaged more by their impossible ideal-ism, than by their eventual rediscovery of the existence and effect of rational authoritarianism and irrational anti-Americanism on the Left. In this, they will be quintessentially American-as-usual. The curse of our national life has been the disjunction of idealism and practicality—and the consequent excessive tension and overblown stature of each: each is dominant in its own good time. Note that the Great Events at Berkeley represented, at most, a revolt against a particular style of administration by a particular group of young ad-ministrators-in-training. I will be most interested to see how much of their idealism they take with them into the darker reaches of the administrations they will inhabit later in life. Or were they just getting it out of their systems? My sharp preference is for practicality among idealists, and idealism when living with the practical people. This is both the true and the useful point of application of individual effort; and this way, the opportunities for creative troublemaking persist for a lifetime.

The youth are not to be opposed because they are foolish. On the other hand, their vital foolishness should not be taken as a second chance for us to be young again. They should be criticized with cutting kindness, as benign as one can manage. When, as they age, some of them refuse to grow up, and their soured idealism turns them vicious, we can drench them in I-told-you-so's and other invective. And maybe they will in fact be the first generation to experience nothing but moral triumphs, with no necessity for learning the uses of practicality. Even if they do not reach the top of that mountain, we can continue our efforts to ensure that they will not fall too low—will never sing the song of the Russian labor camps, where twenty million died in twenty years:

> They finished me, bastards, they
>   finished me,
> They destroyed my youth;
> My golden hair has turned white,
> And I am on the brink of ruin.

IT DON'T PAY TO KILL THE RULING CLASS

REVIEW OF EXISTENTIAL
PSYCHOLOGY AND PSYCHIATRY, 1968

Summary: *There are two reasons it don't pay:* (1) *they are so nearly dead and otherwise uninterested in ruling that they are almost friendly; and* (2) *no one has yet identified, and subjected to similar criticism, the bastards who will replace them.*

You will have noticed that Pure Socialism is now back in fashion, along with sideburns and Nehru jackets. And I have noticed that it bears about the same cultural relation to doc-trinal thought of the Thirties as the Beatnik style of the Fifties did to the original thing of the Twenties. A few more watered-down advances of this kind and we may as well suspend opera-tions. Our fashionable radicals today pick and choose among the materials of the past with the discernment and responsi-bility of network executives planning the next profitable season on television (and I think that's where they learned how to do it).

"It's just that some people care, and some people don't."

"Well, there are the good guys and the bad guys."

"Listen, you either feel it or you don't—I mean the difference between right and wrong."

"This situation stinks. Let's start all over again. Me, I'm the cast-ing director."

"If only we could get rid of the bad guys. . . ."

Thus, the voice of the New Left style-setters.

—Or, if you care to bother, there are complications. The major political complication presented by this absurd century of ours, is— It don't pay to kill the ruling class. Previously, this idea would never have occurred to anyone. Until now, the basic issue of proper moral assertiveness was how to get close enough to the bastards, with a weapon in hand. But the Russian Revolution, the most instructive of them all, was a "successful" experiment finally revising our view of ruling classes in history:

A boss is a boss is a boss.

One class succeeds another: classlessness is a dream.

Those who speak for the proletarians are speakers, not proletar-ians: they divide the class, and they speak for themselves. They are the New Class.

In 1917 in Russia, the nineteenth century ended. With a boom, not a whimper. No more easy hopes; a totally altered world. Fifty or one hundred years of Russia before 1917 amounted to one of the great creative bursts in history—like Greece and Rome and Shake-speare. And it all eventuated in Stalin. The most revealing tragedy of the race, certainly. What it revealed was that your comrade, revolu-tionary blood-brother, committed co-conspirator—your daring, dar-ling ally—might well be a bigger bastard than the sad, weary dunce on the throne. And he rather than you—with your all-out destructive help—might end up ruling: and that rule worse than anything previously imagined.

To sum up: The Russian experience indicates that classlessness cannot be achieved by an act of human will, that to destroy one ruling class merely prepares the way for the creation of another and not necessarily better one. As a consequence, the nature and theory of class struggle have necessarily been altered in essence. It is no longer a sufficient perspective to contemplate the destruction of a ruling class; it is much more important to consider ways and means of living under and with *some* ruling group or other. Rulers we have always with us: the ruled must want to and must learn how to tyrannize over those who rule them: it is not enough to kill them.

If not to kill off a ruling group, then what *is* the political use of violence, if any? There is still war. But with nuclear weapons, war fully enacted is suicidal; therefore, inutile. Indeed, the capacity for ultimate nuclear destructiveness on the part of the Soviet Union and the United States, creating a suicidal stand-off, actually reduces the available power of each when they cannot act together. These two nations could immediately constitute a genuine world government, acting together: that was, remember, the original notion of the United Nations. Not so acting, little wars by little nations are still possible and even profitable—the policemen are preoccupied, glaring at each other.

Given an effective government, violence is absurd as a form of politics. The state, after all, is defined (differentiated from a really big corporation or other "authority") by its monopoly of violence, as well as its exclusive capacity to bestow legality. Still, the selective use of violence to *test* the effectiveness of any existing government retains a certain appeal. One feels like a Philistine to prejudge the creative outcome of such experiments. But tests that do not overthrow, no matter how creative they may be, are merely educational —and, perhaps unfortunately, they mostly educate the existing government in the perfection of its monopoly. I think we are now witnessing this effect in the United States, where our domestic military forces are digesting the lessons of Summer '67's urban violence, and revamping and rearming themselves in preparation for Summer '68. I fear their progress will far outdistance that of the streetfighters. God is still on the side of the big battalions.

The major achievement of urban violence, no matter how inventive or whether occurring in New York, Tokyo, or Paris, will only be to upgrade the position of the police in the established order. This will cost everyone dearly. Put differently: we have gotten used to the states' quiet monopoly, and will miss it.

The violence being practiced on all sides in Vietnam is, of course, a much more complicated matter. The American military is learning once again, what in fact it never forgot, that limited wars are for the birds. This time, however, the lesson goes even deeper—as body-count replaces the acquisition of real estate as the measure of success. Speaking of the display of ultramodern guerrilla violence on the other side, it exists by sufferance of the Soviet Union—that is, by an absence of world government—and still its creators will, at best, inherit a destroyed country. As an American experiment in restrained escalation, given exactly the current world power-situation, Vietnam merely demonstrates—with respect to our issue of the political utility of violence—that such exclusive reliance on measured force is much less effective than previously supposed, and can in fact destroy too much more than it saves.

My point is that for modern man, violence is spiritual, not practical—indeed, a form of ineptly expressed despair.

Violence is not "natural" for us. Apart from boyish fighting—which begins to disappear after puberty when it threatens to become serious—our major experience of it is imaginary, derived almost entirely from the media. When I say violence is not natural "for us," I am thinking of middle class urban America: the affluent majority in its adulthood and out-of-uniform. For others, it may remain natural—or at least actual and recurrent. Among those for whom violence is not real, it must always be imagined in the clothing and the context of those for whom it still is real. There are millions of people in this country who have never so much as held a loaded gun in their hands, whose minds are filled with fantasies of its use by cowboys, gangsters, private eyes, soldiers, and policemen. Perhaps an even more significant example would be barroom fights: when I was young they still occurred in actual bars, although not the better ones now called cocktail lounges. No longer—not even very much in lower middle class ethnic gathering places. Meanwhile, in the movies, the barroom fight has become a major sequence in the repertory of American ballet—like the classical *pas de deux*.

Images of violence, derived from denial of the actual activity, are an aspect of the even more general *yearning for primitivism*. We live lives of such physical constraint, under compulsion of patterned demands directed toward symbol and appearance—far beneath the level of full response—that we cannot resist fantasies of full action, even when these reduce us, which they most often do. The yearning for full, completed physical action is the basic thing: violence is merely the ready metaphor. These full-action dramas are more easily expedited by recurrent images of violence for an audience that in fact experiences none. But with or without violence, the ubiquitous purpose is a fantasied displacement of complication—of the ubiquitous complexity of actual modern living.

This passion to simplify creates numerous forms of reductionism; and many other occasions for misidentity. It is, of course, the essence of Consumerism, of the culture of the media which sustains product-use as a way of life.

Violence is the simplest resolution of anything. Imagine, if you will, a full evening of television in which nobody hit anyone, and no weapons were displayed. Nothing would happen. The obsolescence of characterizations would reach epidemic proportions. Players would sit and stare at each other, speechless. They might even start to fondle one another, out of boredom. To talk to each other about themselves and their concerns, or illustrate their experiences and dreams—well, that kind of interplay would require a whole new set of characters, representing and appealing to an audience that was moved to penetrate rather than deny the complexity of its own existence.

The popular product-consuming imagination finds another use for violence: it serves as the italic of seriousness. Everybody knows that you really and truly mean it if you beat up on somebody. So images of violence in our popular culture are designed presumptively to save it all from untoward sentimentality. On this matter, note that people are sentimental to the extent that they lack grasp of their own current circumstance, and know it. (I have lately taken to measuring my own lack thereof by the amount of sentiment I find irresistible on TV, especially in the ads: my sentimentality about old movies merely indicates how poorly I am enduring the loss of youth.) So violence, as we learn from the media to use it imaginatively, is the indicated way of lying to ourselves about our own ineptitude.

And here we wind our way back to politics—to violence as an aspect of power. The dominant form of modern power is simply organization itself—and that should be understood as organization utilizing deception more than violence, and con more than coercion. The actual use of violence by a ruling organization always constitutes a sad dissolution of the major terms of that organization—a failure of intention. The purport of the state's traditional monopoly of force, for example, is not to enable it to exercise this power continuously: quite the contrary. The successful exercise of the monopoly entails no use except in perfecting and preserving the monopoly, that is, forcefully preventing others from using force. A successful state merely commands—it does not kill. Killing is wasteful and exhausting: in a word, primitive. Deception—the next step up in animal forms of power—is less exhausting than violence; but still more strenuous than candor: the lie-detector test measures increased bodily tensions revealed by pulse-rate, sweating, etc., when lying. Still, despite the obvious savings in energy, few ruling organizations rely chiefly on candor; the state's preference for deception over violence, however, is clear.

The traditional state rests on a monopoly of force; the modern totalitarian state, constituting a creative departure designed to dominate history and not merely to survive it, asserts as well a monopoly of deception—wherein no one may lie to the state about anything, and the state may in its discretion lie to anyone about everything in the ordinary course of business. (Candor is reserved for the announcement of imminent disaster.) In the United States, luckily, the technical advances in widespread deception have had to be shared by the state with the corporate order, which, year in and year out, tells many more lies even than the federal government. But the basic federal jurisdiction is maintained (as in many other areas) under the war powers clause of the Constitution.

It is the alliance of force and deception, in order to perfect the monopoly of each, that particularly characterizes modern totalitarianism—whether voluntary as in this country, or involuntary as in Russia. Himmler's actions were worse than Goebbels' lies, although the latter prepared the way for the former, and neither would have fared as well without the other. With the mixed situation in the United States, the major fabricating power is in the hands of the industrial government, which rules by means of its advertising culture. On occasion, the federal establishment will exert state power to limit somewhat the private quasi-monopoly of lying—as in disclosure statutes. The totalitarian joining of the two powers is probably the most fearsome conjunction; but an absolute separation would create a very unstable social order. Very obviously, the two orders of American government, for better or for worse, are beginning to mesh with accelerating intimacy.

Indeed, it is the signature of our time that politics and media culture are more and more entwined—not least of all in the outlook and behavior of our first affluent and TV-trained generation, who learned, if at all, from the media. I believe that Consumerism is so completely the ideology of this nation, and so deeply embraced as such, that our politics is on the way to becoming primarily a form of cultural criticism: it is an effort to improve the quality or change the character of the product and the programming.

The objects comprising an up-to-date suburban home no longer bear any reasonable relation to any natural or necessary desire for food or shelter; or the rest. They are a way of life; an end in themselves. The *spiritual meaning* of the object—derived from media culture and still existing in that culture even while the object is being used or observed—is far and away superior to and predominant over the object itself as a merely physical thing. We need dozens of detergents and new model can-openers like we need more holes in the head. I mean, *neither* for animal want *nor* human perfection. We require these things and these meanings because together they constitute both the means and the end, the truly transcendent purpose of our lives. Which purpose has been so completely subsumed under the ideology of Consumerism that the best in people can come out under its influence, and even delicate experiments in being genuinely sociable are conducted. We spend our better evenings in submission to our neighbor's demonstration of affluence, meanwhile choosing occasions for profound agreement as to the horrors of Vietnam, air pollution, Time, Inc., the ghetto, etc.

All this is a fantasy of life—as historical religion was for some poorer people. Now my major point is this: Sustaining the fantasy or myth is the *purpose*; buying Duz or killing heretics is merely the indicated *means* of confirming it. One sustains a myth by believing in it strenuously or helplessly—preferably both—and, on occasion, actually doing something to confirm it; that is, sacrificing a piece of putative reality to it. In pursuit of the fantasy of Consumerism presented by media culture, one occasionally *buys* something or even *uses* it seriously as the sacrificial act of confirmation. It is perfectly obvious that no one in his right mind would bother with all that junk if it was not a way of life; if he had anything else to do with himself; if there was another crap-game in town.

All of this was created out of the dislocated hungers of the Depression generations; and then bestowed as the curse of the fathers upon the postwar generations. We were not meant to be pigs and soldiers; it just worked out that way. Too much, too soon: and too little to go on. The tragedy of America is that we became rich before we became a society; and so inevitably confounded and then substituted the one state of being for the other.

I will not attempt to catalogue the mesh of media culture and politics. Many politicians will imitate Ronald Reagan who, with great good fortune, need only imitate himself. I will rush to my conclusion with final remarks about "order" and "crime in the streets" —two notions which, I suspect, will carry the burden of our next working-out of the role of the New Violence in politics, and the involvement of this with media culture sustaining our dominant ideology of Consumerism.

It is, of course, very difficult these days to speak in *favor* of "order." That is because the order apt to be imposed in the cities, in the immediate future, will be very new and very ugly in terms of traditional American images, and therefore will require excessive justification. On the side of the state, the police seem to be dealing with riots in the cities as a military problem: I am told that they are not receptive to sophisticated European techniques of crowd control, which involve a minimal show of violence and careful escalation. Like most Americans, they favor solving problems with heavy hardware.* On the side of the ghetto victims, compensatory fantasies of violence have been given the most absurdly brilliant green light in the long story of political streetfighting. I am afraid that only deeply realistic fear on the part of the ghetto majority can save the situation: there will be no lack of incidents—if necessary, provoked by hysterical black militants. As for the white majority and their newly readied police, the script for the coming summer has been and will continue to be so well advertised that, if August is reached with-

* This notion is belied by the careful actions of trained troops during the federally managed post-King Washington, D. C. riots. But then confirmed by the ethnic class rebellion in Chicago, Summer 1968.

out substantial newscopy, the national disappointment of television-viewers may well be critical.* The fundamental military wisdom which made America great—Don't shoot until you see the whites of their eyes—might be forgotten. Electronic hysteria may mount along with the rise in environmental temperature.

Order will be disrupted; and order will be restored. If this were a revolution instead of a stupid fantasy being acted out by juveniles and other powerless disruptionists, successful revolutionists might be in charge of reestablishing order. As it is, only the military will gain. When disrupted order is recreated, it is of course different; so what? The advertised point is that it be *better*.

Note that our affluent radicals, and their black brethren, talk about "order" only by reference to the Establishment. This personalizes a serious matter; galvanizes envy in the service of foolishness; and conveniently ignores numerous historical examples of postrevolutionary "order." We are witnessing, along with much else, a silly exfoliation of TV-Marxism—just as Beats and Hippies and othersuch represented electronically bowdlerized Bohemianism, literary Modernism for the masses, and similar cultural excess. Give them their head, and we will have a *Brothers Karamazov* breakfast food next year, as soon as the package can be designed. If technocrats are the major captive and rebellious class in Communist countries, our liberal arts majors on Madison Avenue and in Hollywood are the prime counterparts in this country. *And their children.*

Ideas are not exchanged—indeed, language does not occur—in the absence of order. We are all dependent upon some given order; especially intellectuals. The order created by the state, with its monopoly of violence, may be likened to the matter of personal *balance*. Without it, no effectiveness. Social order and personal balance are the Holy Ghosts of existence: the true passage from father to son; the necessary relation between form and content. All else is wayward reductionism. The terms of power have changed so profoundly that even disruption must be calculated carefully. One day soon, four-year-old temper-tantrums will be shrewdly plotted.

Some years ago, the Goldwater intellectuals gave us "crime in the streets." It is the greatest political slogan since Roosevelt's "We have nothing to fear but fear itself." But crime-in-the-streets is not a

---

* Written prior to the King riots, the second Kennedy assassination, and other such events which will have occurred before this copy will have been printed.

Mammy-coo: it is a military slogan: a battle-cry. And President Johnson is already engaged in an effort to preempt it. Which means we are really stuck with it.

This truest slogan of the New Violence may be "imaged" in terms of the blitz campaign on television (early, but to be repeated often) a few years ago favoring abolition of the Civilian Review Board in New York City. Never before so perfect a wedding of media culture and politics. The dramatic presentation in spot commercials of white office-girls being stalked on the streets of New York by blue-collar or unemployed Negroes was so good that the viewer never knew until the last word that a political point was being made, rather than the presentation of the coming attractions of a new thirteen-week series.

I take *this* as the summary image of the New Violence. And be assured that the office-girl is Irish if the cop and the viewer are Irish, Italian-if . . . Polish-if . . . even Jewish-if. We now face the final Armageddon of the American melting-pot. All of us who went to college, and have forsaken all-but-TV violence in favor of all-but-admitted deception, are perfectly prepared to accept colored classmates (and even dusky neighbors who can afford the rent). But no real violence. And what about our brothers and sisters and other cousins who didn't bother and stayed at home, sucking ethnic effluvia—and only a few thousand dollars a year ahead of the black hordes screaming for impossible historical justice?

I insist that violence is not natural for us. But neither is this new condition of well-advertised affluence, which occasions its re-emergence.

The Quondam Peace Issue

Thinking about war and peace is immensely improved these twenty years later. But right after the War, until the United Nations was understood to be a setting for Soviet vetoes, we were fêted with much high-minded liberalism of the kind that bothered to negotiate and sign the Kellogg Pact in the late Twenties. Whatever the devious doings of elite insiders may have been at the time, recently uncovered for us by the revisionist historians in order to boost our flagging disbelief, the rest of the comme-çi, comme-ça foreign affairs public in the United States was trying to avoid a little longer, in order to get ready to face a lot longer, the horror of the postwar world.

You see, my young friends, we did not fight (what a phrase!) World War II merely in order to drop the atom bomb on Hiroshima and get the Cold War in motion by refusing to be reasonable with Russia. Of course we accomplished all of these inevitable military-industrial complex things, but That War—and attendant hopes and fears—had been big medicine for us. It took us a little time to get to work on the big disease its application had produced. (To my readers way-over-thirty: I am sure you have noticed that these baby-faced wiseguys never refer to Our War, neither pro nor con; have no thoughts whatsoever as to its significance, if any; and more or less assume that the world began when they reached the age of pubic intellectual hair. Only the dropping of The Bomb, and other origins of the Cold War—only these were their inheritance from us, only that entices their interest: as if only that happened, way back then.)

In the Forties after the war, before Korea, I had a golden opportunity to make a few hundred dollars: I had an introduction to some big shot at Pocket Books, the going paperback miracle of the day. Sitting in the ante-room, speculating about whether I maybe-might get laid that evening, I suddenly realized that I, personally, was then and there in a classic movie-situation. I was a young man off the streets, about to receive fifteen minutes in which to make my fortune. I decided immediately (they always did in the movies) to overwhelm the son of a bitch with a Big Idea and thus come away clean, if no richer. Give him What? Why Freud was important, even if you were mostly a Marxist? Maybe. And then the electric light bulb lit,* just like in the comic strips—Russia! There was no anthology of stuff on Russia-since-the-Revolution in the drugstores. It was the time of the Soviet takeover of Czechoslovakia; or maybe

* Have you noticed that the very image of an idea in this benighted nation is a sudden bit of technology?

the first Berlin Crisis with its grandiose airlift. Zow-ie! I came-on to the guy like the young Edmond O'Brien in The Web, sold hard like my daddy always wanted me to, and fired him enough to get his agreement to present the proposition to his particular Kafka Committee. Promptly, two weeks later, I had the answer: It was a good idea, but their production time was nine months—business was so good—and by then Russia would be out of the news. (I take great pleasure telling this anecdote in a book published by Simon and Schuster, which still owns Pocket Books.)

❊ JAMES BURNHAM AND THE DENOUEMENT

UNPUBLISHED, 1947

Review of *The Struggle for the World,*
by James Burnham

The New Youth should know about James Burnham, as an example of what can happen to the best of talent and motivation when the devotion to heated atmospheres is uninhibited. (Please forgive a footnote reference: read George Orwell's beautiful essay about him.)

Briefly, Burnham was a very bright teacher of philosophy at CCNY (the Berkeley of those days), and the intellectual leader of the faction fight in the American section of the Fourth International against its founder, Leon Trotsky, and his trade union supporters in this country. The issue was dialectical materialism, as dogma, against a more modern and more American rendering of radical philosophy: Burnham was a Deweyan; Dewey represented an interpretation of Hegel that was both complementary to and competitive with Marx; the intellectuals in the movement desperately wanted a reconciliation of Dewey and Marx (Sidney Hook's early career was devoted to providing this—he was a Marxist, and an actual student of Dewey). That was the intellectual issue, which was aggravated because there was also a practical issue (maybe vice versa), namely, the attack by the Soviet Union on Finland in 1940: Should all 284 of us revolutionaries "support" Russia (in what way was not the issue) because it was the home of the

*socialist revolution, or oppose the war because Russia was
guilty of revolutionary degeneracy, then known as "bureaucratic collectivism"? The obvious American feeling that Big
Guys shouldn't pick on Little Guys was determinative but
unmentionable as such. (I may note that The Kid arrived on
the scene one year after the fact, so all of this was for me at
the age of eighteen as much "history" as it surely is now for
my younger readers, if any.)*

*When he lost the faction fight—which was led as well by a
very witty gentleman named Max Shachtman, who had been
very close to the great man himself, Trotsky, and by Dwight
Macdonald and some others—Burnham turned inside out, as
befits a High Priest suddenly infected with befouled purity,
and tried to become a fascist overnight. He failed, but only for
lack of stupidity. He later succeeded in spite of his intelligence,
and now is a gray eminence of the* National Review.

But in the white heat of his paroxysm, he wrote The Managerial Revolution. *It is a brilliant statement—whatever is wrong
with it, and whether or not or in what degree it is a restate-
ment of Trotsky, or Max Nomad, or any of their friends. If
socialism is noble, and fascism is evil, in Burnham's work we
see some of the relation between the two; begin to understand
how and why principled anti-Stalinism cannot serve as a final
puberty ritual for political intellectuals; and even begin to
glimpse aspects of the modern flow between righteousness and
evil. The similarity between fascism and Stalinism is much
greater in retrospect even than it was then—certainly to the
Russians; and especially to the East Europeans, who have
intimately endured both.*

The Struggle for the World *came later, and was an early
statement of the premises of the Cold War from a sophisticated if melodramatic world-view (in the mode of thought and
climate of concern that prompted Bertrand Russell to recommend a preemptive atomic strike). But it needs to be recalled,
for decent understanding of the quondam peace issue then-
and-now, that the anti-war position in those days owed much
more to Lenin's* Imperialism *than to pacifism; and the effort
to account for the atom bomb in that context was convulsive.
It took a little time to digest the incredible idea that The
Bomb superseded history.*

My review of Burnham's book was written for the Modern
Review, *a monthly financed by David Dubinsky on behalf of
an old socialist comrade, Raphael Abramovitch, who con-*

trolled it. The review was already in galleys when I was sum-
moned to the old Menshevik's upper West Side apartment to
"discuss" it. Like the impressive half of my Russian-born rela-
tives, he was very short and had a marvelously stiff spine. He
was at the time nearly blind. Comrade Abramovitch objected
to my treatment of Burnham on principled grounds, namely,
that I seemed to disagree with Burnham and Abramovitch.
The old gentleman could have killed the review outright; but
instead he took the occasion to display for my benefit his
stylish equipment as a faction-fighter (St. Petersburg, circa
1905). I was so honored and enthralled that I was not able to
give him even a semblance of the opposition for which he hun-
gered. Me bargain with him? I bought the rug being peddled
(and have treasured it ever since).

Never before has history afforded us so many opportunities for being
hysterical in public. Genuine opportunities. And, naturally, we have
not been slow in seizing our chances. Thus—the true pain and fascination of our period. Unfortunately, hysterical expression, while
often a necessary forerunner of the solution of problems, does not of
itself constitute an abiding solution: its real products are pain and
fascination, not answers: it is, then, both cathartic and esthetic.
That is, not without value. When we come upon a person who is
brilliant as well as hysterical, we have found something of great
interest. Something supremely pertinent. Such is James Burnham's
recent book on the atomic crisis.

Burnham's thesis is quite simple—in fact, too simple. But very
forceful. (It has all the seductive attraction of rape, or of a temptation one can no longer resist: let the reader beware.) The point of
departure is the existence of atomic weapons which are fully capable
of destroying Western Civilization; and the fact that a third World
War has already begun. Just as Marxists have always protested the
dissociation of economics and politics, so Burnham protests the false
severance of politics from war. He emphasizes the important contradictory truth that wars begin before they start. We are now at war
with Russia, he says. We can achieve peace only by winning or losing that war. The *politics* of the war will mitigate or heighten its
destructiveness and determine, of course, its historical meaning; but
nothing can stop it. Unless we are so optimistic as to count on an
immediate revolutionary or Utopian "third camp," we must agree
with this broad statement of Burnham's. . . . Or we can give up

politics and view the destructive denouement of Western Civilization as a natural phenomenon similar to a huge tornado or meteor: it will be a bit difficult, however, *to live with the plan of accepting esthetically one's own actual, imminent death*. Most of us will be deeply attracted to any possibility of averting this terrible end.

The essential statements constituting Burnham's thesis are as follows: The kind of atomic war we fear can only be waged by nations possessing an advanced technology of considerable size; there are only two such nations—Russia and the United States. The war between these two great technological areas has resulted from the nature of Communism, which is "a world-wide, conspiratorial movement for the conquest of a monopoly of power in the era of capitalist decline." The only means of forestalling atomic destruction is the securing of monopoly control of all technological areas capable of producing atomic weapons. In practical terms, this means the creation of either an American or a Communist world empire. Since Communism means a totalitarian police terror, an American world empire is preferable. Besides, the latter may become democratic and progressive. *Therefore*, the United States must assume world leadership against Communism and for the preservation of Western Civilization from atomic destruction, using both force and concession as means. This policy of "democratic world order" under American leadership could, but probably will not, be carried out successfully. The most likely resolution of the present crisis will be a full-scale atomic war between Russia and the United States with the latter ill-prepared politically, and thus the probable loser.

I believe we must agree with Burnham to the following extent: We will live under the perpetual and imminent threat of atomic destruction until the relevant technological areas are united politically; only two centers of power exist as aspirants for leadership in achieving this unity—the United States and the Soviet Union (that is, Communist expansion cannot be stopped without opposing to it American economic power, and American or Communist power must be involved in any program of anti-atomic unity). Furthermore, a Communist world empire would bring untold misery to the human race for at least a century, whereas an American hegemony holds out other possibilities. No responsible person will ignore these basic factors which constitute the general historical framework of our atomic crisis.

I think we have arrived now at the point where it becomes quite clear that everything depends on what happens in America. In writing his book, Burnham also saw future events in this country as the pivot of the problem. But the chief merit of his work lies in his description of the world crisis, in his exposition of the abstract logic of the necessity-situation. His main statement about America is simply that it is an immature country—which is both true and important. But from there on his view of the United States is too narrow, mechanical, and unimaginative. *Burnham has presented for America the minimum program to meet the worst eventuality.* All middle-aged property-owners should thank him from the bottom of their hearts—as much for what he has *not* said, as for his brilliant general statement of the crisis. For the rest of us, this is the beginning, not the end, of the discussion.

The Struggle for the World is addressed to the American ruling class. Burnham, with his cataclysmic view of the crisis and his exclusive concern with power, seems not to be interested in the relation of other groups to the creation of an American "policy of democratic world order." He is saying, essentially, that the leadership of the anti-Communist front must be conceded to the group of men who control the basic American industries, since these stand at the core of any non-Communist resolution of the crisis. When not overtly, then implicitly, he advises these our rulers to continue to control the government and people of the United States as heretofore, and to branch out and dominate—by force when secondary concessions do not suffice—all countries not at present within the Communist orbit.

Nowhere does Burnham seriously consider the fascist potential in such an *abdication of politics to power.* That is because he defines politics as "nothing but the struggle for power." I believe that this statement, so central to Burnham's view, is patently false. If politics is *"nothing but* the struggle for power," then all parties to that struggle must be equal politically except in their relation to power. But this can be true only of an individual who, in the political sphere, has no *aim* except power, or who is *unwilling to act* on any other aim than power. *The phrase "nothing but power," is the best possible definition of the essence of fascism.* Power is certainly central to politics, and the struggle for power is always a part of the resolution of any political question; but this is not the same thing as saying that politics is *"nothing but* the struggle for power." The latter statement is simply reductionist nonsense.*

It is from this misdefinition that all of Burnham's errors and distortions flow. He sees Communism *purely* as a conspiracy to achieve world power—and thus absolves the anti-Communist bloc of any necessity for dealing with those festering social problems the resolution of which constitutes the main totalitarian strength. Also, since Communism has always been politics—has always been "nothing but the struggle for power"—Lenin and Stalin can be equated, revolutionary socialism can be "logically" drowned in the sewer of Stalinism. (Burnham throughout fails to capitalize Communism when referring to the Stalinist movement.) And he can dispose foolishly of the question "What *should* be done?" by holding up the toy of Hindu renunciation, the abandonment of all power.—And many, many other neat little tricks.

What is the source of this ugly, oversize distortion of Burnham's conception of politics and, I am afraid, of his picture of life itself? Why does he see nothing but power wherever he looks? He himself gives us the answer: "In the United States, the practical politician despises the men of learning in the political sciences—for there are a few; and the men of learning, blocked from contact with the springs of power, become academic and sterile." But *not* Professor James Burnham, *not* this planetary warrior with a Princeton degree: he knows he is brilliant enough, and quite embittered enough, to more than fill the role of a Machiavelli to the most important and most stupid ruling class in history. And the morality of this exhibitionist act? But morals are only an illusion—power is the reality. Besides, didn't he once upon a time give the workers their chance to make a revolution for him? Of course he did! Having invited God and been refused, he is now free to do business with the Devil.

Burnham was perhaps the primary figure, in this country, in the collapse of the anti-Stalinist Left. There were a number of very good reasons for this collapse—*but there was no moral reason.* It is altogether fitting, therefore, that he should be the one to make a totem of amoralism. But again Burnham uses a genuine and crucial problem to suit his own ends. For it is the penchant for irrelevant morality which so distinguishes Americans, especially those Americans

---

* This nonsense is often indulged in by those intellectuals whose revulsion at liberal moralism has become uncontrollable.

who can least afford it, i.e., those without power. Both the brilliant and the bad in Burnham's thought are primarily directed against this national characteristic: it is the real theme of the book. The break-down of Puritan morality in this country (which Freud as late as the Twenties called "pious America") is not merely a source of excite-ment to Frenchmen, but is a primary factor in the discussion of any American problems. Having said this, it is rather interesting to see that, besides Burnham and his kind, the chaos of the Left has also thrust forward some other purely and excessively Moral Individuals.*

But there are *some* possibilities in this unbelievable situation. Al-though terribly weakened economically, England is not finished in a political sense. The issue in Europe is from now on unbearably sharp; any life left there must be squeezed out into the open. The consequences of the approaching depression in the United States cannot be written off, are bound to shake up the whole situation considerably (and may, of course, hasten the assumption of an authoritarian government here). Both by governmental repression and a to-be-expected swing of opinion, the Stalinoid Left is bound to diminish; these persons need not become apolitical. The anti-labor measures of the Republican Congress may force a reaction from the unions. People may not submit to slavery and death so easily.

In general, the greatest possibility is held forth by exactly that primary condition which Professor Burnham so much deplores—the adolescence of America. If the adolescent is unformed, he is none-theless a lively, flexible being. Adolescence is quintessentially the condition of man which contains the most promise and variety. And perhaps the greatest sadness in life is that men abandon more of themselves than is necessary as they grow away from that time of promise. Germany, for example, was not adolescent as she fell into the mad arms of Hitler, but rather was like a person approaching middle age who suddenly realizes, with a traumatic shock, that all of the real problems of life have gone unsolved. This might have been but cannot now be the fate of America. With the addition of a major depression to the present international crisis, we will have a situation—demanding decision—in which the basic problems *could not be posed more clearly or imperatively*. And the great choice will be made by a people which possesses more unused, primitive vitality than any other in the modern world. This is not the worst we might

* I was thinking of Dwight Macdonald—and some others.

have feared. In a sense, granted the failure of Europe, it is the most we could have hoped for. If, after Europe, we have any faith left in life, the time to exercise it will soon come.*

❊ THE MILITARY-INDUSTRIAL COMPLEX:
IS IT A DANGER?

WNDT/NEW YORK, 1963

In retrospect, 1938 was not merely the year of Munich, and the last hope of preventing war; it was also the year in which the New Deal ended, to be revived and concluded in magnificent anti-climax twenty-seven years later. And 1938 was the beginning of Preparedness, including gimmickry like lend-lease. Ours has been a war economy for thirty years, with no relief except the comic relief of precipitate demobilization, reconversion boodle, the theft of $50 billion in war bonds, and a pause for retooling in preparation for high-class deterrence rather than old-fashioned industrial warfare. The political and economic facts of the thirty-year war economy are monstrous beyond belief.

Along with my opening statement, I have included here some of the supporting facts and observations used in a television debate on the subject of the military. My opponent was a representative of the Hudson Institute—a nice fellow who, I am sorry to say, insisted that Eisenhower was wrong: no, my opponent hadn't noticed a "military-industrial complex."

We know there is a military-industrial complex because General Eisenhower told us about it a couple of years ago—and warned against it—in his farewell speech to the history books.† We can also see it by looking at the scope of military expenditure, currently running at a rate in excess of *one billion dollars a week.*

Now if there is such a complex of elite power in our democratic

---

* Apocalyptic, wasn't I? Then came Korea, missiles, and the New Economics: no more depressions in America—just killing malaise.

† The writer reputed to be responsible for the major speech in question was Malcolm Moos.

order, how does the question arise as to whether it is a "danger"? When and where in history has a big military *not* been a danger? Moreover, our postwar military posture vis-à-vis the Soviet Union, consisting of a competitive and insane exchange of homicide-plus-suicide threats, is admittedly as much of a danger to our own domestic population as it is to the enemy nation.

But the danger is not limited to the possible effects of war with the Soviets. Indeed, it is not properly understood at all by reference to nuclear war—that is not a danger, but an incomparable disaster. No, there are clear and present dangers in the very existence of the military-industrial complex, whether or not we are ever to suffer an exchange of nuclear salvos. That is because this complex of elite power underlies and urges the military point of view, the military resolution of all problems.

The true and immediate danger lies in the *political* character of the military emphasis, which is supported by big industry and serviced by the technological elite. Here, we need some history:

The 1937–38 recession, marking the end of the New Deal, was never properly resolved in political terms. It was transcended by a shift to war production, which has been more or less continuous since then. Thus, the New Deal did not solve the structural problems of the economy which were the key to the Great Depression—the quasi-solution of these has been inseparable from the expansion of military production. Without military spending, our economic history would have been drastically different. In effect, a truce was made between the forces of the New Deal and major corporate power in order to fight World War II. We have, for the past quarter-century now, translated most major issues of the political economy into the terms of this truce—nothing more than a temporary military solution—with the obvious effect that we have become deeply wedded to the military, both domestically and in our foreign affairs. *Because we are afraid to come back to the real problems.*

But the military offers no genuine solution either to the Cold War or to the deeper problems of the domestic economy. In relation to both, it is at best a dangerous and temporary holding-action—to give us time.

Time to do what?

Time to learn to fight the Cold War by non-military means, and time to come to terms politically with our technological snowball of a super-abundant economy. Both have been confronted as military issues—neither is susceptible of a military solution, in the long run. In the short run, each is a great danger. And there you have a political issue so profound that our grandchildren will still be talking about what we did about it, if they are here to talk, and their rulers let them—and if in fact we did anything about it.

Each of the $800 billion and more we have spent under the sign of the military since 1941 might have been exactly necessary (not each of them was) and *still*, the concentrated amalgam of military, industrial, and technological power created thereby, which General Eisenhower called the military-industrial complex, would constitute an extreme threat to our democratic order. That is because—come reason or madness—it is so compelling an institutional commitment to the military view of affairs.

We will know exactly how much of a danger the military-industrial complex is when the time comes to liquidate it. That is, when the threat of serious disarmament is immediate. Or, when we realize to what extent the *successful* prosecution of the Cold War requires non-military initiatives. Or, finally, at that moment when we understand that our economy demands the intervention of considerable federal power—whether or not excused or camouflaged by real or imagined military need.

NOTES:

From Eisenhower's Farewell Address of January 17, 1961:

"Our military organization today bears little relation to that known by any of my predecessors . . ."

"We have been compelled to create a permanent armaments industry of vast proportions."

"Now this conjunction of an immense military establishment and a large arms industry is new in the American experience. The total influence—economic, political, even spiritual—is felt in every city, every state house, every office of the Federal government. We recognize the imperative need for this development. Yet we must not fail to comprehend its grave implications. Our toil, resources and livelihood are all involved; so is the very structure of our society.

"In the councils of Government, we must guard against the acquisition of unwarranted influence, whether sought or unsought, by the military-industrial complex. The potential for the disastrous rise of misplaced power exists and will persist.

"We must never let the weight of this combination endanger our liberties or democratic processes. We should take nothing for granted."

"Akin to, and largely responsible for, the sweeping changes in our industrial-military posture has been the technological revolution during recent decades."

"Yet, in holding scientific research and discovery in respect, as we should, we must also be alert to the equal and opposite danger that public policy could itself become the captive of a scientific-technological elite."

"As one who has witnessed the horror and the lingering sadness of war, as one who knows that another war could utterly destroy this civilization which has been so slowly and painfully built over thousands of years, I wish I could say tonight that a lasting peace is in sight."

FACTS:

In 1961, the whole world was spending $14 million an hour on arms and armies. That equaled $140 a year per person on the planet: 75 million men involved.

From 1950–59, the U.S. spent $228 billion on supplies and weapons—38 million purchase transactions. Military inventory exceeds total retail inventory, and not much less than total manufacturing inventory. Tangible assets of $150 billion. Surplus disposal of $10 billion annually, at 2 per cent of cost—pretty obviously *not* "just another customer."

Seymour Harris, 1959: 1941–1959, $700 billion spent for defense and war. One out of every seven dollars—GNP for period of $5.25 trillion.

In all U.S. history, we—the government of the United States—have spent $1.4 trillion: 90 per cent in the last twenty years. I don't take this as a conspiracy or a mistake, but as an economic necessity. The fact that most of this money was spent on the military is not, however, a continuing, absolute, or undiscussable necessity.

Three-quarters of the prime contracts go to the 100 leading defense suppliers.

In 1960, a House investigating committee disclosed that 726 former high-ranking officers were employed by the 100 leading contractors (1,400 from the rank of major on up—27 generals and admirals with General Dynamics alone).

POINTS:

The deterrent system can, at best, deter the use of nuclear force to spread Communism. It cannot, however, deter Communism. That requires a viable (and even shrewd) alternative to Communism, and of course a realistic one; and our great power unleashed and applied unstintingly to the support of that alternative. This is the real issue of the Cold War—the military part is either an illusion or a disaster, or both.

The Cold War has been misconceived—it is not a military operation. It involves total social competition with Russia, to determine the future society of the whole planet. (Criticize the theory of spending Russia into submission: OK, but not on useless military items.)

We ought to notice the *character* of the present-day military. Its center is no longer the mass civilian army, but *various institutional elites*. This is a general social movement in our society, of course, but it is both accelerated and obscured as it develops under the military umbrella.

The industrial-technological complex alone, without the addition of an immense military which it hides behind, is quite sufficient a danger to a democratic society of liberal intention. So-called private industry in the shape of the big corporation is a form of government; and it is not a democratic form.

The biggest issue in American history, never more so than today, is the power relation between the big corporations and the state. In these big terms, what the military-industrial complex—and the military emphasis it fosters—stands for is the *choice* of big industry and big finance to come to terms with the military side of the state rather than the democratic civilian authority.

We do things in the name of the military that under any other designation would be impermissible politically—assertion of federal coordination and purpose, spending, borrowing, planning, acceleration of programs, etc.

It is essential that the federal government redistribute income and otherwise stimulate the economy, by direct spending as well as other means. It can do this most readily under the military umbrella. Congress hardly ever questions the immense military budget, and hardly ever fails to haggle over all other budgetary items. (Example of the Veterans Administration.) If all these other issues were placed alongside military ones with equal effect, then the military could be dealt with realistically, in terms of its necessities. That is *not* the case. That *is* the danger.

Is a military dictatorship possible in the United States? Apart from nuclear war, this is of course the ultimate danger implied in the existence—and continued undomesticated growth—of the military-industrial complex. This might be called the "Seven Days in May" problem, or the General Walker nightmare. A military dictatorship would run against all of our traditions, but that is not a very good reason for dismissing the possibility. It could come, it seems to me, as the result of any of these three conditions: (1) as the immediate effect of an exchange of nuclear salvos; (2) under the threat of genuine disarmament; and (3) in the convulsive response to a series of cumulative defeats in the Cold War. The first is out of our control; the second will be a great political issue when the time comes; the third worries me considerably, but it is a very complicated kind of time-bomb (and could hardly be discussed here and now).

 LIBERAL ANTI-COMMUNISM REVISITED

COMMENTARY, 1967

I need not set out the questions of the symposium to which this piece provided my answers. The issue is clear enough: Are you sorry now about your Support (that word again!) of the Cold War, whatever it was? Yes and no: mostly I am sorry about my powerlessness, then and now. I am genuinely sorry about all of the lost opportunities, mine and others. The Cold War could have been fought with infinitely more imagination as to initiatives, battlegrounds, allies, and objectives. Instead, it was fought stupid and on-the-cheap, with weaponry limited to military hardware (except for the Marshall Plan). If it was

*worth fighting at all, the country should have been mobilized
—just as in World War II, price controls and all—for the pursuit of objectives by other than military means.* Mere containment was an absurd long-term policy: it assumed the non-
Communist world would stand still, and the Communist order
collapse in awe of our mighty determination.

Yes, I have an inventory of historical sorrows. And—*as always—I weep for America,* my country right-and-wrong.

To answer the questions: Yes, I feel responsible for American policies in Vietnam: I am an American, which for me is not a mere fate,
but a point of view. I have intellectually allowed for and, if it means
anything, have supported the postwar policy of military containment. One Vietnam or another—the containing power being sucked
into excessive support of a nonexistent government—seems nearly
inevitable in retrospect: a time-bomb flaw in American policy from
the beginning.

I most certainly remain an anti-Communist today; although both
Communism and I have changed. For one thing, I would never
favor the use of nuclear weapons in pursuit of anti-Communist
policy, or any other. Most sane men would rather be red, or even red-
white-and-blue, than dead-in-a-devastated-world. However, once
thus-colored—or living in any spiritually devastated world—I would
treasure the option to choose a rich occasion of my own death. But
this heroism, suicidal or otherwise, is a personal choice, not a social
policy.

I am a slave to almost all American policy—foreign or not, dark or
otherwise—as are we all. As for being a dupe, quite the contrary: if
anybody in 1947 had told me we would all be alive in 1967, and with
a chance for our kids to survive us, I would have sneered at length
and in detail.

Communism—any system—is livable, I suppose: half of Europe
even survived the plague. And I can think of a dozen or more social
arrangements right here in the United States that I cannot imagine
surviving, and that would at the same time constitute rapid social
advance for millions of my fellow citizens. The confusion of personal and social policy considerations is now, among us, at an exquisite height: I know women who cannot be diverted from imagining
themselves as mothers of napalmed babies long enough to give substantial attention to their own affluent children: *we lust after primi-*

tive conditions of life. It was that romantic idiot, Gauguin, who afforded our current half-civilized masses the key to historical experience, he, and more recently Mississippi (somewhat more available by Greyhound, but now forgotten).

It is this elevation of primitivism to the status of the sole revelatory truth that provides the core of the New Style in American public expression, including politics. To measure the depth of our fall to primitivism, compare this new kind to the romantic naturalism of D. H. Lawrence—the last of the great romantics, now almost forty years dead. Lawrence *imagined* a new animal man, he did not merely imitate existing primitives (and certainly not men whose primitivism derived mostly from their unnatural deprivations); and he rejected modern industrialism in its fact and its essence. Our current romantics accept all the benefits—including the personal chemical distortions—of the technological order; they owe their stylish existence and most of their ideas to the representational media of the technological society; and their Noble Savages are the enraged victims of ghetto hysteria, and the stunted peasants of the Black Belt.

Liberal anti-Communism, growing out of the history of the socialist movement and more particularly out of the utter rejection of Stalinism by elements of that tradition—as well as the coerced political propriety of the McCarthy period—is not so much attacked as it is summarily dismissed by the politicos of the New Style: dismissed for no better reason than that it is inconveniently inhibiting. (They *are* capable of thinking about it.) This new generation of New Class middlebrows—only gently sprinkled with the paprika of old fellow-traveling maturity and wisdom—believes that Communism is a bogey invented by McCarthy in order to disrupt the Left; and they are not about to be taken in by any such obvious maneuver. In any event, it is not an issue important enough to think about—it will mellow, it has mellowed; what do you mean by Communism; what about lynching in the South; Stalin is dead; Yankee go home; America never does anything right; Ho Chi Minh is an intelligent, well-educated, peasant leader.

Primitive identifications are strangely like projective images, as in the scapegoat theory of anti-Semitism, only benign. They have the desperate object of avoiding the entanglements, or awareness of the entanglements, of one's emotional life (or what is left of it) in the immediate actualities of a rationalistically organized social order, and the accompanying Consumerism. It is all a middlebrow rewrite of selected moods of popular culture—as if some images on television had jumped out of the tube and begun picketing and demonstrating in the living room. The civil rights revolution occurred mostly in the media: the demonstrators were unpaid actors for the networks.

In the context of this absurdly derived and puerile emotionality, it now becomes necessary to re-discuss a complicated historical phenomenon like Communism, as some decades ago it was necessary to delineate the tragic fate of the October Revolution to a movie audience that had just moments before seized upon a Russian Dream as its American one dissolved in the sick ozone of the Depression. Vietnam is our nightmare, just as Soviet power, years ago, was our dream. So be it—even though now the group concerned, centered in the growth industry of education, is many times over more numerous and assertive and powerful than was the earlier generation. This time they are so strong they don't even need Stalin.

Communism is not a matter of indifference, no matter how much it has or will become mellowed. Moreover, its mellowing, such as it is, is the result at least *also* of checked Soviet expansion, and the fact that Stalinism did not find an heir in Europe. Leaving other things aside for the moment, it seems ordinary to me that the necessity of the last battle, Vietnam, should be more deeply questioned than that of earlier ones—like the Berlin airlift or the Italian election of the late Forties. But, in the absence of American counter-pressure, even Stalin might very well have succeeded in building a more durable totalitarian empire.

While Communism cannot be opposed effectively without American power, the purpose of the opposition cannot be to secure the planetary dominion of the patterns of the American order. These are not viable, worldwide, since the two main strands of Americanism—our capacity for technological application, and our freedom to indulge minority cultural and political expression—are both derived from our exceptional wealth, which in turn has a unique basis in our continental history. The planetary issue should not be conceived as either/or—since even mellowing Communism is not a matter of indifference, and non-military Americanism is not yet exportable. The issue before the planet is not to copy an inimitable America, but to suffer the technological transformation with less rather than more damage to the humanity that may survive it. And that is, for me, the vital point about Communism, in *any* of its polycentric forms: it concentrates all power in a purportedly supra-historical agency devoted to technological transformation without any conception at all of the accompanying human damage, and of course without allowing for any expression of any such conception by others. Moreover, in its monolithic concentration of power in the party and over the state, it is politically musclebound (overadministered) *even* in its introduction of the technology, apart from the character of the accompanying social order. This is not acceptable, to humans, except for pure survival.

What is a better way than the Communist way?

Any nationalist way, since that preserves an indigenous sense of the human in the inevitable engagement with technology; the way of any internationalist agency, including that of national corporations of advanced countries, where more technological sophistication than world-view is being exported (e.g., Krupp factory-building or Japanese trade); and perhaps, one future day from somewhere, the way of a truly humane social democracy (which technological wealth may soon make feasible). But the issue is technology: (1) to keep it from destroying us; (2) to make it available to the poor who insist on having it; (3) to preserve options of the survival of indigenous human society in the wake of the devastation that inevitably accompanies the introduction of effective production; and (4) most especially not to accept the simple recapitulation of the past experiences of *any* advanced nation, concerning the primitive accumulation of capital, upon the helpless, greedy, unknowing body of the pre-technological peoples of the planet.

Conceived in this manner, the struggle is clearly with ourselves as well as with Communism. Just as clearly, it is not merely with ourselves, but also with a Communist pattern that is often woodenly stupid, and not even—for all that—as useful to the Third World as idiot American efficiency that cannot as yet distinguish between steel and Coca-Cola.

I am afraid that we are fighting a war in Vietnam for no better reason than that it is what we do best—and somebody has to do something. Both notions are tragically true. There is good reason not to lose the war in Vietnam; there is also good reason not to bother winning it. This war, which now involves Vietnam itself only as victim, should not be won or lost but transcended. The Pentagon desires to prove that guerrilla subversion, or Wars of National Liberation, can be defeated by the determined application of American power: I believe that some can and some can't, and that if we won this one this year the proof of victory would be deeply deceptive. Very crudely, it has already cost too much to be a pattern of anything but defeat. To date, we have proven that we are bigger than France, which everyone knew anyway; and that American power, when acting alone, must be selectively applied—and this was a very poor selection from the point of view even of the Pentagon. We have said that we are prepared to fight for ten or twenty years: what would possibly remain, of Vietnam or of our purpose, after ten or twenty years? Better to destroy North Vietnam next year, or sit in Saigon and wait, than to persist in any such wilful absurdity. The best way to win in Vietnam is to finance Ho Chi Minh thirty years ago.

But the Vietnam experience, however concluded, is a beginning as well as an end. It is an end only of the simple-minded postwar policy of containment monstrously misapplied. But a beginning of *active military world government*.

Notice how much seems to have been forgotten in the recent concentration on the Vietnam overinvolvement—by the liberal intellectual community as well as by the Pentagon. There is an ever-present issue of the survival of the planet which we must strain to recall. It is perhaps still vaguely reasonable to argue about winning a war in Vietnam, or not losing one again; it is simply insane to discuss the winning of a nuclear war with the Soviet Union. Not to fight that war means to make a deal with that enemy. This deal must be, in the first instance, military; it had better be, secondarily, something more. But note that the realistic range of possibility here is from immediate utter destruction, all the way to a horrifying planetary condominium by the two most detested powers in the world (which comprise not much more than one-sixth of the population), the central drama of which will consist of waverings between obnoxious piety and sickening insecurity. The politics of the future necessarily occurs under this black umbrella.

The issue is the survival of the planet, and the pattern of control over its development if it does survive. That is an ultimate and an immediate—therefore an apocalyptic—issue: indeed, somebody ought to make a morning prayer out of it, so that we might properly greet the fresh apocalypse of Everyday. *And this issue is to be met by*

*firm mental opposition to war? And fervent demonstrations in favor
of love and de-escalation in Vietnam? And hating American power
so much that we drift into a benign view of Communist power?*

So I am an anti-Communist who believes that our most urgent
business is to make a deal with the Communists. This may strike
some unilinear logicians as contradictory—as what, in the real world,
would not? Further to pursue this contradiction, as to a non-nuclear
matter, I imagine that if I were a Frenchman in politics I would
affirm and elaborate my anti-Communism *in order to* participate
effectively in the construction of the new Popular Front now challenging, and soon to inherit, the Gaullist state. Thus, and not otherwise, the ugly dialogue of the Thirties continues.

Russia and the United States are being driven together by the
greatest force in organized (rather than organic) human society—
the need of equal powers to cooperate in order to avoid the irony of
neutralization. And the need to recognize the iron law that governs
all anti-suicide arrangements, namely, that if we do not kill each
other, then we damn well must live together, God help us. And if
we spend all of our time and energy threatening each other with
revocation of the arrangement, others with less power will prevail in
our absence.

To conclude: I said the war in Vietnam should be not won or lost,
but transcended. That is, indeed, the effort of the liberal intellectual
community in the United States—to transcend the war with primitive emotional assertion as to this, that, and the other. I propose,
instead, an alternative *policy* that can be lobbied and campaigned
for right here at home, and that will thereby raise rather than reduce
the activists thereof. It should be endorsed by Congress before being
acted upon. It is as follows:

1. The President of the United States shall appear before the
General Assembly of the United Nations and apologize to the world
for our excessively military emphasis in opposing the evil of Communist subversion;

2. A radical change of policy shall be announced, consisting of a
secondary military posture in all instances, and a primary effort to
afford technology and capital assistance to all who desire it and who
observe the planetary peace;

3. A continuing Coexistence Commission under the auspices of
the United Nations with a free agenda for the discussion on inter-

continental television of all aspects of Soviet-American problems, differences, similarities, prospects, attitudes toward this-and-that area of the world, etc., by both private and governmental persons;

4. A congressionally authorized commitment by the United States government, presented to the United Nations, specifying (on conditions to be negotiated) the devotion of a sum equal to 5 per cent of American GNP, or 50 per cent of the last annual increase in American GNP, whichever shall be greater, to a new international development authority controlled according to the extent of contribution of whomsoever thereto, plus whatever sums shall be made available by negotiated reduction of armament; and

5. A one-organization plan for the planet reported upon and/or revised annually as necessary, and in any event not less than every five years.

You want peace? This is the way to fight for it.

You want to fight Communism? This is the way to hit them where it counts.

You want a real fight, or just occasions for primitive hate?

You want to persuade the United States to act its age? Try this way for size.

Or shall we persist—decade after decade—in expecting that the Soviet Union, once we play dead, will accomplish all of this without our assistance?

Is it really up to them alone to save the world?

❀ FACING UP TO THE PRESENT

COMMENTARY, 1968

Review of *Waist Deep in the Big Muddy:*
Personal Reflections on 1968,
by Richard H. Rovere

This says it—and this ends it. You don't buy time at the five-and-dime: you cook it up in your own kitchen, or you do without.

Richard Rovere can write; he can think; he's sensitive; he's been around. And here he makes a brief, strenuous effort to face up to the

Big New Mood that we are all compulsively preoccupied with, that none of us has adequately characterized—Vietnam, riots, the election, boredom, drugs and drop-outs, the hysteria of One More Federal Program, marches against this-and-that, youthful *mish* against aging *mash*. This book is no triumph. But it is the first of what is sure to become a deluge, and it is very interesting—mostly mood and implication, everything pregnant-with-meaning.

The ostensible subject is how Richard Rovere, certainly no "premature anti-Vietnamer," came to oppose the war in Vietnam. His current effort will only put him back in touch with his constituency, however; it will not anoint him, in the Thoreau-Muste-Goodman tradition. It certainly is not, as the dust-jacket argues, "one of the most agonizing documents to appear in recent years." I found it a different kind of reading.

The subject of the book, perhaps, also is: Does the United States really need, can it afford, much of a foreign policy? If this is the question, Rovere's answer is: No. The reasons for the answer are mostly—and eagerly—deferred to Unanswered History, both past and future.* Pierced by the same intergenerational bullet as Mr. Rovere, I accept this absurd position.

It is utterly clear that Vietnam was one war too many for this country. The policy issues are now, therefore, substantially irrelevant. So many intelligent people have seen this, that slowpokes like Rovere and myself must take it as given—whether we join in Rovere's *mea culpa*, or write (or think) our own. But I am saddened to admit that I have no particular respect, no admiration for the fast-fellows who figured it all out before I did—and that seems to be Rovere's feeling too. The last time we went through this kind of experience, as I recall, was when it was overwhelmingly decided that Marxism was old-hat. But what I remember best was Harold Rosenberg's convincing exposition of the observable fact that the earliest mongers of that particular fashion were those who never understood Marxism in the first place. Small consolation, certainly. But, for those who take politics also as a metaphor of something more important, not insignificant.

If I thought what Rovere actually says in his book, his intellectual

* Rovere's attitude toward the Cold War revisionist historians, for example, is to say it isn't important whether the fears of the Forties were real or apparent. I think it's important; but neither am I prepared to engage in the detailed, abstract argument they are clamoring for.

argument, was equal to his "waist-deep" feeling, I would have gotten to it sooner in this review. Anyway, I will get to it now.

"Some of us who were well beyond the age of consent in 1948 and 1950 must now square past and present," he begins. His own effort commences with a chapter comparing Truman and Johnson, Korea and Vietnam. That, it seems to me, is a rather special view of the relevant "past" and "present" which must now be squared, if only because the current past/present turnabout has much deeper roots than the issue of Communism in Asia. The true issue is—and has been since October 1917—what those in the socialist tradition, or naturally attracted to it, would do once that tradition had been taken over, in historical fact, by the future monstrously-arrived ahead of schedule. In the United States, the majority so disposed decided to support the American containment of Communism as a desperate, interim measure. (Meanwhile, like other Americans, we got rich.) Containment, and this special support of it, finally flopped in Vietnam. Naturally, those whose thought did not begin with October 1917 noticed the final flop ahead of time. It's much easier to understand the modern world in terms of The Bomb; and The Bomb, it turns out, provides an intellectual writ of greater jurisdiction than the Bolshevik Revolution ever did.

In his second chapter (of four), "The People We Have Become," Rovere talks about the independent significance of "affluence as an agent of change." I agree; and wholeheartedly when he points out that "this is the first war of the century of which it is true that opposition to it is not only widespread but fashionable." Writing his book for him, I would have begun with this perception, and worked my way back, carefully, to the socialist tradition, its middlebrow fate in America, and so on. But he wrote it for himself, and he goes on to note the importance of television (and the violence of it); that "kookiness of every sort is alarmingly on the rise"; that "there is building up in this country a powerful sentiment not simply against the war in Vietnam but against war itself" (I personally lost twelve months on this idiotic point alone, in my own readjustment); that all this is—let's not kid ourselves—a return to isolationism; and that certainly this society is racist, but that there never has been one that wasn't. He is superbly himself, at his best, when in several choice lines he capsulates the issue of "wars of national liberation"—which Vietnam is, but not the last, since the Soviet Union will certainly continue to stoop to pick up this loose change: "From the Soviet point of view, they are irresistible. They cost next to nothing and drive us Americans out of our minds."

"In 1948, when he was Secretary of State and putting in place the foundation stones of postwar American foreign policy, General Marshall was asked to describe his objective," Chapter 3 begins. Then ensues an insider-paragraph no one could summarize, ending with the following quotation from Marshall: " 'If we could just hold on for twenty or thirty years without starting a nuclear war . . . the world would be a different place.' " This is the heart of the book: the time has passed and the world *is* a different place.

Time. To do what? To survive, certainly: but we bought much more expensive time than that. We bought—or tried to buy—time in which America would become good enough to justify its ruling the world instead of Russia. Period. Now the new generation informs us that our rather abstract experiment bores them. QED. If we had tried harder to explain, if they had tried harder to understand, that: (1) somebody must rule; (2) American rule is better; and (3) Russian rule is worse than they imagine—so what? Clearly, they are not interested in any such subtleties. Scream them to the wind, as an ultimate devotion? No. Give in, and see what the rest of the discussion will be like.

"Marshall thought that the world would be a different place a generation later. The time has passed, and the world is so very different that the fathers cannot convince grown sons, young men born into that other world, that the place ever existed and that its terrors were real." Right. "Communism is scarcely more binding ideologically than monarchy or democracy." Wrong (it has extensive relevance, beyond monarchy and more than equal to democracy). Although he did not change his own view about military containment until 1965, Rovere identifies 1955 as the year in which the world changed enough to render our policy obsolete. In 1955 the balance of terror matured, the first summit meeting was held, etc.—*but*: "Just as it was becoming clear that Europe was out of danger, we began to conceive our mission to be a global one and our adversary to be an ideology." That's neat; I don't know whether it's true, it might be. Anyway, the possibility of *détente* was pursued with inadequate vigor on both sides, and the happenstantial mess of

Vietnam occurred for no better reason than that a bypassed policy had not been changed nor the consequent priorities reshuffled. So, Rovere quite effectively informs us that "whatever moral and political judgments may be made on American policy in Vietnam, what one is compelled to say is that the war there is . . . monumentally irrelevant to what should be the priorities of policy in 1968." Agreed, agreed.

He does not discuss the details of the war in Vietnam: indeed, he does not tell us much about what is wrong with it—only about the used-up quality of the global policy that led us to it, and the fact that he has signed off. But he has a number of excellent observations and insights into it—for instance, on the domino theory: "Some dominos might fall in a certain way because we set them up that way." In other words, an entire Asian policy is at stake—as to which Vietnam may well be only *one* flaw.

I was disappointed, however, that Rovere does not even mention, much less discuss, what I thought was one of the more serious aspects of the war, namely, that military containment relying on limited wars was being tested in its application to "wars of national liberation," that the primary audience for such testing was the Soviet Union, and that the test is now a demonstrated flop. The point about Vietnam is that the war was not won within the required time. If we had won in Vietnam (as the British won in Malaya), we would have heard no more of it. We would simply have had to sit still and wait for the next one that could not be won. And I am bitterly convinced that this kind of sitting still is all that "we" should have expected to receive by buying historical time.

"These are the worst of American times," Rovere concludes. And they will get worse, he feels, because scapegoating the Vietnam folly will bring about "a great purge" and "may be far worse than the McCarthy years." It's possible, but I doubt it. That's an old horror: I think we are in for a new one. Vietnam as the End of Something will be, I think, that great occasion when the American people give up on infinity, turn inward, and observe themselves with delayed loathing. No help for it: it was due. We overconcentrated on making money; then we were equally foolish about what we might buy with it. Now, the whole thing must be thought through all over again, this time with previously-avoided pain present, and surely other unpleasantness as well.

We are a great society—or we are nothing any of us can bear to think of. A great society must entertain great projects. If we are not going to rule the world, then we must remake ourselves. Who (and what) will survive *that* effort?

3

THE OTHER WALLACE— AND THE OTHER McCARTHY

❀ THE FAITH OF HENRY WALLACE

COMMENTARY, 1947

I am tempted to depict our other four-party Presidential campaign in 1948 and compare it to the recent one in 1968 (which was in effect a four-party campaign even if Eugene McCarthy did not finally stand-in for his protest vote). And of course to compare the George Wallace and Joe McCarthy phenomena. I am even tempted to let loose on the mystical sameness of the names. But all that would be too much for the occasion. So I will just set forth here my portrait of Henry Wallace written before his Progressive party campaign of 1948 got under way; and my characterization of McCarthyism written substantially after the fact.

By the time this volume appears, I think it will be clear that, this time, both the Right and the Left are much more formidable than they were on that first test of strength twenty years ago. And, this time, the governing New Deal coalition (whether or not in a Republican Me-Too posture) will survive, if at all, in barely recognizable shape. The center is not holding: Can it reconstitute itself effectively, and in time? Essentially, can the major property and organizational powers finally step forward and reasonably govern the social order they created and have benefited from in such great degree?

❀ HENRY A. WALLACE is the "uncommon man" whom many liberals propose as leader of the well-known Common Man, whose century is supposed to be the present one.

This is the culmination of a development that began in 1940 when Roosevelt forced Wallace on the Democratic nominating convention as vice-presidential candidate, to stand as a symbol of liberalism in his administration. During the war, Wallace relieved the President of much of the task of interpreting the conflict from a progressive viewpoint. In 1944, the left wing of the Democratic party and the Political Action Committee fought to have Wallace retained as their advocate in the government and first in the line of succession. The Democratic progressives lost in a close fight, chiefly for lack of Roosevelt's support. When, after Roosevelt's death, Wallace's time came to break with the Truman administration, he became the symbol of the New Deal exodus from Washington.

Wallace has now become editor of the *New Republic*, which has embarked on an ambitious program of expansion: "I want it [the *New Republic*] to be so simple that high school students can understand it and so sound that doctors of philosophy respect it." Whether or not this miracle materializes, the new *New Republic* under Wallace is certain to become the center of liberal program-hatching in the post-Roosevelt period, at least for a time. "We need to rethink the whole basis of progressive political action," says Max Lerner, one of Wallace's ardent admirers. "If we fail in doing that, the next major depression may lead to a fascist era rather than to another New Deal."

This being the present importance of Henry Wallace, it is well to ask: What manner of man is he? What are the forces that produced him? What are his ideas?

The special strain of American liberalism that nurtured Wallace is not hard to identify. He is Midwestern; for most of his life he was purely a farm leader; religious ideas play a very large role in his political thinking. Just as Frances Perkins was the most successful social worker in the nation, so Wallace is the blue-ribbon product of the prairie land-grant colleges and of the great American populist tradition.

I

The Wallace family settled in Pennsylvania in 1823, coming from Scotland and Ulster. They had been mostly farmers as far back as anyone could remember. Henry A.'s grandfather, also named Henry, came out to Iowa and became a very important figure in the state, being known affectionately as "Uncle Henry." He built up the family's land-holdings and founded *Wallace's Farmer*. The motto on the masthead of this family newspaper has always been "Good Farming . . . Clear Thinking . . . Right Living."

"Uncle Henry" was for the first part of his life an ordained minister of the Presbyterian faith. In 1877, he left the Church in a huff, railing against "church-made sins." His reason for de-institutionalizing himself appears to have been a desire to preach more freely and effectively, and to larger audiences. He did just that. "Uncle Henry's" rhetorical style was original and richly personal. His preaching never consisted of mere hell-fire, but always had a practical, educative emphasis. At the same time, he became a political power in Iowa, taking a leading part in the fight for soil conservation, against freight-rate discriminations, and in other progressive struggles of his day. He served on Teddy Roosevelt's Country Life Commission, one of the earliest governmental projects for improving the lot of farmers.

Henry Cantwell Wallace (Henry A.'s father) lacked "Uncle Henry's" vivid personal qualities, but was a very capable and successful continuator of the family tradition. One writer describes him succinctly: "As a citizen his three interests were the Y.M.C.A., the United Presbyterian Church, and the Republican Party." Henry C. spent a number of years as professor of dairying at Ames College. He later became permanent secretary of the Corn Belt Meat Producers Association. And under his management, *Wallace's Farmer* so prospered during World War I as to earn the nickname, "Wallace's Gold Mine."

Henry C. served as Secretary of Agriculture in the cabinets of Harding and Coolidge, dying in office in 1924. The chief incident of his tenure was a long, bitter struggle with Herbert Hoover, then Secretary of Commerce. The source of their conflict was the fact that farmers were suffering, despite the industrial boom, from the high tariffs of the period and the loss of wartime markets. Throughout the Twenties, the farm interests conducted a huge propaganda campaign for some form of state aid in solving the farm problem—a campaign that was instrumental in bringing about the present system of parity payments. Hoover, on the side of the industrial and financial interests then supreme, was opposed to any really significant intervention in the farm market.

Some form of state planning and control has been an absolute necessity for American farmers since the beginning of the Twenties. Only during a v ~an agriculture now survive in a free market. It was under the influence of this overwhelming fact that Henry A. Wallace's economic thinking matured. And his father's bitter fight with Hoover was one of the reasons he threw his support to Roosevelt in 1932; but he had already switched parties four years earlier.

Henry A. Wallace was influenced profoundly by his grandfather. Indeed, never in his career has he abandoned the essential values of his family background and tradition; he has attempted, rather, to adapt them to modern problems and raise them to a world level. And the simple fact is that Wallace has perhaps done as much with this tradition as could be done. His father once said to the family: "Our Henry has the best mind of any Wallace in six generations."

Even before his graduation from Ames in 1910, he was writing for the family paper about his experiments in corn-breeding, which he began while still an adolescent. From 1910 until he entered Roosevelt's cabinet in 1933, he filled editorial positions on *Wallace's Farmer*. At the same time, he continued his researches in plant genetics—which eventually led him into business. His very active intellectual life and his friendships were centered around "agricultural-college people," the kind who for the past seventy-five years have had a deep influence on all aspects of farm life in this country and, through that, on our national existence.

Though Wallace's mentality was formed by his background, his interests have not been provincial. He mentions studying Bergson's *Creative Evolution* with his grandfather, he admires Veblen greatly —many more examples could be adduced. But even more important in his intellectual development has been the persistent devotion to religious beliefs and the curious pattern established by the unresolved conflict of this religious emphasis with his broader culture.

While still young, Wallace tells us, he began to reflect on the sermons he heard in church; he found them somewhat lacking in logic. This naturally caused an inner conflict, which he disposed of by deciding that a critical attitude in church was improper. He stopped attending services and began a study of Darwinism, but the more he read, the stronger became his feeling of the need for a God "immanent as well as transcendent." (He accepted the theory of evolution, of course.) Wallace calls Veblen "a modern Isaiah," but he also says: "I think there is far more possibility of good in the American businessman than Veblen cared to admit." Darwinism is true, Veblen's thought is true, but—*their opposites are also true!*

Wallace has told us that the book that influenced him most (after the Bible, presumably) was *Revolutions of Civilization* (1911) by W. M. Flinders Petrie, the British Egyptologist. A slim volume, it presents a very simple thesis on historical cycles, maintaining that every civilization has developed and decayed in the course of 1,500 years. Petrie's thesis was derived from a study of works of art, especially sculpture, in Egypt and Europe. The abandonment of archaic forms being his only criterion of growth, Petrie demonstrates the existence of cycles rather convincingly. He also describes the typical stages in the development of a civilization: the sequence is, roughly, from the flowering of the fine arts to scientific creativity and, finally, the accumulation of wealth. At the end of a cycle the old, decayed forms remain dormant until revivified by barbaric forces: "the source of every civilization has lain in race mixture. . . ."

The point of Petrie's book, Wallace believes, "is that democracy by destroying capitalism eventually destroys itself." This is quite an unexpected pronouncement, coming from a liberal leader whose program presumably espouses democracy at the expense of capitalism. But Wallace apparently sees basic economic democracy as historically unfeasible. Essentially, Petrie holds a racist or national view of history, not seeing class structure as dynamic, and Wallace seems to share this view with him. The Egyptologist's proposal for overcoming the elemental cycles of history was to create a biologically superior group to serve as rulers and preservers of culture.

In his first two years as Secretary of Agriculture, Wallace wrote speeches, articles, and books at a tremendous rate. After 1934, however, his rate of production dropped considerably, though he has always remained comparatively prolific. He has published about a dozen volumes in all, including collections of speeches. Except for several technical books and one or two dealing chiefly with religion, his writings are largely devoted to detailed economic analysis and suggestions for economic planning. Most of this literary production was occasioned by contemporary issues—such as early New Deal planning, the question of the Constitution and the Supreme Court, the economics of the war, and so forth.

Judging from his record in the Roosevelt-Truman span, some government people consider Wallace a good administrator, while others assert that his departments were poorly run because he lacked good sense in selecting personnel. He is generally thought to have shown ineptitude in choosing his political advisers. And, contrary to common opinion, many Washington liberals criticize Wallace strongly for what they consider his toadying to business groups. In the course of his office-holding career, Wallace made a reputation for himself as a mystic. There are tales about séances and his interest in yoga. (On his trip to China in 1944, he showed less curiosity about politics than about Buddhism.) In Washington one hears the ominous words—"the Republicans are sitting on a pile of stuff about Henry. . . ."

The change Wallace underwent in office was profound. Let me quote two disparate observations by Russell Lord (who has edited two collections of Wallace's speeches and who claims objectivity in his judgment of the liberal leader). First: when Wallace took office in 1933, he "visibly gained each day in poise, assurance and health." Second: after the first Wallace-Jones dispute, and Roosevelt's rebuke to both, the conservative papers began to count Wallace as dead politically, while liberals were dubbing him a hero and a martyr. Lord remarks, "He seemed more relaxed and tranquil than he had been for years." Wallace, apparently, enjoys receiving power and enjoys losing it. The first exhilarates him and the second relieves him. He has never really conquered the complex problem of his relation to power.

II

Wallace doesn't drink, smoke, tell off-color stories, swear, or play cards. He is a very early riser and a very hard worker. In Washington he often worked in his garden before going to his office in the morning. He is also an "exercise-bug." This aspect of his personality is rather well known—through his newsworthy practice with a boomerang in Washington parks. (It is typical of him that he was not content simply with exercising but also made a study of the theory and history of boomerang-throwing, and on the basis of this research had a special boomerang made.) There are anecdotes about Wallace which reveal him as the kind of person who gets mental satisfaction from submitting himself to gratuitous tests of physical endurance, while other stories indicate that he is quite insensible to the point of view of people who enjoy such pleasures as drinking.

About a year ago at a fair-sized outdoor meeting in Washington, which was being broadcast with Wallace acting as master of ceremonies, this writer had a chance to see him at close range. In the course of the meeting, he introduced perhaps seven or eight speakers and made a speech himself. His voice was warm, familiar, very rich in human qualities, emotional yet well modulated—whenever he spoke into the microphone. But his expression remained rigid, held-in, unresponsive. As speakers passed him going to and from the microphone he lowered his eyes. The impression one received was of an individual lacking any direct, spontaneous relation to the human beings around him. The contrast between this and the qualities of his speaking voice was startling.

This fleeting impression of Wallace is borne out by a much closer observer, and one, moreover, who believes him to be the hope of the nation. Frank Kingdon, liberal commentator and preacher, published a loving study in 1945 called *An Uncommon Man: Henry Wallace and Sixty Million Jobs*. Dr. Kingdon describes Wallace as being incapable of small talk; he habitually and characteristically forces conversations around to intellectual topics. This happens to be true of many intellectuals of a certain type—and one wonders what happens when such an intellectual in government comes up against, say, a "normal" politician.

Dr. Kingdon gives us a striking picture of Wallace facing the Senate Finance Committee at the time of his nomination as Secretary of Commerce. Jesse Jones, fresh from a Roosevelt booting, had to answer questions about his tenure in the Commerce and lending-agency posts. He talked to the Committee members easily and with great rapport. Except for Senator Pepper, they sympathized with Jones; all the world knew they were out to "get" Wallace. Yet all Wallace did in rebuttal was present his progressive planning thesis "straight," hoping for understanding. He took a pretty bad polemical drubbing, coming out of the conference room with little more than the personal knowledge that he was "right." And this despite Senator Pepper's eager leading questions in his behalf.

Dr. Kingdon talks about Wallace's sincerity and "natural shyness." But "shyness" in a public figure of mature age—in a situation of political rough-and-tumble—is a serious incapacity. When, in debate, the flow of Wallace's analytical thought is interrupted by a sharp jab, illogical or insignificant from his view, but expressing the gulf in understanding that exists between him and his adversary, he becomes confused and helpless and can only laugh embarrassedly. His enemies say he giggles.

When one contrasts Wallace's clumsiness in personal relations with his vigorous physical regimen, and with the energetic competence he exhibited in carrying out Roosevelt's policies, one is forced to conclude that he is capable of a creative relation only to his own opinions and power, not to those of other human beings. He seems unable to cope with personal power stemming from others. He often submits to it. More frequently, perhaps, and certainly with more unfortunate consequences, he ignores it.

Wallace is better with tools and with things. He is an excellent technician. When he came to Washington he was a very poor speaker. He became expert at speaking, just as he had at throwing the boomerang. He learns foreign languages well. When he was only seventeen years old he began a series of corn-breeding experiments, based on the theoretical work of some Harvard geneticists, that resulted in the creation of a whole new corn-seed industry. He even published a book, *Corn and Corn Growing*. Writing as market analyst for *Wallace's Farmer*, he became a statistician of ability: on the basis of his analyses he predicted, as early as 1919, a postwar economic collapse. Two books resulted from this technical interest of his: *Agricultural Prices* and *Correlation and Machine Calculation*. Now that we are "entering the air age" he has learned to fly a plane. In terms of technique, he adapts himself very well to the world.

But he is aware that such adaptation cannot satisfy the whole man. *Where technique does not suffice, Wallace fills in with religion.* Nothing is more deeply characteristic of the man than this dual pattern. Yet the very terms in which this duality is posed seem to preclude its resolution. Wallace's self-reliance, his sense of power, proceeds from his technical capacity; his moral nature—the hope he has of fulfillment for the whole man—derives from religious feeling. He has been unable to bring these two points of view together in any rational framework (in truth, his experience has forced them farther and farther apart). He is unable to unite power with right. For that he looks to a Superior Power. This attitude happens to be typical of the whole strain of American mentality that Wallace represents. There is a huge intellectual area in this country that is amoral—characteristically, more by default than by specific intention.

III

Henry Wallace is, I have suggested, the supreme political expression of populism in contemporary American life. This tradition was certainly one of the most important indigenous strains in the life of this country, and one of the best. Culturally, it is not equal to what Poe or Emerson represents, but neither does it lean so heavily on European sources.

Populism was the progressive culture of the small proprietor, the independent farmer. It can almost be said that the United States has had three histories—that of the South's plantation economy, that of Northern commerce and industry, and that of the populism of the West, the ever-receding West. The Western farmers in the Republican coalition, the Homestead Act, trust-busting, Bryan—these are some of the populist peaks in American history. Until Debs and the I.W.W., and apart from the North-South conflict, populism *was* the class struggle in the United States.

The great American frontier had two voices—a raucous, lusty, land-hungry shriek, and the sharp, hell-fire preaching of industrious Protestants. Populism must be explained in terms of the frontier. But when the land was finally settled, only religion remained to populism.

For Wallace, populism is not primarily a social movement: it is a family heritage. The Wallaces, as newspaper-owners, have always been important intellectual leaders in the Midwest farming community. And the career of populism, in the struggles with other power groups in America, is mirrored in the careers and personalities of all three Henry Wallaces. "Uncle Henry" represents the early enthusiasm and force of the movement, before the closing of the frontier made itself felt. Henry C. Wallace stands for the consolidation of ground already won, and the awareness of the impasse reached by the farmers in their alliance with Eastern industrial forces inside the Republican party.

Henry A. Wallace came on the scene to uphold the populist tradition in its period of crisis and decline. *His thought, personality, and program mirror the contradictions resulting from the attempt to adapt the populist tradition to the necessities of modern leadership.* Like labor's, the political strength of the small proprietor was split and weakened by the irrationalities of the two-party system in America. In his change of party allegiance during the Twenties, Wallace reflected this conflict. The farm interests in this country achieved their objective when, under Roosevelt, the system of parity payments was established. But by this very fact they became incapable from then on of offering progressive leadership to our time. They had been fulfilled, made equal; the need that drives toward leadership was gone. During the Roosevelt period, it was made quite clear that it was labor that stood at the head of modern progressivism.

The mentality of populism has always been religious. Religious on the one hand—and yet very practical on the other. Wallace's own grandfather is an excellent example of this combination. Bryan's rhetoric is another: the great populist leader clothed the debtor's cry for cheap money in phrases of ringing religiosity. In the largest terms, the difference between scientific and religious definitions lies in the nature of their explicitness and exactness. The effect of scientific exactness is, obviously, to expand human power over events. Wallace is scientific as to the techniques of manipulating things, but he is religious and abstract in relation to human beings. This may in part be a reflection of the fact that the farmer deals with tools rather than with persons (he has no serious labor problem) and therefore comes to consider his most important practical problems to be technological rather than social. He tends to underestimate the difficulties of social relations and to see the source of human troubles in nature—thus, ultimately, in God, since the farmer accepts nature as *given.*

Wallace's technological outlook is expressed by what is almost an obsession with the possibilities of material abundance. The largest part of his writings is devoted to analysis of these possibilities.

If only industrial technology is allowed to expand, all other problems will automatically and mechanically solve themselves—this seems to be the key to Wallace's political faith. But on the contrary, it is quite *probable* that without the prior solution of certain sociopolitical problems, technology will destroy rather than fulfill us. Wallace, however, faces *these* problems, which are the *human* ones, with primitive intellectual tools (a position, incidentally, that he tries to justify in emotional terms: in 1934, he said "we need a 'heart trust' even more than we need a 'brain trust' ").

The complexity of modern existence demands, above all else, exactness in the description of *human relations*. It is precisely here that Wallace's populist-religious tradition proves itself lacking. And as a political consequence, in part, of his belief in an inscrutable God, Wallace's relation to the power of *others* must always be uncreative and passive. See him delivering that famous Madison Square Garden speech which led to Truman's request for his resignation from the Cabinet. A Communist audience, dominated by pro-Russian sentiments, began to hiss and boo at the very first of his loving rebukes to the Soviet Union. Wallace proceeded to execute some on-the-spot editorial deletions, which included eliminating such remarks as: "The Russians should stop conniving against us in certain areas of the world." He had instinctively surrendered to the *others*. And, at the close of the unedifying Baruch episode, in which Wallace agreed to retract his criticism of the Baruch atom plan and then reneged on this agreement, he is quoted as saying: "My friends would not let me eat crow." Here again, he had surrendered to the *others*. Wallace's political strength, we must remember, is grounded in his role as hero of the Stalinist-influenced liberal.

Being irrevocably committed to the declining populist tradition and knowing that the efficacy of populism depended on the existence of the frontier, he now talks of "moral frontiers." But this implies that the old frontier movement was *not* "moral"—an obvious falsehood. Every social movement has its own object, and its own morality. Actually, Wallace is trying to salvage the morality of populism for historical tasks of which populism never dreamed and to which it is woefully inadequate.

Wallace's free-trade policy in economics is a clear example of his devious way with the essential meaning of populism. Like most liberals during the Thirties, he began, more or less consciously, to advocate the Keynesian program for a controlled economy. A controlled capitalist economy in a democratic country must answer two major questions: how to insure capital investment, and how to maintain wage levels and not conscript labor. High wages cut into profits, and without a high profit return the capitalist simply will not make risky investments. Without going into the economic details, it can be said that, fundamentally, there is only one capitalist resolution of this primary conflict: imperialism—exploitation of foreign markets through overlordship of other peoples. Imperialism is called "free trade" by liberals. In actual fact it is not, and cannot be, any more "free" than the conditions of labor in the colonies and dominated countries with which trade is being carried on.

Wallace is a free-trader of old. But he came to it by another path than did the usual sophisticated liberal. And therein lies our tale. The Iowan began his espousal of free trade as part of a *farm* program. The farmer is forced to sell in a free market and buy in one protected by tariffs—Wallace tells us he realized this "quite early in life." But it should be easy to see that free trade for the farmer is something very different from free trade as imperialism. This first is in the genuine interest of the small proprietor and is the stuff of the traditional populist program in the United States. The second is a dangerous diversion of the progressive aims and program of farmers and labor, leading to the ever-increasing power of international cartels—and to war.

Though he advocates free trade in moral terms, Wallace's morality actually justifies imperialism at the same time—which is typical of what happens when an old morality is applied to a new and inappropriate situation. The contradiction here results from Wallace's inability either to abandon the populist tradition or to ignore—or to solve progressively—distinctly modern problems. Clinging to a particular morality and yet unaware of the immoral consequences of the application of that morality in the contemporary world, Wallace has become a *non-functioning* moral symbol for the progressive struggle of this day. Actually, as a personality, he is in no sense a fighter for human betterment in a world of realities. Rather he represents the final reduction of the religious man. (If one asks what I mean by the reduction of the religious man, let him remember with what indulgence the more self-conscious neo-Catholics and neo-Anglicans of Europe looked upon fascism in its earlier stages.)

IV

The illusions imbedded in Wallace's thought divide neatly under the same two headings of technological and religious.

To illustrate the former, there is his recent book on Russia, *Soviet*

Asia Mission, a report of his fifty-day air journey through Siberia in 1944.

One doubts whether Wallace's credulity and lack of perception have ever been equaled by another foreign observer in Russia. One could go on endlessly citing the details of his gross distortion of the Soviet picture. I will merely outline his perspective of the Siberian frontier.

Throughout his book, Wallace constantly draws irrelevant parallels between Soviet Asia and America's West. This rhetorical device softens the reader up for a very important and quite unfounded generalization: "There exist no other two countries more alike than the Soviet Union and the United States of America." The reason: both America and Russia have had frontiers. From this it follows that "Men born in wide, free spaces will not brook injustice and slavery. They will not even temporarily live in slavery." These words were uttered in a speech at Irkutsk.

David J. Dallin, a liberal anti-Stalin expert on Russia, comments: "It so happens that the recently emerged industry of this region [Irkutsk] has been built and is being operated largely by the manpower of the labor-camps of Eastern Siberia." In other words, the great Siberian "frontier" rests on forced labor and penal sentences—quite unlike the old American one. Thus, in his view of the Siberian frontier, Wallace either ignores or terribly distorts the significant human, political factors. However, he reports on the machines, and especially the vegetation, in great detail.

Toward the end of *Soviet Asia Mission*, Wallace remarks that America is now in the position that England occupied at the close of the Napoleonic era. And he justifies England's nineteenth-century imperialism by the fact that it raised standards of living. This kind of reasoning is totally consonant with a justification of the Soviet police state—if it raises standards of living, which it is likely to do after starving its subjects for a few generations. In other words, technological progress equals progress. (A corollary of this is the notion that nationalization of means of production and wealth is *per se* socialism.) By this criterion any imperialism, any exploitation, can be whitewashed morally.

All this gives us a hint of the real meaning of many liberals' present policy of rapprochement with Russia (workable, however, only if Soviet expansionism were voluntarily abandoned). The Soviets are to be allowed to exploit most of Asia and Eastern Europe in peace, while the Anglo-American powers retain the security of capital markets in the rest of the world—with the sole purpose of raising standards of living, of course. Wallace, the ideologist supreme of Soviet-American rapprochement, sees great possibilities of creating mutual understanding between the two power-blocs by trade. He reports that the Russian masses are very fond of American consumer goods. The formula: Anglo-American imperialism plus Russian exploitation equals Progress.

Wallace's religious illusions, on the other hand, are illustrated in *Statesmanship and Religion* (1934), where he devotes most of his attention to religion. Here he discusses the Catholic theocracy of the twelfth and thirteenth centuries and its effort to realize God's will on earth by subordinating economics to religion—by fixing just prices, fair wages, etc. Wallace says he wants to do this today "on a more vast and more just scale." But—"Perhaps the times will have to be even more difficult than they have been during the past two years before the hearts of our people will have been moved sufficiently so they will be willing to join together in a modern adaptation of the theocracy of old."

In another connection, Wallace quoted with approval a Papal encyclical about cooperation between classes, "reasonable" wages and profits, society as an organism, and so on. Most intelligent people today understand that behind such innocent-sounding phrases lies an extremely dangerous concept of clerical fascism. But Wallace, because of the very vagueness of his religiosity and his almost calculated failure to discern the real factors of power, overlooks the elements of authoritarianism, not only in papal theocracy, but in his own program as well.

But it is in his notion of "unity" that he becomes consistently, if unconsciously, totalitarian in his thinking. "Unity" is absolutely required, he believes—but it can only be maintained by "an effective social discipline." This could easily mean that capitalists must be capitalists even at 3 per cent per annum and that workers must be satisfied with "jobs" and not demand wage raises. Yet Wallace believes "unity" to be possible in a real and lasting way precisely *in a class society*. He defines economic democracy—in one place—as equal bargaining power for business, agriculture, and labor.

Notice, first, that such equality would satisfy only agriculture: for equal bargaining power is as much as the small-farm proprietor can ever hope to attain. On the other hand, equal bargaining power for all classes in our present industrial society could only mean a stalemate, out of which the state would arise transcendently powerful and independent, as under totalitarian regimes.

Implicit in Wallace's thinking is the belief that equilibrium signifies the absence of conflict. But conflict is not an unfortunate interlude or interruption in human history—it is the very stuff of it. Only repression can give Mr. Wallace the equilibrium of his "democratic unity."

Connected with this pernicious "unity" is Wallace's concept of the "common man." It directly follows from Wallace's terms that men must *become* "common," if they are not already so, before they can be united. That is, if in themselves or their conditions of life they happen to have distinguishing characteristics, these must be ignored for political purposes (and, with the mechanization of culture, eventually for *all* purposes—including the vision of self). As far as one can determine, Wallace's common man is simply *homo sapiens*, to be given a bottle of milk, and already "on the march" in a kind of revolutionary way. The common man, moreover, is to be considered only as a consumer in industrial society—not even as producer, which role is infinitely more significant.

In the end, if men actually come to see themselves as common, society will contain not men at all, but just so many parts of the total supply of refrigerators, potatoes, newspapers, and movie seats. Men will not consume in order to live, but rather their lives will consist solely of what they consume. (Perhaps the common man is no more than the imperialist market atomized into units of consumption.) Now, to be a mere consumer demands nothing of the *person*—he is given things, his role is passive. If you are without fault, if you are common—you will be given what you need to exist, including a "job." The notion of the common man can be summed up: become like everybody else, become nothing. This is a long way from the Western concept of the citizen. One wonders what grandfather "Uncle Henry" would have made of Henry III's creature.

To finish, if this dearly loved phrase of Wallace's is a figure of speech rather than a concept, then it is merely a dangerous substitute for analysis. And in our time, mystical political formulations tend to lead to totalitarianism.

V

To arrive at a full understanding of the historical meaning of Henry Wallace's psychological pattern, it may be useful to relate it explicitly to the pervasive modern problem of alienation. Especially since his religiosity, which has spread through his mind like ink on cloth, is above all else a means of wishing the problem of alienation out of existence.

When Wallace switched from the Republican to the Democratic party, he also changed his denomination, becoming an Episcopalian. He made both moves, he says, because he was "against barriers" —against Republican protectionism, and against the anti-Catholic slander directed at Al Smith in 1928. "The world is a neighborhood," Wallace insists repeatedly. Russell Lord, biographer of the Wallaces, once asserted that all of Henry A.'s career could be explained as an attempt to overcome barriers.*

Good enough—but the whole point, of course, is *how* barriers are to be overcome. Wallace does quite well at knocking down the barriers between himself and *things*, but, to reiterate, he is classically unsuccessful in accomplishing this with *persons*. The reasons, as I have suggested, are to be found partly in his farm background. "When I was a boy working in the garden I studied plants as indi-

---

* But not in his recently published study of the three Henry Wallaces (*The Wallaces of Iowa*. Boston: Houghton, Mifflin, 1947. 615 pp. $5.00). This thick, heavily factual volume contains anything and everything concerning the Wallaces—*except* genuine analysis. However, what it lacks in historical understanding it more than makes up for in pure love. In a deceptively mild way, it justifies Henry A. Wallace's every act on earth, from the way he ties his shoes to his ultimate place in our history.

The wealth of misinterpreted and uninterpreted facts in this first full-length study of Wallace became available to this writer only after the present article was completed. A slight note may therefore be in order: "Uncle Henry" became quite a well-to-do farmer and his politics, consequently, consisted more of an effort to dignify farming than to advance the purposes of *radical* populism. As a matter of fact, he began to attack soft-money advocates as early as 1878; and opposed Bryan in 1896. The Wallace relation to populism never included an allegiance to the Populist or Greenback parties. It was, rather, an involvement in populism as a general movement and as the culture of farmers growing out of certain historical conditions, especially the rise of capitalism. In other words, the Wallaces were, to some extent, *aristocrats* of the farming community. This factor requires an emphasis I was not able to give it.

viduals and had a definite affection for them," he tells us. The psychological value of investing non-human objects with affection is that the individual thus achieves a sense of unity with the outside world *and*, at one and the same time, a feeling of his own power—and alienation is overcome.

"We shall never have again a religion of the whole man until there is opportunity for the great bulk of mankind once more to come into a loving relationship with things." This is perhaps the most revealing statement Wallace ever made. The question it naturally provokes in one's mind is: Why "a *loving* relationship with *things*"? The really imperative achievement is for man to gain *control* over things, especially the objects of his own creation, from which commodity-production has alienated him. If anything, men should reestablish a loving relation to other *human beings*. What is the advantage in confusing love and power as Wallace does? Only this, that if by loving things we could gain power over them, we would never be insecure. Anxiety would be banished. But life holds no greater illusion.

VI

What can be said about the future of Henry Wallace? What is the political meaning of his present ascendancy among liberals?

There can be no doubt that he is the chief inheritor of the New Deal-Roosevelt halo. Nor is there any question of the fact that all liberal groups today are crowding around the Roosevelt tradition, to keep themselves warm in its afterglow. As long as this situation continues, even Wallace's enemies cannot dispense with him.

But it should be remembered that the New Deal was composed less of an ideology than of a master politician. We must also keep in mind that if it had not been for the coming of war, even Roosevelt's great talents would have been insufficient to hold his broad and exceedingly heterogeneous coalition together. Nor is it likely that the approaching economic crisis will be a simple repetition of the last one, especially in its political effects. Apart from its freshness and enthusiasm, the essence of the New Deal, after all, was simply public spending. The Republicans would be mad indeed to allow Hoover's gross blunders to be repeated in case the coming deflation catches them in office. One can presume they have learned a lesson;

this time, they will certainly accommodate themselves to the popular demand for "pump-priming."

If this much of the New Deal thunder can be stolen, and if the growing progressive wing of the Republican party has any significance, then the post–New Dealers will be forced, in self-defense, to deepen and expand the definitions of their program. But this will take them farther away from the Roosevelt precedent and, therefore, from the place where Wallace now stands. Is he capable of riding along?

It may be helpful in answering this question to glance at Wallace's pronouncements as editor of the *New Republic*. In his first editorial—"Jobs, Peace, Freedom" (December 16)—he surveyed the general situation and called for "two 20-year plans" on a global scale to eradicate illiteracy, starvation, transmissible disease, and low standards of living. This sounded technological, appeared in a political context, and was actually the ultimate in irrelevant moralism. The *political* problem he ran up against, as always, was Russia—and there again he failed to say anything that was even accurate, much less revealing. ("We cannot hide the weaknesses in our democracy. If we take steps to overcome these weaknesses, then I believe the Russians, believing in the genuineness of our democracy, will move toward greater political freedom." And in a later editorial: "Whenever we meet Russia in Europe, it is not Russia that is the enemy, but the devastation itself.") In this keynote piece, and in those that followed, one witnesses the emergence of a pattern: purely rhetorical resolutions of problems occur more and more frequently and centrally—a certain sign of political helplessness. To be sure, now that Wallace no longer wields official power, he feels the need for a kind of action that was not so necessary in the halcyon days of the New Deal. He therefore talks more now of "progressives" *doing* than of the "common man" *being given*. But the new shibboleth is no better defined than the old one, and equally unhelpful.

In the December 30 issue of the *New Republic*, Wallace spoke out on labor. "My object at all times will be to find a legitimate basis for a sound and enduring industrial peace," he said. When, later, he subtly threatened labor with a fascist reaction to continued strikes in "essential" industries, we began to get an inkling of something more precise behind the vague phrase "industrial peace." Then, hearing Wallace baldly accept the proposition that workers in government-operated industries ought not to strike, while at the same time advancing a scheme for settling disputes that provided for government seizure as the final act, we become alarmed, quite properly, at his notion of a "legitimate" peace—*since the right to strike against the state is the one truly basic issue of freedom confronting the American public today*. That the present leader of the liberals should have exhibited such depthless misunderstanding of the modern state is significant beyond measure.

Wallace has given great emphasis to the fact that he is "neither an officer nor a member" of the Progressive Citizens of America or of Americans for Democratic Action. He calls the conflict of the two groups over the issue of Stalinism "a comedy." However, it was he who delivered the principal address (December 29) at the founding conference of the Stalinist-influenced PCA. In this speech, he spoke of the existence of a struggle between "Russia-haters and Russophiles"—which muddied everything up by putting the issue in black and white—while raising himself to the Olympian somewhere-above-and-beyond.

Later, when it appeared that the liberal split might have a serious potential, Wallace further stretched his long legs to maintain his straddled balance. In an editorial called "The Enemy Is Not Each Other" (January 27), he rededicated himself to the "liberal cause" rather than to any particular group, and made the misinformed statement that Mrs. Roosevelt was not a member of ADA. She was and is, and an officer of that group quickly and loudly said so in print. This blunder only spotlighted Wallace's own reason for hedging on the conflict: political ambition. Mrs. Roosevelt is a widely respected humanitarian, patently uninterested in political power for herself.

It should not be too difficult to predict Wallace's role in a future progressive upsurge. As long as it is more Stalinist than socialist, and more religious than militant, he might well be at the head of it. But he would serve as the speechifying symbol of such a movement, rather than its actual leader. So far he has shown no talent as a practical politician. The actual leaders are no doubt already engaged in jockeying for position inside the trade-union movement.

In the first issue of the new Wallace *New Republic*, publisher Michael Straight introduced the liberal leader with these words: "The *New Republic* was founded to express the promise of American life.

No American can express that promise as well and truly as Henry
Wallace."

Yes—*as* promise.

✸ POINT OF ORDER!

BOOK PUBLISHED BY
W. W. NORTON & CO., 1964

*I was in law school during the big days of McCarthyism and
was completing my first year of practice when the denouement
occurred in the spring of 1954. So you might say I learned law
under the gun. Indeed, my most substantial piece of research
for the* Yale Law Journal *concerned the publicity accorded
Congressional hearings.*

*My position on McCarthyism was complicated by the fact
that I had every reason to believe that a Communist conspiracy did in fact exist; that many liberals had indeed been used
by the Party in pursuance of the ends of Soviet policy; and that
the United States government—any government, including
any future revolutionary government—had the right to defend
itself against any such conspiracy. And I had to maintain these
points while at the same time being frightened and revolted
by the virulent idiocy he represented. The chief consideration
for me, then and now, is that no government in its right mind
would contest a conspiracy in the absurd manner chosen by
McCarthy. Therefore, that was not his purpose in doing it, or
theirs in allowing him to do it. The one governmental right—
to defend against a conspiracy, especially foreign-based—should
have been handled entirely by the FBI; and, possibly, a public
fact-finding agency (allowing for rebuttal testimony and the
right of cross-examination). As far as I was concerned, both
Hiss and McCarthy were guilty—of different political "crimes"
—and I was caught in the crossfire. It is thus justifying for me
that the critical encounter which felled McCarthy was the
confrontation between his private espionage agency and the
official one headed by J. Edgar Hoover. Also, would those who
so hunger after simple views please note that McCarthy was
destroyed by taking on the military establishment?*

The writing on McCarthy that follows resulted from work on the film Point of Order! *It is an Introduction and Epilogue to a book containing a transcript of the soundtrack. The basic work was done initially as editorial consultant on the film and as a draft of a proposed narration-over—which, in the end, was not used. After my narration was abandoned, Richard Rovere wrote a briefer one (also not used), which was appropriate, since I had relied heavily on his marvelous book,* Senator Joe McCarthy. *I was brought into this work on the film by my good friend, Daniel Talbot, its co-producer along with Emile de Antonio. (Screening the kinescope of the Army-McCarthy Hearings—we never got through even a sizable fraction of the 188 hours of verbatim stuff—was a weirdly rewarding experience.)*

The incredible effect of television was, of course, first noted in the entertainment industry; but the Kefauver Crime Hearings of 1950–51 revealed the potential political power inherent in the medium. The Army-McCarthy Hearings were the first time that TV had a direct—and decisive—effect on political history. Since then—oh, so much! And finally, in Chicago in the summer of 1968, social power struck back against the presence of the Big Eye. It is a primary question now as to how long the media can retain the independence that, helplessly, they have exhibited. A fascinating irony, that the networks should have been compelled to assume a progressive historical role. William Randolph Hearst must be spinning in his well-padded grave.

Introduction

Point of Order!—both the startling film (taken from the files of CBS News) and this book authentically portraying the film—is the rendering of the Army-McCarthy Hearings held in the spring of 1954. These Hearings, which consumed the attention of the nation for thirty-six days, were at once the glaring moment of truth in the career of Senator Joe McCarthy and as well perhaps the greatest political spectacle of American history. This was because they were televised—and because the television camera, for the first time, acted as an independent force in our history.

For those who remember, the name of Joe McCarthy need only be mentioned to be appreciated. Likewise the televised Hearings in which he confronted the American people with such terrifying intimacy. But ten years have passed, and the details of the event have faded—only the great essence remains lodged in the memory of those who lived through the television experience of the Hearings. For those who did not, some background explanation of the setting and the circumstance is even more obviously called for.

Who was McCarthy and what were the Hearings?

SENATOR JOE MCCARTHY

He was at one time so important that the man himself and what he stood for constituted a phenomenon known as "McCarthyism." It grew to be the dominant political phenomenon of the day.

It all began about a month after Alger Hiss had finally been convicted of perjury in 1950. The junior Senator from Wisconsin, who was elected in 1946 at the age of thirty-seven, had not yet distinguished himself from any other first-term senators or, indeed, from the general run of people making a career of politics. Then he delivered a speech in Wheeling, West Virginia, on February 9, 1950. He waved some papers—this was to become his trademark—and suggested that the State Department was in the hands of the Communists. Thus began the most meteoric political career in our history.

The fuel for this engine was printer's ink. McCarthy captured the headlines and held them in a vise of continuing and startling accusations for nearly five years. There was a McCarthy story almost every day, certainly several every week. Almost everything he said and did was news in every paper across the country. And mostly what he did was to accuse individuals in the federal government of being Communists, or of having been Communists, or of having associated with Communists, or of being "soft" on them or "coddling" them. For the most part, the accusation and the innuendo were never overtaken by the facts of the case, certainly not any legal evidentiary facts of the case. One can still get a good argument going today on the question of whether McCarthy ever really exposed a single real Communist.

But at the time, accusation alone was quite sufficient—and it was clearly the essence of McCarthyism. With our present hindsight, most people now believe that the most important consideration is not whether or how many of the individuals accused were actual Communists, but just why the American people credited so many of the accusations at the time and were so caught up in the ongoing accusatory process. Anyway, they were. And this was McCarthy's power. It was considerable, and it is hardly an exaggeration to say that he functioned for a time as a supplemental form of government in the United States—as you will see in the course of reading this transcript of the film *Point of Order!*

Mostly it was the mood of the times that carried McCarthy to the pinnacle of power he had reached when the Army-McCarthy Hearings began in April 1954. The deep suspicion and readiness to believe McCarthy's accusations were sustained by the fact that there were a good number of admitted ex-Communists around who had in fact been connected with the federal government in the past. (Some of these people were in the accusing business themselves.) Also, there was a growing accumulation of facts concerning the effectiveness of Soviet espionage, and the employment of local Communists in carrying it out. All in all, enough genuine fact on which to build a mountain of uncritical accusation. And few remembered or seemed to care that it was not against the law to be a Communist, much less to have been one in the past; that it was not *per se* an act of treason. In McCarthy's hands, any past act of association with Communists, or even any sympathy for them, became an act of "implied treason." He operated a star-chamber in newsprint in which he accused, judged, and convicted numerous individuals of this homemade crime. For his purposes, the term "Fifth Amendment Communist" was invented, such a person being anyone who invoked his Constitutional privilege against incriminating himself under questioning by McCarthy's Permanent Investigating Subcommittee.

The deepest level of the mood that made McCarthyism possible was that created by the emotional backwash of World War II. One should recall the great hopes involved in the grand alliance against Hitler—which were cruelly transgressed almost as the postwar world began. A deep and enduring conflict with the Soviet Union emerged; the facts of Soviet atomic espionage during the War itself; and the utterly new and absolute horror of The Bomb. All these terrible and disappointing events joined to create a pervasive mood, a postwar nightmare mood, a national spasm of dismay.

All this was McCarthyism, and no one knew where it might end. Certainly no one knew when the Army-McCarthy Hearings began in April 1954.

THE ARMY-MCCARTHY HEARINGS

By the time of the presidential election of 1952, less than three years after the Wheeling speech, McCarthy was a major political force in the major political effort to turn the Democrats out. They had been accused of "twenty years of treason" and, in a sweeping *non sequitur*, McCarthy and his doings were the proof of the proposition. But when General Eisenhower was elected, the Democratic (or, as both Eisenhower and McCarthy said, "Democrat") "traitors" were no longer in control, which posed a problem for McCarthy.

He could have closed up shop, or gone into another line of business; but he did not. As a consequence, an eventual collision between himself and the new Republican administration became inevitable. Where the State Department had been the primary object of attack under the Democrats, it was in the Army that McCarthy finally concentrated his search for Communist infection under the Republicans. And it was the Army that finally set up the new administration's line of resistance to a rampaging McCarthyism that could not distinguish between a good Republican and a bad Democratic administration.

After a lengthy investigation of supposed espionage at a top-secret radar center at Fort Monmouth, New Jersey, McCarthy turned his attention in January 1954 to the case of Dr. Irving Peress, a dentist who had been drafted and stationed at Camp Kilmer. Dr. Peress, after his induction, had refused to answer certain items contained in an Army loyalty questionnaire. Later, being subpoenaed to appear before McCarthy's investigating subcommittee, he pleaded the Fifth Amendment. When Dr. Peress thereafter applied for and received an honorable discharge, McCarthy became "infuriated" and accused the Army of a "conspiracy" (according to a recent retelling of the story by former President Eisenhower).

And then the fatal mistake was made. Following up the Peress matter, McCarthy called in Brigadier General Ralph Zwicker, a decorated war hero. Testifying under instructions, Zwicker was not able to satisfy McCarthy—who was in fact demanding too much, including a court-martial of Peress, which was impossible in any event. Then McCarthy exploded during the hearing into a personal attack on Zwicker, roughing him up verbally and humiliating him. In this one act, whether or not he knew it at the time, McCarthy had taken on the full power of the elite officer corps of the Army. One of their own had been mortally insulted, and a generation of living West Point ideology turned against the all-powerful Communist-hunter from Wisconsin.

The Army counterattack centered, however, not on the defense of a general but on the career of a private. He was a very important private named G. David Schine, a young man whose family owned a chain of hotels. His crucial importance derived from his very close friendship with Roy M. Cohn, McCarthy's chief counsel. Cohn had brought Schine into the McCarthy investigating group as an "expert" on Communist subversion (he was in his early twenties) and the two young men had taken a whirlwind junket through Europe "exposing" subversive influence in the International Information Administration. This trip made world headlines, and is generally considered to have been the most bizarre and bitterly comic episode in the entire phenomenon of McCarthyism. It occurred, incidentally, just one year before the beginning of the Army-McCarthy Hearings.

In July 1953, Schine received a draft notice; in November he was inducted and sent to Fort Dix for basic training. Cohn bestirred himself to secure special attention for his special friend.

Under the direction of Sherman Adams (President Eisenhower's jack-of-all-trades) and prior to the Zwicker affair, the Army had been preparing a memorandum setting forth its view of Cohn's efforts on Schine's behalf. The Army counterattack began with the release of this memorandum to selected individuals within the government, and then to the press. McCarthy's response was immediate and explosive. General Eisenhower has characterized it this way: "At a press conference on the 12th of March he called the report 'blackmail,' and counterattacked with an accusation that Secretary Stevens was trying to divert the investigation to the Air Force and Navy." He also claimed that Schine was being held by the Army as a "hostage." The circus-train of the Army-McCarthy Hearings was then and there on the rails and rolling.

The Hearings were unique in the conception of their formal structure—and of course beyond the unique, if that is possible, in the way they actually worked out. In a formal way, they were a special hearing before McCarthy's own Special Subcommittee on Investigations, held to hear and report on the charges and countercharges that had been exchanged between McCarthy and the Army. Senator

Karl E. Mundt of South Dakota, ranking Republican member of the subcommittee, occupied the chair temporarily vacated by McCarthy. (The Democratic minority of the subcommittee, which had been boycotting it since the summer of 1953 because of the Chairman's tactics, returned for the occasion.) Since individuals were named in support of or along with the charges and countercharges, the proceedings began with half an aspect of a trial, as well as a fact-finding or peace-making enterprise. It was certainly far out of the ordinary run of Senatorial business. How far out, only the event itself was to tell.

From the legal viewpoint, taken either as legislative or judicial proceedings, the Hearings were a shambles. The lawyer from Boston who represented the Army later said, "a good many irrelevancies were enthusiastically pursued." Irrelevancies, as a lawyer would identify them, dominated the proceedings. They also determined the outcome. Their pursuit turned out to be a superb vehicle for the exposure of personality, motive, method, character—which were indeed the "real" issues of the case and the stuff of a new form of political drama.

In the end, everyone played to the camera. There was very likely little chance under any circumstances that the collision between Senator Joe McCarthy and the United States Army could have been choreographed with optimum decorum. But the television camera—backed up by twenty million voters—made of the encounter something absolutely unique in American law and politics (and entertainment as well). There were two million words of testimony in the Hearings, delivered over thirty-six days from April 22 through June 16, 1954; but more important by far were the 188 hours of visual exposure which accompanied this verbal flow. There is no question but that it changed the history of this country.

It would be anticipating too much of the book that follows to attempt further to background or characterize the course of the inimitable Army-McCarthy Hearings. They were, in a fabulously exact sense, the greatest political show on earth. The passage of time has altered this fact not at all.

Joe McCarthy often began his vote-gathering speeches around the country by saying, "It's good to get out of Washington and back to the United States." *Point of Order!* is the brilliantly assembled story of what happened when the United States came to Washington—by means of television—for a visit with Joe McCarthy.

Epilogue

Joseph R. McCarthy died May 2, 1957. The three years after the Army-McCarthy Hearings ended were all rather consistently and decisively downhill. He never regained his former menace. And without the menace, the remaining elements of McCarthy and McCarthyism hardly hung together at all.

There has been some excessive delicacy in referring to the circumstance, but the truth of the matter (widely known and appreciated in Washington) is that the man was drinking excessively. Indeed, he died of it—unless one wants to say that he died rather of whatever it was that led him to drink so much. If the latter, then one can say that he died of not being the *real* Joe McCarthy any longer (or perhaps having to live too close to the really real one). In any event, he was never the same Joe McCarthy after the Hearings. The camera had done its deadly work too well.

In a formal way, four reports issued from the Hearings on September 1, 1954—a Republican, a Democratic, and two separate statements by Senators Potter and Dirksen. They were diffuse in effect—and in any event unequal to the task of telling the American people what it had found out for itself via television. Also, before the formal reports were released, Roy Cohn had resigned as chief counsel and Senator Ralph Flanders had introduced in the Senate a resolution of censure against McCarthy. After debate, a Select Committee was authorized to consider the censure motion. The chairman named was the Republican Arthur V. Watkins. The Watkins Committee, as it came to be known, conducted hearings of a much more rigorous nature than those involving the Army. Under the firm direction of his counsel, Edward Bennett Williams, McCarthy was fairly well behaved before the Watkins Committee—there was not much effort to adapt Senate floor rules to his own purposes, as in the Army Hearings, with frequent points of order. The Select Committee, in a forty-thousand-word report, recommended censure and on December 2, 1954, the Senate voted, 67 to 22, to censure its colleague from Wisconsin. The grounds were more limited than those originally proposed, but significant enough for all that. His previous influence in the Senate was at an end.

But he never lost his hard-core followers in the country. At his death, some of them more or less accused the President of his murder. It was that extreme. As the irresistible force it was when the

Hearings began in 1954, McCarthyism is dead along with Joe Mc-Carthy. But many of the substantial elements thereof, now strongly reconstituted, are still very much alive today.

In *Robert's Rules* of parliamentary procedure, a "point of order" is defined in this way: "One 'makes a point of order' when he objects to a proceeding as being out of order," which it is "when the rules are violated." In a sense, Joe McCarthy's whole life was one loud scream—*"Point of order, Mr. Chairman!"* His eternal followers in their millions, with lives and views of life based on bygone rules which no chairman can any longer observe, are still screaming their objection to the proceedings "as being out of order." For them, they truly are—and will be. History is the "proceedings" and the "rules" are the verities of the past. For a poor humanity engaged in swift history, a point of order is always tragically relevant.

"Point of order, Mr. Chairman!"

4

▤ POPULAR CULTURE

Introductory

A little history will be appropriate here. The critical method for analyzing popular culture—indeed, the identification of the subject matter as worthwhile—has two disparate sources in this country. The first is indigenous: the esthetic critics of Hound & Horn, for instance, who were entranced by silent film; and, with broader range, Gilbert Seldes, who published a marvelously loving book in 1924 called The Seven Lively Arts. This strand was continued by Otis Ferguson's movie reviews in the New Republic during the Thirties; and among others by Manny Farber and James Agee in the Forties (there and in The Nation).

The second source, more scholarly and formidable, was the theoretical approach of a group of German refugees, most notably Leo Lowenthal, Paul F. Lazarsfeld, and Max Horkheimer. The German scholars had their greatest influence among social scientists in the universities. But they also influenced—afforded another dimension to—the writing of several intellectual journalists who were more or less involved in the first, indigenous strand, and in addition were disappointed Marxists in search of a subject to replace the Coming Revolution which wasn't going to come anytime soon. Add, variously, interest in literary criticism and/or Freud—the other qualifications for "discovery" of popular culture as a fascinating and relevant subject—and you have the following, from whom I and many others learned:

DWIGHT MACDONALD, founder, editor, etc. of Politics, in which he established a column called "Popular Culture"—probably the first of its kind (which should have been continued elsewhere). As best he could, he emphasized the subject and tried manfully to bring *together—and to bring to bear on this subject—the Marxist, Freudian, literary/modernist resources of the highbrows. In an early issue of the magazine (February 1944), he published "A Theory of Popular Culture" that was very big for its day and is still worth reading.* When he had abandoned Politics, *and even tried to give up on the thing itself during the Frightful Fifties, he turned to movie reviews for* Esquire *as a substitute. Dwight was the first to get me involved in the analysis of popular culture; and he handed me a copy of* Studies in Classic American Literature, *by D. H. Lawrence, containing the essay on Poe which states the breakdown of modern sensibility that is the truest source of both popular culture and anyone's understanding of it.*

CLEMENT GREENBERG, *author of "Avante Garde and Kitsch," published in* Partisan Review *in 1939. This was the major piece bringing the two strands together (although that was probably not Greenberg's purpose). Anyway, it is possibly the next most important essay on the subject (certainly for me), after Lawrence's analysis of Poe.*

ELLIOT COHEN, *founder and first editor of* Commentary, *who brought together in his person all of the influences and sources previously mentioned, and intended as a matter of editorial policy to publish as much popular culture criticism in* Commentary *as he could manage. I was one of the group who responded to and benefited from his permissive direction.*

My good friends, HERBERT POSTER *and* MANNY FARBER, *who always viewed everything of ordinary interest—a movie, a baseball game, any middlebrow opinion anywhere, the* Daily News, *subway advertising, and Russell Wright dinnerware—with the full weight of their apperceptive apparatus: from them I learned the most and received the profoundest permission to think about my actual environment.*

ROBERT WARSHOW, *the only one who in a serious and devoted and detailed manner elevated the subject of the popular environment, in his workings, to the highest level of essay-art. On this subject, he was my editor at* Commentary: *no more perfect teacher of the new and difficult ever existed. He was too good to be true, so he died young.*

And finally, HAROLD ROSENBERG, *who has consistently detested Freud, popular culture criticism, and Marxism as anything but a theory of political action—for his superb disdain. When he liked anything in this mode, he found a special reason for it: he once told Parker Tyler that his book,* The Hollywood Hallucination, *proved nothing about movies or other popular art because it was a simple act of genius, to be appreciated and ignored. Harold was totally concerned with the* other *side of Poe which was so important a source of Baudelaire's sensibility. In his approach to the action painters, however, I rather think he was exhibiting the fact that he had found a worthy metaphor to lead him out of the by-then awful boredom of Baudelaire's sensibility and Marxism solely as a theory of revolutionary action. (His beautiful book,* The Tradition of the New, *is so important because by nature he is really such an awful traditionalist.)*

Anyway, I wrote the following stuff for all of the reasons my mentors gave me. Indeed, I could have—any of us could have—written a lot more. One day, maybe we will. Still, this early writing is significant, in my view, at least because of what has happened since. As follows:

1. *Joe McCarthy would not have been brought down so conveniently; the Kennedy government-in-exile would not have been the superordinate power it was, and possibly even now still is; the Negro as celebrity would not have been so certified; indeed, the civil rights revolution itself is literally inconceivable without this intervention of the media in history. And now, after Chicago '68, an absolutely unique set of political issues has been presented to the nation: a fresh view of Northern bossism, in its new connection with Southern racism, and the police of the North—now like those of the South— legally constituted to disrupt the Constitution in favor of local hegemony.* All known or achieved by means of television. Brand new. *Predicted long ago by those who saw the creative political possibilities in the media—and even beyond the classic conjunction of the propaganda/terror factors of fascism.*

2. *High Camp—a primary source of silly modern style—is entirely indebted to this early critical effort, especially that of Manny Farber. (Susan Sontag, take note.)*

3. *The generational conflict, whatever else it is, centrally involves the effect of the media differently on different generations. Without a method of understanding the human effect of the media, we are*

literally foreclosed from essential understanding of our children's experience.

4. *Apart from its more obvious practical utilities, taking mass culture seriously for purposes of analysis (at least) had a major high-culture effect: it cut down the native snobbery of American high-brows. The literary highbrow was the prototype and laboratory of future forms of snobbism for new elites, whatever else he was. In one sentence, it is simply too easy to constitute oneself an elite in this low-grade nation: I am against the easy way.*

5. *Culture, of whatever kind, is now too important to the powers that are, to remain as free as it was even twenty years ago in the United States. So, what is happening in the Soviet bloc (selective repression) is apt to happen—differently, of course—here. We had better prepare for it. That means, among many other things, not to go perfectly for broke toward the highest of the high, and damn all the slowpokes—and to hell with all the social cost—along the way. We must pay better attention to the popular modes, thus to participate in the creation of the inevitable new restraints, which may serve for us as form did for our forebears, since nothing else, apparently, can. And what expression (beyond mere release) without form? Anyway, the whole intellectual endeavor is now becoming "political" in a new way: we have responsibilities for new constituencies. Intellectuals have grown up and become a political force.*

Somewhat sanguine thought: The slaves of Madison Avenue have created a whole new grammar of visual art with their superbly "meaningless" commercials for television. (They are the true heirs of Mallarmé.)

On my way out of literature into the law, I taught the former while thinking about the possibility of the latter, at Bard College, 1949–1950, at $2,800-a-year-they-should-drop-dead.

I taught this and that—and a course called "The Analysis of Popular Culture." It had to be the first one for literature students hereabouts. On campus, they called me "Pop Culture" (I was twenty-five): I took them to movies, instructed them how to read the Satevepost, analyzed Crime and Punishment as a hot detective story, and so on. All of this to high-class literature students who were insulted by the suggestion that they read Tom Jones (one of them burst into tears at that particular suggestion: she felt that my failure *to name* The Trial *was a brutal put-down). My purpose was to train them away from the schizophrenia of popular/highbrow two-mindedness. They failed, but I didn't. I got a deeper grasp on why I shouldn't have tried. And it only took one year at that despicable price.*

Middlebrows of Yesteryear

❀ ARE YOU *PM*-MINDED?

PARTISAN REVIEW, 1944

This piece is a perfect expression of my youthfulness. Not being young any longer, I couldn't write it now. On the other hand, having been just that young then, I don't think I need change a word of it.

❀ OF THE newspaper *PM* it can be said that its "inner life" consists of liberal-reformist pleas and reveries, but that its objective framework is that of acceptance of the existing social order and acquiescence in the new American imperialism. We know that imperialism abroad has been paired, historically, with "popular reformism" at home. But this new American imperialism, appearing so late upon the scene (a scene to which another determining element, the fascist technique, has been added), can be expected to produce an abortively "original" reformism. With our nineteenth-century capitalism fading into a museum-piece, the formal expression and design of the social order will become increasingly "modern," all of it catching up with Hollywood. *PM* is simply one of the more obnoxious outcomes of this special historical situation.

PM's relation to Stalinism is significant because of the latter's dual —reformist and totalitarian—character. The newspaper generally adheres to the Stalinist line, though at times it is "critical" of both program and leadership. It is under no compelling bond to use the more extreme absurdities of a line created by remote control. Because of their totalitarian source, the Stalinists operate with a more rigid logic than the *PM*-ers, who are closer to the tradition of sloppy liberal thinking. (They have retained very little of the good in that tradition—aside from the useful habit of muckraking; and some fancy words from the democratic dictionary, which, unless one has never heard them before, are about equal to zero.) *PM* is a local variation of Stalinism, representing its sensitive rather than its mechanical adaption to the American milieu.

Sam Grafton and Max Lerner are, I believe, the main stylistic sources of *PM*. The former is the fount of that cute "simplistication," or sophisticated baby-talk, which has crept into so much liberal writing—an attempt to make banalities palatable. His column appears in the *Chicago Sun*, but not in Marshall Field's New York outlet. *PM* reprints the really good ones, though: "We have reached the stage now where a good sneeze will finish off the Vichy government in France." He's quite talented at this sort of thing. I wish he'd do *Barnaby*; or Eve Merriam's *Short Snorts*.

But Grafton is seen to be a lightweight indeed, compared to Max Lerner. Max Lerner writes books about ideas; he also engages in other intellectual pursuits. For instance, he makes up fairy tales. He recited one over the radio, not long ago, called "Fable of the Skulls." It begins: "Once upon a time there was a man in Germany," and it tells about how this little fellow wanted to be big. "And so he built himself a mound of skulls" and then little guys in a lot of countries did the same thing, "but there was one country, the United States, that had a peculiar prejudice against letting people build mounds of skulls." But I had to change the station just when the fairy tale got to the part about Don't cash in your War Bonds, you're cashing in your country (or something), and didn't hear the end.

Max Lerner is not simply "fantastical," though. When the gods conferred at Cairo and Teheran, he wrote one of those editorials of his. I'm sorry to say it was largely devoted to enthusiastic nonsense. But he did offer up the next-to-last paragraph to certain "unsolved problems," like India. Then he concluded: "But this is jumping far ahead of the story. For the story is a serial, and a good serial, and a good serial reader must learn to contain his impatience while he enjoys his suspense. And what magnificent serial writers the United Nations powers and their leaders are." We lost politics at about the second bounce. It's like an easy and interesting game, you see. And the five million Indians dead of famine must enjoy their "suspense," patiently rotting in British-dug graves, while the next round of the game is prepared . . . or while Max Lerner writes another editorial, with his affectedly naïve style, mildly manufacturing "sincere logic," which consists mainly in the use of popular figures that catch on quickly; the repetition of a word or rhythm in successive clauses, rocking the reader into a nice feeling of security; and the sweet aura of a hopeful commonsense that will surely carry us through.

The opening paragraph of an editorial by I. F. Stone called "Meet John Smith" is a classic expression of a strain that permeates the entire mentality of PM-ism: "Meet John Smith. He cannot be described as an imaginary character, since there are 11,000,000 of him in uniform." Alternative pseudonyms are Joe Doakes, G. I. Joe or Josephine, etc. These have a delightful feel of simplicity and concreteness: Just another guy, like anybody else. Actually, they are just simple: by no strain of the imagination can they be considered concrete. They are, in fact, the wildest, most unwarranted abstractions that a first adventurer into theory could dream up. But notice how Stone insists that "John Smith" is not an "imaginary character." This whole technique of simulating realistic thought is part of something larger among PM-ers—their chummy, oversimple attitude, with which they seem to be saying, "We're no better than you, we scratch under the arm, yawn at concerts," and so on.

PM's attempt to bridge (or ignore) the class contradictions of its audience, leading as it does to a simplistic and hazy kind of populism, is responsible for much of the paper's cultural vulgarity. In neither art nor politics can folksy journalism overcome the elements of alienation in society. But PM tries all the same. Examples: (1) The "OK, Joe?" cheesecake they print every week: "We just can't get Esther Williams off our minds, Joe. You and us both, eh?" Just as if they graduated from the same whorehouse together. (2) Two adjacent photographs, the first of a handsome Frenchwoman who "wears a bathing costume made of mottled green parachute silk. This invasion material is much sought after in France." The other is of a pitiful refugee family, one of the several millions on the roads of Europe.

In the entire American press, probably the all-around worst column is William McCleery's "DEAR JOE" letter that appears in the Sunday Magazine Section of PM. It is signed "yours as always,

BILL, William Jennings O'Brien." In the thing that got in the July 2 issue, BILL is concerned over a possible schism between soldiers and civilians after the war: "Then, as always, it will be the good guys vs. the bad guys. And already the bad guys are trying to split the good guys apart." Toward the end he gets nostalgic: "But some day the last Kraut will yell *Kamerad* and the last Nip will blow his poor miseducated brains out and the war will be over. And you will come home."

How long, do you think, before BILL "will blow his poor miseducated brains out"?

A desperate friend of mine who worked on *PM* for a short while tells me this is the question standing first with *PM*-ers: "Is this guy *PM*-minded?"—a question which sums up all that they are or ever will be.

The following editorial warning was part of a prologue to six pages of threatening Depression photos, printed while *PM* was stumping for the Kilgore Bill (August 9): "An unhappy America, economically awry and socially unstable, will hardly be a Good Neighbor, almost certainly will be tempted to ease its internal tensions by imperialist forays abroad." Not today, you see—but tomorrow, maybe. The *PM* mentality is not simply philistine: it is eclectic, and will utilize any kind of critical idea. But always incorrectly—epigone-fashion. They cut off ideas from their moorings and exhibit them like toy-balloons. They sell words, make commodities out of ideas. Nothing is dirtier.

❀ BURGUM'S PLOY

PARTISAN REVIEW, 1947

Review of *The Novel and the World's Dilemma*, by Edwin Berry Burgum

The following review, little thing that it is, caused me considerable trouble—on two fronts. First, the Bosses at Partisan Review *returned the submitted draft for beefing up, with the editorial comment, in effect: We thought you were a hatchet-man. (That's when I found out I had become one.) Second, I was going with a very pleasant girl who, I subsequently found out to my dismay, was being analyzed by Burgum's wife. Gevalt, the consequent high-level discussion.*

Of these little concatenations are the quicksands of literature concocted. (But even in the awful glare of hindsight, one survives: she was a nice girl, it was a lousy book.)

The American literary section of the NKVD has recently dressed itself in double-breasted pin-striped suits and come out into the genteel open again. We have, for instance, the new fancy quarterly, *Mainstream*. And we have Edwin Berry Burgum.

Who will read this book? I mean, *besides* the core of the faithful and those few strollers-in who find themselves in a bookstore and imagine they ought to read something sometime about the novel or the world. Well, I am afraid that there is a sizable group of middle-brows—people not vitally interested in either modern literature or modern politics—who are determined to improve themselves by reading just this sort of book. And their effort will, as a matter of fact, pay them back in coin that they well know how to spend. For the chief result of reading *The Novel and the World's Dilemma* will be the strengthening of their conviction that the only thing worth reading, anyway, is *PM*. Because what Mr. Burgum does is to take fifteen great, near-great, and questionable writers and show how most of them didn't quite manage to end up on the side of democracy. Or, to put it straight, the book is a careful accounting of how the major novelists of the twentieth century and of the United States failed to join the CP.

(I would like to take time out at this point to compliment Mr. Burgum. He is the cleverest Stalinist I have ever read. He commits very few of the obvious crude blunders so typical of Stalinist "literary criticism." While considerably overrating Richard Wright, for instance, he is hip enough to criticize Max's speech at the end of *Native Son*. And he is firmly seated on the rickety bandwagon of psychoanalytic jargon. But, of course, he reveals himself only too clearly as a vicious fool in his horrendous piece on Kafka.)

The book is chock-full of "decadence" and "democracy." These blocks of cement continually turn up as substitutes for literary judgment. But, in Mr. Burgum's case, I suppose it is just as well. However, old pieces of cement are not, in my opinion, the core of the book. The core of the book is that Mr. Burgum believes "that all functioning truth is ideationally platitude, and that what is important is that the platitude be true and functioning." Now if we clear away the debris, we are left with the statement that truth is platitude. Or, to complicate the matter, that truth is platitude when it has a relation to real life, that is, when it functions. To extend this revelation, for Mr. Burgum every statement that is not a platitude is either not true or does not function. If some of us are so non-professorial and non-Stalinist as to read Proust and Joyce for their *disproof* of the notion that truth is platitude, Mr. Burgum, we can assume, reads them to reconvince himself of it. With the horse facing him and running backward, he has the assurance of having already arrived wherever he is going.

The theme of this book is the frustration of the ideal in bourgeois society; this, especially, should not be handled with mittens on. Unfortunately, that is just what Mr. Burgum has done—being, as he is, content with platitudes. But it is only with the failure of the Russian Revolution, and the consequent advent of fascism and war, that up-to-date despair begins. And here, of course, Mr. Burgum releases a loud and long "Include me out!" He prefers the zombie optimism of the Stalinist myth.

❈ WISHING WILL MAKE IT SO

COMMENTARY, 1947

Review of *The Miracle of the Bells,*
by Russell Janney

Best-sellers should be reviewed and analyzed on a regular basis. If this were done, a method could be developed, along with a cumulative history of the fantasy-institution itself, that might well afford important insights into the changing moods of the nation. It has not been done; pure snobbery of the literary people capable of doing it is the reason. If I were running a magazine, there would damn well be a regular column devoted to best-sellers.

John Brunini, director of the Catholic Poetry Society, says, "This is a story of God's grace, originating in the simple goodness and faith of a young girl, spreading in ever widening circles through the lives of many and uniting individuals of all classes in a new sense of brotherhood." The publisher considers *The Miracle of the Bells* to be a novel "of joyousness in life that will sweep the reader into a delightful liberating experience. . . ." A Protestant minister of New York—it is a Catholic book—went so far as to compare it with *The Robe*, calling it "one of the finest examples of practical, real Christianity that I have seen in modern fiction." One hundred twenty-five thousand copies have been printed. It is now number three on most best-seller lists.

Russell Janney, the author of *The Miracle of the Bells*, has been a press agent and writer of song lyrics; he was producer and co-author of the very successful operetta, *The Vagabond King*; he even published stories in Mencken's *Smart Set*. His extravaganza is filled with anecdotes about well-known figures, and many boastful references to great names.

It tells the story of Bill Dunnigan, the greatest press agent in America, who brings the body of Olga Treskovna, the purest female and best actress of America, to Coaltown, the worst mining town in the country, for burial. The first part of the book is a flashback to the love story of the press agent and the actress, which was ideal, rather uncomplicated, and completely unconsummated. With her death, there begins an exhibition of power by the press agent: this becomes the real substance of the book.

The mind at work here is trying to convince itself—and succeeding—that for the loved object, death is better than life. Olga, still suffering from tuberculosis contracted while working in a mine, kills herself by overwork in the movies. She wants to finish a picture on schedule—to achieve something rather than to live. Dunnigan is partly responsible—he knew she was sick, and yet he did not urge her to abandon the role in the film which he got for her. Now, because its star has died, the picture is not going to be released; Dunnigan has been fired—he is a jinx. In order to get his job back and the film off the shelves, Dunnigan pulls a stunt. Olga wanted the bells of all the churches rung at her funeral. The press agent decides to keep them going for four days.

From this point on, the story becomes one of booming ecstasy, ending at last with a funeral service attended by thousands, including movie stars, governors, Jack Dempsey, and anyone else the average person might like to have at his funeral; all this is broadcast, photographed for the newsreels, etc., etc. And during the four days that the church bells ring, everything and everybody is changed by Dunnigan from badness to goodness, from failure to success, from hate to love, and so on. The movie producer, a Jew, releases not only the film to the world—assured of the greatest box-office success ever —but also a torrent of money to Dunnigan; a poor priest becomes a national hero—and rich; those who happened to be well off "B.D." —Before Dunnigan—learn the value of other things than money; the union leader, a bully and an atheist, gets a punch in his face and goodness in his soul from Dunnigan—and so on and so on until the reader is ready to jump under the bed. Dunnigan gets his job back with a raise, and repeated visits from Olga's ghost. Oh, yes: there is also a miracle.

The plot's intent is reflected in the actual writing technique. In the first part of the book, as the love story is being told, Dunnigan's mind continually strays from immediate unpleasant situations to recall sentimentally important experiences of his past. Later, when things are going about as well for him as could be imagined (literally), his only real trouble is that Olga is dead. This difficulty is resolved by frequent chats with her ghost. The flow of the plot is nothing but the activity of setting up and knocking down straw men. Bad people appear so Dunnigan can make them good; problems arise so Dunnigan can solve them.

Because of the relation it constructs between illusion and reality, the book reads more like a movie than a movie looks. Reality is introduced only for the sake of illusion and in order to have something to pervert. (The power of the movies is to make unreality very real: given the naturalness of the actual celluloid images, their order of arrangement can depart from reality at will.) What begins as a banal, unregenerated contrast between "the sordid reality of selfish interests" and "the pure world of spirit"—between Bad and Good, in other words—undergoes a strange development. Selfish interest and goodness are no longer contrasted, *they are united*. The main vehicle of this unity is success; nor does the author bother to distinguish between religion and success. And the quality of *sincerity* is completely lost in this unifying process. It becomes irrelevant.

What we observe here is the absolute futility of using the simple terms "good" and "bad" as a means of understanding the world. These concepts can function only within a structure of knowledge that would assure us what "good" and "bad" mean *in practice*—and it is such a structure that we moderns have lost, perhaps irretrievably. In its absence, the use of these naïve terms can only be referred to a context of wishes. The world is simplified out of all relation to reality in order to enable Mr. Janney and Hollywood to approve of it as "good." (Good for whom and for what?) Here art loses sight of everything except the wish. Under the influence of Hollywood, and books like *The Miracle of the Bells*, culture becomes nothing but the interplay of childish wish with the superficial appearance of reality. Art becomes a means of deceiving and drugging us, so that we begin to live, as adults, either non-emotional or childish lives.

Mr. Janney's fantastic piece of fiction is significant not only in that it shows the effect of the movies on other cultural media, but also for the relations it suggests between religion and Hollywood. Dunnigan is in part a press agent for religion, wanting to "put it over" the same way he sells movies. He is continually saying that religion and the theater both put on "shows"; he calls God the "Great Producer."

Hollywood's resources for producing illusion—movies, movie money, and the persons of its actors and actresses—have been employed in recent years, as we know, by political parties and the government. In *The Miracle of the Bells*, these same resources are used to popularize religion. If we understand that illusion has always been a primary aspect of religion, as well as of politics; and when we realize that the movie machine is far and away the most effective illusion-producing force in our society—has become, in fact, the great secular religion of our time—then it appears obvious that religion, like politics, must exploit the Hollywood mechanism or else decline further in its power. But this will mean that religion trades increasing ineffectuality for increasing vulgarization.

Highbrow culture in America, leaning heavily on Europe, has never succeeded in creating a truly profound and satisfying national image; nor have the various American folk cultures been capable in modern times of rising to a national level. But now, at last, it appears that Hollywood and commercial culture may actually be able to manufacture this unified, national image. The political meaning of all this is enormous and obvious. While folk culture is the masses' own expression, and while highbrow culture at its best always penetrated the reality of the mass in order to stimulate it, this new commercial culture demands a passive attitude. Democracy comes to mean not that the masses will create their own heaven on earth, but that they will enter one already constructed by their exploiters. Men will not pay homage to the gods in themselves, as D. H. Lawrence demanded; they will worship in distorted mirrors the reflections of what they have not been.

The Miracle of the Bells is written in baby-talk superlatives, like an advertising blurb: to sell a fake, insane image of our life. Do the living human beings who create these childish wish-pictures actually believe in them themselves? Or is it possible that this book is nothing but a money-making hoax? For our present purposes, it makes little actual difference one way or another: as has already been pointed out, sincerity is irrelevant to the whole book, internally. But it seems quite likely that the paranoiac delusions of grandeur that constitute the character of the press agent actually do belong to the man who signed his name to the book. A ghost writer is at least a craftsman and would have used more restraint than did the author of The Miracle of the Bells. The trouble is that Mr. Janney ghosted his own book.

Ladies

I am, of course, misanthropic. (But more of this later.)

✿ THE DREAM LIFE OF THE NEW WOMAN

COMMENTARY, 1949

> This is my best unappreciated piece. Because it very nicely, delicately, even generously, sets the stage for a major modern discussion. Which no one then, or since, will have anything to do with—the men out of fear, the women mostly out of triumph. . . . Well, one day we will all get back on the track.

The avowed purpose of our popular culture—the Hollywood film, the current best-selling "historical novels," the radio soap operas—is to afford its avid consumers a quick momentary satisfaction of their fantasies; and the box-office returns sufficiently attest to their sensational success in their chosen role. By that same token, such "escapist" culture, being wish-fulfilment, should tell us a good deal about the unfulfilled wishes—the dreams, the desires, the aspirations—that currently stir the hearts of the millions, as well as throw light on the hidden ideals and thwarted ambitions in our modern society. For wishes change with the changing conditions of life; *our* "wish-fulfilments" are not the same as our fathers' or grandfathers', except in the most generalized sense: the wishes expressed on the screen, over the radio, in our novels, are the wishes generated by the problems of present-day life as lived by real people.

The fact that people might wish for other things if they had the power to construct their own wish-fantasies, or if other kinds were presented to them, is beside the point; these are the wishes they accept and act on. And even when it is granted that the consumer of popular culture may to some extent be two people—the one who goes to the movies or listens to the soap operas and the one who leads the rest of his life—still no one can really escape from himself altogether; and indeed the value of escape through fantasy—of "escape" as we know it—would be negligible if the total "loss of oneself" were possible. Fantasies are in essence passive, quick, and easy fulfilments of one's present self.

The "historical novel" is a typical product of this popular culture. It has had a long and varied career, giving expression to many different kinds of fantasies. In its modern and popular form, the historical novel has been little employed as a genuine instrument for understanding history, which in part was the effort of its founder, Sir Walter Scott, who recreated the medieval world in his novels not only because he preferred it to his own, but also because he wished to fructify the experience of his day with the values of medieval or aristocratic society. Instead, the form in our time has been used as a paper-house of historical facts in which current fantasies could be lodged.

Most recently, beginning with *Gone With the Wind*, a new type of fantasy took up its quarters in the "historical" novel; with *Forever Amber* it had its greatest glorification.

Called in the trade the "breast" novel, because there is usually a very bosomy picture of the heroine on the dustjacket, the current historical novel is often written by a woman and is always about a woman. The heroine is endowed with unbelievably strong "sex appeal." (As of the famous Amber: "There was about her a kind of warm luxuriance, something immediately suggestive to men of pleasurable fulfilment—something for which she was not responsible but of which she was acutely conscious.") She is very independent-minded; she has a great deal of trouble controlling her turbulent instincts; she is profoundly amoral; and she is "on the make" not only sexually but in her career (of this more later) with what at times amounts to religious frenzy. These heroines go at men and the world with such abandon and with such concentrated self-interest that their activity can only be compared with our great Western Expansion, the rape of the American continent. And, in truth, these Amazons of fiction are engaged in conquering an area which can justly be compared to the virginal American continent, nothing less than what used to be known as "a man's world."

Let us take three recent examples* of this new use of the historical novel as a vehicle for the fantasy projections of the "new woman" and—always keeping in mind the *magnum opus* of the tradition, Kathleen Winsor's *Forever Amber*—try to discover the typical patterns of meaning they may contain. If we succeed, we should gain some genuine insight into "what women want," those actual women all about us today who are willing and eager to dream this dream of the "new woman."

The Wind Leaves No Shadow is about a woman named Dona Tules, an actual figure in the history of the Southwest in the 1820's. Dona Tules was a poor Mexican girl who rose to be the mistress of the governor and the greatest gambling queen in Santa Fé. She also came to exercise considerable political and financial influence in the Territory. Her story, while presumably true, is altogether similar in emotional pattern to those of the heroines of our other two novels. Her original capital in life is simply an exceptional degree of sex appeal. At first this causes her trouble, for early in her career she is threatened by an intense, criminal-type male, who kills her husband and rapes her, and whom she in turn kills. The husband was a "nice

---

* *The Wind Leaves No Shadow,* by Ruth Laughlin (Whittlesey House); *Mistress Glory,* by Susan Morley (Dial Press); *The Furies,* by Niven Busch (Dial Press).

guy" who gave her love and tenderness, but was unable to make his way in the world. After his death, Dona Tules fights her way to success all alone, relying heavily on her original capital.

On the dustjacket of *Mistress Glory* (our second example), one reads: "Someone was found to look after the children and the author did nothing but live in a sort of fevered dream until the entire manuscript was completed." The book does have a hot, fevered quality. And it differs from the others in that it is not primarily a fantasy of sexual freedom or a get-ahead-in-the-world fantasy (although it is also these): its basic emotional theme is the total intertwining of sex and aggression. It contains more purely perverse and pornographic emotion, and there are many more bizarre plot elements than is usual. For instance, the book opens with the heroine being conceived on her mother's wedding night, and by someone other than the husband. And she is born and raised in a bawdy house. Her entrance into the *haut monde* of early nineteenth-century London takes place under equally unusual circumstances: she is engaged to breed an heir for her aristocratic grandfather. At the end of the book, the author kills her off: she jumps, in flames, from the burning house of disrepute, dying "with a last unearthly surge of joy, transcending all things. . . ." For the rest, the book has all the usual elements.

The third and final book, *The Furies*, was written by a man, Niven Busch, who wrote *Duel in the Sun*, later made into the great movie flop of the same name. While *The Furies*, like the others, is devoted to the grand-scale trials and tribulations of an independent woman, it differs from them in being a father-daughter story as well. And so it is more a novel, less a pure fantasy—"closer to home," figuratively as well as actually. The heroine, Vance Jefford, is enamored of her father because her dead mother had ignored her and favored her brothers. She becomes like her father, who prefers her to his sons, when he offers her a share in managing his huge ranch. But this male role requires, for one reason and another, that she give up sex, which she more or less willingly does—until her father makes known his decision to marry again. Then she turns on him, and the rest of the story concerns her struggle with her father and her eventual triumph over him. Unlike our other heroines, Vance is not much of a sexual meanderer. She achieves success by more masculine means—through shrewd, cut-throat business practices. Vance Jefford, like Dona Tules, is supposed to have been an actual historical personage; the story begins in the 1870's and is set in the South-west.*

T. C. Jefford, Vance's father, is the only character in all of the three books who is, strictly speaking, a character at all. The rest are never realized as persons; one never forgets that the events that are supposed to happen to them really happen only in the mind of the author, and sometimes in the mind of the reader. But this is beside the point, since we are not engaged here in aesthetic criticism, but in an attempt to elucidate fantasies. It is only necessary to point out that the substance of these books consists not so much of characters and events as of occasions for emotional release. For example, the Restoration world of *Forever Amber* is important—is "there"—solely as an opportunity for the expression of the vague, disembodied feeling of licentiousness.

For the "new woman" of these novels, marriage is no longer the chief objective in life; she is not content to handcuff herself and her destiny to some man for realization. Like a man, she achieves happiness and success for and by herself, using members of the opposite sex in the achievement of this purpose just as men do. The fantasy of independence is, of course, not new; what is new is chiefly the intensity with which it is taken up, the turbulence, abandon, and amorality with which the girls pursue their independence. Judging from our material, the new woman is guilty of a profound unrealism in her excessive concentration on purely mental images of sex: she has "sex in the head" to such an extent that there could not be much of it elsewhere, not to speak of the distortion represented in this notion of how one achieves success in the world.

While marriage is no longer the dominant end-in-view for the new woman in this new pattern, it continues to play a significant role in her life: it now serves as the bridge between the family and the larger social world where one can be an individual; it is the easiest, most acceptable way of leaving home. At least the *first* marriage is this bridge (perhaps this fact can bring us closer to understanding the impressive rate of divorce in America). It serves this function for all three of our heroines. With Vance Jefford as with Dona Tules, this first marriage has a spiritual sweetness not very strongly accented in their subsequent relations with men, as if the authors wished to

* Note that this basic format has been repeated by Barbara Stanwyck in a recent TV series.

prove that their heroines at least tried to do things according to the rules. But both husbands are economically inept, and both are killed by the strong, criminal "man in the background." Glory's husband is also killed by this dark figure. In each case, the death of the first husband is what really sets the novel going, by turning the heroine free to make her way in a world of free enterprise.

This first-marriage complex offers other opportunities: at a critical conjuncture, the author reflects for Dona Tules—"Ramón had possessed her heart. Her body was no more important than the corn-husk around a tamale." Women must go through a baptism by marriage.

Certainly in *Forever Amber* marriage is presented as something horrible, not merely bad: this attitude appears with special force in Amber's case because she has no occasion to confuse first love with first marriage, which confusion *is* made by our other heroines. Later marriages are either business maneuvers, breathing spells for the hard-driven independent woman, or a kind of self-ironic regression to femininity after independent status has been attained.

At any rate, our new-woman novel undeniably reflects the changed meaning of marriage. Since we are dealing with a fantasy process, it is not necessary for the female reader to have put marriage to all of these uses in order to participate in the fantasy. It is enough that she has viewed—or has had the impulse to view—the successive periods of her own marriage in ways emotionally equivalent to those of our heroines. These novels let us see the way women have come to regard men, including their husbands.

Success for our heroines is essentially similar to success for a man, except that personally they must not be masculine—aggressive, but not masculine; instead, they function as extraordinary sexual objects —concentrated libidinal magnets. Just as in the old-style historical romances the young hero often advanced himself by attracting the favor of a countess or queen, so our heroines get ahead by shrewdly choosing the objects of their abandon. Dona Tules becomes the mistress of the governor, Glory of the Prince of Wales of her day, and Amber of Charles II. Otherwise, their success is that of a man. Dona Tules wants to set up her own gambling salon and "not share her bed or money with any man," and she succeeds. Glory achieves success on the stage, and later as a partner in a crime syndicate. Vance Jefford wrests her father's ranch from him—with the help of her lover, it is true, but even men must take on partners in order to conquer the world.

But, on the deepest level, success, when it comes, is still felt to be important primarily for the relation it has to men. Success as such is really secondary. (Many male figures in fiction have also claimed to see the matter this way.) The woman who is successful as well as sexy can hardly be beaten: she is in a position to make as much of her independence as can be made of it, and to avoid as many of its terrors as possible. But it is important that this independence itself remains valuable for the variety and intensity it introduces *into her relations with men.*

We have now come to the heart of the matter. In her fantasies, the new woman is toying with all the possible relations she might have with men, from all-out Don Juanism to utter masochistic devotion. This is because, as D. H. Lawrence pointed out, men have themselves become so vacillating in their notions of what they want women to be that the women, out of pure disgust with trying to be six things at once, have taken the matter into their own hands. They are thinking of being what they themselves *want* to be, and of making the men like it. This, I suggest, is at present the real core of present-day female "independence." Whatever the socio-economic causes, the new motivation toward independence is not so much a positive interest in freedom as a disgust with the ineptitude and indecision of men in dealing with their—the women's—problems, and an effort to solve it by female initiative in the relation between the sexes, an initiative ending, however, in submission.

Let us look in these terms at some of the many relations our authors have dreamed up for their heroines. In the forest of bizarre emotions of *Mistress Glory*, we have our heroine hired to produce babies and, instead, simply satisfying an appetite. Later she corrupts stalwart workers and students, and drives an elderly music-teacher into a helpless frenzy. At one point, she forces the man who keeps her to understand "in his heart . . . that she was the master, not he. . . ." And finally she turns over to the police a man with whom she had this so auspicious beginning: "He uttered a moan, low and fierce . . . he ripped at the cloth of her costume with all his strength." There is also a poetic playwright in the background who is distinguished by the fact that she doesn't go to bed with him. One could take example after example from our three novels. But this would become tedious. Let us simply recognize that our heroines are explorers in the new-found land of female option. *Forever Amber,* the classic, is a veritable comic strip of a young lady's possible relations to men.

Who are the male leads in these movies of the mind? What kind of man is the prevailing type? In *The Wind Leaves No Shadow,* it is Don Manuel, last governor of the Southwest under Mexican rule— "He made other men seem puny and impotent." T. C. Jefford, father of our heroine Vance, dominates the male landscape in *The Furies.* And in the fevered world of *Mistress Glory,* we have Innocent Paradine, lord of London's criminals, as the lodestone of Glory's abiding interest. All three are strong, ruthless, and as self-sufficient as leaders of men should be. They are all men who will "stop at nothing" to gain their ends; and they exercise a kind of hypnotic charm over other men. All are engaged in big projects in the world of affairs. Each, in a sense, is an oversized male personalization of objective social and economic forces—a bit evil, a bit inhuman. But all end badly, being killed or losing their positions of power, or both.

In all three cases, however, the man is a major factor in the woman's coming to power. The process by which the man serves this purpose takes up the first half of each of the books; the latter half is devoted to the struggle between the man and woman, with final victory going to the woman. Even when they are not present in person, these men serve as the dark forces in the background around which the mood and much of the action pivot. They are the very problem of maleness, mystically conceived.

Here again, *Forever Amber* gives us the whole thing in classical proportion. Amber's relation to Lord Bruce Carlton expresses not only the pure essence of this male-female relation so typical of the whole genre, but also perhaps contains the final meaning of the New Woman's fantasy life. If we are inclined to view this life sympathetically—"sympathetically" from the male point of view, that is—then the emotion which generates the image of Lord Carlton can certainly be interpreted as a desire on the part of the women, despite everything else they do and don't do, to give themselves submissively and devotedly to some "really male" man. On the other hand, the absurdly idealized image of "maleness" which our heroines have created might also be taken to suggest that they are interested in submitting to the male *only* in his "ideal" form. In any case, independence is seen only in masculine terms: female independence is clearly modeled on the ideal male, or it measures its rewards in its achieved relations to the male. For the new woman, "independence" and "masculinity" seem irrevocably tied together; there is no sign of any fantasy to be independent as a woman.

There are profound social causes, which need not be entered into here, for the breakdown of traditional female roles. It is a waste of time to try to resolve the predicament of modern women with a single grand gesture—"Back to the kitchen, home, and children!" A good number of women don't want to go back to the kitchen (that is, to the life of the submissive homemaker); many women cannot go back; others try and are unable to stay there. Moreover, there is no metaphysical reason why they should go back. The home and the family are undergoing a profound process of readjustment to the overwhelming consequences of mass society, industrial economy, and planetary politics—especially here in America, which is in the vanguard of all these movements. To tell women to save themselves by re-identifying with the old forms is, to put it simply, reactionary —like telling men to return to the church, or the small town, or the farm. We are all, men and women, in the new world of big-city civilization up to our necks, and to hunger after the past is both dangerous and useless. Moreover, we built the cities; and they express something we want.

In our inspection of popular historical fiction, we have seen evidence that women are much concerned—even in their mechanized daydreaming—with this question of their new, more independent ("alienated," if you like) condition. We have observed also that marriage for the new woman, or the woman in this new condition, is no longer an absolute value, but rather one instrument among others; and that a woman's "original capital" is not her virginity, as in the conventional bourgeois view, but plainly and predominantly her "sex appeal."

But, most important of all, we have seen that women in their quest for freedom and a new self-expression have not escaped from the male ideal: they still hanker after male leadership, and when they assume control over their own lives, they tend either to take a man's attitude toward themselves, or else to require that the world contain somewhere the real embodiment of their absurdly ideal notion of masculine power—toward which, however, they remain ambivalent.

Now, the matter of controlling one's own life is all-important for the issue of independence, since that person is most independent who has the most secure control over himself. But self-control means to keep one's instincts in hand as required by modern society; and this tends to work against the sexual interests of the individual. A system of control which does not permit the expression of sex is worse than useless: it is pernicious in every human sense. A woman's pattern of psychic control must be different from that of a man if it is not to contradict her sexuality. A man, sexually, must be able to *give* through the barricade of his control; a woman must be able to *receive*, even to *invite*—after so many years of over-simple "feminism," women themselves are coming to recognize this need.

How *receive*, how *invite*, how be independent *as a woman*—this is the basic issue for the modern independent woman. In emerging from her eternal night of submission into the daylight world of individuality, she has assumed male modes, has continued to identify with men, even though this identification is now active and aggressive. This is no good because it is not female—that can be said even if we are not prepared to say what *is* "female." The problem for the modern woman is precisely to *discover* the "female," to develop a mode of individuality and independence suitable to her own sex. The bosom novel gives us clues only as to the dimensions of the task, but none as to its solution.

❀ "WOMEN TALK TOO MUCH"

MODERN REVIEW, 1947

An editorial, written as an employee of the Modern Review. *But it expresses a spirited defense of feminine freedom, so I thought it should be included—as a bit of exotica—in this collection.*

Andrei Vishinsky,* the Russian confession expert who was elevated

* To our younger readers: this son-of-a-bitch so-called lawyer was the prosecutor at the Moscow Trials.

a few years ago to the position of first spear-carrier to Commissar Molotov, believes that "women talk too much." Now this is a crucial question that has slipped unsolved down the long corridor of history, and it must certainly be of great advantage to have an opinion on it from a person who has shown such infinite skill in getting well-known speakers to keep quiet and to talk, and to say just the right things, and at just the right moments.

Vishinsky revealed his opinions on the matter some time ago to a Mr. George Okulitch, who was serving as a Canadian military attaché in Russia. Mr. Okulitch had married a Russian woman, and when he sought permission for her to return to Canada with him, and was refused, he requested an explanation from the Deputy Foreign Minister. Vishinsky replied—a bit flatly and petulantly—that it was "the duty of a Russian woman . . . to produce Soviet children —not children for the Canadian Government." After relieving himself of this kernel of "Marxist" knowledge, Vishinsky went on to denounce the whole category of Russian women who would marry foreigners, describing them as "the wrong type to be examples of Russian womanhood. They try to exchange the hardships of building Russia for the ease of other countries. *Women talk too much and thus they give the wrong impression of the Soviet Union.*" (Our italics.)

On the face of it, this statement looks like a *non sequitur*—but this is only appearance. Actually it conceals but thinly the staunch Communist principle of the equality of the sexes. That is, *any Russian* who talks too much—man or woman—is apt to give "the wrong impression of the Soviet Union." If this seems to contradict the pronouncement that "the duty of a Russian woman is to produce Soviet children," it is only because of one's lack of dialectical understanding.

And now at last we have the answer to our ancient question concerning female vocal cords. Yes, women talk too much—*when they get loose!* The thing to do then, obviously, is to keep them at home. But certainly Comrade Vishinsky wants nothing so reactionary as *Kirche, Küche, Kinder.*

Socialist metropolitans, *red* borsht, and little Bolsheviks—ah, that is, dialectically speaking, another and a quite different matter.

❀ A COUPLE OF NEW KITTENS

UNPUBLISHED, 1955

I wrote this evenings while getting started in the practice of law in order to satisfy my wife's desire for a new couch. It was done for my friend and client, Bernard Wolfe, who—in another desperate effort to get out of writing Billy Rose's newspaper column—had arranged a certain amount of money to put out a slick thing to be called International Arts *in three major languages, or something grandiose like that: the pigeon went back to straight pot before the first issue could be printed.*

If Hollywood exists at all, it exists through fantasy about women. The synonymous center of dreams, as it has been for some few thousand years, is our little girl-friends, the ladies, the vamps, the vari-structured little cutenesses. However much they may have appeared as unappetizing egg-shapes to Schopenhauer (who nevertheless had some little appetite for them), to the rest of us they have been the true chickens of our dreams, to the point where as everyone knows there are only two kinds of women left: real ones and dream ones. And the two come together, as a regular thing, only in Hollywood.

One of the great mysteries of social life is the operation of the peculiar selective principle by which one woman is, as an image, preferred over another—on Eighth Street, on Fifty-seventh Street, and particularly on Sunset Boulevard. Whether it is Russian prima ballerinas, English music-hall favorites, or American movie stars, there is some profound process at work which in the end goes far toward defining the audience itself—the *national* audience. That's us: and the process reveals some of our dreams.

For instance, Audrey Hepburn and Grace Kelly have hit Hollywood and all us other dreamers like a ton or two of orchids. Miss Hepburn has already acquired Academy Award honors, and much conversation time; Miss Kelly is "in," just one year behind. And the awarders are fortunate that the Dutch tulip bloomed earlier than the American beauty rose, or else the tinsel Solomons might have had to split the Oscar in two. Audrey has come on like the zaniest Sarah Bernhardt in years, while Miss Kelly from Philadelphia is presently reminding movie audiences that we all married for good and sufficient reasons, that one's own bedroom is not necessarily the last refuge of the scoundrel. Even the wriggly Marilyn Monroe, with her somewhat vested interest in the American national game, has not been able to slow the tigerish advance of these two new little kittens. (In her first movie of note, *The Asphalt Jungle*, Miss Monroe was, all unknowingly, the first of the new kittenish movement.)

I call them kittens because—the one with her big head and bean-stalk body; the other with her small apple face and Vassar frame—both have this in common: that each has projected upon the American scene a new intimate cuddle-up quality, a kind of scramble-all-over-you feminine presence. Miss Hepburn has simply ignored the standard American stereotype; Miss Kelly has done something even more interesting and unusual—she has attempted to explode it from within. She, particularly, has made something new and exciting out of the regular American movie embrace: *her kiss is fresh.*

The really original quality of both girls is that they do not achieve their effects by hip movements, or the other usual wiggles and bulges. (Both have nettled the Hollywood pros, and encouraged Christian Dior, in being considerably less than violent by way of the bosom.) They are both extraordinarily mental and facey in their projection. The usual Hollywood sex number is the image of a pretty, immobile face perched uneasily atop a body having a primitive life and expression of its own. These new girls, however, utilize trained and controlled bodies to achieve the facial, vocal act of crawling all over you. They saturate the audience with the idea of femininity (each with her own notion of it).

I might quote Parker Tyler here, one of our more original film critics. In setting a *point d'appui* for what he termed the modern somnambule movie heroine, he referred to Lillian Gish as a human canary in her giving forth of the feminine state. He pointed out that in the typical Griffith movie "Miss Gish . . . became a permanent lyric of jumpiness." That was how she came on, how she seized attention and made her feminine presence felt. The modern gambit, epitomized by Hedy Lamarr and Lana Turner and, later, Elizabeth Taylor, is a simple one. It is to be as thoroughly beautiful as possible all at once, and in the same place. A static, purely pictorial approach. The other big way of doing it, as previously mentioned, is to sit the civilized Ipana head on top of an ignorant but independent body which, under its own laws of motion, makes various anti-social suggestions, more or less subtly or openly. The few conventional facial gestures only accent bodily postures and turns. The signal virtue of our two new kittens is that they have neither frozen the face nor unleashed the body but have attempted to make both subserve another purpose, namely, to foist forward the pure *idea* of femininity. To achieve this, each girl has seized upon the soft waywardness and eye-centered come-on of a kitten to symbolize what she thinks to be feminine. So they are, in a sense, young character actresses, portraying women by means of a feline conception of what it is to be A Woman.

Miss Hepburn is also a ballet dancer. She doesn't point her toes and arch her back to set off the delicate movements of hands and arms, however; she arches her incredibly slight frame as a pedestal for an immense head, with broad and mobile features. Given the proper lighting and costume, she is all eyes, mouth, and forehead. And, it must be said, she mugs: like a Negro jazzman playing for college kids. She mugs cuteness, and zany adolescent wisdom. Still, it is an effective technique. I doubt that Bogart, in twenty years or more of solid professional endeavor, has ever before been upstaged so disastrously as he was by Miss Hepburn in *Sabrina*. Not only upstaged, but so entirely upset that he barely stumbled through his part. He of course was terribly disadvantaged by being unable to smile. Holden, who can grin handsomely with the widest of them, came off much better. And in *Roman Holiday* she made a special point of standing in front of Gregory Peck during most of the picture. Indeed, she ran circles around him romping—with the four paws of her big face—just like a kitten.

Speaking sociologically (and searching up a piece of history), probably the most distinctive thing about each of them is the strong, stiff spine, and the arched neck pregnant with care and awareness. (Again, the mental and personal quality of sex.) The strong back makes them look to most of us very much like ladies, even aristocrats. Miss Hepburn does derive from some form of Dutch nobility; Grace Kelly's credentials are somewhat more plebeian. *Time* magazine reports that she wore white gloves on her first Hollywood job interview: probably inhibited the couching director from undertaking the usual Cook's Tour. Miss Kelly's voice has the pure accent and authority of a Vassar or Wellesley senior, seasoned of course with the strengthened lungs one gathers in a dramatic school. Since her voice is not in the mode of street English, it passes with most American movie-goers as Eastern, wealthy, and high-class.

(After all, how many American men have actually had the unique pleasure of dating a Vassar girl?)

Miss Kelly does come from Philadelphia—but did not attend Vassar or Wellesley. Her father is a substantial citizen there, but not Main Line: he is a successful building contractor, and a figure in the local Democratic party. (A very intriguing literary parallel occurs here, namely, Eileen Butler in Theodore Dreiser's Cowperwood books. Intriguing but inaccurate, since Eileen was of the Old School, and possessed a beautiful animal vitality.) Without picking over the details of her background, it is clear that the main thing is the stubborn Irish chin. In the context of that pert-nosed little blonde dollface, the strong chin gives an uneasy but reassuring feeling to most of us weak modern men. All reports indicate that the chin symbolizes something real—determination, and so on: on her own word, Miss Kelly thinks of herself as stubborn. The chin helps her put distance between herself and the Ipana ads.

There is one other noteworthy fact out of her background: she was extremely fond of her dolls as a child. This is important because Miss Hepburn has had the international temerity to divulge to an interviewer that she did not like dolls. She was, as they say, a tomboy.—When dealing with Hollywood things, one never knows of course what is make-believe and what is sort-of-real; what is before or after the fact. The secret of Hollywood, and the single key to an understanding of it, is that time-sequence is irrelevant; which is why no one ever will write a non-business history of Hollywood that is anything more than chronology. Hollywood dreams can be returned to historical time only as part of a larger social history.

The differences between the two girls are, in their own way, as marked as the similarities—and more challenging, since one naturally wonders how two such unusual and meteoric successes could have occurred in such close conjunction, if not derived from the same atmospheric conditions. The thought occurs that perhaps it is not American taste that has changed, but rather that Hollywood has not perfected the star-making process to the point where it can pull kittens out of its cornucopian hat at will. There is no question that a big-push publicity drive is under way regarding the both of them and, at this writing, particularly Miss Kelly. But publicity drives are not an excrescence upon the Hollywood truth (it may be the other way around): at the very least, these campaigns are an essential part of what one actually sees on the screen. This is really an egg-or-chicken question; and thus irrelevant. Because even the great Garbo was a creature of publicity: a recent series in *Life* magazine revealed a school of thought holding that she generated the desire to be alone only after being informed of the same by her press agent. After all, there is no good reason why such excellent publicity (the naming of essence) should not catch on with her, just as it did with the rest of us.

The chief difference between Miss Hepburn and Miss Kelly is the simple one of nationality—if you can call the difference between Europe and America a "national" difference. While Hollywood has always been voracious enough to consume both foreign and domestic females, the vagaries of the monster's appetite have not lacked significance. Miss Hepburn's eccentricity, and even bizarreness, is not difficult to connect with her formative years in the occupied Netherlands: one can see the "developed" taste to which she is a response. (It is understandable, even compelling, that she is underfed.) Miss Kelly, on the other hand, operates within the classical framework of the cute American blonde, the ideal of American beauty. That is the theme she varies. Miss Hepburn composes her own atonal scores.

Grace Kelly is an even more central phenomenon than might be suggested by her classical cuteness. It can hardly be irrelevant that in five out of her seven motion pictures she played the role of a wife, and her wifeliness was in each instance the core of the matter. In *High Noon* she did not want her husband to do his duty and chance being killed; in *Mogambo* she nearly broke her marriage vows, as what good wife nearly wouldn't, with Clark Gable; she stood still almost long enough to be completely destroyed by her husband in *Dial M for Murder*; and in *The Bridges at Toko-Ri* she presented a superbly pure image of wifeliness—as far, in a clean-cut way, as Hollywood has ever gone in this direction.

She was wifely almost beyond endurance in *The Country Girl*. This was a good role for her and it will get her the Academy Award; but she overacted badly in a number of scenes. This was not all her fault, however, since the rich roles provided by Odets brought out the acting beast in all three principals. She plays the wife—described as "loyal, steadfast, devoted"—of a weak drunken husband, Bing Crosby. She is a wife like other people hold down a job: it doesn't pay well, my efforts aren't appreciated, but after all we have to keep the cars rolling, etc. She is supposed to look slatternly in the picture —to expose how rough life is; but of course it takes more than the absence of lipstick to fool a sophisticated audience. Everyone knows it's Grace Kelly in disguise.

In *The Country Girl* she uses her chin, is effectively belligerent. This turns out to be peculiarly attractive, especially as the story progresses and she emerges as a heroine. Which leads to the high point of the film, and a revelation as to Miss Kelly's appeal. She is kissed by Holden (not her husband) who is overwhelmed by the beauty of her wifeliness. Just before she yields to what a kiss is supposed to do for people, she shouts indignantly at him, *"You're holding me!"*— much as an irascible housewife would say to the delivery boy, "But I ordered *Idaho* potatoes!" The effect is startling: one remembers all of a sudden that Eve was somebody's wife, too, and that that part of the Bible story actually has a modern point.

She is quite a combination: the square-shouldered, straight-necked carriage of a Vassar girl; Eastern educated diction; soft kittenish features; wifely dignity; a classical cute blonde; and doll-faced belligerence. And coldness, that wonderful sexual distance that Garbo had (but which they will never let her exaggerate and elaborate as Garbo did).

Her difficulty is in being too standard an American type, which can and does at times obscure her originality, although it also tends to make it more effective. You know, the closer you are to an audience, and acceptable because you are similar to it, the greater your chance of saying what it did not expect to hear. But if you are too close, too well camouflaged by similarity, the audience may not be listening when you finally inform it—*"The juice of Egypt's grape shall moist this lip."* And then scream, *"Husband, I come:/Now to that name my courage prove my title!"*

Movies

I can't imagine having survived this wonderful life in America without movies. What would I have done with those critical 10,000 hours in this land of opportunity? (Television, for me, is mainly news stuff and old movies: I didn't even get my own set until 1961; and my first experience of the medium was standing in a crowded taxi-driver's bar on Fourth Avenue and Twenty-eighth Street watching Virginia Hill and Rudy Halley do their stuff.)

Television is the best way I can think of temporarily to forestall mass insanity; but the movies of my youth—ah, that was the velvet-glove approach to our belovèd (and ancient) neuroses!

❋ THE HIDDEN MOVIE

COMMENTARY, 1947

Review of *From Caligari to Hitler:
A Psychological History of the German Film,*
by Siegfried Kracauer; and *Magic and Myth
of the Movies,* by Parker Tyler

I was bowled over by Kracauer's book, at the time. Twenty years later, I am sure I would not tolerate or enjoy the psychologizing nearly so much. But the idea of enriching social /political history with movie insights is still very compelling to me—and some kind of psychology must, I suppose, afford the bridge. On second thought, however, history centrally involving the movies should itself be presented primarily in film. The "cost" of translation to words is too great. But who, in my generation, could even imagine the possibility of speaking through any such expensive medium? That would be like taking a taxi from Chicago to New York. (We were word-men—which is one of the reasons movies were so wonderful.)

If reviews still have something to do with what to read, let me urge you to read Parker Tyler's first book, The Hollywood Hallucination.

In both of these books the primary assumption is made that movies are peculiarly suited to the expression of unconscious tendencies, and that, on analysis, films can be made to reveal mass psychological preoccupations. Also, both authors (but especially Dr. Kracauer) believe further that even the pattern—not only the substance—of the mass mentality can be divined by a subtle, interior investigation of movie plots and action. But here the similarity between the books ends.

The framework of Mr. Tyler's criticism is intensely personal, and his mode of expression is surrealist. Dr. Kracauer, on the other hand, is a scholar, and his investigation exhibits a consistent unity of purpose, which is to depict the conflicts in the German mind that eventuated in Hitler. His study owes its superb form to the diversity of social materials which he uses in its construction.

The thesis of Dr. Kracauer's heavily documented work is that the German film under the Weimar Republic exhibited a consistent concern with a duality which he identifies variously as tyranny-chaos, submission-rebellion, etc., etc. Under the stress of this concern, which was produced by a political impasse and consequent social deterioration, the German mind as pictured in the films showed a psychological regression. That is, there was a decreasing degree of willingness and capacity to seek a realistic *social* solution of personal problems. Dr. Kracauer asserts that a concept of genuine freedom was never presented on the German screen, although there was manifest a tendency groping toward such a solution.

After outlining the small beginnings of the German film, and the impetus given to the industry by the needs of World War I, Dr. Kracauer divides the period 1918–33 into three sections. The character of the first or postwar period, extending from 1918 to 1924, was determined by Germany's isolation from the rest of the world, the short-lived burst of freedom of the German "revolution," and the devastating inflation. The middle class retreated into a psychological shell, which was mirrored adequately by the studio-produced fantasies of the time. The early works of Fritz Lang and the unique *Cabinet of Dr. Caligari* are examples. From 1924 to 1929, the German cinema reversed itself completely, becoming just as much externalized as formerly it had been internalized. The chief figure of this stabilization period was G. W. Pabst, whose realistic technique owed much to the early Russian films of Eisenstein and Pudovkin. The deeper themes of the postwar period became more veiled and distorted, but did not disappear, in the realistic productions of this second period. With the help of the Dawes Plan, German trade had revived; the face of reality became more attractive. But it was a false prosperity—nothing really had been resolved.

The economic collapse of 1929 set the stage for the last act of the

Weimar Republic. The cinema of the immediate pre-Hitler period (1930–33) showed a growth of purely escapist productions and of an unreal optimism more or less alien to Germany. But there were also direct manifestations of the approaching denouement. The paralysis of the stabilized period dissolved: "As in the postwar period, the German screen became a battleground of conflicting inner tendencies." There were films of pro-Nazi tendency, and there were even Communist films such as *Kühle Wampe*. But in the end, authoritarian leanings and other aspects of psychological retrogression won out. "The impact of pro-Nazi dispositions seemed to upset all sober considerations." Especially the sober platitudes of the Social Democrats, which "lacked the support of strong emotions." And once Hitler was in power, the fictive characters that had dominated the Weimar screen began to emerge in actual life itself.

The most impressive aspect of Dr. Kracauer's book is his method. *From Caligari to Hitler* contains a history of the film industry and constant references to the objective political and historical events taking place in German society as well as careful analysis of the thematic material and recurrent symbols of the German film. While by no means ignoring aesthetic values—in which the German film of that period was relatively prodigal—Dr. Kracauer's main emphasis is consistently social and psychological, and the result is a superbly well-rounded work, extremely provocative and rewarding. Even more than the actual history itself, the method employed will be of great value to American students of the movies. (Included in the volume is the author's widely remarked monograph, "Propaganda and the Nazi War Film," published in 1942 by the Museum of Modern Art Film Library.)

It is method that also affords the most pertinent point of comparison between Dr. Kracauer's book and Parker Tyler's *Magic and Myth of the Movies*. Method, and also the fact that one writer has described, with systematic thoroughness, the cinema of a German society that no longer exists, while the other gives us occasionally brilliant impressions of the movie-mill of an American society that has not yet fully come into being. Mr. Tyler's criticism is valuable exclusively for its brilliant sparks of insight, its occasional poetry, its often amazing suggestiveness. That is because he does not write within a framework of objective fact. He is, as a matter of fact, forever writing a drama of critical self-consciousness. (He concludes the present volume with a recapitulation of its critical content, which he forces into the senseless mold of a "Scenario for a Comedy of Critical Hallucination"—an exhibition quite embarrassing to any reader more interested in the movies than in Parker Tyler.)

In his first, very brilliant book, *The Hollywood Hallucination* (1944), Mr. Tyler's psychoanalytic-surrealist approach paid huge dividends; the book contained so much inspiration and poetry that it really could not have been other than it was. But it seemed apparent that if he was to write a sequel, his work would have to move in the direction of a broader system of reference. Mr. Tyler himself was aware of this, and his effort in the present book is to relate his insights to the magic and myth of primitives, especially as described by Sir James Frazer. But all this adds very little enlightenment, and anyhow was implicit in the first book. He should have moved toward greater social relevance.

Instead, Mr. Tyler has moved away from it. Nothing could illustrate this better than his shockingly bad analysis of *The Grapes of Wrath*, under the cute chapter-title of "Mirage of the Sunken Bathtub." When he points out that a motive in the plot is a desire on the part of the underprivileged principals for cleanliness and modern plumbing, he is not incorrect; but he is off the mark to a fantastic degree when he uses this motive as a key to the whole movie and, by inference, to the struggle of dispossessed classes. Such cynicism is not even amusing. And it reveals only too well the manner of his use of psychoanalytic terms.

This manner is somewhat more fruitful, however, in the analyses of *Mildred Pierce, Double Indemnity* and—expecially—*Arsenic and Old Lace*. Mr. Tyler also catches certain essential psychoanalytic qualities in his dissection of war films, but here again aspects of a nervous system are substituted for an entire body. And in a section saucily labeled "Schizophrenia à la Mode," his loosely held psychiatric terms get completely out of hand and write a chapter all by themselves. The piece called "Supernaturalism at Home," in which he attempts to demonstrate the other-worldly meanings of many movies, is not so much right or wrong as simply dull. It shows, once and for all, I believe, that Freudianism, and the understanding of myth derived from it, explains poorly any phenomenon *when used in isolation*. Mr. Tyler does something that Freud never did, that is, he substitutes the dream—in this case, movies—for life itself. Which is only to fall victim to the intention of Hollywood, since the heart of the movies as a social phenomenon consists in their great technical capacity for furthering the dissociation of dream from purpose (which dissociation industrial society itself creates). Whoever concentrates on dream-desires in isolation from actuality simply recapitulates in reverse the basic maladjustment of our society—which is that our process of social and intellectual "growth" slowly but inevitably denudes the real world of imaginative (or dream) elements. These latter then lead a disembodied existence of their own, of which the movies are the chief objectification.

It is well known that actual life requires a purpose; it is not so widely understood that one does not live without dreams. The human being persists in dreaming no matter what his condition may be. But his condition is most satisfactory when his dreams are allied with his real-life interests. Without this interactive alliance between dream and purpose, we are forced to divide ourselves and live in two worlds that are more or less disconnected. And our creativity is severely limited. The consequence is the pursuit of purposes that are not informed by and do not satisfy our dreams, and on the other hand the acceptance of dreams we can never realize: thus the atomized, passive individual of our day.

When Mr. Tyler subscribes to a "theory of meaning as essence rather than as form," he accepts the purposeless dream and invites a cloud of meaninglessness to settle over actuality, since genuine meaning is created not by essence or form, but by the dream-essence objectifying itself in the form of a realistic purpose. Dr. Kracauer, however—the German catastrophe notwithstanding—is willing to wait and hope, to analyze and to plan for a new organization of dream elements that will restore an acceptable *emotional* purpose to life. No other kind of purpose will do.

The greatest crime of bourgeois society is that it raises its children to believe that nothing remains left over to contend with when the compromises of "adjustment" are made. We grow up unprepared to deal with our unactualized dream-desires, which are fully as much a part of our lives as the career success we achieve by our compromises. In some form or other, our dreams are forever with us. It is Dr. Kracauer's thesis that failure to deal with this fact may lead to the transformation of the actual world into a fascist nightmare.

❊ THE DREAM ENTHUSIAST

VILLAGE VOICE, 1958

Review of *Agee on Film*, by James Agee

*Whenever I would meet Jim Agee at a party, we would im-
mediately engage in an intense, low-voice conversation about
movies—there was a new quality to the freeze of Alan Ladd's
face in* Shane; *Jimmy Stewart should never have tried to become a sexy Will Rogers; Wanda Hendrix signals a deep pause
in the tortured progression of American sexuality; the brilliant
casting in* Red River *was, like Mercutio in* Romeo and Juliet,
*too much for Blank-Blank to maintain; how do you like that,
the Frogs are imitating us, now—and so on, until someone
would interrupt. And that's all I knew him, except stories
about him from Manny Farber and Herb and Willie Poster.
But he loomed large, since he was a Real Writer and yet made
Real Money working for* Time: *on the rock of his being, the
youthful category of "sell-out" was smashed, for me, once and
for all.*

*He was a sweetheart, utterly inoffensive in his drinking—
the nicest lush you could ever hope to meet (and I've met a
few). He was one of those, like Parker Tyler, who probably
went to the movies at the age of five and "fell in," never to
climb out. (I could never get clear with myself whether my
feeling about them was There-but-for-the-grace-of-God, or
simple envy.)*

James Agee's reputation has grown considerably since his death a
few years ago of a heart attack at the age of forty-five. In his lifetime,
Agee was a uniquely enthusiastic and emotional stylist: his personal
qualities of intensity, sweetness, and terrible sincerity were almost
always present in his written work, and many readers established the
habit of forgiving him his excesses. Early in his career he achieved
success with a volume of poetry and the highly reputed *Let Us
Now Praise Famous Men*, a lyrical picture of Southern sharecrop-
pers. Through most of the Forties, he wrote regular movie criticism
for both *Time* and *The Nation*. In 1948 he got into movie work
directly, most notably in collaborating with John Huston on the
script of *The African Queen*. His posthumously published novel, *A
Death in the Family*, won the Pulitzer Prize in 1958.

Not only was this dead writer's posthumous Pulitzer success about a death, but also his greatest popular success during his life, a beautifully evocative homage to the silent comedies of the early movie days, concerned a dead art form. This article, "Comedy's Greatest Era," appeared as a cover story in *Life* in 1949 and, according to the publisher of the present collection, "received one of the greatest responses in the magazine's history." It was probably the most successful piece of movie criticism ever published. It contains superb appreciations of Mack Sennett, Harold Lloyd, Harry Langdon, Chaplin, and Keaton; is unequaled in its descriptions of the indescribable gestures of the great silent comics; and convinces one, as nothing else can, of the continuing relevance of the proposition that the art of the movies is the art of movement and that the advent of sound has hopelessly "stagified" the movies, locking them in the death-grip of the most unrealistic "realism" ever and all but ruining the medium as art.

This fabulous piece of popular writing is the first of 186 long and short bits of movie criticism collected in *Agee on Film*. These include another *Life* feature, on John Huston; an article on *Sunset Boulevard* from the English *Sight and Sound*; a somewhat general piece on popular art called "Pseudo-Folk," which caused considerable comment when it appeared in *Partisan Review* in 1944; 38 pieces from *Time* and—the bulk of the book—144 which were published in *The Nation* between 1942 and 1948. Altogether it is a very impressive and worthwhile collection, being one of the few sustained efforts by a capable imagination to come to terms with American popular art. I don't think Agee succeeded in his effort (no one does), but his failure—very much in the nature of a tragic passionate love affair—is as deeply meaningful as anything we have in this area of American writing.

What Agee tried to do was to combine in one sensibility the attitudes and understandings and purposes of the best of high culture with a desire for (and an appreciation of) popular art, or his own idea of an uncreated popular art. In his effort to hammer out the elaborate grillwork of this imagined sensibility, he chose, or there were available to him, *movies as a subject and rhetoric as a means*. I think the artist who makes a choice of (or a surrender to) rhetoric—whether he is Wallace Stevens or Dylan Thomas or James Agee—is a man whose need for emotional expression is so immediate and compelling that he will sacrifice the world to it, if the world means restraint; and of course he continually faces the danger thereafter, whatever his initial sincerity, of sacrificing more or less of meaning and coherence as well. The rhetorical pen can always wag the rhetorician. Agee was a really superlative one—the reader can become truly enthralled with the pyrotechnics of his style—and he has all the virtues and failings of his tribe.

The movies are as appropriate a subject as rhetoric is a means for the emotionally compelled person (not to say the victim of emotionalism). With their bigger-than-life images and ubiquitous recollection of reality, they are an easy or even irresistible source of emotion; particularly *forbidden* emotion (in the dark anonymity of the theatre) and especially the emotions forbidden the highbrow by his superior taste. Consistent with the sensibility he was building, Agee wanted to deny himself none of the popular emotional participation afforded by the movies and none of the grandeur of great art. What a task he set for himself, and what a morass of miswedded if often brilliant perceptions he ended up with! But again, what talent and real love was devoted to this project of bridging the gap between himself and the popular audience with his thrust of grandiloquent rhetoric.

Agee was a frequent victim of his own enthusiasms: mostly because of a terrible eagerness to find evidence that the movies were the great art form of our century, much as poetic drama was for the Elizabethan Age. So parts of André Malraux's *Man's Hope* are "Homeric"; Mozart and other great names are dragged in here and there; *Shoeshine*—"a true tragedy"—renews his faith in "the germinal force of Western civilization"; and so on. Even when you agree with him, he can say too much and makes you feel uneasy, as in his elaborate praise for Huston's *Treasure of the Sierra Madre*—just "short of unarguable greatness." His so frequent use of the lost-possibilities or the way-it-should-have-been-done approach, although he is often enough convincing, becomes just plain boring. The apologetic it-stinks-but mannerism also palls and irritates by unconscionable repetition. Attempting to respond within an infinite spectrum extending from Homer to Val Lewton, he is compelled to apologize for anything he just plain likes, and every melodrama must be labeled "intelligent trash" before he can get on to what's good about it. His enthusiasm for the excellent wartime documentaries, e.g. *Desert Victory, San Pietro, Western Approaches*, leads him to say that, given a lack of photographic pretension and hokum, the straight material is "automatically poetic"—to my mind an aesthetic impossibility. But what is basically wrong with trying to see all movies as more or less egregiously unsuccessful works of art on the same level as Shakespeare's plays is that one then misses a great deal of what movies *actually* are, not what they sometimes have been or could be—that is, that they are bureaucratically produced machine-art, an unending fantasy about our own false view of our real American selves. In this meat-and-potato view of movies, the lies afford at least as much nourishment as the occasional glimpses of reality or achievements of art. The infrequency of the latter means, inescapably, that we go to the movies for the former as well, if we go at all.

At the heart of Agee's style there is always a reaching, a sometimes beautiful and sometimes gluttonous effort to find or recapture a piece of the past, a lost or a dead thing, or simply something unattainable. He has the Southerner's sense of the past, a certain amount of Faulkner in him. More than anything, he reached for the past and probably unattainable coherence of the artist and his audience, that lost community of interest apparent in the early silent comedies, the early Griffith, the early Russians, the Shakespearean theater, and the Southerner's mythical belief concerning the ante-bellum South. In this, he follows the Gilbert Seldes tradition in popular art, but he carries the shattering burden of all the differences between the Twenties and the Forties. He tried very hard; and particularly when you consider that his own daily existence was split in two between the nonsense of his Time, Inc. job and the license of his *Nation* reviews, you must recognize that there was true necessity behind his effort toward a unified sensibility. It was not easily undertaken, nor was the rhetorical enthusiasm easily indulged in; he was deadly serious throughout. His commitment to the rigorous values of high art was unequivocal, his search for achievement and means in popular art unceasing, and his contempt for the middle was deep and complete. He made a lot of mistakes, but there are some wonderful things in his writing, and after all he was trying for something most people have given up on. There was something heroic about his effort.

❀ THE LOUDER REALITY:
BEHIND THE BUSY MIRROR

REVIEW OF EXISTENTIAL
PSYCHOLOGY AND PSYCHIATRY, 1966

This sums up what I learned from the movies, put in its proper context of general urban hallucination. The first version was done talky-talky at the First Annual Aspen Film Conference (August 31, 1963), the transcript published in a subsequent volume of Proceedings. *This more careful and elaborate rendition was prepared for a conference of the Association of Existential Psychology and Psychiatry on "Electronic Recording and Reality in Psychotherapeutic Research" held in the spring of 1965.*

I had a ball at that weekend meeting in the Colorado mountains. The casting was excellent, consisting of a thoroughly impossible mix of industry executives and Creative Persons. So I moved quickly (I spoke early) to establish my role in the proceedings as a loud, shifty, only occasionally benign centrist. There I was, a literary man, dropping highbrow names on one hand, and—as a former attorney—mumbling sympathetically about business matters, on the other. (It happened—no choice of my own—that during my five years of practice most of the big transactions with which I was involved concerned the movie industry: Rita Hayworth's suit against Columbia Pictures, the United Artists' underwriting and, later, purchase of the Warner Brothers pre-1948 library for television, and the Loew's proxy fight of 1957. So I knew something about the business side of the matter, as well as having been an inveterate movie-goer and amateur critic for most of my life.)

I cannot honestly claim to have turned the proceedings around, but I made my mark—and helplessly they kept coming back to it, whenever acrimony threatened to touch the keys of the cash register. Besides, no fast-talking weisenheimer is going to loom too large at a film conference attended by Jean Renoir, a major charm stylist and living embodiment of the Great Days; King Vidor, with his pure American newspaper-reporter sensibility risen to cinematic heights capable of challenging, medium for medium, Hemingway's similar sensibility enlargée; a current goddess, Eva Marie Saint (what a doll!); and John Housman, a true Hollywood-Algonquin type, letting us in on *how he and Orson finally managed to put together* Citizen Kane. *I made my mark, I held my own. But what a magnificent opportunity to let both sides have it—after having been on the receiving-end myself for thirty years.**

Come to think of it, this was about the time I stopped going to new movies, and sank into that special generational experience of nostalgic re-viewing on after-news late showings. The modern stuff—my cold-bath was Goldfinger—is not for me: I mean, I can enjoy and/or be impressed by it—but structure a life around it, like in the old days? Baby, it's all yours. Including The Graduate, as nifty a piece of movie-stuff ever put to overexposure, partly written by my old pal, Calder Willingham, the wild kid from Georgia I met at the University of Virginia in 1941. (That Calder, he'll never grow up.)

On movies, one further point: My first several years in New York, I went once a week, more or less, to the Museum of Modern Art for their film repertory showings. I saw Intolerance, I saw Caligari and Anna Christie—I saw lots of stuff. I got Calder to join me in becoming a charter member of Cinema 16 —and to quit with a money-back demand, after they showed one Maya Deren and two Unesco releases. (We right-thinking types have undone an incredible number of opportunities, even in my lifetime.)

Movies were a false community. But they were a community of a kind. This was the edge they held on the reality of the time.

How they did it, was to postulate a concentrated ninety-minute super-reality. Later, they reached for a three-and-a-half-hour one. But only after the coming of television was the double-feature consolidated into the blockbuster. The effort did not avail: the blockbuster is nothing but gorgeous and edited television: and television —being, unlike the original movie form, an invasion of the home— is presuming to become a fairly complete substitute for undefined reality. Being "complete," its dynamic is to be busy rather than pre-

---

* At a darling party on a mountainside, I finally discussed censorship with a leader of the censoring organization. I opened a major attack, setting the stage skillfully for later blockbusters. This he had heard before: he giggled—politely (which I had never heard before). We got delightfully drunk together. I still remember him warmly. I am constitutionally incapable of engaging in a serious discussion of the censorship of anything, since then. (*Bless him!*)

cise or concentrated. Indeed, television has been so busy becoming what it is that, compared to what the movies were, it is decidedly retrograde. It consists mostly of serials which are mass-produced B-movies in which standard parts are utilized. This creates both lowered costs of production and also the hypnotic endlessness which, thus far, defines the medium. I think this is no more than a primitive beginning, however—movies, too, began with serials—and that the louder reality of the re-created world now based on television remains substantially undefined.

To be weighty and historical for a moment, the encroaching problem of the quality of our lives can be characterized as that of industrial Byzantinism. Briefly, the opportunities for affluence will make idiots of us all, if we do not let the barbarians in. So much power and resource as America now possesses cannot simply be placed in some kind of power-and-resource bank, there to be held against a rainy day. Such deposits destroy the banker—and all of us within the affluent sector are bankers of a kind, whether we know it or like it or not. The kind of surplus-for-living we in America have now had thrust upon us, is a dynamism, a continuously threatening transcendence, a monster and a master beyond all previous ones. Happiness, I must tell you, is not a warm puppy: it is the white teeth at the front end of the tiger whose tail we hang onto for our very lives.

While we have been thinking over the character of our new lives, the tiger has led us into fabulous rituals. Ritual, we should remember, is the only non-money life-bank known to man. And it is a bank, history often tells us, from which withdrawals are neither encouraged nor facilitated. Then what happens? Well, first there's a run on the bank; then the priests or bankers are detested; in temporary puzzlement, people live a little in down-to-size, hand-made realities; some actual history occurs; and finally somebody starts a new bank.

Our popular culture, now centered around television, will always be deeply compelling because it is our only community with our inferiors, especially including our inferior sense of ourselves. The factor to reckon with here is that genuine community can never be elitist: community reaches to the limits of identification. That is the present definition of community as it was formerly the obvious definition of God. If I choose *Partisan Review* instead of television (I don't, incidentally), I am simply expressing my putatively superior taste in a choice between two false communities—because I have to

have at least one to get through the rest of the day—just as intellectuals of previous periods ordinarily ended up choosing one false god
or another.

In the law, we say that the rationalistic hypocrisy accompanying
pragmatic change is the "genius of the common law"—and, considering all of the other possibilities, it is. Beyond law, with conscious
human beings generally, we may say that the tendency to heresy is
the special genius of human history. Our popular culture is a hodge-
podge of heresy—an incompetent outpouring of the human demand
for a god for each period of the day. At one moment, it will be the
miracle of a new detergent or toothpaste or mouthwash or shampoo;
at another, the need is for a long sojourn at the wailing wall of domestic misuse; later, an avenging angel waves a tommy-gun or a Colt
.45 in the direction of solvency; then a half-hour of teen-age barbar-
ism convinces us again that age is not the unmitigated disaster it
seems to be; just before bedtime, serious men reassure us as to the
complexities of history which indicate, very likely, another such day
as this one was (some of the shrewdest political nuances occur in the
weather report, if you listen carefully); and then, with the louder
reality silenced, we are free to roam beyond the busy mirror of the
present—all the way into the warmer unreality of the movies of our
youth.

With such programming, Richelieu might have succeeded in creating a France beyond the recurrence not only of the wrong Louis,
but even of Charles de Gaulle.

Art of any kind, even the best kind, is a re-representation, a misrepresentation—in sum, a false community. But, at its best, it is a
true false community. You find this a contradiction? I wonder why.
Truth is a function of mentality: the truest truth of all is not the
lightest bit of a substitute for the littlest banal piece of reality. And
real community is an event, not an idea. But false community is an
idea—that is why it is false. Some of these ideas, however, are better
than others. And one or another is necessary, because we do not
survive well without at least one. Therefore, we are in the business
of making judgments of value as among false communities. Therefore, some are even truer than others.

Perhaps all art and even all consciousness, no matter how we play
with the truth, is a re-representation of reality. In my present daring
mood, I am tempted to agree with Charles Péguy, who said: "Every-

thing begins in mysticism and everything ends in politics." However that may be, as mechanical devices lead us closer to a fuller verisimilitude, a process of once-slow change finally overwhelms us: *the reality being re-represented is lost.* Modern politics, then, would be an attempt to recapture reality through action—mysticism the attempt to do so by standing still (achieving inaction) creatively.

The initial loss of reality is much facilitated by living in cities, where the traditional reality of nature is obscured in its own physical re-representation—as brick and mortar, and chrome and plastic, and other fantastical materializations. Interestingly, natural community is one of the early losses of the city: cities are made up of migrants. The abandonment of natural community is part of the price of admission to the never-ending re-creation of human nature and its environment, which is the drama of the city.

But verisimilitude—whether by mechanical device or by the more laborious and dangerous method of building a city—is tyrannous and objectionable. Indeed, it can be totalitarian. To be brief, it presumes an identity between idea and fact which we are not used to, which is presented without our permission or participation, and which is strangely less believable as it becomes truer. I think this explanation helps to explain, for example, the response of abstract art to the advent of photography: the more serious people became more and more hysterical in their effort not to be "taken in" by encroaching verisimilitude. I think that ordinary and less serious people have, with the ordinary and less serious means available to them, responded similarly to the encroachment of the city.

What is the difference between a city and the photograph of a city? I suggest that the difference lies in the quality of belief bestowed on each: the initial unreality of the city is certified as "real" by the photograph. And these issues of belief are different from others in that both are presented as unalterable facts rather than as subjective notions produced by other human beings. To someone who has never lived in a city, the photograph of one would be taken as an imaginative offering or imposition—as somebody's idea of something. But if you live in that city, the photograph will very likely be taken as fact-truth—and is felt to be the same kind of imposition as the city itself is. Conceive the city as the alterable fault of City Hall, however, and you may walk away from the photograph muttering about lousy artists or presumptuous cameramen. And—

here Péguy is clearly correct—you cannot finally and seriously do the one without also doing the other. Man-made realities and their misrepresentations cannot be kept separate.

As with the arts of the city, so with the managers of verisimilitude —Who runs City Hall, and with what ends in view? More precisely, with what image of *me* in mind, if any. And what can I do about it if I don't like it. (That is, what can I do about it besides learning to like it.)

Note that under the effects of modern technology, the previously clear line between environment and culture is obscured. And that line, further note, is a basic one, since it separates dream from actuality. Now wait a minute, you reflect in a cool objecting mood, if that particular line were lost, everybody would be nuts—by definition. We don't have the time or the courage to face that issue directly, but I would suggest that the line has indeed been obscured, whatever that may do to our definitions; and that the issue replacing this previously compelling and obvious one is a choice of acceptabilities —nearly a matter of fashion. It is we on the outside who decide who is to be put away on the inside—or *vice versa*—and we change our minds on this subject frequently, and according to the vagaries of fashion. Certainly fashion, and other indeterminate compulsions, have already created acceptances and disallowances as to the content of cities, of environment/culture, of who is in and who is out of almost anything. And these choices are not based on any simple Rouault-line between figure and background, dream and actuality.

Religious cultures provided handicraft public dreams—and also the hand-made conventional line between these and reality. With active photography and the movies, our public dreams became subject to the startling dynamics of industrialism. When mechanical verisimilitude replaces mysticism, the dream is unleashed upon reality. The difference between a lyric poem and six hours of television is a difference past comprehension. Without much comprehension, we can confidently say that it is different men who take each as their different cultures. I would now like to characterize these industrial dreams, and indicate some of the avenues of solution for the unitary persons who—because of the nature and need of community—understand that they must live as *both* these different men.

Technology does with our dreams what it does with other aspects of our lives—it rationalizes the production of consumption items and administers their application. But our dreams present the most intractable material with which the rational administrative order must deal. Also, the American gluttony for dreaming far surpasses our world-famous predilection for creature-comforts and shiny objects. All this has the consequence that in the production of dreams our rational administrators rise to levels of incompetence they seldom achieve elsewhere. I tried but could not bring myself to agree with Newton Minow's characterization of television as a "vast wasteland": he saw it as an unsuccessful effort at adult education. Viewing it more pertinently as Dreamsville, USA, the candid observer is struck not with the absence of discussion shows and other cultural events, but with the helpless messiness of the programming. It is one big bowl of chop suey, resulting from the frantic pursuit of a buck by means of the primitive manipulation of happenstance. It is like an unending visual magazine put together by a team of overworked, drunken editors who refuse to speak to each other about any subjects except gross receipts, dividend disbursements, and year-end bonuses.

For instance, given the terms of the game, I don't object to the commercials. They are often enough technically superior and visually more interesting than other segments of the endless show. They certainly consume no more time than one spends finding the text in *The New Yorker*, or distinguishing between the ads and the pictures in a picture-story in *Look*. Apart from big events like the Kefauver or McCarthy hearings, and the great assassination weekend, most of the artistic innovativeness of television has been in connection with the commercials. As for the rest, it is mostly derivative—lifted bodily from the movies (probably half the TV time in the country is devoted to movies, anyway) and the ancient art form of parlor visits by strangers. Even the big events are not that much better than the commercials, when the organization has time to get the equipment in position and plan the representation, as with the Churchill funeral and the Johnson Inauguration.

It is true of our national popular culture generally that the manipulation of the dream and the representation of objects of consumption are hardly separate aspects of the same thing. Mostly, they *are* the same thing. Remove either, and the other will be changed substantially. Which is why I always preferred movies to the *Ladies' Home Journal*. In pre-television movies, the presentation of consumption items was skillfully woven into the text, so to speak. In this, it was more like the photograph of a city, and less like an ordinary real estate ad with pictures.

It should be clear by now that I am one of the old-fashioned fellows: I used to "go to the movies," and doing so was important to me. I think the movies were the "pure case" of popular dream culture—that is, the two decades or so of American talkies, ending with the triumph of television in the Fifties. I saw the end coming in 1951 when I was in law school, and my classmates were a few years younger than myself. After dinner, one of them suggested we all "take in a flick." I didn't know what he was talking about, but I was game for anything in those days, so I agreed. I was horrified to find out he meant let's all "go to the movies." How I learned to detest that phrase! It meant the end of my movie-going days. I was damned if I was going to lower myself to "taking in a flick"—which, it turned out, meant first preference for a French or Italian film or an American thing compounded of the worst elements of each—something as awful, say, as *The Barefoot Contessa*. I withdrew in dignity, nurturing my hard-earned honor as a former slave to movie-going. "Take in a flick," yet! Me—who had seen a hundred and seventy-five Tom Mix serials, every Bogart since *The Petrified Forest*, and every Cagney since *Public Enemy*.

The central institution in American society is something called "Success"; and its sustaining myth has been Individualism. The movies that were important to me, I now see with hindsight, were a development of the post-Depression fate of the myth of American Individualism. I bought my ticket and entered the communal darkness of the theatre in a state of desperate loneliness; I dreamed along with millions of other communityless Americans; and I believe that most of us emerged, after two decades, older and wiser and more shrewdly adjusted, as individuals, to the louder reality of the city. We dreamed our way past the dangerous edges of the myth. I don't think Hollywood ever intended to give us that much for our money. In the delirium of dollar-fever, they goofed. It was as if the machine answered the machine-tender with something like sympathetic consideration. Because of the difficulties of administration and the accompanying distractions of making a buck, this is potential in all dream-machines, I suggest—even television. Machines, like children, mirror the underlying Us when and if we fail to interfere effectively.

The real difference between high art and the lower commercial or industrial stuff is the quality and effectiveness of the interference. We will return to this point in a moment; but first I want to tell you about what happened in the movies, especially from *Little Caesar* to *The House on 92nd Street*. It is relevant to the subject we are speculating about this weekend—the relation between reality, the actor, and mechanical devices of re-representation.

The simple form of the myth of Individualism in the movies appears as the Cowboy. For background, I will only suggest that the Cowboy was romanticized because Mr. Horatio Alger Himself became unbelievable. Before that, the actual cowboy was a dirty bum —a hobo, a seaman, a social Houdini. Anyway, after Cotton Mather and Horatio Alger, the Cowboy became the Purest Thought of which Americans were capable. He was a fellow with a horse, a frying-pan, and a gun. His basic connection with anything real or recognizable was the gun: the horse was a farmer's memory, and the frying-pan dispensed with women altogether. He had one change of clothing. But he had the gun: this was the single symbolic connection with the city, with complicated civilization. In many of the best Westerns, the chief character is the gun—especially to be mentioned is that sophisticated but loving rendition of the crypto-Western, *Destry Rides Again*.

The Western is not hard to understand—it is almost as pure and obvious, in the American context, as Hemingway's hunting and fishing scenes. The esthetic problem was to engage this emotional stream of myth closer to home, as the farmers' stay in the city lengthened into decades. The occasion for the solution was the apocalyptic Depression, and the symbol was the Gangster. In essence, the Gangster was a denuded Cowboy: his horse had been shot out from under him, somebody had taken away his frying-pan, and all he had left was his gun. And no scenery: the picture begins with him arriving in the City. He gets off the bus with one change of clothing and the gun, and there are no Open Spaces: this being the City, all "spaces" must be opened by him.

Probably the greatest single piece of movie criticism written in this country was the five pages in *Partisan Review* by Robert Warshow, called "The Gangster as Tragic Hero." Nearly twenty years later, I find it as startling and brilliant as on the first reading. Bob Warshow was a friend of mine: as were the two other leading American critics (after the *Hound and Horn* group and Otis Ferguson), James Agee also dead, and Manny Farber still kicking. Farber is unequaled in being able to perceive a significant piece of business in a film; Agee's rhetorical enthusiasm for film as an art form is equaled only by the esthetic criticism of the Twenties. But Warshow saw film just as I did, only better: he saw it as a bonanza of an opportunity to penetrate the emotional history of one's own time. Which he did, as for instance in his brief essay on the gangster film.

Warshow begins with the proposition that there is a duty to be happy in America, and that our organs of mass culture naturally undertake to meet this responsibility. Then he notes the just-as-natural countervailing force in our culture, the need "to express by whatever means are available to it that sense of desperation and inevitable failure which optimism itself helps to create." This the gangster film has done in unparalleled fashion: "From its beginnings, it has been a consistent and astonishingly complete presentation of the modern sense of tragedy." The genre consists of a repeated pattern which "creates its own field of reference." The gangster film does not concern "real" gangsters: "What matters is that the experience of the gangster *as an experience of art* is universal to Americans." And that is because "The gangster is the man of the city . . . carrying his life in his hands like a placard, a club . . . he is what we want to be and what we are afraid we may become." The essence of the gangster is that he uses violence to achieve success, but he "is doomed because he is under the obligation to succeed, not because the means he employs are unlawful." To succeed is to be alone—"the successful man is an outlaw"—and if you are alone you will be killed. Thus, with the gangster catharsis enacted, we value our failure.

The gangster film itself had a definite death: it was so in tune with its audience, unconsciously, that it could not be repeated successfully today. When Edward G. Robinson in *Little Caesar* dies in 1931, his last words are pure brutal wonderment—"Mother of God, is this the end of Rico?" Some years later, in *The Roaring Twenties* —a film about the end of the gangster era—Cagney lies dead on the street in front of a cathedral, and a cop with a notebook in hand asks the dead man's girl, "What was his business?" "He used to be a big shot," she says. The final and absolute end of the gangster film I date, however, with Cagney's *White Heat*, circa 1949, in which the basic idea of the gangster was self-consciously psychologized. In this absolutely wild film, the mother was the head of the gang, and Cagney is loudly psychotic from the first reel. And he dies not in the traditional burst of sub-machine gun fire—he is blown up in an oil factory, grinning hideously as the flames, etc., etc.

Meanwhile, the general development of the myth of Individualism and the problem of Success was creatively refurbished in 1940 with the great private eye film, *The Maltese Falcon*. Here, American City Man is no longer a gangster, but not yet a soldier or a cop. He is positioned in between. Indeed, everything is ambiguous about him except one thing: he wants to do a competent job. This is his substitute for big money, big success, big sex, big anything. He can die, it is clear, only through lack of male cunning and other incompetence. With the private eye film—hundreds of which were made during the Forties and early Fifties—the City Man has become a semi-professional with a code of competence centered around the job-at-hand, which affords control over his environment *and* his own impulse to get too much out of life. I date the end of this genre with Mickey Spillane, whom I would rather not discuss at length—certainly not before a group of psychiatrists.

Meanwhile, the cop-film arrived, during the War, with *The House on 92nd Street*. Here, Individualism is the permissive gift of organization. Law and order triumphs as team-work and machine-work: it is a highly bureaucratized form of law and order. The fascination of these cop/organization films consists in the variety of machines and the efficiency of organization: you identify with these, not with people. A recent and very successful example of this type has been *The Untouchables* series on television, high-grade B-movies which presumed to go back and rewrite the gangster film from the viewpoint of a law-gang. Now, with something like *The Man from U.N.C.L.E.*, this genre encroaches upon science-fiction, becomes bizarre as well as sophisticated, and includes a charming layer of silliness. Efficient organization, I predict, is becoming funny in popular culture—not yet the high macabre humor of *Dr. Strangelove*, but still increasingly funny in a bizarre way.

Well, besides being at the end of this talk, where are we? I think my over-all point has been that dreams, and the ideals and ideal-images they contain and enunciate, are a large part of the louder reality, and properly so, whether or not we think we are participating in a religious culture. In a man-made world which includes integrally the machine-made re-representations of it, dream is so much a part of reality that we need a new approach for those occasions when it is still important to distinguish the two. Let me put it another way:

Technology is transcending traditional religious dualism by destroying nature, both inside man and in the outside world. The result has been to unleash dreams and dreaming upon the destroyed worlds. The one virtue of dualism was that it presumed to keep dreams off the streets. Nothing can presume to do that now. So the "new approach," I feel, must follow Freud's prescription for dreams, which I take to have been affording them greater acceptance and applying a higher order of criticism to them. And this must be done socially and politically—on the streets—and not just in the dream-doctor's quiet study.

On your specific subject, my suggestion has been that mechanical reproducing devices merely facilitate the unleashing of dreams by: (1) fostering the deception of verisimilitude; (2) compounding the cultural felony by, so to speak, photographing a photograph; and (3) reproducing the disorder of the management of the city in the "pictured" re-representation of it—on television, for instance, by the absence of the artist—so that it is no longer true enough that in dreams begin responsibilities. In sum, tape and film are magical only if you are not yet aware of what technology has *already* done to the world. With that awareness—but only with that awareness—they become stimulatingly ordinary, and may even be a means of salvation, since they are especially suited to the imaginative manipulation of technologized reality.

And what about the quieter realities of cultural elites? Fine, no problem—except one. That is, how to establish communication between all dreaming realities, and the possibility of community among all dreaming men. That is an old religious problem, now reconstituted on a new technological basis. Indeed, the pattern repeats itself startlingly, on the new basis. Where once the church introduced great distortion in mediating between God and man, we now have the corporations and other bureaus for the administration of dreams and ideals. Instead of the Borgia popes, we had L. B. Mayer and some others; and now, I am sure, have numerous curia of network executives, and so on. Elites-out-of-communication, for one reason or another, tend to become corrupt—one way and another. Especially in America, which is a democracy *or else:* can you imagine this country without its belief in democracy—without that potential, or preoccupation, or whatever it is? The mere thought is enough to make one's head spin. In a democracy, one must always search for the proper relation between popular and other values—

between the worlds made by lesser men and the superior worlds imagined by our elites. But never either/or: that would be crazy.

And especially in America, the better elites perform a great function—sometimes nobly at great cost to themselves, and sometimes less nobly in spite of themselves. Snobbery is their problem: but their value is that they are concerned with *form*—old form, fresh form, frenzied form, form without content, but nevertheless form. And that is very important for us, with our general lack of inherent form in American life. So, view them, if you must, as laboratory technicians of form, and try to forgive them their bad democratic manners, and the fact that, spinster-like, they tend to dry up sooner than their coarser fellow-countrymen.

The future of American culture, as with everything else in this country, lies with the great organizations—which, incidentally and lest we forget, are still made up of individuals, I think. In popular culture, I expect to see giant diversified entertainment organizations —"private" commissariats of culture. Notice how block-booking quickly reappeared, after more than a decade of movie anti-trust litigation, in network television—which, with its great captive audience, is little more than block-booking. With all our dreams held in these fat organizational arms, we may one day look back on the historical mess of Hollywood movie-making as a great Golden Age— because the director, or the producer, or even the great star who carried the script in his face, was a single esthetic organizing factor unavailable to the NBC-MGM-Time, Inc. of the future.

It may soothe us to imagine what may lie behind *all* the busy mirrors: it is the terror of creation. And I rather think this is primarily the terror of creating more and better mirrors, before the reflection of life, in our unanimal settings, ends. I wonder what else it might be.

Anyway, we are too busy or too vain to abandon the mirrors. I know I am. I remember pausing on my way out of the Loew's Sheridan in New York City some years ago, after having submitted to a real stinker. I shook my fist at the screen: "You win this time, damn you! But I'll be back." And I will.

5

▋ MOSTLY LITERARY

❀ DASHIELL HAMMETT'S PRIVATE EYE

COMMENTARY, 1949

As an apprentice literary critic, my impulse was always to write about life-size fellows rather than to nibble at the giants. It would never have occurred to me to write about Dostoyevsky; and when I did think seriously of doing a study of D. H. Lawrence, the issue was posed as the adoption of a nearly life-long career—before one word was written. (The grant didn't come through, and I went to law school instead.) But I have incomplete studies of B. Traven (1944) and Jerome Weidman (1949) and one hundred pages of notes on John O'Hara (1958). I like the life-size fellows. (The biggest one I ever started on was Byron—because I had an idea about him that made him life-size.)

Literature is like law to me in that both were training grounds. But in fact they have a deeper, impersonal connection: each concentrates excessively on words as such, and together they are the finer-honed tools for grasping the power and sensibility of life if you rely substantially on words. (At another time, theology and then philosophy would have done as well or better.)

After nearly a full life of it, I do not recommend the attempt to grasp life with words. Not words primarily. We are not ready for that level of faith.

On the other hand, what is (I really don't know) a muscular or institutional triumph without a well-wrought line or two of celebration or despair, or both?

About Hammett: He is one of our greatest popular writers since Poe's weird stories and Melville's tales of the sea, but obviously I cannot prove any such horrendous statement here.

(Incidentally, this piece received considerable editorial assistance, more than usual, from Robert Warshow.)

✿ THE FIGURE of the rough and tough private detective—or the "private eye," as we have come to call him with our circulating-library knowingness—is one of the key creations of American popular culture. He haunts the 25-cent thrillers on the newsstands, he looks out at us grimly from the moving-picture screen, his masterful gutter-voice echoes from a million radios: it is hard to remember when he was not with us. But he is only some twenty years old. His discoverer—his prophet—is Dashiell Hammett.

In the chief critical history of the detective story written by a fellow-believer—Howard Haycraft's *Murder for Pleasure* (1941)— Dashiell Hammett is placed centrally in "the American Renaissance of the late twenties and early thirties." Except for the fact that this "Renaissance" started a bit late and ended a bit soon, it coincides with a much larger cultural and social impulse that (except for the Depression and the consequent preparation for war) was the most significant feature of the inter-war period. Culturally, this impulse would include, defined in the most general way, the productions of Hemingway, Faulkner, Dos Passos, Farrell; the critical work of Edmund Wilson; the "brain trust" aspect of the New Deal; and the whole complex of expression connected with the diffusion of Marxist ideas and the growth of political consciousness.

But what began as a revolt of the individual sensibility against the whole ideological pattern allied with American participation in World War I (the great "debunking") ended in bureaucracy, Stalinism, proletarian literature, lots and lots of advertising-Hollywood-radio-popular-magazine jobs, and—another war.

The relation between Popular Frontism and popular culture is not accidental; the kind of mind that is able to construct commercial myths without believing in them is the same kind of mind that needs to construct one great myth in which it can believe, whether it is the myth of Abraham Lincoln-Franklin Roosevelt-Walt Whitman-John Henry, or the myth of the Socialist Fatherland, or some incongruous mixture of the two. And the tenacity with which the creator of popular culture holds to this myth—in the face of all the facts which precisely his "sophisticated" mind might be expected to understand—is the measure of the corruption that this one great "ideal" is supposed to cover. Nor is it accidental that these members of the "working class," when threatened with the loss of their fantastically lucrative jobs, should be able to speak in all sincerity of being threatened with starvation because of their political convictions. For what holds this uneasy psychic structure together for the living individual is that American Nirvana—the Well-Paying Job. In America, a good job is expected to be an adequate substitute for almost anything; in an industrial society, the job is the first and last necessity of life. And American society is not only more industrialized than any other, it also embodies fewer traditional elements that might contradict the industrial way of life.

The ascendancy of the job in the lives of Americans—just this is the chief concern of Dashiell Hammett's art. When tuberculosis forced him to return to writing, it was his job experience that he drew upon; and his knowledge of the life of detectives could fit easily into a literary form that had at least as much in common with a production plan as with art. As soon as he got a "better" job, he stopped writing. And, as we shall see, the Job determines the behavior of his fictional characters just as much as it has set the course of his own life.

The most important fact in Samuel Dashiell Hammett's biography is that he worked off and on for eight years as an operative for the Pinkerton detective agency. Hammett claims that he was pretty good as a detective. (He was involved in several "big" cases, including those of Nicky Arnstein and "Fatty" Arbuckle.) We may take him at his word, since detective work is the only job—including his writing—at which he ever persevered.

Hammett seems to have come from a farm—his place of birth is specified only as St. Mary's County, Maryland, and the date is May 25, 1894. But he received his slight education in Baltimore, leaving school—the Baltimore Polytechnic Institute—at the age of thirteen. His jobs, in more or less chronological order, were: newsboy, messenger boy, freight clerk, stevedore, railroad laborer, detective. During World War I, he served in Europe as a sergeant in the Ambulance Corps and contracted tuberculosis. He spent two years in hospitals; and his disease finally forced him to abandon his career as a private investigator. Until he began to write in 1922, he worked as advertising manager for a small store in San Francisco.

Apart from one tubercular hero and one dipsomaniac (both of

whom are also investigators), Hammett's fictional characters are derived almost entirely from his own experience as a detective.

His first detective stories, built around the nameless figure of the "Continental Op," were published in pulp magazines—*Black Mask, Sunset,* and the like. Hammett was one of a group of detective-story writers who had begun producing violent, realistic material in opposition to the refined puzzles of such old hands as S. S. Van Dine. These postwar stories signified a sharp turn from the genteel English tradition toward the creation of a "lean, dynamic, unsentimental" American style (although, as George Orwell has demonstrated, the English too were solving imaginary crimes in new ways and in new settings). Hammett took the lead in this development.

He published five novels between 1929 and 1933. Together with the short stories written concurrently and earlier, these novels constitute almost the total body of his work. He has been phenomenally successful: his books are still being reprinted and most of his old stories have been dug up and republished. But he has written almost nothing in the last fifteen years. Since 1932 he has wanted to write a play, to begin with, and then go on to "straight" novels; he has said that he does not admire his detective stories. Hammett has been in Hollywood off and on since the early Thirties.

There is an obvious coincidence between the beginning of Hammett's sojourn in Hollywood and the de facto end of his literary effort. Moreover, his job in the West Coast magic factories (at a reported $1,500 a week) is not strictly a writing one; he is employed as a trouble-shooter, patching up scripts and expediting stories, often when the film is already before the cameras.* Until 1938, Hammett seems to have been exclusively occupied with his joy-ride on the Hollywood gravytrain, but in that year—it was the height of the Popular Front period—he was seized by "political consciousness." Already forty-four, he had spent six of his best years in Hollywood instead of writing his play, and thus was more or less ready for religion.

Unlike many victims of the Popular Front, Hammett went on following the Communists—up hill and down dale: Popular Front —No Front—Second Front. We can only assume that his need is great. During the war, he was president of the League of American

---

* This was also the work of Odets and Ben Hecht—an interesting point about overqualified talent in Hollywood.

Writers and as such occupied himself lining up talent behind war activities in general and the second front in particular. He also joined the army. At present he serves as head of the New York branch of the Civil Rights Congress, a Stalinist "front" organization; most recently, his name turned up as a sponsor of the Cultural and Scientific Conference for World Peace, held in New York in March.

The core of Hammett's art is his version of the masculine figure in American society. The Continental Op constitutes the basic pattern for this figure, which in the body of Hammett's work undergoes a revealing development.

The older detectives of literature—exemplified most unequivocally by the figure of Sherlock Holmes—stood on a firm social and moral basis, and won their triumphs through the exercise of reason. Holmes, despite his eccentricities, is essentially an English gentleman acting to preserve a moral way of life. The question of his motives never arises, simply because it is answered in advance: he is one of the great army of good men fighting, each in his own way, against evil. Who needs a "motive" for doing his duty? (Holmes's love for his profession is never contaminated by any moral ambiguity: he is not fascinated by evil, but only by the intellectual problem of overcoming evil.) With Hammett, the moral and social base is gone; his detectives would only be amused, if not embarrassed, by any suggestion that they are "doing their duty"—they are merely *doing*.

The Op is primarily a job-holder: all the stories in which he appears begin with an assignment and end when he has completed it. To an extent, *competence* replaces moral stature as the criterion of an individual's worth. The only persons who gain any respect from the Op are those who behave competently—and all such, criminal or otherwise, are accorded some respect. This attitude is applied to women as well as men. In *The Dain Curse*, the Op is attracted deeply only to the woman who has capacity and realism—and he fears her for the same reason. So Woman enters the Hammett picture as desirable not merely for her beauty, but also for her ability to live independently, capably—unmarried, in other words.

But the moral question is not disposed of so easily. Hammett's masculine figures are continually running up against a certain basic situation in which their relation to evil must be defined. In *Red Harvest*, for instance, the detective doing his job is confronted with a condition of evil much bigger than himself. He cannot ignore it since his job is to deal with it. On the other hand, he cannot act morally in any full sense because his particular relation, as a paid agent, to crime and its attendant evils gives him no logical justification for overstepping the bounds of his "job." Through some clever prompting by the Continental Op, the gangsters—whose rule is the evil in *Red Harvest*—destroy each other in their own ways. But it becomes a very bloody business, as the title suggests. And the Op's lost alternative, of perhaps having resolved the situation—and performed his job—with less bloodshed, grows in poignancy. He begins to doubt his own motivation: perhaps the means by which a job is done matters as much as the actual accomplishment of the job.

One of the most suggestive aspects of this situation is that the Op's client hinders rather than aids him in resolving the evil. For the client is the capitalist who opened the city to the gangsters in the first place, to break a strike. (This ambiguous relation to the client is characteristic in that it further isolates the detectives; suspicion is imbedded like a muscle in Hammett's characters, and lying is the primary form of communication between them. In two of the novels, the murderer is an old friend of the detective.) If the Op were not simply *employed*—that is, if he were really concerned with combating evil—he would have to fight against his client directly, to get at the evil's source. As it is, he confines his attention to his "job," which he carries out with an almost bloodthirsty determination that proceeds from an unwillingness to go beyond it. This relation to the job is perhaps typically American.

What is wrong with the character of the Op—this American—is that he almost never wrestles with personal motives of his own. The private eye has no private life. He simply wants to do his job well. One might think he was in it for the money—but his salary is never made known, is apparently not large, and he isn't even *tempted* to steal. Each story contains at least one fabulously beautiful woman— but the Op goes marching on. If he is a philosopher of some peculiarly American *acte gratuit*, a connoisseur of crime and violence, we never know it, since we are never permitted to know his thoughts. So, while this character often holds a strong primitive fascination because he represents an attempt at a realistic image of a human being who succeeds (survives not too painfully) in an environment of modern anxiety, he is, ultimately, too disinterested—too little involved—to be real.

It is interesting, in view of the importance of job-doing to the detective, to remark the reasons for this lack of personal motivation. What the Op has as a substitute for motives is a more or less total projection of himself into the violent environment of crime and death. And by "projection" I mean that he surrenders his emotions to the world outside while dissociating them from his own purposeful, responsible self; he becomes a kind of sensation-seeker. So, despite all the *Sturm und Drang* of his life, it remains an essentially vicarious one, because the *moral* problem—the matter of individual responsibility or decision-making in a situation where society has defaulted morally—is never even faced, much less resolved. The question of doing or not doing a job competently seems to have replaced the whole larger question of good and evil. The Op catches criminals because it is his job to do so, not because they are criminals. At the same time, it is still important that his job is to catch criminals; just any job will not do: the Op has the same relation to the experience of his job, its violence and excitement, the catharsis it affords, as has the ordinary consumer of mass culture to the detective stories and movies he bolts down with such regularity and in such abundance. His satisfactions require a rejection of moral responsibility—but this in itself requires that he be involved in a situation charged with moral significance—which exists for him solely that it may be rejected.

Hammett must have felt the lacks in the Op, for the detective figures that follow—Sam Spade in *The Maltese Falcon*, Ned Beaumont in *The Glass Key*, and Nick Charles in *The Thin Man*—all represent attempts to give his character a more genuine human motivation. And this attempt to intensify the meaning of his detective was also, naturally, an effort on Hammett's own part to express himself more deeply.

"Spade had no original. He is a dream man in the sense that he is what most of the private detectives I worked with would like to have been and what quite a few of them in their cockier movements thought they approached. For your private detective does not—or did not ten years ago when he was my colleague—want to be an erudite solver of riddles in the Sherlock Holmes manner; he wants to be a hard and shifty fellow, able to take care of himself in any situation, able to get the best of anybody he comes in contact with, whether criminal, innocent bystander or client." This statement of

Hammett's in his 1934 introduction to *The Maltese Falcon* could have applied equally to the Op, except that Spade is more fully realized.

Spade differs from the Op primarily in the fact that he has a more active sexual motive of his own. This sexual susceptibility serves to heighten, by contrast, his basic job-doing orientation. So when Spade, in conflict, chooses to do his job instead of indulging in romantic sex, he takes on more dramatic meaning than does the hero of the Op stories. That is, a new, definite motive has been admitted to the public world, and its relations to that world explored dramatically. But Spade *always* chooses to be faithful to his job—because this means being faithful to his own individuality, his masculine self. The point of the character is clear: to be manly is to love and distrust a woman at the same time. To one woman, Spade says, "You're so beautiful you make me sick!"

The very center of Spade's relation to women resides in a situation where the woman uses her sex, and the anachronistic mores attached to it, to fulfill a non-sexual purpose of her own, usually criminal. It is this situation in *The Maltese Falcon*, coming as the climax of Spade's relation to Brigid O'Shaughnessy, that is the supreme scene of all Hammett's fiction. Its essence is stated very simply by Spade as he answers Brigid's—the woman's eternal—"If you loved me you would . . ." "I don't care who loves who," he says. "I'm not going to play the sap for you."

In his great struggle with Brigid, Spade must either deny or destroy himself. Because of the great distance between his *self* (summed up in a masculine code grounded in a job) and *others* whom he loves and does things for (women or clients), Spade is seldom able to act "normally" in significant situations. His choice is usually between being masochistic or sadistic—unless he simply withdraws his inner sentient self from the objective situation. It is his job that so alienates him from life—and yet it is his job also that gives him his real contact with life, his focus. If his emotions released their hold on his job, he would find himself adrift, without pattern or purpose. On the other hand, the job is obviously a form of—not a substitute for—living. This dissociation of the form of one's life from the content of actual life-gratifications is symbolized excellently by the fact that the Maltese Falcon—around which so much life has been expended and disrupted—turns out to be merely a lead bird of no intrinsic interest or value.

•

Ned Beaumont of *The Glass Key* is Hammett's closest, most serious projection, and the author himself prefers *The Glass Key* to all his other books—probably because it was his chief attempt at a genuine novel.

Loyalty is the substitute for job in *The Glass Key*. And the factors of masculinity are a little more evenly distributed among the several characters than in Hammett's more purely detective-story writing. Beaumont is not a professional sleuth, although he occupies himself with getting to the bottom of a murder. Furthermore, the book ends not in the completing of a job but with the hero and heroine planning marriage. We never know whether Beaumont's motive in solving the murder is loyalty, job-doing, or love. However, because the motivation is more complex, though confused, it is superior to that in Hammett's other work.

Beaumont is Hammett's only *weak* hero. He gambles irrationally, gets nervous in a crisis, and seems to be tubercular. The issue of the masculine code is therefore presented in him more sharply and realistically. Unlike the Op, Beaumont is directly involved in evil since he is sidekick to a political racketeer. His relation to the woman involved is ignored over long stretches of the novel, and when Beaumont ends up with Janet Henry we are surprised because unprepared emotionally—although the development is logical in the abstract. It makes sense as consequence rather than as conscious purpose. All in all, *The Glass Key* is an expressive but very ambiguous novel. And this ambiguity reflects, I think, Hammett's difficulty in consciously writing an unformularized novel—that is, one in which an analysis of motives is fundamental.

The ambiguity is also reflected in the style, which is almost completely behavioristic. "He put thoughtfulness on his face"—and one doesn't know whether he is thoughtful or not. We are given various minute descriptions of the hero's breathing process, the condition of his eyes, etc. Hammett employs the technique, I presume, as expertly as it can be. But it is a poor one to begin with, being too often a substitute for an analysis of consciousness—being, that is, the *distortion* of such an analysis. (There is only one story in which Hammett shows us the processes of thought in his characters—*Ruffian's Wife*—and it is an embarrassing failure.) But just as consciousness is a weakness for Hammett the man (his conscious mind has been dominated by mere formulas—Stalinism, the detective story, etc.), so analysis of consciousness would appear the same for Hammett the artist. And, of course, he is not wrong. Consciousness is either accepted as an essential, growing factor in the structure of one's life, or else it suffers continual distortion—not by accident, but inevitably.

Beaumont's friend, Paul Madvig, is also his boss and his superior in strength and manliness—almost, indeed, a homosexual love-object. The factors that make Beaumont succeed where Madvig fails —in getting Janet Henry—are therefore extremely important: Beaumont has more awareness of the pretensions of higher society; he banks more on cunning than on pure power; he prefers silence to lying; he does not protect the girl's father-murderer but fights him. Beginning with more weakness than Madvig, with defects in his male armor, he is eventually a more successful male because of his capacity to approach the objects of his desire indirectly—to work upon their relations in the real world rather than remaining fixed on the intrinsic qualities that his desire attributes to them. This factor of cunning and restraint, of knowing when to talk and when to shut up, when to fight, when to run, appears, then, as the final fruit of Hammett's brief but not unrewarding engagement in literature. The private investigator's shrewdness emerges finally as more important —more reliable in a pinch—than his toughness (which in Ned Beaumont is reduced to the power to endure rather than the power to act aggressively).

Now such an indirect road to satisfaction must be supplemented by consciousness—by which I mean a comprehensive hypothesis as to the nature of real life, based on as accurate as possible an understanding of the environment—or else it is likely to become frustrating beyond endurance. We can assume this alliance between our deep desires and a carefully defined world *on paper*, intellectually; but can it be *lived?* Or, a less ambitious question, can it subserve the creation of an aesthetically unified novel?

In the case of Hammett, the answer apparently is no—not without great distortion. For Hammett, in *The Glass Key*, got only as far as the experience of the vital need of knowing (beyond the horizon of the job). He then collapsed—quite completely. Instead of following his literary problem where it was leading him, he preferred to follow his new-found Hollywoodism down whatever paths of pleasure *it* might take him. He postponed the attempt to resolve those problems with which life had presented him. But it was, it could be, only a postponement, and after a few years he came upon Stalinism—that fake consciousness, fake resolution, perfect apposite of Hollywoodism—and crossed the t's of his lost art.

Nick Charles, the hero of *The Thin Man*, spends more time drinking than solving crimes. If he does his job at all, it is only because Nora, his wife, eggs him on for the sake of her own excitement. Nick is as indulgent of his wife's whims as he is of the bottle's contents. Ned Beaumont's weakness, which was at least to some degree a product of moral consciousness, becomes in Nick Charles the weakness of mere self-indulgence, the weakness of deliberate *unconsciousness*; thus literal drunkenness becomes a symbol of that more fundamental drunkenness that submerges the individual in commercialized culture and formularized "progressive" politics. *The Thin Man* was very successful, as I have noted. It is a very amusing detective comedy. But whatever the book was publicly, to Hammett himself it must surely have been an avowal of defeat. He had to give up Ned Beaumont, because Ned Beaumont was almost a human being and *The Glass Key* was almost a novel. It is Nick Charles who survives best in the atmosphere in which Hammett has stifled his talent.

❊ THE HOUSE WE LIVE IN

NEW LEADER, 1947

Review of *When Boyhood Dreams Come True*,
by James T. Farrell

Farrell was the last of a great honorable tradition in our half-educated nation—the street boy who gave up football at an equivocal moment and wrote a major honest naturalistic novel instead. Naturalism was the great and vital democratic form of art. I still like it (when it's good)—and I can still use it, if need be, to take the temperature of my democratic sentiments. But the form was upended by movies, especially the incredible effect of movies in dominating creation of the kind of life that naturalistic novelists might otherwise write about. In brief, we made do with reality for one hundred years—and then they took that from us, too. (Naturalism may be dead, but telling the simple truth is not. It is just that there is no longer any particular point in calling this "fiction." Better to know what you are talking about, and have one or two big ideas that you can't shake. Then you inhabit that great new area between democratic novel-writing and working, say, as a reporter for a newspaper or some other big reality-dominating institution.)

Dreiser, I have been told, wept daily for twenty years for America and for Russia; Farrell got up early in the morning— too early, really—and wrote some more about that, and other things.

This collection of short stories (which also contains a full-length play) is Farrell's nineteenth published volume and his sixth book of short stories. It in no way alters the straight line of the author's literary career, nor does it reveal any possible new direction of his. Farrell's method here is as factual and objective as ever; all of the genre will be familiar to anyone acquainted with Farrell's other stories. (The only variation I noticed was "A Summer Morning in Dublin in 1938," which is not a story at all, but a report on housing and living conditions in the Dublin slums.) The author continues his recent tendency of writing more often about writers. The average age level of his characters seems to have risen—it would now be found to lie somewhere between twenty and thirty. The well-ordered quality of Farrell's later prose, which so helped to sharpen the early novels of the Danny O'Neill series, continues to become more and more didactic and distracting in the present collection: it has become, unfortunately, an excellent means of clarifying the obvious.

Most of the stories are connected in a vague way by a similarity in general theme, which might read: When-boyhood-dreams-come-true-better-they-shouldn't. The first story, "The Power of Literature," is a demonstration of the truth that literary success is only literary success, that literature has no great salutary effect on the lives of people. The irony of the story is like a well-scrubbed elephant, i.e., neat but heavy. "Willie Collins" is one of a dozen portraits Farrell has done of a Chicago petty-bourgeois egocentric ass. It has more humor and less strength than some of the others. The longest piece, "Two Brothers," is also the best. Set in the usual Chicago-Irish environment, it is nevertheless effective and interesting. The title story,

about an embarking soldier's last night in New York, is not too good
—it promises more than it delivers. "Fritz," a portrait à la Dreiser's
Twelve Men of a postwar German youth, holds a large primitive
interest which is never fully satisfied. For the rest, there is a sentimental story about a little boy having his dog taken away; a star
basketball player with gonorrhea; a less-than-Sinclair-Lewis sketch of
an American businessman in Paris; a depressing story about an unsuccessful college graduate.

The play, *The Mowbray Family*, is a very inclusive exposure of
Park Avenue Stalinism before the Pact. All of the right elements are
present, and they are well put together theatrically (the play, I am
sure, could be acted much better than it reads). But it never becomes more than a very good propaganda piece. An anti-Stalinist is
pleased that someone wrote such a play.

Farrell writes about common people in a common world, and he
does this writing with phenomenal *accuracy*. I do not agree with
those critics who identify honesty as Farrell's primary quality. We
expect honesty from all serious writers and, within *their* own terms,
our expectation is gratified. (No one is honest "in general.") Farrell
is not simply honest—he is not merely the common denominator of
serious artists—rather he is, above all, *accurate* in his portrayal of
common life. Which is always of some value, sometimes quite exciting and revelatory, and often boring. In his last novel, *Bernard
Clare*, which concerns a young writer's first mix with New York,
perhaps 40 percent of the relevant experience is ignored or left unex-
plored. But the rest is presented with entire, even fabulous, accuracy.

Now accuracy is not the same thing as art, but it *is* a basic material
of naturalistic art. It lacks only depth and proportion to become art.
Farrell, unfortunately, has only a sense of what is important—he
lacks a feeling for proportion. In these terms, it is understandable, I
think, that he should write many beautiful scenes and many mediocre novels. Farrell's basic criterion, as he himself has said, is
"Truth." But what does this mean? When Flaubert made himself
humble only to "Art," did he thereby write untruly? Of course not.
Then what is the difference between art and Farrell's "Truth"?
Simply that a man as artist must reshape experience more drastically
than he would as truth-teller.

This leads us, necessarily if not obviously, to the question of the
writer's audience. Farrell does not write for the highbrow intellec-

tual, as do most serious artists today.* He has said that he has no particular audience, and that it is dangerous to have one. But dangerous or not, an audience is indispensable. Further, I would suggest that even Farrell has an audience, and that it consists of his Chicago self and the individuals who peopled his Chicago environment. They are the ones to whom he is forever telling the truth. Otherwise, why would he write about his own experience so explicitly—this having, as it does, such patently undesirable consequences? If this were not his audience, then he would seek other forms for his experience than the common ones in which they occurred (with the mere addition of truthfulness and didactic clarity). And if he ever seriously undertook this search for form he would find himself, like most other searching artists, squirming in the straitjacket of his *deeply admitted* cultural isolation.

On the other hand, many highbrow writers, if only they might confess it, would like to do just what Farrell is doing—simply to tell the truth about it all. But I sympathize more with their restraint than I do with Farrell's lack of it. "It all" is not that important.

❊ O'HARA AND AMERICA

NEW LEADER, 1958

Review of *From the Terrace*, by John O'Hara

When I walked away from my law career in 1958, I didn't know I was quitting for good. I thought I was just screwing-off for a few months and would subsequently search out a lighter halter. But something inside me knew better. Just to flex old muscles, and to pass the time of day, I read or re-read every word by or about John O'Hara, intending to write the first thorough study of our master of the short story and most ambitious social panoramist.

My choice of O'Hara resulted from three simple facts: I always enjoyed reading him, and I was determined to indulge myself before getting back to the law. I detested Hemingway's dominance, and was convinced of O'Hara's superior value.

* This was a silly thing to say.

*And I wanted to prove, once again, that it was the highbrows'
rotten attitude toward American experience that induced their
shameful neglect of O'Hara. (Their line about him was to say
that* Appointment in Samarra *was "a minor modern classic"
and nothing much since: how many times I heard this slogan-
opinion repeated!) I went to see Lionel Trilling, perhaps the
only highbrow critic who appreciated O'Hara. He told me how
much trouble he had caused himself in trying to undercut
literary snobbishness in O'Hara's favor. It was a frightening
tale. Anyway, it frightened me, and I chickened out: I just
didn't have the money to buy the time to write a book that
could only hurt me. Ah, the darling little tyrannies of free
thought in America!*

*I salved my conscience by going out of my way to write re-
views of his next three books—in the* New Leader, *which pays
a bagle-and-a-half a page. (The first of these reviews was in
fact written originally for* Commentary, *where Marty Greenberg turned it down—I have this in writing—because my
opinion differed from that of the lead review in the* New York
Times Book Review.)

As the third major production of his second literary career, O'Hara
now presents us with an immense novel, with a half-million words as
good as ever, and some of them among his best. The book covers a
span of fifty years. Its elements of unity are primarily these: It is
about America, it is about Alfred Eaton, and the subject is love.
There is no "story" in the plotted sense but rather a historical narrative of a man's existence—going back to an honored tradition of the
English novel—where one looks back over an entire life and touches
on most of what he has seen and known.

It has not been fully appreciated that the offerings of O'Hara's
second literary career—*A Rage to Live, Ten North Frederick,* and
now *From the Terrace*—are this kind of historical novel. O'Hara's
public image is still too closely associated with his very modern, early
novels (*Appointment in Samarra, Butterfield 8*) and his recent stories. In his later books, O'Hara, who is now fifty-three, emphasized
the first two or three decades of this century, although *From the
Terrace* is carried through to the late Forties.

Alfred Eaton is a golden boy of the Eastern upper classes. He
represents all the promise of life embodied in a well-favored young
man—high enough up in the social order so as not to be disadvan-

taged in any important way, and yet not so highly placed that life ceases to be a question of winning and losing. He is handsome, a Princeton man with Ivy League training in manners and dress, and enough money so that he need never work. His father's mill is pre-eminent in his native town of Port Johnson, Pennsylvania (named after an ancestor). Through a friend at Princeton he gains entrée to the just-under-the-top level of New York society. His business career is made up largely of a Wall Street period as a Morgan-type partner and a wartime period as Assistant Secretary of the Navy.

The main locales are Princeton, Philadelphia, New York, Long Island, Washington, and Los Angeles, besides the usual small-town Pennsylvania. Alfred Eaton is the first of O'Hara's major male characters to have left his Pennsylvania home, as O'Hara himself did, and act out his life on the larger American stage.

This is the outside of Alfred Eaton. But much more than before, O'Hara has here gotten inside of his character. In addition to his usual expert social description, O'Hara has tried to give us the detailed history of the inner affectional life of a man who was never very far from the center of what O'Hara believes to have been the American life of our century. An utterly impossible task, of course, but what a magnificent thing even to attempt!

I will only indicate the ground covered in this long emotional history, which I found always interesting and frequently admirable. The story begins—somewhat slowly—with Alfred's lack of father-love, proceeds through self-discovery away from home, objective apperception of his parents, early tragic love, the beginnings of thorough sexual engagement, a single college comradeship, a period of sexual Bohemianism, the passion and disintegration of a first marriage, and a long overly ideal love affair. The conclusion of this history is bound up, ambiguously, with the sense of the title; Alfred sits on a terrace and looks out upon the landscape of his life, and at that point it is substantially over.

Of course one cannot review O'Hara without reference to sex. Perhaps no other writer since D. H. Lawrence has shown such preoccupation with this subject. Although less inspired and less poetic than Lawrence, O'Hara in his work has produced a beautiful descriptive catalog of American sexual life.

From the Terrace adds substantially to this catalog: it begins with reference to a childhood perversion and ends with a lady reputed to be expert with an electric vibrator; in between, there is an incredible amount of expertly described and believable fornication and exotic sensuality, both within and without the "confines" of marriage. The main "point" of the novel, however, is that love is the true basis of morality and that evil people are sensualists who do not or cannot believe in and practice love. This is not a new idea, but it is a believable one.

The development of Mary, Alfred's first wife, from a poised, virginal debutante to an accomplished sensualist is one of the strongest portraits in this richly provided book, and the short description of her as a fortyish woman, completed in her fate, is writing of the highest order. I mention this because O'Hara's commanding capacity in the fictional portraiture of American women is as neglected by his critics as it is unequaled by his comtemporaries.

His men are another matter: He has been struggling too hard and too long with the theme of the gentleman, not of fundamental importance in America in any event. His best male figure is the outsider Irishman, but unfortunately, the Duffy of *From the Terrace* is not nearly as engaging as Mike Slattery, the politician of *Ten North Frederick*. A lower-class counterpoint in the new novel, Tom Rothermel, begins well enough but then is simply thrown away. Rothermel is a CIO intellectual, and O'Hara doesn't like or understand intellectuals (he likes the CIO). Thus, when he does not ignore them, he commits gross distortions in presenting them. This has consistently been a major fault of his work.

Another American facet O'Hara does not understand as well as sex, women, and society—as Lionel Trilling has pointed out, no one understands American society in the drawing-room sense as well as O'Hara—is business. There is much more business milieu in *From the Terrace* than in any of O'Hara's other books. But I am afraid he misses the point. The heart of a businessman's existence is in the action of the game, less personal than O'Hara sees it and indeed often quite impersonal, and always more exciting to the true believer than any cocktail party or any new woman. O'Hara is more interested in the businessman's clothes, his clubs, and his women—he is overly eager to get them into their extracurricular activities—and misses the main thing, the anti-sexual as well as anti-social passion for the game itself. For the real businessman, sex is only one among the many emoluments of office.

From the Terrace is O'Hara's most ambitious book. The unusual thing about this writer is that, through thirty years of writing and thirteen books, he keeps getting better—although this is not quite obvious to many people who are confused by the stardust of *Appointment in Samarra*, anointed too soon a "minor modern classic." In fact, that poorly constructed book, published when the author was twenty-nine, could be fitted in a corner of any one of his last three books.

When O'Hara published *A Rage to Live* in 1949, it was his first novel in eleven years—years he had devoted largely to short stories, of which he became a master, and Hollywood–New York partying, in which he was also quite adept—and bigger and better than all his previous novels. It also was the beginning of his second literary career, which, so far, has given us well over a million words of the truest, broadest, most expertly rendered picture of American society, sex, and circumstances that our literature affords.

❊ O'HARA IN A DESCENDING SPIRAL

Review of *Ourselves to Know*, by John O'Hara

Since John O'Hara started writing novels again in 1949, the continuity in his work has been a preoccupation with the concept of the gentleman in America, and what (God help us all) certain kinds of women can do to him. Even here the theme of adultery predominates, or is pivotal, as in much of his writing. But in his second career—after the Hollywood dunking—the idea of the American gentleman has been nagged and worked to death. His fascination with this character-type is truly awesome. Reading any of the four big novels he has done in the last decade, or viewing them in tandem, one wonders just what he has been trying to get at with these portraits of his dullish gentlemen. Salts of the earth, noble Romans, principled stoics, washed-out bridges between the prewar worlds and the modern, they are finely carved wooden figures that never really get up and move. They are nothing like the vital images in his beautiful and elaborate gallery of women (most of whom are not very gentle).

Julian English, for example, the hero of his first novel, *Appoint-*

ment in Samarra (1934), was well-born, upper-classy, and so on—but a wild drunk who destroyed himself in short order. Joe Chapin, the principal figure in the later *Ten North Frederick*, also drank himself to death—but at an advanced age, and in a quiet, calculated, reasonable way. Something had happened to O'Hara: His own wildness disappeared from his personal life and survived in his fiction almost solely in his women. The result, for the men, has been gentlemanliness—and for O'Hara a value found in the restraint of principled men who are the moral force holding society together.

Ah, but the women! His imagination has suffered no hardening of the arteries regarding them. They swish across the pages of his later works, the darlings, in uninhibited profusion. If anything, the encyclopedic range of female types and propensities in O'Hara's vision has broadened and lengthened. There are agate-efficient social lionesses, middle-aged ladies competently prepared for life's later romantic opportunities, bulldog mothers, dirty little girls, ideal ingénues, madams and whores and kid-sisters, and a full Sears, Roebuck assortment of wives—any size, shape, or class, and in all states of spiritual disrepair.

We have Grace Caldwell Tate of *A Rage to Live* (1949), a small-town aristocrat and fallen demi-goddess, containing an awe-inspiring force of sexual love—one of the most compelling portraits of a fully alive, sexual woman in our modern fiction. Then Edith Chapin, the killer-wife of *Ten North Frederick* (1955), a brilliant characterization, both powerful and subtle, of the possessive woman; and Kate Drummond of the same book, the unreal ingénue who gladdens a gentleman's autumn. In *From the Terrace* (1958), we are presented with the most interesting of the later O'Hara gentlemen—most interesting because drawn at greatest length and most ambivalently—and a complete convention of female types, including Alfred Eaton's two wives, the first of whom grows into a very exciting, rapacious and mature sensualist, the second of whom never really grows at all.

And now we have *Ourselves to Know*, with the dullest gentleman of them all, situated in the smallest Pennsylvania town O'Hara has yet written about and with the dirtiest little heroine in the entire O'Hara gallery. Another way of introducing this new book would be to say that John O'Hara has finally written a whole novel about a man who remained a virgin until the age of twenty-seven. The story, briefly, is focused on the gentleman, Robert Millhouser, who shoots and kills the dirty little girl, who was his wife, because she had been adulterous. He kills her for the same reason that he married her at an advanced age—because he had waited too long for love, because he had incurred too deep a debt of loneliness, because his character required the punishment of isolation. There is considerable psychological insight in this portrait of a disastrously lonely man: The author evokes some of the real quality of the coldness and emptiness of that inner abyss.

Hedda, the dirty little girl, is well drawn, vital, and thoroughly believable: O'Hara makes her sexual evil a concrete human quality. (She is a descendant of Gloria Wandrous of *Butterfield 8* who was ruined at an early age by Dr. Reddington—"within a month he had her sniffing ether and loving it"—but Hedda has no saving graces, and she manages to do all of her own corrupting.) The gentleman's mother is a standard O'Hara woman-of-strength, which means excellent. The depiction of the system of power in a small town is fascinating and has the usual aura of authenticity—not as good as the high quality of the political scenes in *Ten North Frederick*, but still very good, especially in the legal aspects of the crime (better, by far, for instance, than anything in Cozzens' *The Just and the Unjust*). And there is also a detailed and surprisingly sympathetic portrait of an Oscar Wilde or Ronald Firbank litterateur, a *fin de siècle* homosexual.

The structure of this novel is more involved and artificial than any of the previous works: A young man, the first-person narrator, serves as Millhouser's foil in telling his story. Because of this interview-confession device, the story is told in a rather disconnected fashion and, like *Ten North Frederick*, begins at a point closer to the end than the beginning. For most of the telling, the first-person narration is either baldly abandoned or irrelevant; it functions chiefly, when at all, to let the author project the quality of a detective story or a psychoanalysis, or just to be self-conscious about the process of reconstructing a life-story. If one recalls a more successful use of the creator's self-consciousness as part of the narration—say, André Gide's *The Conterfeiters*—he sees immediately the reason for O'Hara's relative failure. In Gide the self-consciousness was integral because he was writing a novel about a novel-writer writing a novel. O'Hara is not, and the self-consciousness never really becomes more than a mere device.

But, apart from its ill-advised structure, the book contains a great deal of value and interest, as does all of O'Hara's work. Though this is the least successful of his recent books, it reveals again that his median level is very good indeed, and has been consistently so over a thirty-year career.

Ourselves to Know will be reviewed badly by the highbrows not because it is the least successful of his recent novels, but just because it is one of them. I cannot think of any important contemporary American writer treated quite so shabbily and with such consistent tastelessness by the "better" critics. (The chief exception is Lionel Trilling, who appears to have been wearied by his thankless, uphill effort to induce the highbrow audience to stop disgracing itself in this matter.) But it does seem obvious now that since *Ten North Frederick*, O'Hara is not improving. *From the Terrace* was not the book its size would have led one to expect and the present effort is even less successful. Regrettably, O'Hara seems to be repeating himself in a slowly descending spiral, and reaching too far for birds he cannot catch.

❊ O'HARA'S RAGE TO PRODUCE

NEW LEADER, 1961

Review of *Sermons and Soda-Water*,
by John O'Hara

"I want to get it all down on paper while I can," says John O'Hara in his introduction to these three novellas. Now that is necessarily an ideal rather than a genuine literary program, but O'Hara is certainly making a manly and masterful effort in his chosen direction. *Sermons and Soda-Water* is his seventeenth book in about three decades. Whatever else one thinks of him, it must be recognized that O'Hara is one of the most serious and devotedly ambitious, productive craftsmen in the country today. At times he strikes one almost as a man possessed. With a mission, that is, to tell or evoke the truth about it all.

What he has gotten down on paper here, in these three long stories, is a passel of evocative truth mostly about New York in the Thirties. The second story, however, is more Gibbsville than otherwise, and is probably the best of the three. It is called "Imagine Kissing Pete" and appeared last fall in *The New Yorker*, thus marking the end of an eleven-year mad that started with a despicable louse-up review by Brendan Gill of O'Hara's *A Rage to Live* in 1949. This story covers about thirty years of misery of two mismated Gibbsvillians—a disrespected young man, and one of the beauties of the crowd who marries him to spite both herself and a dashing New Yorker with inadequately honorable intentions. Pete, whom none of the girls could imagine kissing before his marriage, turns sexually wild soon after his honeymoon and more than imagines kissing a number of the girls. This is a story of triumph over adversity, but Pete's activities in this direction are not the special triumph of the story. That triumph is simply the survival of the misbegotten marriage—through much downward social mobility and considerable accompanying infidelity. Finally the war saves the situation (as it saved many situations) and there is a happy ending—one which I found very affecting, but each reader I suppose will have to decide for himself between its sentimentality and its esthetic truth.

Along the way, we are given a description of what O'Hara himself was doing the night of the country club dance at which Julian English threw a drink in Harry Reilly's face and thus set in motion the course of events leading to his suicide in *Appointment in Samarra*. (Almost all of O'Hara's books since 1949 contain some reference to Julian or his wife, Caroline. In a way, "Imagine Kissing Pete" is the Julian English counterpoint story: Pete McCrea had more reason over the years to kill himself than Julian did, but he lived on through the sewer of the Depression and other disorganization, and he and his wife sort of won out. It's an affirmative story.)

All three novellas are first-person narratives told by James Malloy, who is O'Hara himself throughout his writing; but "Imagine Kissing Pete" is the only one of the three that is at all fictionalized, that is, contains scenes in which Malloy is not present. The other two—"The Girl on the Baggage Truck" and "We're Friends Again"—are virtually straight autobiography, including more Author Self-Consciousness than anything else of O'Hara's. James Malloy as character and narrator first appeared in O'Hara's famous early story, "The Doctor's Son." There are later a number of short stories featuring Malloy, and he appears briefly in several novels (including *Butterfield 8*: O'Hara covered the news story on which the Gloria Wandrous tale was based, so Malloy appears as a reporter at the end of the novel). Before *Sermons and Soda-Water,* the only other long Malloy story was *Hope of Heaven,* O'Hara's Hollywood novel, published in 1938. This book was not well received, and O'Hara seems to have been quite hurt by its reception: He did not publish another novel until eleven years later. I think he is generally quite sensitive to criticism, and apparently a bit more so about a book in which he felt he was revealing himself.

In the present novellas (especially the first and third ones), he has returned to the autobiographical format of "The Doctor's Son" and *Hope of Heaven*—with a vengeance. These two stories—which are connected by several characters other than Malloy—are substantially memoirs. Even in "Imagine Kissing Pete" we learn (again) that O'Hara was "the only boy in our crowd who was not away at college" (page 9); that he was not able to live on his early magazine writing "without a steady job" (page 17); that his forced retirement from night life "was not nearly so difficult as I had always anticipated it would be" (page 71); etc. This reflective, personal tone results in a certain amount of fatuity, but I for one forgive it all for the deep sincerity of the underlying impulse: a very talented man trying to encompass all his experience that he finds significant.

As in all of O'Hara, it is the portraits of women and the more or less feminine sense of social connections that, despite some pretty obvious failings and a certain aimless lack of intensity, induces one to feel the presence of a big talent and significant voice. "The Girl on the Baggage Truck" concerns an aging movie queen for whom Malloy serves as a press agent in and around New York. (He did an excellent short story on this theme many years ago.) We meet her first as a nervous, tough-talking broad who is losing her hold on stardom and fairly anxious as well about her boy-friend—and this, that, and the other. In the end, after a disfiguring accident, she comes through as a woman of character. All believable.

There is also in this story the beginning of the portrait of Polly Williamson, a Boston type of lady of stature, who appears again and more fully in "We're Friends Again." This third story also contains a very nice sketch of Malloy's girl-friend in a "synthetic" New York affair, a minor Broadway actress built like a subway kiosk, and indeed almost as superb as the movie queen. And also in the third story there is a portrait of the woman who is the key, Nancy, the *so* beautiful woman who would "much rather be admired for her brains." In search of this admiration, the beautiful Nancy domineers intellectually and even manages to kill one husband and shape almost entirely the second shapeless one.

This last is Charley Ellis, the narrator's upper-class friend, a drinking companion who went into his father's Wall Street firm although he wanted to write; for Malloy, "he provided anecdotes about the rich . . . the kind of information I liked to hear." (There is so much Author's Self-Consciousness in these stories that we are even given a character sketch of the author's source of information.) But Charley Ellis is a well-drawn, affecting character in "We're Friends Again."

Once again, I got something from this outsider-Irishman's feeling about what it means to be rich (O'Hara is rich now, incidentally, but that isn't the feeling he is writing about). I much prefer his guesses to Fitzgerald's. But also I must confess that his picture of Junior Williamson, who appears as a really wealthy kind of Rockefeller, doesn't amount to much—except a paragraph or two intimating why or how women are impelled to help him get the pleasure he demands. And that's O'Hara, I think: He really knew Ellis, but he had only met Williamson.

There is a curious thing about these stories: I was struck by men weeping. Pete McCrea cries because his wife appreciated a gift, and that is the turning point of his marriage in "Imagine Kissing Pete." Malloy is also weeping as part of the happy ending of that story. "We're Friends Again" gets moving when Charley Ellis produces tears of grief for his dead wife. And when Ellis, successfully married, tells Malloy in that story that he, Malloy, is "the lonesomest son of a bitch I know"—his actress had just walked out on their synthetic love affair—there are immediate inexplicable tears.

"A writer belongs to his time, and mine is past," says O'Hara. "In the days or years that remain to me, I shall entertain myself in contemplation of my time and be fascinated by the way things tie up, one with another."

Fascinates me, too.

6

▌ SOME PSYCHOLOGY

❁ OF BEING AND NOT BEING

NEW LEADER, 1948

Review of *The Psychology of Imagination,*
by Jean-Paul Sartre

*My self-consiousness committed me to psychologizing in all
its varied forms quite early in life. (And there was, of course,
my basic training as a marriage counselor beginning at the age
of seven.) I began reading Freud in adolescence and, in
short order, was analyzing dreams as a parlor trick. My own
psychological problem was quite clear to me—I lacked self-
confidence, also known in those days as having an inferiority
complex. So I eagerly believed that as soon as I managed to
admit all of my faults to myself (and anybody else who would
listen), and succeeded as well in talking myself into the grand
idea that I could do whatever I wanted to do if only I tried
hard enough, I would be cured.*

*Of course, I was not the first modern healer to believe in
cure by infection.*

❁ THIS VOLUME is quite unlike the other things of Sartre that
we have seen in English. There is little of the freshness and excitement here of his series, *What Is Literature?*; and the use of existentialist ideas provides less interest and fewer original slants than in his
analysis of anti-Semitism and the nature of the Jew. As a matter of
fact, despite the still-provocative sound and movement of existentialist thought, the book is dull. It is unforgivably technical and academic. And if an over-size pun was intended by such unimaginative
use of language in a work on imagination, it must be said that this

pun thuds to the floor very early in one's reading. (Unfortunately, the writing is bad enough so that one cannot blame it on the translator.) Other admirers of Sartre will be as disappointed as I was with the Ph.D. thesis quality of the volume. Published in France in 1946 under the title *L'Imaginaire*, it was probably written under the Occupation; and, indeed, one easily imagines the German censor (or the impossible life of that time) behind M. Sartre's manner of writing. This is a guess, but a generous one.

The first point of the thesis is that consciousness is made up of semi-discreet *consciousnesses*, among which there are no cause-and-effect relationships; and these consciousnesses are all intentional. One consciousness is said to "motivate" another. This definition immediately allows for the making of a fundamental distinction between the image, and percepts and concepts. In the image, the object "never precedes the intention" and "consciousness never precedes the object"; moreover, "the intention reveals itself to itself at the same time that it realizes itself." Another important distinction between the image and the perception—which "represent the two main irreducible attitudes of consciousness"—is that "What is successive in perception is simultaneous in the image. . . ." The specifically existentialist view of the image enters, however, with the application of the concept of nothingness: ". . . it presents its object as not being." And, later, he states "the essential characteristic of the mental image: it is a certain way an object has of being absent within its very presence." So "the negative act is constitutive of the image," the image is always essentially "unreal," and "the real is never beautiful." Etc., etc.

Sartre writes about many types of images, and he rediscovers the same essential characteristic in all of them. He does this by continually contrasting perception and imagination; on the basis of this contrast, he constructs a dichotomy of being and not-being, the real and the unreal. He devotes surprisingly little attention to the comparison of the image with the concept. While the discussion of this problem is vague and unsatisfactory, what he seems to be saying is that the image is a derivation of conceptual knowledge in that it "is like an incarnation of non-reflective thought." Knowledge "debases" itself in the creation of the image: on inspection, the image reveals nothing that was not previously known. Debased or imaginative knowledge is knowledge that has "become unhesitatingly non-reflective":

". . . when knowledge combines with affectivity it undergoes a debasement which is precisely what permits it to fulfill itself."—But who or what dissevered knowledge from affectivity in the first place, thus making the debasement of knowledge necessary?

The choice of the word "debasement" is very revealing, I believe. Because it implies "pure" knowledge, knowledge in a pristine metaphysical state, knowledge that is not "debased" because it is knowledge *qua* knowledge, uninvolved in the compulsion to fulfillment. Why this word "debasement"? Why not rather say that knowledge elevates or completes itself when it becomes flesh and bone in the flux of existence, helping to form desire in its effort toward fulfillment? We have the answer, I think, when we notice the similarity the emotional tone of this word has with that of two of the most familiar terms in the existentialist vocabulary: "nausea" and "absurdity." Existence—"reality"—is always essentially nauseating and absurd for the existentialist. And presumably these terms are not used lightly, they represent a metaphysical definition of reality. Existence is not nauseating on Tuesday and absurd on Friday, but nauseating and absurd *everywhere and all the time*, whenever we are conscious of it.

I, for one, disagree totally with this notion. What is nauseating and absurd is a certain metaphysical attitude toward reality, not reality itself. Reality, existence, life—this is not nauseating or absurd but merely mysterious, unknown. And the unknown is nauseating only from a certain intellectual point of view—from an excessively rationalistic attitude that insists on experience having a form which it simply doesn't have. I have experienced this nausea which Sartre emphasizes so much, but I recognize it as the product of self-disgust with my own rationalism; or of a hatred I am not prepared to feel or express—an impotent hatred toward a society which deprives me of my right to live life fully. But it is not reality which is nauseating, only certain configurations of reality, specific events. As for existence being absurd, that is a little more witty and a little more "correct."

Knowledge obviously "debases" itself when it is chiefly interested in being pure and when it is forced to do what it is not interested in, that is, contribute to the fulfillment of desire. And that is what Sartre pushes it to in his insistence on *engagement*. So the necessity of engagement "debases" knowledge. The desire not to desire life, but the duty of putting oneself in a position to be raped by it—this is what it comes to. The real desire is purity, metaphysical certainty.

In *The Psychology of Imagination*, M. Sartre denies the existence of the unconscious in a footnote.

❈ THE ROOT OF THE MIND

TOMORROW, 1948

Review of *What Is Psychoanalysis?*
by Ernest Jones

The problem stated in this little review is a big one—and it persists. Indeed, for my part it is more significant today than it was—or seemed to be—twenty years ago. The closer-in from the stars to the center of man one gets, the more science-as-ideology—as the one exclusive way to approach or think about anything—strikes me as absurdly excessive, an all-too-human form of rigidly optimistic will. Certainly the bloom on the rose of science is all gone for me. As a young man, however, I was a Deweyan believer, and I welcomed all the scientific trellis-work of Marx and Freud and other big men whose thought in fact impressed me for much better reasons than its scientistic frills. Today, I am hard-pressed to keep my cool confronting (or ducking) the mindless reductionism of the going scientism of New Class professionals, which identifies reason with science in order not to be burdened with the former at all on any terms but their own.

Since the very earliest days of the psychoanalytic movement, Ernest Jones has been its foremost spokesman in the medical profession in Britain. This brief essay, re-issued now after twenty years with a short addendum, is an attempt to outline the content and significance of psychoanalysis for the uninitiated layman. While it is often simple to the point of banality, it is nevertheless authoritative and comprehensive, though very sketchily so. The book is probably the clearest and easiest-to-read introduction to the subject that has yet been written by a major figure in the movement: certainly it is simpler than anything Freud ever wrote—simpler, and much less interesting, than the *Introductory Lectures,* for example.

Dr. Jones sets out by sketching the history of psychoanalysis, in which he emphasizes that Freud's "belief in determinism was thorough-going." This is a very important point, and Dr. Jones is candid enough to state that psychoanalysis cannot be dissociated from the whole vexed question of free will. The rest of the book is divided into two sections in which first the content and then the applications of psychoanalysis are discussed. Under the first heading, the essential discoveries of psychoanalysis are stated and somewhat adumbrated: regarding the unconscious, repression, sexuality, dreams, etc. In the latter half of the book, the importance of psychoanalysis for various fields of inquiry and practice is indicated—fields such as medicine, sociology, literature, religion, etc. In his conclusion, Dr. Jones says: "Psychoanalysis is . . . essentially a genetic psychology. It traces the evolution of our primordial instincts into the elaborate patterns of our conscious activities. Darwin established the continuity between man's body and the rest of life on this earth: Freud has done the same for the human mind."

Well, what *is* psychoanalysis? Today, when it is not only accepted but tends to dominate intellectual life, and even competes with political ideologies, it is obviously many things to many people. The most general descriptive definition of psychoanalysis, and the one the largest number of people would be most likely to accept, is, I believe, that it is a movement which aspires to create *a science of the unconscious*. And, indeed, Dr. Jones writes: "The essence of Freud's discovery is his exploration of the unconscious, a concept which before his work was an empty term." This is correct—but let us remember that Freud's exploration was carried out under the metaphysical aegis of scientific determinism. Here we have it, then: psychoanalysis is the scientific exploration of the unconscious.

But what is the unconscious? From one point of view, it is the id—"the fount of mental energy derived from the instincts . . . the quite undifferentiated basis of the whole mind." From another, it is *a collection of thoughts* which are not permitted into the area of consciousness, which are deeply repressed. The unconscious nevertheless is that "from which emanates the energy of the whole mind. . . ."

So psychoanalysis is science exploring the very source of all human creativity that expresses itself through the mind. Science, however, has existed and prospered thus far *on the basis of the fiction that it was "objective," unconcerned with values in their subjective context*. The source of creativity, however—the unconscious—is just this source of all positive values: it *is* the "subjective context" of values. Science, with its fiction of objectivity, has held to one value only, that of creating more and better science: its credo has been "science for science's sake." What happens, then, when psychoanalysis takes the source of creativity as its subject-matter—that is, examines exactly the area of experience which science has heretofore excluded from contributing to its formal structure? It seems clear to me that either science must change or else it will never succeed in understanding the unconscious. That is, science must alter itself if it is to give us the *kind* of understanding of the creative unconscious which will allow and stimulate its fullest expression. This is the point at which science must pay its debt to mankind for ever having uncovered atomic energy—the *chef d'oeuvre* of "objective" science.

❀ WHERE WILL MAN?

UNPUBLISHED, 1966

Review of *The Ways of the Will: Essays Toward a Psychology and Psychopathology of Will,* by Leslie H. Farber

Leslie Farber is a very dear friend of mine. I wrote this review because his book was not getting the attention and understanding it deserved. It still is not, which is absurd. The review was written for Book Week, and finally turned down by reason of that most dread of all editorial diseases—assured "knowledge" of the content and capacity of the potential reader's mind.

How does one describe, in order to recommend, a really important book? There are in fact so few that one first doubts the perception, then denies the presumption, and finally demeans the actual reading.

With *The Ways of the Will*, I will resist all three errors, and begin by introducing the author: Leslie H. Farber has been a psychoanalyst for several decades, currently a training analyst with the traditional Institute in Washington, D.C., chairman of the Association of Existential Psychology and Psychiatry (a group identified with the name of Rollo May), and a former leading official of the Washington School of Psychiatry (the Sullivanian group in Washington). I mention this sort of thing because it is in fact earned, and is generally thought to be significant. I feel free to do so in the instant case because, as I believe, his book is really important, and I would not want the slightest odor of lack of qualification to interfere with the reader's perception of this fact. Also, in a professional way, the book will first be thought of as important because it is a strong attack on current psychoanalytical theory and practice. For this layman, however, the book is to be recommended not alone for its professional insight, but more especially for the quality of language: this is prose of the highest order, equaled by only a handful of writers in any profession.

The author's literary talent, joined with the materials of his special professional work, has led him back to the basic conflict between theology and science. The following may serve to capsulate his starting point: A great deal of the disinterest in God that we inherited from the nineteenth century—*and the accompanying disparagement of everything involved in religion that was not reconstituted by science*—derived from animus against the anthropomorphic image of an *intervening* Divinity: that is, God as the Master Politician of the Universe. It was not those who believed in God who caused all the trouble, but rather those who presumed to speak for—and against—Him.

Science led the attack; which was won. We still suffer inordinately from the awful victory—because the initial loss of the values of religion was so thoroughly identified with the primary gain represented by science, that the latter's eccentric pinpoint view of human life was first taken to be full insurance covering the entire loss. The two earthquake events were childishly confounded. But now that the loss of God is being separated out from the success of science, the rediscovery of primary non-scientific human experience—often desperately called "existentialism"—is again the order of the day throughout the endeavor of human consciousness. (Now that He is gone, we may at last truly understand Him—and, best of all, without the notions of omnipotence rigidly associated with Him.)

The major difficulty in rediscovering the human, in the wake of the devastation of scientific victory, lies in redressing the balance between the definition of man as object and as subject. Science refuses to concern itself with the latter (or even to allow much office-space for those who would). But it is quite willing, meanwhile, to construct models of man as an active mechanism, which presumptively include the "real" residue of man as subject. Leaving aside the more puerile excesses of positivistic science, the primary category by means of which this daredevil science has attempted to encompass and restate the subjectivity of man has been that of the unconscious mind. In order to accomplish this without abandoning the theory of causation, the unconscious mind has been understood as the persistent past (Freud's idea). But there is a trap here, namely, the inevitability of the proposition—Know the past, know a man—which leaves nothing to subjectivity, and does leave modern man still pondering whether and when to see himself as a caused object or an acting subject. Since to common understanding he is obviously both, it finally dawns upon us that the greatest devastation of science has been effected by what we may call its "imperialism of language": even at the genius hand of Freud, we have been forced to *speak* of ourselves as caused object, in our most precious and precarious moments as acting subject.

Where better to reconstitute and make room for the old language, or to begin the creation of an appropriately modern one, than in the psychotherapeutic chamber—that close, careful staging area of man's new sense of himself? At least, so the hopeful layman imagines. Not to disappoint the hope, Dr. Farber (for his own good reasons) accepts the burden—all the while insisting that it is a finely ironic measure of the various misdirections of science that all the risky and ultimate issues involved in the aliveness of man's spirit should have been smuggled into the psychoanalytic office as symptoms of mental illness, there to seek a "cure" through the deft application of word-pills. But so it has happened; and so he will deal with "this astonishing situation" in which even "moralists and priests and theologians are now turning to the psychoanalyst for their definitions of man." He does so by means of a brilliant and subtle series of essays in retranslation, from medical symptomatology back into terms concerning the human condition which can be used by acting subjects. (Thus, his talented sense of language is crucial both for his therapy and his philosophy.)

The chief term is an old and honored one: *will*. "Will has been the category through which we examine that portion of our life that is the mover of our life." Will being the new/old word for the "causality within," Dr. Farber deploys it delicately (and convincingly) to displace large pieces of Freud's "libido" and Sullivan's "anxiety," which are the primary subjective-cause terms of these two great psychoanalytic thinkers, and consequently the persistent preoccupation of the profession (and its patients). Indeed, his primary insight is that "without a clear and explicit conception of will as responsible mover, we tend to smuggle will into our psychological systems under other names—this contraband will being usually an irresponsible mover of our lives." The second most important principle governing the action of will, in Dr. Farber's view, is that the more we will what cannot be willed, the less other faculties of mind —intelligence, imagination, and so on—are available in helping us to come to terms with our difficulties: will ignored or improperly deployed leaves us, in effect, mentally muscle-bound. Also, he suggests (in a fascinating comment on Freud's early statement concerning the famous Dora case), will discussed only through the metaphor of sexuality demeans and distorts both. But his attack on the dominant anxiety theory goes to the heart of current analytic practice, and in his central essay, "Will and Anxiety," he could not be clearer: "*Anxiety is that range of distress which attends willing what cannot be willed.*" Confusing the categories of will and anxiety means that we abandon our best leverage in dealing with our distress resulting from either, and end up experiencing much painful "anxiety about anxiety." We live not in an Age of Anxiety, Dr. Farber asserts, but in an Age of the Disordered Will. He has no single pill for undoing the disorder: but his subtle depiction of the ways of the modern will offers much toward liberating understanding itself from its forlorn participation in the distorting process.

In the context of his enlightening (and exciting) theoretical discussion, the author continuously includes—it is very much of a piece with his method of exposition—portrayals of psychic condition which are sustained at a very high level of dramatic narrative, and occasionally reach poetic intensity. This is especially to be noted in "Despair and the Life of Suicide," a superb dissection—and *rendition*—of modern despair (which includes a close analysis of a speech by Kirillov, the suicide in Dostoyevsky's *The Possessed*). The latter part of the book, beginning with "Martin Buber and Psychoanalysis" (the seventh of ten essays comprising the collection) and continuing with "The Therapeutic Despair" and "Schizophrenia and the Mad Psychiatrist," contains a shrewd and candid picture of psychiatric practice, with the central example being the intractable problem of treating the schizophrenic. In relation to his exposition of will as "responsible mover," however, the condition that most deeply engages his attention—he returns to it throughout the book —is hysteria: indeed, he seems to understand schizophrenia as very much like hysteria-plus-frozen-panic. Hysteria, of course, was the disease that first and most deeply engaged Freud's attention; and, in this sense, Dr. Farber has gone back to the very beginning in his revision of traditional theory. (In "Will and Willfulness in Hysteria," it is clear that he sees this condition as the disease of the disordered will *par excellence*.) The collection also includes the author's rather famous essay on modern sexuality, "I'm Sorry, Dear"—a parable of the well-willed body involved in the brightly lighted affair between the Ideal Sexologist and the Lady of the Laboratory— which is reputed to have provoked more reader-comment than any other piece that ever appeared in *Commentary*.

The sense of the modern will set forth by Dr. Farber—most essentially, the awful, intricate power of the adult educated mind to destroy the body it worships, in pursuit of rigidly conceived wholeness—was presaged, I believe, by the whole mood of D. H. Lawrence's work. But Lawrence was a Romantic—indeed, the last and perhaps the greatest of the Romantics—and to his seminal dissection of the modern will he opposed a massive and overwhelming counter-image of beautiful animal wholeness. Not so the sadder and wiser psychiatrist who wrote *The Ways of the Will*—who did not, like Lawrence, run from the heat but stayed in the kitchen (and may, as a result, have been burned a bit: as who is not who stays?). Lawrence was such a great man that he was in fact *two* great writers: one, the last and most relevant Romantic—projecting not mere landscape, but essentially the inner natural sense of the living animal; and two, the first great analyst of the immense horror of twentieth-century will—our newly exaggerated ability to manufacture frozen bits of "reality" merely by wishful insistence. As we honor let us forgive the mere psychoanalyst who, with a special sense of responsibility, concentrated on what he most had to offer (as merely *one* writer) by way of showing our immediate danger of substituting the willfulness of conscious will for life itself. The grand perspective beyond . . . well, who knows? For Lawrence, the Real Sex led nearly to God; in the psychoanalytic kitchen, however, the "quite preposterous situation arose in which the patient sought treatment for *ejaculatio praecox* or impotence, and the healer sought to find out whether he liked his partner." In any event, Dr. Farber has preserved—for those who can use it—the theory of the Lawrencian framework: in his first essay, "The Two Realms of Will," he allows not only for the modern conscious will that may consume us, but also for that earlier and deeper existential will which is our essential sense of direction in life (rather than our wilful grasping of the objects which seem to comprise it).

The modern conception of will so successfully expounded in Lawrence and now, differently, in *The Ways of the Will*, is so difficult to grasp because we are so accustomed to seek causes that we characteristically invent them ahead of time, and can hardly imagine our participation in an uncaused event. But that is exactly what we must imagine in order to bring some better order to the modern will. The alternative is not merely the absence of the natural spontaneity of the Romantics—that is long gone—but the final atrophy of any ability to act (or remember what we did) without a prior script. (This script, incidentally, tends to be excessively celebrative and ennobling, in a greedy way.) We hardly understand will any longer because so much of our living that we dare to remember is so completely and consciously willed that the writer on will seems to be talking about everything all at once: his subject—like that of love or power—is too common to be comprehended. When, for example, Dr. Farber in his widely discussed "I'm Sorry, Dear" gently suggested that the exchange of nascent affection for rigid behavioristic ideals—the gift to the twentieth century of scientific sexologists—threatened to produce a nightmare of perfected onanism, many disputants in turn exchanged the issue of will, which had been raised, for the issue of ideological commitment to the female orgasm, which had not been raised—except as an example of the disordered will. If life has become so self-conscious that it is about to be equated with the movement from one preconceived self-image to another, then our integrity at least requires that we take note of our own *causing* participation in this process: that is, the action of our will—instead of merely excusing it all in terms of our ideals or anxieties. (Indeed, if we are in fact stuck with this sort of thing as a way of life, then we damn well better have a much more sophisticated conception of will —just to get through an ordinary day.)

In the final essay, "Perfectibility and the Psychoanalytic Candidate," the matter is pinned down closest to home. Dr. Farber is a training analyst, and so responsible in a direct fashion for the quality of the next generation of practitioners. The author had included, in the essay on hysteria, a marvelous little picture of hypnosis—and the enchantment it holds for young psychiatrists. Then, further setting himself apart from Romanticism, he said: "Let us remember that at the same time Mesmer was discovering Nature's magnetic forces within himself, Shelley was augmenting his own powers by merging with the west wind." So how does one deal with young men, while at the same time maintaining a proper distance decreed by one's hard-earned awareness of the idiocies of Romanticism? Along with other things, teach the young men the notion of the *impossibility* of the literal achievement of ideals—along with teaching them, necessarily, the intoxicating stuff itself. (Indeed, without this, "participatory democracy"—for instance—will forever remain a cheap slogan.)

And here the disordered will connects up with its social cousin —our typically sloppy understanding of political power: the analogue of the individual psychology of will is the social psychology of power. In each instance, reductionist historicity—the genetic fallacy of the scientific mood—is an expression of the inept normative statement in terms of causation; and we acting subjects end up churned and buttered as between a catatonically conceived past and an hysterically idealized future. (Like Freud, Marx was also a nineteenth century scientist, with words of causation set to do the work of the will.) And, once again, the young men will exhaust themselves (and destroy their troops) trying to become their ideals; while middle-aged masters spend three decades undoing the short enthusiasms of youth. When—*how*—will this end?

When the power that once was God's is seen to lie *between* two human beings—especially of different generations—and nowhere else.

7

VIEWS FROM A LAW OFFICE WINDOW

❀ PORTRAIT OF A BUSINESS GENERALIST

COMMENTARY, 1960

I had more damn fun doing this piece! The guy liked me, and I liked him (and each of us, in his own circle, known as "difficult"). What it was, we are both arrogant talkers; and since neither of us was selling or buying anything, we just talked— arrogantly. Such zest we had: him to grab the world, me to understand it. I still remember him fondly. At one point he squeaked an incredulous look at me and asked whether, really, all I wanted was to write about it? (Lack of capital is not, according to the rules, a legitimate inhibition—you are supposed to put together a proposition and go out and sell it somewhere.)

In our society there is a money-barrier like the sound-barrier in flight—not how much you have, but whether you finally understand it. Money is mostly markers for the peasants—although women genuinely enjoy spending it, and can even devote themselves to this activity. And it is fun of some kind, certainly, to throw a crumpled hundred-dollar bill at a head-waiter's puss. But very few people who really make money really make it in order to spend it. (To command by actually buying is soon understood as a rather cheesy form of commanding.) For me in fact, money means what it does for most people—an absence of poverty. But I know that most important money in this country has little to do with that. And most people who have broken the mental money-barrier have done so by being near a lot of it and having some substantial sum of it (most

*who have it, incidentally, have not broken the barrier—by a
long shot). I am immodest enough to inform you that I am
one of the few people who has managed merely to imagine the
meaning of money in America.*

❀ SUCCESSFUL CORPORATE lawyers like to be described these days
as "generalists." This new term has a touch of magic for them—it
seems to catch the essence of their drastically changed role in shep-
herding money and men of money through the green pastures of the
new American property system. The word is not derived from any
military analogy, but comes directly from "general"—meaning not
specific or particular. We have come so far along the road of special-
ization and "expertise" that it is now a new and somehow different
thing *not* to be an expert. The role I speak of is really that of a
pseudo-non-expert, since the lawyer-as-generalist must be quite currently knowledgeable about tax law, corporate law, the securities
market, and what's going on around town and in Washington. He is
in fact quite expert about the broadest matters affecting the fortunes
of men and corporations; but his expertness is not attuned primarily
to specificities. So he is a generalist—one of the more significant
forces creating and caring for our managerial system. He kind of
manages the managers, with their permission.

The root distinction to be made here (which of course goes far
beyond the role of lawyers) is between the manager of actual production and the manager of the *purpose* of production. If we were
talking about the Soviet Union, the difference would be easier to
describe: in that special society, all the managers who manage the
managers are hierarchically organized in the Communist party; their
roles are more easily identified. The production superintendent of a
factory in Russia may very possibly be a member of the Communist
party, but if so, he is still under the direction of someone above him
in the party who is charged with managing the purpose of production. In America the distinction is not so clear; and the confusion
comes from the fact that no one will admit that he is doing anything
other than trying to make a profit. Making a profit means making
money, and money is made both in producing and selling goods *and*
in orienting a corporation more effectively to the selling of paper.
First you produce goods and sell them at a profit; and then, in effect,
you sell the profit. The latter is sometimes referred to as selling

paper, and managing it is a very different matter from managing the actual production of goods. Here enters the generalist.

Now, among generalists, each individual is special, and can serve only as a rough example of the type. Yet, looking for a real generalist, whose actual career I could portray, I think I've found a good one.

Arnold M. Grant is what one might call a "pure" generalist, who has pursued his role with a creative vengeance, probably because it suits him so neatly in a personal way. A highly trained lawyer who helped build a substantial New York–Los Angeles law firm, he doesn't "practice" law as that term is understood by most other lawyers who do. For example, if there is a federal securities registration to be accomplished as a part of an over-all transaction which he is engineering, he acts like a client and hires a law firm to do it. (But he acts like a lawyer toward the corporate client in coming to the decision that a registration is called for in the first place.) Of course, he also edits the work turned out by the law firm he has seen fit to hire. The generalist's own staff consists largely of himself (with his briefcase) and a harassed secretary. He has relations, however, with more than one leading New York law firm; and on a five o'clock phone call from him, a complement of several men will be put to work for the night, drafting the necessary papers. The generalist certainly offers ordinary legal advice, but quite incidentally. What he actually does, sitting tense and urgent at the corporation president's elbow, is to guide the asset value and earning power—his truest, most important clients—into that reality of realities, After-Tax Money; with this ultimate purpose of production consummated, his work is done—except for the mop-up job of making sure the new values are not lost.

Mr. Grant's own description of his work is somewhat simpler: when asked pointblank, he says that he "merchandises paper" or "packages property." But most of us need to have the meaning of these laconic phrases spelled out. And to elaborate them is to tell the long, intricate, important story of our entire business system. Most values in our business civilization are represented by various pieces of paper—money, bank deposits, stock certificates, debt instruments, deeds, and other contracts—and the heart of the whole story is how and why the value of a particular piece of paper is established. In our paper economy, merchandising paper and packaging property is the most highly rewarded activity open to men of mind and talent. No wonder, then, that it has become a fine creative art and undergone exquisite development.

Mr. Grant is a tall, trim, high-voltage individual in his early fifties, a man of considerable charm, and a talker to call the wind down. As if to complete the symbol of the special (yet general) career he was to mark out for himself, he got out of law school in 1929—that last-of-the-old-world year. In those woebegone days it was something of a curse to be a lawyer; many young lawyers took it as a favor to work for peanuts or even promises of peanuts, in order to get experience. But litigation was also a bigger thing in those unprosperous days before the New Deal and taxes, and anybody with a license could litigate. Like other determined young men of that time, Arnold Grant amassed a considerable amount of trial experience.

In 1943, he went out to California on behalf of a big electrical outfit in New York to negotiate a contract with the Kaiser shipbuilding interests. This agreement, which covered the construction of thirty C-4 troopships in Richmond, California, turned out to be so complicated that Grant was induced to stay out there to interpret its provisions and supervise operations under it. He worked around the clock for nearly six months—and learned the lessons of a lifetime. (So often a man gains insight or perspective that amounts almost to a spiritual conversion as a result of an extended and concentrated involvement in something, anything.) Grant dates a major turn in his career from the time of this experience as a production supervisor; he began then to learn his trade as a generalist. The primary insight he derived (with considerable surprise) from this engagement was that you didn't have to be a highly seasoned production man to understand costs or efficiency and make actual contributions to production. Without ever putting on a construction helmet, dealing only with paper and job-foremen, Grant found that the "general point of view" could be crucially helpful in the building of ships. He discovered, for example, that it had previously been necessary to rip out the electrical installation in a hull, because the sheet metal—or maybe it was the plumbing—had to but hadn't gone in first. You don't have to go to engineering school to solve that problem—just find out who is responsible for initiating installations of electricity, sheet metal, plumbing, or whatever, call them in and introduce them to each other, and procure a statement from each as to what job precedes what other job. The general point of view is not always complicated—but it *is* always general.

In the course of his California experience, Grant also had the opportunity to appreciate the inner financial workings of the creation of the Kaiser empire, which was one of the first and certainly the most flamboyant in the new context of government procurement together with deadly high taxes. It was his introduction to the overriding importance of public relations, to credit as the true way of business life, and to what he calls "astute" tax thinking.

About this time he was, along with many others in the business world, contemplating the revolutionary new facts of life—the 90 per cent-plus tax rate on personal income and the corporate excess profits tax. It was obvious that money wasn't money any more, and that any wealth to be acquired would have to come by way of capital gains. But the consequences of the new situation were so startling and extensive that, the human mind being the habitual thing it is, not everyone—even among those who were trying—could think the problem through at the time. For example, if capital gains were to be the new source of wealth, then both the demand for capital gains opportunities and their value would spiral up. That certainly meant a new bull market in stocks was in the making—the market was still low, so buy. Grant called a meeting of a dozen well-to-do clients and put to them the proposition of forming a substantial syndicate. They turned him down—and, worse, talked him out of going in on his own modest net worth. He admits that he has ever since been a very difficult fellow to talk out of anything that he has seriously figured for himself.

California looked good to him—the new air travel put the attractive climate within national reach—and at the end of the war he opened a branch office there. He became quite successful in short order. His modest explanation (he is not a particularly modest person) is that Hollywood is like a small town in that news travels fast, and a reputation can be made overnight. He notes another special thing about Hollywood—that the big earners out there live with the knowledge or fear that their days are numbered ("You're as good as your last picture"), and therefore they are under a compulsion to do what's right and do it right away—all of which makes them superlative devotees of fashion. Being one of the first New York lawyers on the scene, he quickly became fashionable. (There is a nice vignette to be written about the popular displacement in the past few decades of the historic phrase "Philadelphia lawyer" by the new and more magical "New York lawyer.") Without disagreeing with Grant's own explanation of his success, I think at least two additional factors should be noted. One is his personal charm and vitality, along with the generalist's aura of knowingness; and the other is that Hollywood was at that time practically a sanitarium for big-income people near-fatally wounded by the new tax rates. They needed a modern tax-thinker, and Grant was it.

He was, in fact, one of the first to incorporate personal income in Hollywood—i.e., to expand the use of the corporate device to translate personal income into appreciation of corporate shares which could be disposed of at capital gains rates. The way this worked—mostly for the very biggest stars—was to set up a corporation which then employed the star, and produced and owned the movie—all this done, however, under elaborate contracts with the studio. These independent companies (in the Forties, not today) were little more than tax and bookkeeping forms, since the studio retained control over everything important. But when the movie was completed, and before the corporation began to take in any income, the shares held by the star could be sold to the studio at a price reflecting the appreciated value of the completed film. The gain was taxed at the comfortable 25 per cent rate. It was a wonderful lawful loophole while it lasted. So good, in fact, that the success of Grant and others in its use led to the adoption in the late Forties of the "collapsible corporation" provision of the Internal Revenue Code, which was supposed to make the maneuver impossible, and in fact did make it considerably more difficult.

Once the gorgeous vision of "capital gains" caught on, however, the enthusiasts became irrepressible. Everybody wanted to be a corporation—and in fashionable Hollywood if you were not one, you were just not with it. Although the high-C phase of this song ended in the late Forties, the deeper music of capital gains has of course lingered on.

But the generalist moves with the time: indeed, he is in a kind of lock step—but a step or two ahead—with the gentlemen in Washington. He is charged with appraising the general situation, meaning the whole situation, and properly relating the different factors thereof. The logic of inversion (the basic logic of psychoanalysis and detective stories) is central to his role: it is incumbent on him to remember what everybody else is forgetting, to look for what isn't there, and to test every proposition by formulating and fooling around with its opposite. Capital gains became such a thing that Grant's biggest problem with non-corporate clients was to get them to take another look at the possibilities of ordinary income, which had been more or less lost sight of in the frantic shuffle. (An entrée to this prosaic approach was to remind the client that there had to be actual *gain* along with a good capital gains plan—that some of the latter just looked good on paper.)

A lively producer, director, or star would come to him in a creative panic demanding that the government take less. He wanted capital gains—a percentage deal, options, something big-business like that. Grant would say in effect, What are you going to do with your capital gains and how much do you want? (It is really astounding how effective simple questions are in this esoteric area: perhaps a generalist is simply the person who retains an ordinary capacity to ask simple questions in extraordinary circumstances.) Invariably the answer would be, I want to be a millionaire—to be secure. Whereupon Grant would patiently explain that in order to accumulate $1 million at the capital gains rate one had to take in $1,330,000-plus; that the safe return on $1 million capital was $50,000 gross, or not much better than $25,000 after taxes—an income that would keep *somebody else* very comfortably in a 4½-room apartment. (The explanation might continue much longer, for the magic lure of Being a Millionaire expires slowly.)

The answer, after that, would be deferred compensation, which incorporates incontestable delights. Grant would advise the favored client that an employment deal with the studio could be worked out whereby he could get one, two, or three thousand a week until hell froze over, which is excellent day-to-day money even after taxes—and as secure as mundane things can be. One of the beauties of this deal, and a great selling point to the studio, is that the difference between what the recipient gets now and what he gets eventually is interest-free money for the studio to work with; and part of the risk can be covered by cheap term insurance.

First item: with x thousand dollars a week, after completing the multi-picture stint, you can lose your job or even experience reasonable failures without undue panic (in other words, you earn the long view). Second item: with, say, $2,000 a week you have an income equal to 5 per cent on $2 million, and you can afford to speculate on real capital gains opportunities as they come along. Third item: your family is, without further question, utterly taken care of. To sum up: it isn't the millions, but the income on the millions, that makes life beautiful. The charming thing about this is that it is still a fresh idea, as the capital gains panic continues.*

High-income individuals are obviously a dramatic part of a lawyer's work; and the ordinary mortal, in his casual or bemused efforts to comprehend wealth and the property system that produces it, finds it easy enough to identify with those anointed ones who possess the fabled incomes. But the real call upon the capacities of the generalist is made by the asset value and earning power of corporations. In our generalist-lawyer's relation to these, people are only intermediaries—the client you talk to is a person, but the Real Thing you work for is not.

In 1948, Grant made perhaps the most crucial "generalist" decision of his career. He was at that time a senior partner of a sizable New York–Los Angeles law firm, and making more money than he could spend. But not more than the government could spend; he says he felt like a slave to overhead. So he in effect walked away from it and put himself on what he calls "50 per cent free time"—meaning he is committed to clients of his firm for only half his time, the golden remainder being available to "anything good that comes up." Plenty has.

He has designed, engineered, and executed a substantial number of big deals—including the purchase of the Empire State Building from the Raskob estate, a $50 million private transaction. But of course there are a lot of people around who put deals together—I suppose a Murchison hears from several of them every day. What Grant has done more especially has been to create for himself a role

* Grant worked out his first deferred compensation arrangement for a leading male star in 1946. The technique caught on. In its annual reports on executive compensation (based on studies of half or more of the companies listed on the New York Stock Exchange), the *Harvard Business Review* states that 17 per cent of the companies had deferred compensation deals going for top executives in 1955, 26 per cent in 1956, and a full one-third in 1957. Quite recently, the Internal Revenue Service stopped struggling and has abandoned its finickiness in reviewing these arrangements, which means they are finally "in."

as a kind of total adviser to corporations—a role which, as far as I know, is duplicated only by similar quintessential generalists and by the more imaginative investment bankers. He is usually retained as financial and legal consultant to the board of directors, and frequently goes on the board itself. His generalist purpose is to alter, orient, and organize both the enterprise itself and its appearance to the financial public, so that the inherent values will be recognized and will become marketable. The Wall Street term for this is "merchandising paper."

The kinds of situations and solutions involved in the process of "merchandising paper" are too numerous to tell about, or even to catalogue. I shall content myself with offering two case histories in which Grant played an important role. The first concerns a leading company in the postwar office-building boom in the revolutionized urban real estate market, which in New York City alone has transformed the face of midtown Park Avenue and Fifth Avenue in a single decade.

The company I speak of is the Tishman Realty & Construction Co., Inc., a third-generation family enterprise (Julian Tishman began building tenements in 1898), which is currently 53.5 per cent publicly owned. Tishman claims several firsts in the new bonanza market—that the 22-story office building it put up at 445 Park Avenue in 1947 was the first to be erected on that street of streets since the late Twenties (and thus started the fabulous trend); that it was the first fully air-conditioned structure in New York City; and, more important still, that it was "one of the first" to be financed by the "sale-leaseback" method, which perhaps more than anything else distinguishes the current real estate market from the ill-remembered one of the Twenties.

Just as people were slow to get into the postwar stock market because of the lingering odor of 1929, although it was a totally different market, so also it took effort and clever merchandising to get across the even greater differences between the two real estate markets. But, to tell the complicated story briefly, the difference from which all other differences flow is the present practice of major corporations of signing long-term leases for substantial prime office space, frequently several full floors. (One has only to stroll up Park Avenue from Grand Central to Fifty-seventh Street to realize that this small stretch is becoming the plush headquarters of the corporate world, comparable to the blocks of Wall Street which for nearly a century have been known as the center of the financial world.) The corporations go for the long-term leases these days probably because they have greater confidence they will be in business fifteen or twenty years from now; the government in effect pays half the cost of fancier, fully integrated headquarters offices; there is no good reason any longer (and a number of disadvantages) for leaving the main office in Keokuk where the first plant happened by chance to be located. Business, as distinct from production, is concentrated in the largest cities, with New York first.

A lease for twenty years with the signature of General Motors on it is as good as money—better, in fact, since the new leases include escalator clauses which provide against rising taxes and labor costs, and so contain a built-in hedge against inflation. Before the era of the big lease, the amount of money a builder could borrow on a mortgage was ordinarily two-thirds of the appraised value of the land acquired and the building to be constructed. The additional one-third had to be supplied out of the builder's own pocket (equity capital) or by means of an expensive second mortgage, when that was available. Today, the mortgage lender will take into consideration the value of the long-term leases as well as the land and building, and so is willing to lend more than two-thirds. This of course reduces the builder's investment—and there have been some wonderful instances where, after a brief period, the builder's investment has been reduced to zero by the time construction was completed.

The legal device for effectuating this marvelous maneuver is the "sale-and-leaseback," which substitutes for the conventional mortgage. What happens is that instead of mortgaging the land and building, the builder sells it and simultaneously leases it back from the purchaser, usually an insurance company. Because of the added value of the long-term corporate leases, the insurance company is willing to pay a purchase price of more than two-thirds of the cost of the completed building—on some occasions, the full cost. The rental that the builder is required to pay to the insurance company under the leaseback is sufficiently smaller than the net operating income on the fully rented building to allow for a good profit. The margin of profit on the leaseback is like an owner's equity under conventional mortgage financing. Instead of paying mortgage interest and amortization, the builder—now a lessee—pays rental. This gives him a tax advantage in that he pays deductible rent rather than non-deductible amortization. In a reversal of roles, the insurance company—now an owner—gets the right to depreciate the cost of the building, which is just about as good, taxwise, as amortization of a mortgage. In the year 2000-something, the insurance company ends up owning the land and building free of any leasehold. (Grant himself half believes the big life insurance companies will finally own the better part of Manhattan Island in fee simple in 50 or 100 years.) This whole financial operation is in effect underwritten by major corporate tenants. It's a beautiful thing.

In fact, it's so good that a lot of people who should have known better wouldn't believe it at first. They just couldn't see it: they remembered the Thirties as a dreary procession of reorganizations in bankruptcy of almost every major building put up in the Twenties in New York City. Many investors were determined not to be burned again. One consequence of this backwardness was that Tishman's stock was selling for $8 million in 1955 (400,000 shares at $20 a share), although the new proposition had already been proven in practice. Two years later, when Grant's generalist work was done, the stock sold for $37 million. Recently, 1,900,000 shares were selling at about $25 a share, or better than $47 million. The $29 million or $39 million difference is "merchandised paper," and real as rain.

How was it done? On one level, it can be said that the existing values of the business were properly presented. On another, that conventional backwardness was overcome by conventional forwardness. But the heart of the matter was the merchandising of corporate values—bringing certain facts about the operation, and their interrelations, to the attention of the financial public. For example:

• People were overlooking the highly important fact that substantial cash was being generated by the company under the guise of depreciation charges. Depreciation deductions are taken and allowed for tax purposes on the theory that as each year passes buildings "wear out" and decrease in value—but in the postwar real estate market almost all buildings, including the oldest, have increased in value. Viewed practically rather than conventionally, this depreciation-cash was similar to net profits after taxes and dividends—and on this basis the company had developed over $23 million from 1945 to 1956 which (cash alone) was $15 million more than the stock was selling for.

• Tishman regularly showed important profit in capital gains on the sale of older properties, but apparently the public discounted this because such profits usually appear on operating statements under the heading "non-recurring gain," which is the conventional accounting designation. It took the financial community a little while to realize that these profitable sales were a recurrent feature of Tishman's business—and that they also indicated a significant upgrading of the company's inventory (that is, the company was replacing not as good old buildings with better new buildings).

• The better this inventory became, and the more depreciation (really profit) that was taken, the more the company's assets were undervalued on its books—balance sheet entries are conventionally set at depreciated cost. With the most successful sale-leaseback deal, no cost at all would appear on the books, because the future profit was based on a lease that entailed no continuing investment, and so would not be an asset at all! Since the balance sheet understated the appreciated value of properties, $29 million of assets actually had a market value of about $70 million.

• In the real estate market of the Twenties the big danger, and what ended up by collapsing the whole endeavor, was that the builder had to hock everything to get the necessary second mortgage and equity money. But in the new market, based on long-term leases and sale-leaseback, lenders have allowed the builder to insulate each transaction in a separate corporation, without any extra guarantees or collateral. So if a particular deal goes sour, other profitable enterprises are not dragged down with it. A very important difference.

The pattern of concealed values was brought out in the open, and the means of trading in the paper representing them were facilitated. First, the annual report to Tishman stockholders was overhauled (the one for 1955 began, unpardonably, with a "Submitted herewith" and went on to the deadly "I am pleased to report" and "It is most gratifying to note") and turned into a potent exposition of the new market and Tishman's position in it. These reports, which are required by the SEC, have come to be recognized as a blessing rather than an imposition, and now are widely used as publicity vehicles. Also, Norman Tishman as president of the company told the new story with considerable effect to the influential New York Society of Security Analysts—and, as usual with addresses to this group, copies were distributed to the market community and through them to the buying public. So the story got around.

Then, the floating supply of stock was too small—only 400,000 shares, well over half of which were held by the Tishman family, employees, and so on—with the result that infrequent trading and erratic price changes marred the market for the stock. So the 400,000 shares, selling at $20 a share in 1955, were split 2-for-1 in December of that year; a 10 per cent stock dividend was declared in January 1956; another 5 per cent increase in December; a second 2-for-1 split in June 1957; and another 5 per cent dividend in January 1958. All this cutting up came to about a 385 per cent increase in paper, better than 1,500,000 additional potential pieces of it—each of which has been selling recently for $23-$25! During most of this time, the aggregate cash dividend was not noticeably increased—although after awhile there were some extras.

(Stock splits—and stock dividends, which have the same effect— are among the weirdest phenomena of the current market. In 1944, there were twenty-two splits-or-dividends on the Big Board, six in the popular 2-for-1 range. The movement hit its peak in 1956 when there were 290 in all, including sixty-five 2-for-1'ers. Again and again, the increased aggregate of shares will sell for more after the split, although nothing real has happened except that paper has been cut up. The whole strange phenomenon is supposed to have started big after a 2-for-1 by General Motors in 1950, when it was noticed that twice as many pieces of paper were somehow more valuable. Cheaper stock and more of it increases the floating supply and trading volume generally—you might say it enlarges the game by letting the pikers in. Tradition has always made the round-lot—multiples of 100 shares—somewhat magical, and cheaper stock broadens the base of round-lot trading. So all by itself more paper means greater volume which, in this market, moves the price up.)

So, complicated values inhering in the whirl of modern paper property were coherently presented, and the Tishman company had an up-to-date coming-out party. This "merchandising" program was not at all hurt, of course, by the fact that 1956–58 were Tishman's best years for earnings. But there's the whole point, for the business generalist, who knows that earning potential is the heart of paper value. He feels sometimes it is downright wicked to allow innocent stockholders to sell a piece of paper, all unknowing, at a fraction of its value. But you have to get up and *move*, to make it clear to the stockholder.

Grant has a firm belief that property must be made available in the proper "package" in order to be appreciated, in order to be taken at its inherent value. This has nothing to do with hustling stock through excessive puff in the selling, or indeed with any of the various elements of a Madison Avenue hard sell. Proper packaging of paper values is comparable, rather, to effective writing: instead of lumping together a miscellany of ideas, moods, and burble, one can, by prior analysis and sensitive use of language, present a rhetorically coherent expression. The analogy to the classical sense of rhetoric is quite apt: by packaging, one creates a rhetorical bridge between the existence of property values and the market for them. (The old word "rhetoric" does not have the same meaning of falsification as the modern word "propaganda": the Greeks understood that it was one thing to discover the truth and something else again to make it known to people not truly prepared to understand it. Rhetoric is not false simply because it is rhetoric.)

Packaging means—to be academic for a moment—both the legal form property values are given, and the combination of actual values within a legal form. As in the previous real estate example, the legal form would be a conventional mortgage or the newer sale-and-lease-back device; the values within the legal form would be land-bricks-and-mortar alone, or those usual elements along with long-term leases. In one sense, the story of packaging is probably co-equal with the history of property and contract law; but in modern times at least, we are becoming much more aware of what this history of our law was all about—especially under the bursting proliferation of corporate and tax forms.

One of Grant's fondest feats of packaging was the "spin-off" of S. Klein Department Stores, Inc., from its parent, Grayson-Robinson Stores, Inc. (A spin-off is more or less the opposite of a merger—an approved device under the Internal Revenue Code for making two companies out of one, in a tax-free transaction.) Klein's is a famous and very profitable low-price store located in New York City's Union Square district. This fast-action department store—which has more than one "discount riot" to its credit—pioneered a number of modern merchandising concepts, including low-overhead self-service, cash-and-carry department-store selling, and what came to be known as the discount house operation. It is a cash business that turns over its inventory money twelve times a year, and has a bare minimum of fixed assets.

Grayson-Robinson is a chain of nation-wide specialty stores which started out in California and is still concentrated in the West. It runs a good business, but has nothing like the fast profitable turnover of Klein's. Grayson, again unlike its former subsidiary, has a high asset value—mostly leasehold improvements on its more than 120 stores. The market value of its stock has always been less than its book value (net worth according to the balance sheet). After the spin-off, Grayson sold on the New York Stock Exchange for about one-third of book value—Klein's sold on the American at thirteen times book.

Grayson acquired the Union Square store from the estate of the founder in 1946. The new management updated and expanded the low-price, mass-selling policies initiated by Samuel Klein decades before in New York's famous working class area. And they made a lot of money. But the Klein operation was, so to speak, under the lid of the more widely known (outside of New York) and less flamboyant Grayson-Robinson business. Moreover, Klein's profit capacity was seen always in relation to Grayson's heavy asset investment. (Following the usual practice, Klein was carried on Grayson's books at cost; and the management prepared consolidated financial statements which lumped together the operations of the two businesses.)

When he came into the situation, Grant recognized that this was clearly the wrong package. Utilizing one of the generalist's first principles—that two plus two seldom equals an obvious four in financial matters—and being a tax man aware of the spin-off technique, he decided to lift the lid and present Klein in its own true package. It took a year of hard work to accomplish this: the details make interesting lawyer-talk, but would probably bore or confuse the lay reader. As an example, there was a large insurance company loan the obligation on which had to be parceled out between the divided companies, and that took months of negotiation. It is much easier to merge two separate companies than to make two out of an existing one.

But it was worth all the work, because Grant's idea about the proper package turned out to be right. From the announcement of the intention to separate the companies to the date of the actual spin-off, when new shares of Klein were distributed share-for-share to Grayson stockholders (and while the lawyer-work was going on), the price of Grayson stock went from $7 to better than $20. After the spin-off, Klein sold at $13 while Grayson (without Klein) stayed at $7. There were about 800,000 shares of Grayson outstanding, worth $5.6 million at $7 a share—and when 800,000 shares of Klein emerged from out of the Janus-head, $10.4 million in paper value appeared from "nowhere." Three years after the spin-off, the range of Grayson averaged about $12 and that of Klein about $18, so the whole fresh package went from $5.4 million to $24 million.

That's an example of "packaging." (There are many others.) Perhaps the concept can be summed up in this way: never sell a pregnant mare for the price of an ordinary horse. Or: the whole is equal to the sum of its parts—yes, but only for the generalist who ignores the *given* whole, studies the parts carefully, and does his own addition.

Grant is so completely the general expert that he can both enjoy and profit immensely from his nice involvement in our property system, and also stand off and look at it objectively. When in a mellow mood, his favorite image is that in our business system we are playing a "kitty" poker game—the kind he says he played throughout college. In this sort of poker, something from every pot goes into a kitty, and after enough action has been had the kitty is divided up among the losers—and you can start playing again. Otherwise, there would be one or two big winners and no more poker game. By the percentage to the kitty, of course, he means to refer to the annual tax-bite, which the government in effect distributes to the losers.

But as with a lot of people these days who are perceptive as well as successful, not all of his moods are mellow, and he is both uneasy and discouraged that Americans are continuing the conventional poker game even after the Russians have challenged us to a much more serious—and exciting—competition. For production rather than merely paper profit. (He takes the continuing bull market as proof of our lack of seriousness in meeting this challenge, of our concentration on paper rather than production: and maybe in his musings he also remembers those wartime days back in Richmond, California, and thirty important troopships.) A life-long liberal Democrat, and active in both of Stevenson's campaigns, he is not one of those in his party who have been lulled or enticed into a spiritual me-too-ism by eight years of Prosperous Nothing. He thinks we're in trouble and that we ought to get busy doing something about it. In the present unusual circumstances, too much business as usual could end up ruining the business system.

It is strong medicine for a man who has prospered under this exciting productive system to stand witness to its fall into ignominious second place. I suppose he feels he did not become a successful generalist, a "pure" manager in the liveliest managerial system of them all, to see "his" enterprise lose out almost without a struggle to imitative and amateurish upstarts. But he is enough of a generalist to be able to see that exactly that is happening. And, like many others in his fraternity, he will ponder the question, *Why?*

❁ A BREED APART

COMMENTARY, 1962

Review of *My Life in Court*, by Louis Nizer

Here, I could write a whole chapter, if propriety permitted. The great Loew's proxy fight of 1957—now in the textbooks as Campbell v. Loew's—was the highpoint of my legal career. Frankly, I was tall in the saddle—and for the weirdest reasons (at least for the way they taught it at Yale Law School). I had the original thought, at just the right moment, that everybody should stop futzing around. It saved the day. Although it was obviously correct, no one was more surprised than I was at how well it worked. But a lesson, a real lesson. The stuff that goes on Up There? It is very much like Life—in the neighborhoods or in the novels. Quite similar.

It is fairly crazy Up There. It was just like living in a third-rate novel—with hurry up, finish it, and get to sleep—that is, the action of the narrative and the act of reading the narrative all mixed up, as with a so-so detective story. In the Loew's fight, I ran-ran-ran for three months—literally logged eighty hours of time-charges in six days of fabooble with the SEC in Washington—and when it was all over, all I knew was that I was tired. I guess that was the true end of my legal career: the next big thing they laid on me was indescribable—so I quit in the midst of trying to describe it.

The so-called "evil" of what I was doing never made the slightest impression on me—to this day I don't know whether it was or it wasn't, and I couldn't care less. I was a professional, and damn good at it: sufficient unto the day. But the over-all silliness—and, sadly I must say, the specific treachery of my colleagues of and in the ongoing activity—raised my gorge to a level of decisive awareness. (I often feel that firm moral prin-

ciple is merely the peasant's sense of esthetics: certainly, in my own life, I have been infinitely more daring and decisive and disruptive in social circumstances because I was revolted or bored, than ever I was in slavish observance of principle: tell me witty stories, and I'll go out on a shrewd-steal with you tomorrow.)

I was twenty-one when I reviewed an early book of Nizer's—and thirty-four when (an overworked lawyer) I knew him day-by-day as a boss-colleague in the Loew's proxy fight. I had enough to worry about doing the SEC-type thinking for that over-the-hill movie-gang without being edgy as to whether the boss-man might finally recall my nasty review of his book written thirteen years previously. Thank God, he never did; things being different today, I hereby remind him of it. Nizer wrote a number of books like the one I reviewed—rich addresses to negligence juries—before he got around to My Life in Court, which was so good I spent some time trying to figure out who maybe wrote it for him. Well, he probably wrote it on his own. But I know enough about ghostwriting, having done quite that much of it, to excuse the question coming to mind.

No matter how much the nine out of ten lawyers who never go to court may deny it, and no matter what legal entrancements they may find to occupy themselves meanwhile, the pure, true, and transcendent legal event is a trial. And the work of the sorrowful 90 per cent consists entirely of imagining what would happen *if* the contract, the letter, the prospectus, or other piece of paper ended up in court. Trial lawyers, the really good ones, are a breed apart. They are like intellectual matadors or fifty-mission war aces. Whole firms are built around a single one, because the mystique of a trial-winner is a great lodestone for clients who are money-winners. The money in legal practice, however, does not come directly from trying cases—and the best lawyers are always those who keep their clients out of court. But every once in a long while . . . the gauntlet is offered and cannot be refused. Then you run for Simon Rifkind or Bruce Bromley, Milton Pollack or Louis Nizer, or somebody who carried a briefcase for someone who was trained by Max Steuer. That is, if you really want to win, and can afford to pay the price. Trials are frightfully expensive, because there are thousands of man-hours of

highly trained work behind the blue-serge baritone who finally initi-
ates what is still one of the great secular mysteries of our way of life
with the portentous, "May it *please* Your Honor . . ."

No one ever told me that Louis Nizer was another Max Steuer,
but everybody knows he's very good—one of the better ones around
today. His book tends to prove this point; and has much besides to
recommend it to the general reader. Properly read, it is an occasion
for some real understanding of the trial man. Haphazardly or
naïvely read, it is interesting, instructive, and even exciting. I don't
pretend to understand why it has become a best-seller—except that
it is good, which wouldn't alone accomplish that; and was also superbly launched, which might. I do see very well why something
from it has already been scheduled for a Broadway production this
fall: television has revived our interest in law, and rightly so: great
trials can sum up a generation, being both political and artistic
events. A trial is the basic prototype of intellectual drama—fuller
and richer than the dialogue: less rational and Platonic, more emotional and human.

My Life in Court is not "one of the great legal autobiographies of
our time," as suggested by Max Lerner. It is hardly an autobiography
at all, legal or otherwise. It mostly consists of a dramatic retelling of
about eight or nine of Louis Nizer's legal victories, but: (1) no defeats; (2) no story of a career; (3) very little that is personal—hardly
anything more than how he managed to get to sleep before the sum-
mation in such-and-so; and (4) it is basically the trial man putting
himself on trial for the benefit of the public, all roles choreographed
by the same prime-mover. The big victories heralded and dramatized
are Quentin Reynolds' libel case against Westbrook Pegler; several
divorce actions including one of Billy Rose, a foot fetishist, and a
John Jacob Astor; a song plagiarism involving the classic "Rum and
Coca-Cola"; another libel action brought by the refugee anti-Nazi,
Professor Friedrich Foerster, against Victor F. Ridder, publisher of
the *New Yorker Staats-Zeitung und Herold*; a couple of choice negligence cases; and the complicated struggle for control of Loew's,
Inc. The long section on divorce is a bit of an anomaly in the book,
since it is a rather broad (and surprisingly good) discussion of law
technique in matrimonial matters—rather than the dramatic narrative of courtroom action. The plagiarism case is effective for showing
how much *hard work* can be consumed in a more or less ridiculous
litigation. The negligence cases are quite good, but are included, I

imagine, because of the author's deep pride in the almost impossible triumphs—especially the first one, in which an unheard-of victory was gained against an obstetrician (you can hardly ever get a doctor for careless practice, because you need another doctor to testify as an expert and they just won't). The weakest section is that of the libel case concerning Nazi sympathies (but most noble and important to the author, who years ago wrote a defense of the Morgenthau thesis on Germany).

The narrative of the Pegler trial is far and away the best of the collection. It convinced me that this trial could stand nomination for one of the most significant of our generation—because, as in the Hiss case, the issue was deeply imbedded in the personalities of two combatants, and was tragically impossible of resolution by a legal judgment. Nizer sees it as a hard-fought vindication of one of his kind of people against a popularly detested troublemaker; and also, naturally, as his achievement of the largest libel award of punitive damages in American legal history. But the true fascination of the Reynolds-Pegler conflict lies in the deeper nuance and profounder inevitability of the clash of journalistic-literary values. Reynolds was one of the most popular, well-liked, big-time journalists in the country, almost a nice Ed Murrow; as Nizer says, he had even had a private dinner with Churchill. (There is an awful lot of name-dropping in this book.) But no intimation of anything more than a popular-magazine talent, with a "Me, the People" posture. (For example, out of topical foolishness he spoke in favor of the Russian Army purges.) Pegler, on the other hand, can hardly be characterized without libeling him—so I won't try. But he is probably one of the most talented stylists appearing regularly in American newspapers. Both started out together years ago in the Heywood Broun coterie. (One of the charges of libel was that Pegler said Reynolds bathed in the nude at Broun's Connecticut country place, and proposed marriage to the widow on the way to the burial—also that he was pro-Communist, a coward as a war correspondent, etc.) Pegler's hatred of Reynolds is almost too understandable, because Reynolds had the kind of success that, in a better world, Pegler (for talent) deserved even more; but that, in this world, he (out of abrasive feeling) had disqualified himself from achieving. Pegler was too talented, even too "serious" in a distorted way: these right-wing hotheads are nothing if not emotionally interesting.

Although Nizer never admits it, in an equivocal way the case from his end was almost too easy. Pegler was the classic sitting-duck for cross-examination: he could get a job, anytime Hearst readers tire of him, as a demonstrator in law schools. Nizer succeeded so well as a cross-examiner that several times Pegler nearly struck him when he approached the witness stand too closely. This goading technique is indicated by the following:

> I found that one of the easiest ways to reveal Pegler's extremism and irresponsibility was to question him about men who were genuinely admired and draw his denunciation of them.
>
> Q. Did you rely on General MacArthur with respect to . . .
> A. No, I don't think he knew head to finger side what he was talking about . . .

The baiting was required in order to bring out the malice which supplies the legal basis for an award of punitive damages—the libel itself was fairly clear from the beginning, and there were no actual damages. Sitting-duck though Pegler was, Nizer showed great cleverness in taking fullest advantage of him. For example, the legal answer to Reynolds' complaint initiating the lawsuit repeated and embellished the original libel (apparently it was touched up by Pegler himself, who published part of it in his column), but Nizer shrewdly let it stand instead of moving to have it changed, because it confirmed the malice and also implicated the Hearst companies more directly: they were finally charged with $75,000 of the $175,000 award by the jury.

One might imagine oneself, in the role of cross-examiner, letting up after awhile on someone like Pegler. But not the real trial men. They are a breed apart. The essential difference was once characterized for me by a man who was as good a craftsman as any I have ever met. I was assisting him in a frantic injunction action and, in a reflective mood, he insisted on formulating the reason he was not a top-flight trial man. "I have the brains, the legal sense, and the imagination," he admitted, staring at the ceiling. "But I just don't have the jugular instinct—and you can't learn that. You have to be *born* a tiger and *then* go to law school." Not just any old tiger, you understand, but one with supple language, an actor's projective sense of himself, a quick instinctive intelligence, a degrading intuitive sense of popular values (certainly for the jury actor), an unerring feel for an opponent's psychological weakness—all built around and serving a tiger's passion to win.

The last case in the book concerns the struggle for control of Metro-Goldwyn-Mayer (Loew's, Inc.), which Nizer masterminded on behalf of the management. He tells the story well—but I happen to know that it is a much better story than the one he tells, because I was a line lieutenant in the army under his command. The fight for Loew's was a massive donnybrook—not comparable at all to a single courtroom action, no matter how intensely engaged in. (The over-all maneuvering did include several lawsuits, as well as hearings before the SEC: Nizer says there were twenty-six hours of oral argument on motions, etc., along with eighteen sizable legal briefs.) What happened was that the great Louis B. Mayer made an attempt to regain control of the company he helped to make great, using a young protégé and a free-wheeling Canadian millionaire to front for him. They nearly succeeded by undermining and then taking over control of the board of directors. The management strategy was to call a special stockholders' meeting in order to retake control of the board; the opposition tried everything in the book (*and* one or two of the supplements) to prevent this meeting—they never seriously undertook a counter-solicitation of proxies, much to our surprise. There was no letup from July until the meeting was finally held some time in the middle of October. Backstage at the Loew's State Theater, where the meeting was appropriately held, the tired tiger retained his fierce devotion until the last proxy was counted, the last vote-counter's affidavit signed. Then it was all over, the "real movie people" had won, Napoleon had not reached Paris, and we all gathered at Dinty Moore's for a victory celebration. One of the kind of things Louis Nizer doesn't mention about the practice of the law is that some of us ended up needlessly insulting each other.

❈ BRANDEIS, THE JEW

WASHINGTON POST, 1964

Review of *Justice on Trial:*
The Case of Louis D. Brandeis,
by A. L. Todd

David Riesman, who clerked for Brandeis, once told me that
the great man's devotion to The Law was such that he regu-
larly declined invitations to dine and talk with President Roose-
velt—during the mid-Thirties, yet!—at the gatherings of Rather
Interesting People the President regularly invited to the White
House, because that would make it difficult for him to get
back to his lawbooks at six in the morning. I have read some
lawbooks (and even got up at six in the morning once or
twice), and so can never forgive the hero's execrable taste—or
ever again view him as a hero.

On January 28, 1916, President Woodrow Wilson sent the name of
Louis D. Brandeis of Boston to the Senate for confirmation as an
associate justice of the Supreme Court. On June 1, the Senate duly
confirmed by a vote of 47 to 22. It was a firm party-line vote, with
only one Democrat defecting, and a handful of Progressives led by
La Follette supporting the nomination. The intervening four months
had presented to the American public a headline-spectacle of a kind
previously unknown in our history. The quality of a man's character
—purportedly that alone—had become a major national issue. Perhaps not until the Army-McCarthy Hearings in 1954 were we to witness a similar all-out political fight cast in terms of the national moral
evaluation of a single individual.

In a rough historical way, the Brandeis confirmation fight was
America's Dreyfus affair. This would have been enough for one symbolic event—to qualify Jews as a reservoir for recruitment to the
highest positions in official society. But the Brandeis matter involved
a great deal more.

First, the nomination represented a major effort by Wilson to entice the Bull Moosers into the Democratic party. (The Brandeis
nomination was "cleared" only—and secretly—with La Follette and
Gompers.)

Furthermore, the major section of the Jewish vote was corralled for the Democrats, more or less irrevocably. At the same time, an immense step in favor of the polyglot meritocracy was taken, since apart from symbolism the overriding fact was that Brandeis possessed a superlative talent of the kind that a community fails to reward only at its gravest peril.

Finally, and perhaps most portentous of all, the long travail of what might be called "the Americanization of the Supreme Court" was begun. And, in even longer perspective, Brandeis' appointment signaled the beginning of the reversal of the then-established perversion of the 14th Amendment—back from Corporatist "due process" to the original "equal protection."

This episode in our history is retold by Todd, in the style of the new palatable history—more or less novelized. In this instance, less novelized rather than more, because Todd is a journalist who has discovered the glory and infinity of real research, and seems to love it. His book consequently relies a great deal on the remarkable correspondence of William Howard Taft, who was a leading spirit of the organized Brandeis opposition; and it is, as Todd confesses, "incomplete," because certain relevant papers have not yet been made available to researchers.

Most notably, Wilson himself is a minor figure in the story, which can be taken to indicate a genuine aversion to easy novelization. But it's a wonderful story, and the author's presentation is certainly readable.

He builds his story around an adequate center—the fact that the Boston-Wall Street upper class, Anglo-Saxon–Protestant opposition to Brandeis relied on the proposition that if they questioned his fitness he was ipso facto unfit, without further "evidence." They had deep difficulty understanding the resistance, especially from their own kind, to this self-evident proposition.

Elihu Root said: "He has no moral sense." Root, the man who, more than any other, created the illegitimate corporate cabal in this country, said this of a man whose outstanding fault was his excessive moralism.

Of ironies such as these, a better book than Todd's can be written.

✿ STEREOTYPE AND CARICATURE

UNPUBLISHED, 1963

Review of *Powers of Attorney*,
by Louis Auchincloss

*The editorial reception of this piece and the following one were
the occasion of my break with the* New York Review of Books.
*With hindsight, I can think of a dozen good reasons for that
event; at the time, I was overwhelmed by one—who the hell
were they to tell me how to write about lawyers?*
NYRB *(for short) is probably the most significant new publication in this country in quite some time. It has corralled the
New Mood and brokered a number of other fashionable forces,
at the putative highbrow level—and that's the best there is with
the growing gourmet market.* Ramparts *is a special, not-really-
unfamiliar type of crap (as are the Catskills of this kind of
intellectual Show Biz, the various Free Presses here and there
around the country). But* NYRB *is something else again: with
the fullest borrowing from the going celebrity system, it represents a primary breakthrough in the power-use of modern snobbery—the first truly effective style-demagoguery directed toward the new intellectual masses. It (or something very much
like it) could even become the* Time, Inc. *of the new redneck–
Ph.D. generation.*
That NYRB *also is a very good literary publication—and certainly fulfills its original purpose of making up for the slack in
American culture so forcefully represented by the dominance
of the* New York Times Book Review *section (*NYRB *was
launched during a New York newspaper strike)—is beside the
point. That is, beside my point: namely, it is not the big thing it
is because it reviews books so well (although using an inordinate
number of Englishmen to accomplish this):* NYRB *is big because it mobilized—even discovered, a bit—the existing forces
of chic affluent radicalism and directed these toward fresh expression. All honor due. But—it has used this primarily English literary thing as one piece of a snobbish pattern (even the
format was designed in imitation of the* New Statesman *which,
happily, was also cheaper than ordinary American printing)
devoted in silly subservience to the New Mood, almost all of
the kooky elements of the New Politics, and to New-This and
to New-That. Which reveals its sources: jet-set realism, the*

current ideology in service to upward-mobile idealism (a new New Yorker). That almost everyone from the old Partisan Review gang has gone along with this, even as fairly junior partners, is to my aging eyes incredible—and therefore significant beyond-compare. Like it or not (I don't believe all of the people doing it care for it in any intrinsic way), there it is. Mobilize modern snobbery, and you have a major door-pass to enter the big-money tent. (You see, the people with money are coming to us to find out what is currently "in": they can't be sure, any longer, just because they have money.)

Louis Auchincloss is a surprising writer. First he surprises you with his crudities; and then with an unexpected insight or characterization. The most surprising thing, one realizes on reflection, is that his subjects are so good but his connection with them so hesitant that one suffers a continually frustrated expectation that something is always about to happen; with the final effect that you are equally surprised when it does and when it doesn't. (I was even taken back a bit to discover, on opening this book, that the current collection of stories is the twelfth volume to be published by the middle-aged Mr. Auchincloss.)

As they say in the trade, a very uneven writer. For instance, many of these stories hardly pretend to be much more than slick fiction fortified with B-1. Then why get exercised about them, as I am obviously getting ready to do? Because he nags me. Because the stories aren't bad enough to be dismissed, just as they aren't good enough to be wholly admired. And because the author is an exceptionally exotic item in the American repertoire—a trained and involved Wall Street attorney, a genuine fourteen-karat representative of the historical upper class, and a persistent writer of so-so fiction who concentrates on both milieus as subjects. Now how can any self-respecting member of the New Class (e.g., me) dismiss such a writer? Given the law and the upper-class background and the intimations of future performance, you can't just call him a pretty good slick writer, and go on about your business. He *is* your business.

Powers of Attorney consists of twelve stories joined by common characters and a common setting, namely, a big downtown law firm called Tower, Tilney and Webb. (I have been told that Mr. Auchincloss is an attorney with Sullivan and Cromwell, and that "everybody" at Sullivan and Cromwell recognized themselves and everybody else in an earlier novel about a big law firm, *The Great World and Timothy Colt:* the big man at Sullivan and Cromwell, one of the nation's leading law firms, is Arthur Dean: the Dulles brothers have been partners there: so much for that sort of thing.) The firm grew to importance under the guiding hand of Reginald Tower in the great past; he had been a surrogate (judge in a court dealing with wills), which is the best ever if you want to connect up with the owning classes. The great old Tower, himself fully probated in the period covered by these stories, remains as a mahogany memory, but the vital power of the going firm is Clitus Tilney, the current generalissimo of everything. All this can be certified as good sociology. Law firms are like that. But the author has presented his particular grand old man as a kind of noble savage of Wall Street, fiercely painted with bold streaks of noblesse oblige. I will have to enter a demurrer here. I don't think they are quite that cute—and I suggest the author doesn't quite manage to think so either (as for actual feeling expressed).

The first and last stories, with Clitus in the center of each, are good cases for my brief on this point. Clitus would like to get rid of one of his partners who is a bachelor and drinks—in "Power in Trust," the first story, reprinted from the *Satevepost.* Well, now, this fellow, Hyde, is a rather common savage of a lawyer—he likes fees and winning cases, and he doesn't much care for all this morality stuff, or the more noble savages who do. Issue is joined over a garden variety type of extortionate settlement claim in a big estate matter: Clitus is outraged that Hyde has taken on the representation of the claimant. Also, he went to kindergarten or dancing school with the widow. So in order to block the "shyster," his partner, he advises the widow surreptitiously and everything ends so well that Hyde's suicide would have been an anticlimax. Hyde not only took on the wrong client just to make money (ugh), but in angling for the settlement he employs "delaying tactics" (ditto). Feature that! The double-cross by Clitus, in truth, is unheard of in the law; while Hyde's actions are standard operating procedure. But the author wants us to compare evils and persons and ultimate purposes. To this end, he provides us with information such as that, at a low point in the fortunes of propriety, Clitus "and his wife went to a private harpsichord concert in an old brownstone on lower Park Avenue." To me, that sounds like a real estate ad, not serious fiction.

The moral ambiguity of the first story (not to say viciousness

pasted over with stereotype) is matched I think by the sentimentality of the concluding one, also about Clitus. Called "The Crowning
Offer" and not previously published, it has to do with the grand old
man's youthful dream of ending up as a benign old professor rather
than a grizzled old attorney. Oh, to escape the hurly-burly of noblesse oblige on Wall Street and to impart to eager young men in
sylvan glades the wisdom that is choking one; that is, as fund-raising
president of Barnes, one's upstate alma mater. But, no, it cannot
be—because it turns out that one's heir apparent plotted the whole
damn thing. In the first story, Clitus yanks the rug on a drinking
bachelor shyster; in the wrap-up story, he foils a subtle rug-pulling
attempt on himself. The main thing is to stay in office, even though
certain noble impulses must be held in check to do so. Ah, but the
whimsy: his noble wife says, "I, too, had a yen to go to Barnes. I,
too, had that fantasy." (I, too, think he should have stayed put.)

The ten stories in the middle are all, one way and another, better
than the two about Clitus—even Clitus himself is more interesting
in his more realistic appearances therein as boss. The second story,
"Power of Suggestion," is very well plotted for the nightmarish
issue of who gets a partnership when. But even though he has something good going, his tin-ear can't hear it: "Horace . . . have you
ever stopped to consider Barry Schilde's future in the firm?"—this,
to the fellow with whom the speaker shares an office! Later on, however, when the nervous hero, Jake Platt, is advised that he and not
Barry has been tapped, Mr. Auchincloss beautifully characterizes the
moment by referring to the tender of partnership as "the offer that
in its very making, carried the germ, already recognizable, of a lifetime of anticlimax. . . ." As I noted earlier, a very uneven writer—
who is very hard to dismiss.

There is also a sketch of the no-talent nephew of Surrogate
Tower, an amusing *New Yorker*-type story (that was published in
The New Yorker). And one about the old office-retainer, the Surrogate's former secretary, who certifies her preference for bygones by
torturing the new no-talent nephew. "The Single Reader," a weird
and engaging effort concerning a diarist, is quite good in the old-
fashioned way of Maupassant. Mr. Auchincloss tends strongly toward skillful, tricky plotting; he has a real talent for it. But I had
the distinct feeling, musing about his technique, that his plot-con-
trivances trap him too often into flat characterization. Not always,
however: least often is he trapped when his subject is an older woman

or a younger man. For example, "The 'True Story' of Lavinia Todd" (from *Cosmopolitan*) is an excellent twisteroo about a bypassed wife who takes up writing as a form of therapy, telling in her writing how and why she was put aside in the course of her husband's success. The wife is quite good, the husband is pure cardboard. The young man in "The Mavericks" (the only long story in the book), which concerns the lower classes of the office, is sincerely well drawn. This is, however, the least fancily plotted of the collection.

What I finally come up with is this: Mr. Auchincloss tends toward stereotype and caricature (notice the connection, in that stereotype is a pre-image not derived from observation or fresh imagination, while caricature is a stereotype broadened, after the fact, into a revealing or at least funny image). This is one of the most surprising things about him, since one would expect this from an outsider, but looks to an insider for the opposite, for precise and distinguishing detail. Caricature, intended or otherwise, is involved in both the best and the worst in the book—the worst being Clitus Tilney's wooden nobility. The best is far and away the caricature of the bull litigator, Waldron P. Webb, who appears in (and rises well above) "Bed and Board," a divorce case twisteroo from *Cosmopolitan*, as well as "The Ambassador from Wall Street" (also from *Cosmopolitan*) about a summer colony set-to between two aging pedigreed ladies. Webb is a hilariously glowing caricature of the lawyer's angry aggressiveness. He is delightfully exaggerated, downright Dickensian. There are intimations of others, but Webb is the one instance in which the author, beginning with a stereotype, progresses well into imaginative caricature. It may be significant that Webb is not upper class in origin: one is tempted to say that (for the author) he has "imagined insides" instead. The point is that the author seems able to get at this true stuff of fiction only through the large keyhole of caricature, but hardly at all descriptively.

Louis Auchincloss does not seem to have very many ideas he is willing or able to express about members of the upper class that they do not have about themselves. He really doesn't have much of interest to say about them (neither is there much occasion for an enthusiastic hallelujah about his insights into the practice of the law—he sees it through a gentlemanly haze). That, of course, is not good enough for big fiction. On the other hand, maybe there just is no news from Up There. In any event, Mr. Auchincloss has an indicated direction when he finishes with his disappointing efforts to share his insider's view of the law and the fancies. He has a comic talent, and a developing technique of caricature to go with it. That is largely reserved for the future, however; *Powers of Attorney* indicates that the author's present efforts are still bogged down with the stereotypes of his milieus, not yet risen to deliberate caricature.

Mr. Auchincloss' failure to present his upper-class people freshly may mean more than that he doesn't hate them or love them enough; or that his talent is not equal to the task. It may mean that they are not very interesting once you get to know them, and not nearly as important as many of us living downstairs have tended to believe. It's distinctly possible. A correct reading of American history, in which the patricians have accomplished so little since the Civil War, would suggest this conclusion. Perhaps all they stand for is safe, elevated consumption. It's a horrible thought—but this is a zany country, and we may finally have to admit that all those decades while we were envying them their security of consumption and opportunity for achievement, they themselves were only concerned with the former.

On this point, a comparison of Auchincloss and John O'Hara is irresistible, even if it means being more unkind than I care to be to the author of *Powers of Attorney*. Why is O'Hara so much better? Well, he has an infinitely superior ear and eye, and a number of other capabilities associated with "talent." But that doesn't satisfy me. You can't understand very much using "talent" as an analytical term. The real difference between the two writers is *passion*. The heart of O'Hara is hunger for what he imagines the uppers have— that is the motor of identification that makes his writing go. Auchincloss either knows they don't have it, or no longer finds it tasty. Maybe you can only desire it if you don't have it—close enough to taste it, like Fitzgerald and O'Hara, but not right in there wallowing in it like the true belongers. And maybe, more profoundly, the secret of upper-class existence here is a uniquely American secret, like the white whale Ahab was chasing or, less delicately, the lead bird that induced such violence among Dashiell Hammett's people in *The Maltese Falcon*.

❀ WHERE THE ELITE MEET

UNPUBLISHED, 1964

Review of *The Wall Street Lawyer*,
by Erwin O. Smigel

Yale Law School is a major source, along with Harvard and Columbia, of the aggressive talent that gets deployed on Wall Street. The system has been so finely honed that one is wearing rep ties and working sixty hours a week before one ever knows what hit one. Anyway, that was my experience.

The school has a great reputation—mostly deserved, but not properly understood. Mainly it's another Harvard, a high-talent trade school; but this essential activity—running an elevated railroad to Wall Street—is carried on under cover of some additional liberalish holier-than-thou educational activity. This is in fact quite useful in making up for some of the deficiencies in one's college curriculum. I wasn't having any of that. The fact is, I was fascinated by the law—that is, the character of legal thinking—and I was fortunate enough in my first year to have two great teachers: Harry Shulman, who taught me how to read a case, and Grant Gilmore, who taught me how to read a statute as if it were a line of French Symbolist poetry, which is what he taught before he switched to law. That was all there was to learn, really; apart from law review work, the last two years are an unnecessary bore and should be joined half-and-half with on-the-job training.

As an example of the college-supplement stuff in my day, Eugene Rostow taught a course on economics and various aspects of its relation to the law which was often described by upper classmen as Galloping Keynesianism 201; so I stayed away from it. I also stayed away from Fred Rodell's course on how to be a stylish writer even if you are a lawyer. Foolishly, however, I did not stay away from the Yale Law Journal. The reason? Greed—pure upward-mobile oil. Of the thousands of annual law graduates, three are truly anointed: the editors-in-chief of the Yale, Harvard, and Columbia student law publications. Also, to a lesser degree, the thirty-or-so members of each class at each school who make the board of editors.

I will write about this in my next book; here I will pause to state, firmly, that the vicious system of physical hazing practiced at elite military schools (as described to me long ago,

with respect to The Citadel, *by Calder Willingham—and for
everybody else's benefit in his novel,* End As a Man) *is as
nothing compared to the mental hazing which constitutes the
core of law school/law review endeavor. Since the only reason
you went there was to be successful, they really have you by the
nuts. Two points: (1) control of the law review process is entirely in the hands of the winners in the class immediately
ahead of you, and no one else; (2) making the review and/or
becoming an officer of it can affect a lifetime career decisively,
and certainly has an immediate cash value on graduation of
several thousand dollars.*

    Calder told me the sophomores at The Citadel *dunked his
head in a toilet bowl. I now tell him that at least he did not
have a spiritual struggle to find out what kind of bowl it was.*

There is something drastically wrong with sociology. Even when I
was reading and enjoying it, I suspected this. In the end, the literary
people who always louse it up are right: what is wrong with sociology
is that the practitioners have left too much of the people themselves
out of their study of society, and this can't be right. I don't believe
they did this maliciously, or even on purpose: I think it was an accident, a monumental oversight resulting from a hurried devotion to
method—that terrible modern hunger to become systematic and statistical and scientific and get a raise. So in the study of society I
think we are going to have to get back to an emphasis on impressions of people, only using notions of large historical dynamisms for
elements of structure. The proper study of man is man—still by
men, not alone by sociologists.

I finally enunciate these morbid reflections because I have just
read an excellent sociological study of me. Well, that's a bit much:
The Wall Street Lawyer is actually a study of the twenty largest law
firms in New York City, and I was for a time associated with number twenty on the list, which was not only last but also atypical (too
many Jews, located uptown, not enough big corporate clients, mostly
liberal Democratic). But even so, I felt included in the study: I did
go to school with, and practice against, the downtown *goyim*. I feel I
know, in addition to the law-review Jews in elite New York practice,
this more important group which we began in law school and continued thereafter to refer to as "the white shoe boys": they wear
white shoes at Yale. (I should also admit that the author had been
through my firm by the time I arrived in the spring of 1956: indeed,

I remember the fellows in the office telling me about the funny questions he had been asking; I was sorry to have arrived late: I was filled with funny answers.)

As a comprehensive description of the form of big-firm practice, this study is solid and commendable: for the massive interviewing and card-shuffling and editing effort involved, extending obviously over many years, it is even awe-inspiring—and mostly accurate. And as a statement of the "logic," so to speak, of the recruitment, training, and career-making of an intellectually distinguished power elite, the study may have range and interest beyond the field of the law. I hope so. For one thing, because our society is such that we really must try to understand our elites; for another, because I seriously believe (whether parochially or not) that the legal elite Professor Smigel describes so thoroughly is far and away the most important intellectual elite in American society—because it inhabits the area where more true intellectual ability exists in a genuine working relation with more true power, than anywhere else. If you would like to see what American intellect and power look like when hooked up in tandem, look to the life and work of the Wall Street lawyer (who, most significantly, does not stay in Wall Street: which, paradoxically, is the major part of his power).

Elite law, centered in Wall Street, is a subculture that is transported extensively around and about the upper reaches of power in our society. Now this point is not lost on Professor Smigel; but Professor Smigel does get more or less lost in the middle of it. He notes, for example, that one big firm had eight hundred alumni: he recognizes that the big firm is in large measure a postgraduate training center and a very high-level employment agency. Few associates ever become partners: most of these men are not "failures" in any recognizable sense, but go on to well-paying and often better-paying jobs with corporate and other clients; and one's "certificate" of years spent at Cravath, etc., is the next essential step after the Yale or Harvard or Columbia degree, even including the law review officership and the Supreme Court clerkship, if you happen to be that creamy. And here is the problem with methodological sociology: Professor Smigel describes the outlines of this process accurately, but he seems not to understand it at all. Or, what is more likely, he does not *express* his understanding of it because he cannot find a legitimate place for it within the narrow confines of his method. This is very unfortunate.

Big-firm law is to be understood only in terms of the profound conflict between intellect and the client's fee, with the latter (as much as may be) firmly in control. The point about Wall Street is that it has corralled the cream of each. The big firm successfully manages this by operating an intense exploitation of the one, and a beautifully elaborate spider's-control of the other. Professor Smigel elaborates the fact that these firms have had to become training institutions in order to attract the top graduates; but he nowhere notes the very major consideration that "alumni" infiltrate the corporate client and thus ensnare it eternally for the firm, albeit at wonderful salaries.

In carefully covering the elaborate ground of recruitment, the weeding-out process, and the organization of work-patterns in the big firm—constituting the bulk of his book—he is, for instance, satisfied with one arguable diary quotation from the early nineteenth century to establish that lawyers worked harder in the old days. The hell they did: besides, law was a totally different matter in those days, like much else. The professor was taken in by the partner-statements about the cost of training of associates (the client pays for it all, with vigorish, even at the lowest level), and so missed the most obvious and important factor in the whole system—the simple, vicious exploitation of associate talent and energy. Now the exploitation in elite medicine is even worse—the big surgeons get everything, while the interns and residents who do the work barely get eating-money and are practically live-in servants—but the rather nice salaries the elite law associates receive are utterly misleading, certainly for the purpose of comprehending the system, presumably Professor Smigel's purpose. The ten or twenty thousand a year is ridiculous money for the work done and hours put in, when seen in relation to the unearned profit to the partners. And there are a number of partners who hardly do any "work" at all; all they do is hold on to the client, which is the main thing (and which is the main reason they bother administering intellect and the training system at all).

The tradition of unremitting hard work in the fashioning of the elite was begun long ago at Harvard. Also there, and also long ago, was begun the recruitment of representatives of the upper class into the law so as to provide a basis of appeal to "their own kind" (who, having so much money, make wonderful clients). But more and more in recent years, superlative brains and other ability were added to the recruitment mix. The resulting elite is nonpareil: if I were still a thoroughgoing Marxist, I would call it the intellectual directorate of the ruling class. On second thought, I think I will anyway: I cannot imagine any really big corporations or funds or fortunes not utilizing the subculture of the members of this elite. It is an important part of American history that as much intellectual culture as our ruling groups have had—*applied to their purpose of rule*—has been supplied largely by lawyers. The Wall Street lawyer (formerly known as "the Philadelphia lawyer") is the supplier to the top. From the point of view of intellectual culture only, and certainly since the Civil War, one may even reach a little and say we have had lawyers *instead of* a ruling class: these servants were *that* important.

In an early chapter detailing his method and technique, Professor Smigel says that he interviewed 188 of the 1,700 lawyers in the twenty biggest firms, and then sought other information "in much the same manner as the social anthropologist studies primitive tribes. . . ." Now why that should strike anyone as a shrewd approach is quite beyond me. Primitive tribe, indeed! The only thing even barely "primitive" about this particular tribe is the money-lust which is its organizing principle, and that he hardly notices. What he concentrates on, instead, is the standard Ph.D.-type issue of "whether the 'free' nature of the profession is threatened by the growth of the large law firm"—that is, Individuality vs. the Large Organization. He finally decides that the individual lawyer remains an individual even in the big firm because recruitment and weeding-out produce a homogeneous type and because high-class thinking is necessary and therefore welcomed in elite law, all of which leads to something he calls "creative conformity." And besides, I might add, if they weren't good, there are a number of fast Jews around town (maybe Italians, too, nowadays) who would be pleased to knock over their clients—as they used to in the old days, the great old golden days of the giant-killer stockholders' derivative suit undertaken by the likes of Max Steuer and David Podell, who were so good at it that Wall Street passed a law against it. If organizational fat ever comes to dominate the big firms, it will be because they have secured for their corporate clients a few too many protective statutes of this kind. (Otherwise, when Big X Corporation gets in real trouble, it will again bypass the retainer firm and, as in the old days, send out a call for "a smart Jew lawyer"—many of whom, incidentally, are not really Jewish at all, just smart. But *very* smart.)

He missed so many of the really important "inner" points—and I notice that I am having so much nostalgic fun reminiscing—that I will have to bring myself to an arbitrary halt. But just this last one, on his Big Issue of the independence of the individual in the large firm: Who needs it? Actually, it's very easy to be independent—and you thereby become a mark for more and harder work. And if you are as smart as you have to be to carry the load, it will soon occur to you that since you are not getting any more of the fee for your effort, maybe you are not as smart as you thought you were. From which, along with the natural incompetence of some others, is derived the elaborate arsenal of gold-bricking and corner-cutting which no one seems to have mentioned to Professor Smigel. In *his* Wall Street firm, every associate privileged to do so nibbles on the partner-carrot all day long, seven days a week. Oh, yeah? There were a few finks; but mostly the partner-thing was for golden boys and operators, and a few men who were not smart enough to realize they were killing themselves for a carrot. (Maybe *that's* why there are so many alumni.)

I could go on and on supplying elements of the soul that is missing from this book. Or I could retrace my steps in a more strenuous effort to do justice to Professor Smigel's great effort and considerable descriptive achievement. But instead I will conclude by restating my main proposition: What is really wrong with sociology is the frightful yearning for *structural* truth that it honors and encourages, whereby the revealing and really important *textural* details of human living are actually suppressed, even when known. This inevitably makes the work-product official and apologetic. I cannot abide this kind of perception: it is so decisively wrong as to be downright objectionable. On any reasonable view, on any human scale, sociologists express and suppress inversely. *The selective principle is exactly wrong,* so that they are saved if at all only by their inability to observe it perfectly. They are not dull or stupid: they are bull-headed. Or, more precisely, professional about life itself—an unforgivable sin.

(This being a short review, compared to some of the briefs I have written, I am reminded of the most grating line of all in New York practice: nine out of ten times when I was lucky enough to be waiting for the home-going elevator at 5:30, some guy would rush past me with his arms full of papers and smile a colleague-sort-of-smile— "What's wrong—*half*-day today, Dave?")

❀ LEGAL SURVEY

COMMENTARY, 1967

Review of *The Lawyers*, by Martin Mayer

No comment. (This guy and me don't like each other: I tried to be fair.)

With this sizable book representing a six-year effort, Martin Mayer takes his dearly earned place as America's leading amateur lawyer. When he wrote his book about advertising people, Mr. Mayer did not have to become an advertising man himself. Nor did he, in my recollection, exert himself to touch all bases (anyway, compared to advertising men, lawyers have more bases than Ty Cobb chasing Jackie Robinson for decades could touch). We may suppose, then, that law compels Mr. Mayer more deeply than advertising; and we may just note (though I detest this kind of irresistible psychoanalytic thing) that both his parents are lawyers—which suggests, of course, that to become a lawyer (without jeopardizing his amateur status) he did not have to go to law school—for the good and sufficient reason that he had been raised in one.

Mr. Mayer has attempted a comprehensive survey not only of lawyer activity—how much money in negligence practice, how many lawyers in Washington, what a night school is like, etc.—but something like a survey of the law itself. It must be a hundred years or more since any single legal scholar has undertaken a *survey*, as distinct from a characterization, of American law with examples. We have some encyclopedias in the law, but they run to dozens of oversized volumes, and have little status among the better technicians. By its very nature, the law cannot be surveyed; it makes sense, if at all, only as it is *given* sense—most often through an argument in a particular case, or, in law-review/treatise work covering a larger problem or an entire field, through a consistent prejudice which lawyers like to call a "policy argument." What then is Mr. Mayer's argument? I am kindest to him if I say that I do not find any in the book that is consistent or coherent; but I start to be unkind if I say that the book is swarming with the kind of practice-argumentation that one can overhear at any time of day or night in any good law-school dormitory (this being far and away the primary educating factor in the initial training of a lawyer).

The Lawyers starts with a general introductory chapter with a barrage of fascinating facts about the profession. *Did you know that* . . .

• An estimated $4 billion was spent on legal services in 1966?

• Three-fifths of the lawyers in New York City are Jewish?

• Lawyers live longer than most people?

• Although their business is drafting contracts, 55 per cent of law partnerships are governed by unwritten understandings? (This is the best fact in the whole book, by far.)

• A leading Boston lawyer took cash instead of stock—on a collection job in the early days—from Henry Ford, yet?

• The median annual income of 300,000 lawyers was $13,000 in 1966?

• The "right" price for an average lawyer's time is $25 an hour?

Throughout *The Lawyers*, Mr. Mayer gives us a lot of this sort of thing (including a whole chapter on law publishers, which is fresh and excellent). But the defect of this virtue is that Mr. Mayer's approach to the law is merely inquisitive, and based merely on his own energetic eccentricity. Thus, in his chapter, "The Business of the Courts," a cause of action is defined in one helpful sentence, and motions are dealt with by means of a complaining quotation from a former judge and the author's timely reminder that the key to successful motion practice is the Christmas present to the clerk. In his chapter on torts, the nature of "loss of consortium" is firmly fixed in mind with the parenthetical remark that it is "a fancy word for sexual intercourse: courts have even worried deeply about how much a wife is entitled to if her husband's accident deprived him of one testicle." Tax lawyers are concentrated in New York City, we are told, "because taxes and the money market are closely related." (Nothing else?) The Robinson-Patman Act gets two paragraphs in which space is found to note the FTC's "lawyer-like ignorance of the significance of actual marketing practices" but no space is found to mention the political reasons for the initial passage or subsequent immovability of this absurd statute, nor is there any mention of the presence of numerous economists on the Commission's staff.

The most characteristic fault of this book is the presentation of a fact or a statement which presumes to inform us as to law and lawyers, but which in truth misleads through inadequacy. Here is one example of many: "Associates may talk to clients, but they are almost never authorized to sign letters of opinion." Associates (i.e., non-partner attorneys) do indeed spend long hours talking to clients and writing letters, all of which has nothing to do with signing opinion letters (which they also write). An opinion letter is the basis of a malpractice action, like an accountant's certificate; it is always signed in the firm name by a partner identified as such, to ensure the firm's liability; no client in his right mind would accept an opinion letter (they are expensive) signed by a non-partner, because such a signature would leave open the factual issue of authorization in a subsequent malpractice suit. Now my point is that Mr. Mayer should not have included this fact without an explanation; in the absence of the latter, nobody is being informed of anything, and the statement as it stands is a senseless *non sequitur*.

And then there is Mr. Mayer's famous quotesmanship. To be succinct, the talent he displays is in the gathering, not in the deploying. It fascinates me that, as a journalist, he uses quotes the way a mediocre win-the-argument lawyer cites cases—except that he usually argues both sides of each case. This frequently enables him, with a wordy show of fairness, to give a double Bronx cheer to single aspects of the profession. On many other occasions, the point of this Indian-giving method of composition seems merely to be the obvious convenience it offers the harassed writer actually to use all the index cards he has collected. Mr. Mayer's gathering-instinct is catholic, to say the least; and while I personally have no prejudice against gossip, I did wonder occasionally about its value to the lay reader; anyway, many of the juxtapositions are jarring even when the word-of-mouth or library quotes are individually intriguing.

I don't mean to suggest that Mr. Mayer doesn't have his own opinions on a great range of matters connected with law and lawyers —even a good number that are not subsequently retracted. Here, I am the eccentric: my problem is that I just don't agree with very many of them. For example, he follows Alexander Bickel on reapportionment, and seems to favor Herbert Wechsler in criminal law: I did not, do not, and will not. But there are also a good many straightforward views expressed which I would both hope and expect that very few lawyers might consider acceptable. Most spectacularly, Mr. Mayer finds the presumption of innocence functioning primarily to inhibit intelligent discussion of crime; and he assures us that

95 per cent of adult defendants in serious cases "have unquestionably done *something* for which they could properly be punished by
law" (his emphasis). Nor are matters any better in civil litigation—
"where both sides are usually more or less right" (my emphasis, this
time). Not only lawyers but numerous philosophers are apt to object
to his definition of justice—"The only possible operational definition of the word says that justice is the visceral reaction of informed
people." In fact, he is generally bilious toward the entire adversary
system. Deal-making, maneuvering, etc., before trial (and plea-
bargaining in criminal law) he everywhere takes as evidence that
trials aren't important anyway. This reveals such a profound misunderstanding of the essentially symbolic nature of the legal system,
the role of lawyers in it, and its role in society, that one is almost
embarrassed at taking the book seriously at all.

If we think of a book as something more than a collection of
interesting facts and quoted opinions, then *The Lawyers* must be
judged a monumental failure. In America, we are all trained from an
early age to make do without ideas, with facts alone. This has been
the essence of our journalism—and much else besides—and nowhere
can the method have been more monstrously misapplied (by one of
its most expert devotees) than in *The Lawyers*. One simply cannot
write about the law without a unifying idea—or at least the serious
search for such an idea. And unifying ideas about the law do not
come as a gift in this country, because we have practically no juris-
prudence: we have the reminiscences of technicians and Big Bosses,
a handful of literate judges, scores of brilliant professors in special
areas (few writers among them), Roscoe Pound, and David Riesman. Hardly a tradition. And Martin Mayer has not managed on his
own to make up for the lack of it.

Saddest fact of all, he clearly has a deep and complicated feeling
for the subject, which I honor. But I must aggressively suggest—recalling that we are noting the failure of a method, not a man—that
this most earnest, hard-worked expression of the feeling resulted in
an impossible and dangerously misleading book.

❧ CLIENTS AGAINST LAWYERS

HARPER'S, 1967

> *This is the cute half of a not altogether cute piece I wrote about my legal career for* Esquire *in 1963. The other part is now serving as a jumping-off point for a new book, a strenuously serio-comic effort to explain the nature of the law to laymen, as I discovered it—me, basically a layman even with a good degree and training—and to make a point or two about the relevance of lawyering in this particular nation.*

What happens between lawyer and client today goes something like this: The lawyer sits at the elbow of the businessman while contracts are being negotiated, that is, while a deal is being made. Then, once the principals feel an agreement has been concluded, the lawyers assure them it has not. After much further negotiation, the lawyers "draft the contract"—*reduce the deal to written law*—and pass it back and forth accompanied in each passage by increasingly minute argumentation (e.g., "We believe in all fairness that the law of Luxembourg should govern in the event of non-performance under Para. V [c] [ii]" etc., etc.). Once they have decided that neither party can be further hoodwinked or bullied, the typist prepares many copies to make "doubly sure" (making doubly sure in this special fashion is 28 per cent of law practice), and the clients sign all of them. Then they smile at each other and shake hands, while glancing sidelong at their lawyers, who are still scowling (it's part of the fee-action). This little drama, in numerous manifestations, is the beginning of law—perhaps, even, the final heart of it as well.

Lawyers and clients don't really like one another. Oh, they *act* friendly enough—they play golf, eat and drink, nightclub together, and so on. But they really *can't* like each other: the forces that bring them together preclude it. The client owns things or has power or both, but he comes to the lawyer because he needs the latter's brains and savvy to protect and otherwise make sense out of what he owns or controls. In brief, the client feels, If you're so smart, why aren't you rich? While the lawyer (knowing that this is the way the other feels) reverses the proposition and replies silently, Since you're so rich, why aren't you smart enough to do without me?

There is another aspect to the relation. A very smart lawyer* once advised me about going to law school. "Don't," he said. "You'll get terribly bored with it. It won't hold you, intellectually." I tried to explain how ambitious I was trying to be; that I was already fairly well bored with being an unplaced, general-purpose intellectual; and I added, somewhat petulantly, that everybody had always said I would make a good lawyer.

"Okay," he said, "but go home and ask yourself one question, very seriously—are you a big enough son of a bitch? Because that's really what it takes—not to practice law, but to like it. The lawyer is a kind of witch-doctor, a shaman, to the American businessman. The client comes to you feeling guilty about what he's done or is getting ready to do, and one of the things he is paying you for is to carry his guilt for him. He's going to leave that in your office with the rest of his problem, with the technical part of it. The only satisfied client is the one who has convinced himself—with your help—that *you* are the thief, the conniver, the guilty party. You have to be a very aggressive son of a bitch to put up with that sort of thing. And unlike a psychoanalyst, you know, you're stuck with the projection—you don't get a chance to straighten him out later on."

He was right, too, as I later found out. Anyway, I went home and thought about it, realizing with some embarrassment why it was that everybody had always said I would make a good lawyer, and I ended up convincing myself that the law was the only safe place for somebody with my special talents. As it turned out, compared to the very best in the field, I was only moderately well qualified. I may say, moreover, that I used up all my meanness during my time in the law and have been a sweet, gentle, irrelevant, all-purpose intellectual ever since.

Once in practice, my comprehension of the client took a very practical turn, since I did not find myself with a great deal of time for sociological speculation. While learning my trade I did note, however, that clients lie a great deal. In the arduous process of preparing for trial, for example, half the show is to entice your own man into revealing more than selected items of the story, and doing so sooner rather than later. A smart young lawyer soon recognizes what lies behind his client's faulty memory and other fumbling: the guy is

* David Riesman.

just marking time waiting for you to indicate *which* lie is apt to win the case. Many clients seem to feel that is the only clear and substantial reason for hiring a lawyer in the first place. Anyway, it's the reason they understand best (and are most prepared to pay for).

This kind of interview can easily degenerate into an extremely sophisticated ballet, since the lawyer must know the facts in order to advise as to which fabrication will earn the fee (a really good lie, after all, is only an edited version of the truth), but he wants the client to take full responsibility for the lie. Otherwise you get blamed morally as well as financially if the case is lost. (Perjury charges, much less convictions, are extremely rare in civil actions.) A style worthy of Diaghilev has been worked out whereby the attorney says, wistfully, "Gee, that's too bad. If he had offered the money when your wife—in fact, any witness" (*brief pause*)—"was still in the room, we might have him on a unilateral contract. As it is, we're stuck with *quantum meruit*"—the latter made to sound like rubbery pizza. There are infinite variations on this little *pas de deux*. Of course, not everybody is a toe dancer. A colleague once told me of a flat-footed client who answered, in effect, "Okay, my wife *was* in the room," followed by several minutes of awkward silence.

As in all professional work, the activity of the lawyer breaks down into two categories: (1) handling the client, and (2) doing the work. These cannot be separated in fact—that would jeopardize the fee and other interpersonal communication—but must be kept distinct conceptually in order to accomplish the actual work. The point is that the client is not really very important but he doesn't know this and, since he is incapable of believing it, you are not permitted to tell him, not even with a slightly elevated eyebrow. As a consequence, in the best-run offices there is a wholly needful division of staff labor between the legal technician and the client-man. Unfortunately, the man who handles the client is closer to the source of income and so gets much more of it (like premium pay for combat duty). Since the technician thinks *he* does all the "work," this can create a very nasty situation within the office. In point of fact, this intra-office tension is the price paid for the smooth front of professional mystique presented to the outside gullible world.

What happens, without this division of labor, is that the client barges into the office, claps his hand to his forehead, and shouts,

"He stole from me!" or, "He's going to steal from me!" or, "I'm having trouble stealing from him!" *

The client is very emotional, even though he may be dissembling. Very soon, if not immediately, it becomes clear just what he wants from you. If perchance you are too busy (or the fee is too high) to go out and shoot his tormenter right now, then perhaps he will settle for some absolutely brand-new form of Chinese torture to be set in motion early tomorrow morning at the latest, and would you please describe it in exquisite detail now; don't rush, he has the rest of the afternoon to devote to this problem. If you are a client-man, you begin to sell him the sympathetic junk he wants. If you are a technician, you might, being frightened by his hysteria, begin to explain to him that the law does not always or so easily permit such forms of convenient homicide. Also, clients tend to get quite confused about whether they are appealing to a lawyer's sense of justice, or his ordinary desire to get a little bit richer as soon as possible. Inexperienced men or young lawyers, who begin immediately to turn their minds from the "client-problem" to the problem-of-the-client, can be stampeded into forgetting the point of the whole matter as regards this special fellow, namely, the fee.

Besides the fee, all the lawyer needs from the client is certain selected facts (selected by the lawyer, that is). But the client is filled with nagging irrelevancies, and quickly becomes a pest. He's always on the phone wanting to know what's happening, although if you told him the truth he wouldn't know what you were talking about, since he's not a lawyer. So you turn him over to the client-man, if, happily, there is one around. If not, you turn on the client-side of your brain, and sell some more of That Stuff. But the client is irrelevant. I realize that there is no legal practice without clients, but still he is irrelevant to the actual work of the law—when there is any other work than keeping the guy happy or well-conned. (It should be perfectly obvious by now that I was no good at all when it came

* Better than 90 per cent of the problems in law practice have to do with money—what we call property rights—rather than with personal rights. In most places, criminal law is practiced as a professional obligation, since most criminals can hardly support themselves, much less a lawyer as well. Marital problems are handled by amateur psychiatrists, or as a professional favor to otherwise hopeful and well-heeled clients; and civil rights and civil liberties are there for a handful of enthusiasts.

to peddling the mystique: no desk-side manner, so to speak. I had some kind of horrible compulsion to try to explain what was happening, and what I was going to do next, and matters like that.)

The key to the lawyer-client relationship is the way lawyers think. This is actually rather interesting for its own sake. Since the medieval head-of-a-pin fellows were displaced, technical legal thought amounts perhaps to the most advanced and highly trained misuse of the human intelligence we have as yet achieved.

The client is interested in his own actual situation; the lawyer is interested only in translating that human situation into legal terms. This is proper professional practice, and you begin to learn how to do it in law school. For the first few months the process is very weird, and the student is quite disoriented. Then all of a sudden you get the point: *nothing real is involved*. What is substituted for "reality" is "winning the argument." After you get going and when you get good at it, the less reality in the winning argument, the tastier it is. Many almost-good lawyers go under at this point—something springs loose in their heads, they literally identify unreality with legal logic, and then they feel they must, poor souls, bull their way through the rest of their professional lives. They are perpetually recurring victims of a dream of the Completely Unreal Bullheaded Winning Argument.

Put another way, it is one thing in law to figure out the substantial issues—they usually come down to *Did he or didn't he?* and *How much?*—and quite another to discover the points on which to fight out the case. These are made up of rules and precedents more or less irrelevant to the human, or readily recognizable, substance of the case. For instance, in jockeying for the settlement price in a matter I worked on many years ago, it became important to get a court order to examine the president of the defendant corporation in New York rather than in Los Angeles. The former was inconvenient for him, and he was a man who liked his convenience, to say the least. We won the argument, with a fancy arrangement of precedents, by working out a noble theory about the perfect relationship between venue, state of incorporation, and principal place of business. (It was so good I hardly understood it myself, although I created it.)

If we left the matter here, it would be very misleading because you would be free to imagine that winning the argument and defining reality were somehow still or eventually related, as in other areas of thought. In the law, they are not. That is because, in law, you never really win the *argument*. You only win the *case*. And this, in fact, makes other good lawyers try twice as hard to win the argument on the *other* side the next time. In the law, you win the argument only by reference to the past, almost never by reference to present reality. (When the latter happens, as in major revolutionary cases, scores of law review articles are written to prove that it didn't happen or shouldn't have happened—in the best articles, both.)

This is the character of legal argument—*not* the character of the best lawyers. Because (I will finally admit it) the best lawyers are exceptionally intelligent people, among the most intelligent our society permits to come into being. *They are the best because they know what they are doing instead of believing in it.* They have to, to win all the unreal arguments.

The client, please note, does not win arguments; he wins only things and conditions. What the laity considers to be the most distasteful characteristic of the lawyer—his cynicism, his ability, even devotion, in *advocating any cause*—is exactly the measure of his achievement. In their own terms, lawyers elevate themselves professionally by arguing, at different times, opposite sides of the same great issue. Some achieve even more, and sit in judgment in the matter on a third occasion. This seeming triplicity is the ultimate in the law, for the lawyer; but the general public is revolted.

Perhaps the greatest difficulty the client has in understanding the law and the lawyer is that he cannot get over his initial assumption that there is a major difference. There is none. *The law is what lawyers do.* Very good lawyers, who know this, waste absolutely no time at all trying to find out what the law is (and infinite time figuring out what the cases say, and can be made to say). They just do it, i.e., go about trying to win another argument. Many unimaginative lawyers, it is true, slavishly imitate past winning arguments, from which derives the quaint notion that such arguments are the law, and are distinct from the lawyer making them. The greatest professional satisfaction comes from nibbling away at such ancient winners, and finally overturning them. (Justice Holmes called this "the genius of the common law"; he liked to talk like that.) As a quick and important example, the clear old rule for the responsibility of corporate managers to stockholders—the great winning argument of an earlier day—had been to adapt the analogy of the strict accountability of a personal trustee. But corporations are much more complicated than personal trusts, and a series of smart, well-paid lawyers began to chew away at the edges of trustee accountability by frightening judges with the prospect of the detailed review of corporate affairs (as in a trust accounting). Thus the principle arose that courts will not question matters of "business judgment." This principle, which began as a minor exception, is now so dominant a winning argument that the only fun left is trying to prove that the business-judgment rule does not cover absolutely *all* forms of corporate theft. Meanwhile, no one outside of the law reviews even has time to suggest that this game be interrupted long enough to devise some relevant rules for corporate responsibility today.

I used to have the recurrent fantasy, when I was practicing, that one day I would get out of the office-library and into court, carrying my own briefcase on a big matter involving some dramatic issue of justice (not just which of the Bobbsey Twins got mommy's money). My opening statement always began, "Now look, fellas . . ." and continued with a dazzling plea to the opposing attorney and the judge to join with me in a great creative human effort to knock off the professional happiness pills and dispose of this matter so as to further the progress of humanity and American culture, and save everybody a lot of time and wasted effort. It was really a major address in favor of non-legal thought. This fantasy helped me to realize my deeper motivation: all I had ever wanted to be, it turned out, was an ordinary itinerant preacher. Let somebody else tend the dogma; somebody who was really interested enough in the power derived from an expert manipulation of it.

Dogma and power, these are the two opportunities presented by the law as such. At the top of the profession, the first requires great technical accomplishment and consequently affords a technician's deep satisfaction. The second, of course, has been the stuff of rulership throughout the ages; in the hands of a top-flight lawyer, it is today cleanly and beautifully sophisticated.

As an extreme example of dogma in the law: a partner once caught me staring out of the window and as punishment gave me the crud-job of revising purchase-order "boilerplate." This is the trade name for the fine print nobody reads (it's unreadable, on purpose) which is printed on the back of contracts of sale. "Read" it sometime. It's incredible—an accretion of disclaimers derived from ancient but still nerve-wracking decisions on implied warranties, breaches entitling revocation, consequential damages, and similar horrors. The funniest part is that the various boilerplate on a request to quote, an answering quotation of price, the final purchase order, and the post-final acceptance language on a shipping order, may well create such a bowl of legal chop suey that no one is able to sue on anything; it's much like two dinosaurs in ultimate and impossible approach, or two obese lovers who can't get close enough to smooch. In too great a degree, law is rationalism gone wild, rationalism as symptom. *Oh, to romp in the green fields, away from the madness of men!*

True enough, there are definite satisfactions available to members of the metropolitan legal elite. Some few lawyers even make some real money, even practicing law. But it is a demanding and even exhausting career. The *distinctive* advantage of the law is the opportunity to use your intelligence-as-trained in the course of each day. All skill involves intelligence, broadly defined; what I refer to is intelligence narrowly defined, more specifically as the capacity of abstract reasoning and imagining: *the intellectual's intelligence*. Every day you go into a good law office you have another chance to prove to yourself how smart you are, and to make a nice living while playing this game.

But it is rather hard for a grown man to spend his whole life playing games with himself; particularly such an egotistical one as proving again and again an element of superiority which you know you began with. After a time, one develops a strong desire to accept it as proven and get on to something more interesting or worthwhile or at least less enervating. In the law, this is mostly to move over into the client's game in areas where intellectuals are reluctantly welcomed—to take on a more direct participation in the system of business and state and other institutional power.

There is a big change under way in the legal profession, which reflects the even bigger change in society: in general, toward the managerial preoccupations of administering a complex technological society. In brief, the elite lawyer is becoming a structural trouble-shooter in business and other administration. Since the law is what the lawyer does, this is changing the nature of law itself. The law has become more a matter of administration, and is becoming noticeably less concerned with the proper tending of dogma. In the end, this process will possibly result in the creation of new dogma or ideology; meanwhile, we have all become empiricists.

The legal world has become infinitely complicated and specialized since the New Deal—all that legislation, all those administrative agencies, the war taxes, in sum, all those *jobs*, derived from all that *lack* of precedent. Not out of liberal commitment but just to keep one's head above water, the whole legal process became unavoidably functional to an untoward degree.

Many members of the legal elite have relied on this shift toward administration to move out from practice proper into governmental work and even politics; to the law schools as a newly paved road to advanced political and other institutional participation; to executive-advisory positions directly with the institutions, whether corporate, charitable, foundation-academic, social action, labor, new financial, or whatever. The effect of this has been that the lawyers have reconstituted themselves as the advance guard of the New Class in America. It is not advertising, magazine, or book publishing executives, not union or civil-rights activists, not movie or television producers, not teachers, stock salesmen, or new-money-men, and not even the foundation and academic hustlers—but lawyers who remain the only general, inevitable and utterly practical vanguard of the intellectuals in the West. They will do anything, anywhere, and, if you pay extra, also come on for a five-a-day as the high priests of property and propriety, to the guaranteed satisfaction of any and all paying audiences.

It isn't the oldest, but it *is* the most professional of professions. Doctors, for example, are inevitable idealists because, hard as they try and no matter how dollar-driven they may be, they cannot get away from the anxious fact that animal existence depends on their work; they cannot avoid being the technicians of life-and-death. Religionists and academics were long ago housebroken and isolated, to stop the spread of spiritual infection; this is so clear that it is sometimes hard to recall that many of them did not at the outset welcome their trained irrelevance as if it were some kind of fulfillment. But the lawyer, dealing almost always with the most pressing nonsense of the human race and almost always calling on his ultimate capacity of intelligence and word-use in the service thereof, is the one perfect professional.

We've been at this game a long time, you see; and we've gotten very good at it. Also, our product, all in all, is still more important in this country than these other and newer forms of morale-building.

The dream of justice is still a greater dream than that of mouth-wash purity. Thurman Arnold, with Falstaffian tenderness, has said, "The function of the law is not so much to guide society as to comfort it." I would add: comfort in part by entertaining. We were the first entertainers on the frontier, only later sharing stage space with snake oil/laudanum barkers, blackface minstrels, and other con men. Law is an eternal dream, and indulging it as a form of personal expression remains one of the big differences between utterly bureaucratic societies, like Russia, and our messily bureaucratic one. The administrative mode will win out, of course; but the better lawyers will exact a handsome price, in more ways than one. As always with the smart boys, the client pays.

8

SOME POLITICAL ECONOMY— AFTER LAWYERING

❀ FACTS AND FICTIONS OF
U.S. CAPITALISM

THE REPORTER, 1959

This is my single most successful article. It has been antholo- gized a number of times and also used, rather often, for the purposes of teaching. It was the essay from which my first book, The Paper Economy, *was evolved. After my unrealized work on O'Hara (and one piece of fiction), this was what I sat down to instead of standing up, putting on a clean shirt, and getting another job in the law. (Not a living, you understand—neither the essay nor the book that followed; for a living, I did some classy ghost-writing. Literature, I tell every young man who sounds like he might be tempted, is a lousy racket, win or lose.) My girlfriend knew a guy who knew a big man at* The Reporter, *which, I had heard, paid ten cents a word: on that you could get rich—selling a million words a year.*

❀ WE SEEM, as a nation, to be committed equally to increasing production and deceiving ourselves about our productive system. The realities of the American economy are massive and dominant in our way of life; and they are extraordinarily dynamic and original in their evolving nature. But the rhetoric we employ to describe this core activity of ours is overwhelmingly obscurantist: reality and image are hardly within hailing distance. To put it simply, we suffer from an astonishing amount of downright mythical thinking about money and property and basic economic organization. While we all know that America manufactures as much as all the rest of the world, the words, images, and ideological structures we use to represent to ourselves what we are and what we do tend to be a quarter, a half, or even a full century old. Old, irrelevant, and misleading.

This stricture applies to liberals and socialists as well as to NAM publicists and their businessmen backers. Indeed, to be fair, one should credit many of the centrally placed executives and managers with a distinctly superior though unshared comprehension of our economic system. As for the rest of us, we seem to have been too busy enjoying its beneficence to have bothered to examine its realities. It is about time we began.

The falsification of economic reality, buttressed by the laziness (or something) of the educated, is becoming a highly organized, even essential instrument of policy—and that is always dangerous, politically, morally, and intellectually. To obscure, as a matter of policy, the existence and nature of the dominant power in a society is to undermine the basic creative sources of social life. This falsification presents America in the classic image of free enterprise and private-property capitalism; its consequence is to conceal the incontestable fact that we are dominated by great faceless corporations "owned" by no one and run by self-designated "managers."

There is a great deal of talk on Madison Avenue these days about the "corporate image," which means giving a humanized face to these impersonal structures. And the New York Stock Exchange publicists are pushing hard the idea of a "People's Capitalism," which has as much to do with capitalism proper as "People's Democracy" has to do with democracy proper. The purpose of these maneuvers is to plug some of the more gaping holes in the traditional web of justifications which, before the New Deal, was deemed sufficient in itself.

What is being simultaneously justified and obscured is the revolutionary emergence of a new American property system—and the fact that the men in control of it, the managers, occupy unexampled positions of power and privilege which are not based on entrepreneurial accumulation or private ownership, to which they were "elected" only by their peers, and for which they have been answerable only to history.

The managers of corporate industrial wealth and the big-money funds—along with their expert advisers—are the ones who are creating the new system; they run it, and they also best understand it. They know everything worth knowing in a practical way about money, property, and basic economic organization—because that's what they manage. They milk the pre-tax dollar and thread their way through government regulation on behalf of all sizable funds or forms of wealth. They are personally intimate with the intricacies of the fragmentation of property ownership and the alienation of capital because their very existence derives from those crucial changes in our property system.

What are some of the things the managers "know" that the rest have not gotten around to learning? We had better—because of their elaborate nature—avoid the subjects of the tax-torn dollar and other government regulation. But we might take a straight look at property as such. And here the invitation to understanding reads: *Nothing is very private in a mass society, including property.*

Advanced or even adequate thinking about property by the people who manage it requires what might be called a non-possessory or non-owning frame of mind. As any good manager knows, ownership is irrelevant—the main thing is control. And frequently control is created or ensured by means of *giving up* ownership or by having certain others own the property. Management control of big corporations, for instance, is based on a dispersal of stock ownership among as large a public as possible: AT&T has 1,600,000 stockholders, no one of whom owns more than one-thirtieth of 1 per cent. The Ford family retained control over Henry Ford's creation only by giving its stock in the company to a foundation; if it had held on to ownership, it would have lost control. Sears, Roebuck is controlled by company stock held in the company's pension trust: here the management consolidated its position by "giving away" huge sums of money. Managers manage, they don't own.

In a modern law school, some of the best all-around fun is had in arriving at a definition of property. The faculty considers it a first essential for the development of legal technique to tease the apprentice lawyers out of their ordinary received notions.

First off, the basic image of property—land and things—is pooh-poohed; then the search for a definition is carried through contract rights, choses in action (unrealized rights, including claims in court), and other intangibles. The class then thinks it has the answer: property is rights—called property rights or, in the short form, property. This is the point at which the modern professor enjoys himself most, and to confound the class completely he pulls out a case in which a property right is recognized and enforced by a court for the first time—a good one is the early radio broadcasting case in which a court first held that the right to broadcast a description of a baseball game "belonged" to the baseball club, could be disposed of by it, and could not be pirated by a party lacking contractual privilege from the "owner." Then the *coup de grâce*: Did the court enforce the club owner's right because it was a property right, or was it a property right because the court enforced it? A smile settles on the professor's face, and the pot of gold is indicated: property is a right of use or disposition which will be enforced by a court. On that day we are men; and the legal elite is then prepared to go out, tautology in hand, and grow rich defending and creating such rights.

But a whisper of doubt remains as older tautologies assert themselves: land is land, to own is to own, and all property, like land, is supposed to be owned. Yes, but less frequently nowadays by any one person. Take land, for example: the bank holds a first mortgage on the suburban home, the contractor has a material man's lien, various governmental authorities hold tax liens, the niece of the guy who sold it to you is suing you because her uncle didn't have the right to convey it, and you hocked your equity in order to post bond for your brother-in-law. Who owns the house? Why, everybody who has an enforceable right to its use or disposition; and all the possible rights in and to the home, the whole bundle, add up to *the* ownership of it. In our crowded, mobile society there has occurred a very extensive fragmentation of property ownership.

Some things are too big to own. If the suburban home is too much for me, and a car is too much for an industrial worker, then General Motors is too much for a Du Pont, and Standard Oil of New Jersey is too much for a Rockefeller. The use of the word "ownership" in referring to an agglomeration of industrial capacity like General Motors is, to put it kindly, overripe. And the simple designation of our system as one based on "private" property is not merely overripe, it is a calculated deceit. The managers know that the ownership of General Motors is irrelevant, but their spokesmen spend millions attempting to convince us that General Motors—and all publicly held American corporations—are owned by, you guessed it, the people-public. When they say "owned," they mean for us to "feel" the word in the utterly primitive sense. As Keith Funston of the New York Stock Exchange remarked to a group of advertising men, this "is a very humanizing bit of news."

One can face the question "Who owns General Motors?" if one will face the answer—"Nobody." But that is inconceivable, you say. Our training in property thinking (or lack of it) induces a certain horror in contemplating anything so big and so valuable walking around unowned! We abhor the vacuum of non-ownership. But how *could* GM be "owned"? The total assets of this corporation amount to nearly $7 billion and the market value of its common stock is in excess of $13 billion. There are more than 750,000 stockholders. A control block of stock, usually put at between 20 and 51 per cent, affords a means of translating ownership into control; but this is a feature of the aggregate, not of individual shares—and the courts so recognize it. When Du Pont disposes of the major part of its holdings in the company, there will not be anything like a control block in the GM situation.

The notion that GM (or any one of the great majority of our public corporations) is "owned" proceeds from the time-honored assumption that to own stock is to own the corporation. If we examine this old-fashioned "self-evident" truth empirically, we note that what the public stockholder actually has is three double-edged rights: (1) he can sell his stock at a profit or at a loss; (2) he can receive or fail to receive a variable dividend; and (3) he can vote "Yes" or "No" on certain issues affecting control of the corporation and the disposition of its properties. The first two items indicate that he owns a negotiable instrument of a certain character—consisting of an "iffy" return on capital and a lottery ticket on market appreciation. Let us look more closely at the third item, the only one of the three that even looks like ownership of the corporation itself. What does the stockholder's vote mean? To skip over several stages of a dull argument, it means that the voter can effect changes of control over "his" property, the corporation, or it means approximately nothing. Can he do this? The answer is "No," not unless an ambitious, well-heeled syndicate mounts a campaign to do so, and thus gives *him* the opportunity to support *them*. This does not happen at all often.

A mite of ownership, indeed. Especially when one considers that the essential difference between the incumbent and contending control groups is apt to be that the one has been at that particular trough for a period of time and the other has not. Moreover, in the absence of blatant mismanagement or special business reverses, it is next to impossible to unseat an in-group that is on the alert and well advised by experts. Unlike a campaign for political office, the "ins" have at their disposal not only the corporate patronage but also the corporate treasury; and the voting apathy of the citizen is a form of frenzied activity compared to that of the lottery-ticket holder. As a recent writer so felicitously put it, "The modern proxy contest is at best a device for tempering autocracy by invasion." Following the New York Central and Montgomery Ward fights, in theory the SEC put the final kibosh on the matter by promulgating proxy-fight regulations which ensure that only nice people fighting a good clean fight may now do battle in the arena of what is charmingly called "corporate democracy."

The fundamental meaning of private property is private control over the property one owns, and all the stockholder owns is a share of stock. The corporation is not private property—only the share of stock is.

Twenty-seven years after the publication of A. A. Berle and Gardiner C. Means's *The Modern Corporation and Private Property*, the crucial lessons of that landmark work have not been generally assimilated even among the educated. The processes there described have in the meantime undergone an extensive development. These were adumbrated by Mr. Berle in a brilliant little essay written for the Fund for the Republic a couple of years ago, in which he states flatly that the American corporate system now represents "the highest concentration of economic power in recorded history." The ever-present factual ground of his thinking, which simply cannot be repeated often enough, is that 150 corporations hold sway over 50 per cent of American manufacturing, based on asset values. On the same basis, "about two-thirds of the economically productive assets of the United States, excluding agriculture, are owned by a group of not more than 500 corporations."

The liberal view since the Progressive era has been that big corporations mean big capitalists. The point that has to be gotten into the liberal skull is that the manager is not a capitalist at all: he is a new fish.

The day of classic capitalism based on private property is gone. This is not a matter of ideology, it is a simple question of observable fact.

In comprehending the demise of the private-property system, it may be helpful to think of property as being of two kinds—"thing-property" and "rights-property." The former would be the plants, machines, railroads, buildings, etc., most of which are organized in great corporate units. The latter would be pieces of paper, like stock certificates and bonds, representing certain direct entitlements relating to such property. Now we have to complicate the picture a little by indicating a third, hybrid form of property—liquid capital organized in huge blocks, mediating between corporate thing-property and personal rights-property. An example would be the $13 billion or so in mutual funds (growing at the rate of $100 million a month). The point here is that a mutual fund would be capable of exercising ownership control over thing-property, but no one could exercise ownership control over a big mutual fund. The same would hold true of many banks, insurance companies, and pension trusts.

Now, as a consequence of the dispersion decreed by the estate and income tax laws, and the raw fact that corporations and big-money funds get bigger and bigger, there is observable *an increasing fragmentation of rights-property and an increasing concentration and accumulation of thing-property (and hybrid-property)*. Rights-property remains private, but it is just paper—somewhat like money, except that it earns and changes in value. Most thing-property is not private, because it is not owned by private persons and, as we shall see, it does not exist, in the last analysis, for private purposes.

It is beyond the scope of this essay to indicate the concentration of rights-property, but a few facts may help to suggest the truth of the situation. The Stock Exchange propagandists tell us, and we should believe them, that there are more than ten million American stockholders. They tell us nothing, however, about the concentration of holdings. Now besides the fact that everybody knows that Nelson Rockefeller owns more stock than most gas-station attendants, we do have some 1957 Federal Reserve Board figures to help us out. At that time, the Board reported that there were 56.1 million spending units in the United States, and that 11 per cent of these owned some publicly held stock. Only 3 per cent, however, held investments valued at more than $10,000, and no more than 8 per cent of the units had an annual income of $10,000 or more. Which bears out what everyone knows anyway, that the distribution of the ownership of income paper is something like the distribution of income itself, only more so; and there is almost none of this paper at and below the median level of income (except insurance, life-and-death savings, etc.), where the imperatives of consumption are absolute.

The psychology (if not the fact) of private-property ownership goes very deep; as Mr. Berle has suggested, we are "the most violently private-property-minded country in the world." There was a profound truth in Jefferson's image of a democracy as a society of small property-holders—even if in our day it is so impractical as to be tragic. If a man plants himself firmly upon the rock of his property ownership, he has an independence, and a sense of secure equality with other individuals similarly situated, which indeed does make him, as Jefferson believed, the truly anointed member of a democratic community. Now on what rock does the highly paid corporate executive stand, with his expense account, his stock options, his pension plan, deferred compensation, and death benefits? He stands on the "rock" of his acceptability to his board of directors and other superiors in a bureaucratic hierarchy. No rock at all; so he buries himself in work, in the immediate present of power and privileged consumption.

We should not confuse standard of living with accumulation. The 30,000 corporate executives earning $50,000 or more a year (as reported by *Fortune* a few years ago), and indeed all the managers, have excellent and even magnificent standards of living. Mr. J. A. Livingston, a perceptive financial writer for the Philadelphia *Bulletin*, thinks that the "tax-sheltered managerial elite" is "an over-privileged class in a democratic society." But they are workers and spenders, not accumulators. They don't build family financial empires any longer—the estate and income tax laws, and the corporate bureaucratic organization of wealth, have seen to that. Somebody could doubtless still build a temporary empire by merchandising a frozen daiquiri that can be drunk under water. But such events no longer characterize the system.

Free enterprise, motored by that hallowed value, individual initiative, and based on private property for real, has become a minority sector of the economy; still noisy, exhilarating, and important, but no longer the big show. Also, it is quite significant that two of the more substantial success stories of recent times—Reynolds Metals and Kaiser Aluminum—each involves government beneficence as well as individual initiative.

Perhaps this point that the important managers are mostly not important accumulators can best be made by recalling what the old days were like—before the Pecora investigation and New Deal securities legislation, for instance. Describing the business system in the heyday of American capitalist accumulation, in *The Theory of Business Enterprise*, Thorstein Veblen devotes several choice pages to the "accumulation of wealth" by corporate executives. His point was that the corporation men made their fortunes by trading in the stock of the corporations they managed. To this end, their purpose was served by a "discrepancy . . . between the actual and the putative earning-capacity of the corporation's capital." So the directorate gave out "partial information, as well as misinformation" to create such discrepancies. If this was not sufficient, some actual mismanagement could be indulged, if desired, to depress the stock. In those days—what the liberal muckrakers called the "robber baron" period —great fortunes could be and were accumulated.

And today? Apart from taxes, Section 16(b) of the Securities Exchange Act of 1934 imposes an absolute liability in favor of the corporation with respect to any insider's short-swing profits in such transactions (which are a matter of public record). Where statutes are not sufficient, the revolution in the corporate common law effected by the brilliant practitioners of minority-stockholder litigation ensures that the managers remain housebroken, as they have been for some decades. This does not imply that insider information is not valuable today; one should not underemphasize the extent to which the corporate world has learned to live with restricting legislation and litigation; but the fact remains that control of a corporation is not the paved highway to an accumulation of great wealth which it once was. Now it is, by and large, just a very good job, in terms of both power and material welfare. But the power is based on position, not ownership; and the material advantages are standard-of-living advantages—nothing really important in the way of accumulation. (Not more than enough to support one wife and a lazy son or two after one's death.)

Top corporate executives, and other important managers, typically have choice long-term employment contracts as well as many lucra-

tive "fringe" benefits. The contracts and benefits afford them substantial security, but they do not amount to "owning" the job—any
more than union seniority and grievance procedures mean the
assembly-line worker "owns" his job. We would like to possess these
important things because, in a way, "everything" depends on them.
Some of us want and need the security that a sense of ownership
gives so much that we kid ourselves into the belief that we do indeed
own what we need to own. For example, a woman who needs to feel
that she possesses her husband will literally think and feel a "property right" in him. This happens to be a property right that, to a
considerable degree, the courts will recognize. But they have not
come around to accepting much of the ownership quality in our job
tenure.

It will come, however, because insofar as we move away from private property and are bureaucratized, we become defined as a society
of jobholders—all of us, from the quarter-million-a-year executive to
the subsistence laborer. In a certain fundamental sense, both are
proletarians: an increasingly comfortable proletarianization is America's gift to the modern world.

The issue is: We can belong to the job as proletarians, or the job
can belong to us as individuals. (I don't think Sweden is going to
give us a middle way on this issue.) As jobs come more and more to
be *owned* by the jobholder, there will develop an increasingly elaborate structure of rights and duties with regard to jobs-as-property: a
system of *law* will develop, just as happened in the epoch of bourgeois property after the transcendence of feudal forms. I think this is
a more likely outcome than that the human race should manage to
dispense with the sense of ownership and property entirely—dispense, that is, with identity in depth between self and thing.

Meanwhile, union members are as much concerned with seniority
rights as with wage demands, the secretary home-furnishes her office
niche, and the medium-level white-collar worker measures the size
and newness of "his" desk against all comers. (Note that many ad-
vertisements for new typewriters, postage-meter machines, etc., are
directed to the office worker rather than to the boss.) And also
meanwhile, what the junior and senior managers "have" is simply
their qualifications to be managers. "Qualification" takes in a great
deal—in some corporations it includes the character and social standing of one's wife. It is this compulsion to qualify that has created

W. H. Whyte's "organization man" and David Riesman's "other-directed" group man. It is obvious that their dominance as social types is tied to the decline of private property.

What are the aims of the big corporations that dominate our national life? They are bureaucracies, so they have, at least in the first instance, the purposes of any bureaucratic structure: (1) to maintain itself; (2) to grow bigger; and (3) incidentally to accomplish the function that justifies its existence. The profit motive of corporations—their basic vestigial connection with capitalism proper—subserves all three of these bureaucratic purposes, but especially the second. Corporations are, after all, mainly a means of accumulating and maintaining wealth in an organized form: they are the only remaining legal form of a perpetuity, apart from the sovereign state itself. But there is no perpetuity in the ownership or the control of corporations.

The difference between an economic organization like General Motors or AT&T and a $10-million or even a $50-million corporation is not the simple additive one of size. At some point, a change in quantity becomes a change in quality, and a new property form is created. Moreover, a smaller corporation may drag along or fail, and only a limited number of people are hurt; but the giants cannot be allowed to fail, and indeed they cannot be allowed for long to function at much below their optimum capacity. National production and the fate of a people would be decisively affected.

Little corporations get bigger—by accumulation, by merger, and simply because we have an expanding economy. At a certain point, they transcend their original nature and then two crucial economic events occur simultaneously: there has been a new addition of $X million to the sphere of quasi-public or unprivate property and a subtraction of the same amount from the private-property, free-enterprise sector. Note these facts: between 1949 and 1954, the number of mergers tripled. In recent years, two-thirds of all mergers have been of small companies into larger ones with assets of over $10 million. In this sense, as well as more obvious ones, the quasi-public giants are destroying free enterprise and private property. The tax law, as well as many other economic factors, has contributed to the formation of mergers. The tax-free reorganization sections of the Tax Code, which allow for the non-recognition of gain or loss in certain major corporate transactions including mergers, provides positive encouragement to the growth of bigness.

Also, bigness is bigger than any balance sheet will reveal—since many smaller companies are organized in constellations around the giants. There are undoubtedly a number of auto-parts manufacturers and other suppliers that might just as well constitute themselves as divisions of General Motors, for all the make-believe independence their freedom entails. (Some giants have purposefully organized their industries in this way as a defense against the antitrust laws, as well as a means of keeping the unions in line.)

The problem of bigness has been with us since the building of the railroads a century ago, and of course it was a great political issue in the trust-busting era around the turn of the century. From that day till this, the liberal view has been to prevent or disperse the concentration of economic power, rather than to accept it and control it. This has been the impulse behind a considerable amount of fundamental legislation—the Sherman and Clayton Acts, the Robinson-Patman Act, resale price maintenance, the setting up of the Federal Trade Commission, etc. Whatever else may be said of this great effort to preserve capitalism in its classic image, it must at least be pointed out that it has failed. It may have slowed down or in some cases deflected the basic trend, and it certainly made a lot of lawyers rich; but after fifty years of this sort of thing our economy is more than ever dominated by big corporations. If the program is justified as a form of public subsidy to free enterprise in the form of small business, similar to our approach to the farmers, then it is perhaps acceptable. But as a comprehensive program or theory, it is mostly irrelevant to U.S. society.

This liberal attitude is based as solidly on the atavistic myths—of free enterprise and private property—as any NAM speech is. Each group is working a different side of a street that runs through a ghost town.

Marx and Veblen among others were quite right after all in one fundamental insight; industrialism was bound eventually to burst out of the straitjacket of early capitalist forms of property—if not into socialism, then into "Americanism." An industrial system, as distinct from an ideology or way of doing business, has a dynamic of its own, which is just simply to be itself, to produce efficiently. As long as a society can afford not to produce—is able to deny the industrial dynamic—it can join any property system and any economic ideology it may whimsically desire with the actual system of industry. But when production becomes imperative, any form of property and any ideological element may be required to give way. Give way in fact, of course, not necessarily in name. Which accounts for many of the misnamed facts in our industrial picture.

The end of capitalism in America as a recognizable entity results from three major historical events—the Great Depression, World War II, and this endless Cold War involving continuous competition in production with the Soviet Union. Many good Democrats feel that the New Deal saved capitalism, but that is putting things wrong end up: corporate concentration saved (and imperceptibly transcended) capitalism, while the New Deal merely saved the corporations, by making it possible for them to produce again. That remains one of the primary functions of our federal government—to keep saving the corporations. It is unnecessary to refer in detail to the numerous means the government has used to bolster purchasing power, or to help organize corporations among themselves. To indicate the scope of the latter, Mr. Berle asserts that "Roughly two-thirds of American industry and much of American finance is controlled by a formal or informal Federal industrial plan."

Not only do corporations regulate themselves through government agencies and similar devices, but it is a fact—to be obscured only by conventional thinking—that the very existence of an AT&T or a GM or an RCA is in itself a form of economic planning on a national industrial scale: True, such planning has no broad or socially debated purpose, and is subject to no exterior responsibility other than the brute verdict of events—but still it *is* that rationalized economic planning so dear to the hearts of older socialists. (It seems an amusing irony that the creepiest part of creeping socialism should be its daily augmentation by the corporate managers.)

So, among other things, the imperatives of production result in an accelerated corporate rationalization of the economy. Let us state these imperatives seriatim, so as to recognize their overwhelming force:

• Thou shalt not allow another Great Depression.
• Thou shalt produce fully and efficiently.
• Thou shalt compete globally with the Soviet Union—a competition whose key terms are not merely tons of steel and numbers of

automobiles but the purposeful organization of production and the rate of industrial growth.

• Finally, thou shalt raise and spread the American standard of living.

Almost everything unique about our system results from the action of these imperatives. Since they cannot be expected to diminish, it is fair to assume that we will continue to change in the direction already marked out. We may all see the day again (as with the NRA) when the president of, say, General Motors insists on more "socialist" control over industry. After all, what's good for the country may also be good for General Motors—at least for the *people* of General Motors, if not for the Thing Itself.

So that's our unnamed property system, still woodenly or deceitfully miscalled "private." But is all this a word game? No. The issue is, first, to recognize the existence of this crucial power now held by corporate and other managers, and then to request them to justify it to us. Power must be legitimated, otherwise any talk of law itself, much less democratic citizenship, becomes absurdly irrelevant. There are two somewhat contradictory "legitimations" of corporate power current today, one obscurely explicit and the other largely implied: (1) it doesn't exist, and (2) it "works."

The claim that it doesn't exist derives entirely from the word "private": corporations are private property, and thus are assimilated to an older system of justifications. This view leads one to the truly remarkable proposition that the personality of a young executive (and that of his fiancée) is *not* private, but the multibillion-dollar telephone system *is!*

The legitimation of corporate power because it "works" amounts to what is probably the lowest level of ideology yet reached by man in his brief but painful rise from the prelingual slime. To coin a lawyer-like phrase, it is unanswerable, contemptible, and irrelevant —and is to be understood as meaning nothing more than *You got yours, Jack.* As long as Jack accepts the statement, it is indeed unanswerable—and we are well on our way to accepting unlegitimated power at the very center of our civilization. The worst effect of the lack of legitimation is, as C. Wright Mills screamingly asserts, that ideology and then ideas and finally mind itself become irrelevant to national life. And this is profoundly frightening.

The subject of politics is power. Probably the main reason there is no longer anything recognizably like significant political activity in the United States is that those who would engage in it have failed or refused to confront the facts of national power. They don't or won't see where it is. Let us hope that this situation is transitory, that like the genteel poor we were temporarily embarrassed by insufficient ideological funds.

The most deeply disturbing aspect of our situation is that nobody is holding a gun to our head: we are *free* to engage in politics—and indeed we were as a nation created free in order to do so. But to pick up our birthright requires at least a significant number of us to indicate with reasonable frankness and accuracy *what* the basic national power is, *where* it is, and *who* the stewards of it are. If the subject of politics is power, the means is ideological discussion, argument, and conflict. Now in this grand activity many things and many qualities are useful, but one is absolutely indispensable—namely, vital ideology itself. And that's our problem: our ideologies have become so irrelevant to the facts of life that it is all the ordinary citizen can do to stay awake while the great debate about our fathers' world goes on.

❀ OWNING AND DOING

UNPUBLISHED, 1960

Review of *Power Without Property*, by
Adolf A. Berle, Jr.

My intellectual debt to Berle is considerable—and I have acknowledged it at length in The Paper Economy (*see pages 217ff.*). *In addition to the statements contained in this review* (*written originally for* Commentary), *I would also like to acknowledge my disgust with the standard pop-radical attitude toward Berle, which seizes on his attempted justifications of the corporate system to forgo the effort to assimilate the other 90 per cent of his work—which stands unparalleled for its insight into modern property forms.*

Property is no longer the key to the modern world—but it is the key-concept of some major traditions of thought that are and will continue to be used in our effort to understand the modern world, e.g., Marxism and American lawyering. I was quite pleased to discover that I was a better lawyer for having been a Marxist. Although he deals with much else, I think property is the central concept in Marx's writing; in the law, it is almost the only useful—and regularly used—idea. (As one consequence of this, good, well-trained lawyers are smarter, I think, than other middlebrows—who did not take their youthful Marxist Study Groups with sufficient seriousness.)

Adolf Berle is the leading authority in this country on one of this country's most profound theoretical issues: the relation of power to property. His credentials as our most advanced thinker about the unique features of the American property system go back a quarter-century to a landmark work, *The Modern Corporation and Private Property*, written with the distinguished economist, Dr. Gardiner C. Means. Professor Berle also holds impressive practical credentials, having occupied important positions in both the La Guardia and Roosevelt administrations; he is a practicing attorney; a leader of New York's Liberal party; and he was one of several Columbia professors who augmented FDR's original brain trust. But he is and will be best known as the chief exponent of the still startling proposition that at the center of American capitalism are great organized power structures which, on any reasonable terms, are not capitalist institutions at all. To put it simply, the major public corporations are not "owned" by anyone. It is only necessary to recall that private property has always been the fundamental premise of historical capitalism to realize, or at least begin to realize, the revolutionary implications of the Berle proposition.

In the present collection of essays, Mr. Berle again carries forward his effort to work out these implications. The results are frequently fascinating; and only on occasion disappointing. He does not achieve here the pointed, compact brilliance of, say, his brief 1957 essay, "Economic Power and the Free Society," published by The Fund for the Republic. I find this writing somewhat uneven: he does not sustain the brilliance of insight and exposition of which he is capable; he too often pursues when the bird has been caught, and stops in his tracks when the reader still has the scent. But I believe this may be accounted for more by the nature of the quarry than of the hunter. However this may be, his achievement is always considerable. Besides, when a man has an intellectual tiger by the tail, all twistings and turnings are relevant—so long as he holds on.

Having stated a "balanced" view in the preceding paragraph, I am now free to unleash my enthusiasm for the book. It contains enough insight and stimulation for two volumes each twice the size. The entire exposition is beautifully relevant to what is, and will each year become, increasingly apparent as the one political issue of the age—the character of economic power and the right of the democracy to demand its organization and use for social purposes. One of the great achievements of Mr. Berle's approach to this issue is that he ends up with a description of the industrial system (sufficiently accurate and comprehensive) whereby political intervention on the part of the citizen is seen as natural, necessary, and historically sanctioned. He thus restores us to the sanity of a *political* economy by pointing out, simply, that we already have one; and he asserts that, in the human scale of things, it works rather well. In so doing, he incidentally undercuts the classical black-and-white conflict of capitalism versus socialism—by showing, among other things, that the actual system contains much less of the one and much more of the other than ideologues on either side will admit. Which probably accounts for the fact that his approach has not gained greater currency than it has: it lacks the excitement of *Götterdämmerung*.

But it unquestionably suits the temper of the American people better than either classical position—since it is mostly a careful if dynamic picture of the system which that temper has created or tolerated. By dissolving the private-public lockjaw of the classical positions, it both invites political intervention on occasions when the citizenry desires it and observes that absolute intervention by the state is not at all necessary to achieve our democratic purposes. His view even incorporates an "inevitablist" element by holding, on rather good historical grounds, that we always do get whatever political intervention is in fact necessary. This is New Dealism-after-the-fact, grown to philosophical-historical proportions, but based on an infinitely more sophisticated comprehension of the entire actual system than was available in the Thirties.

In his previous work, Mr. Berle has pointed out again and again that "two-thirds of the economically productive assets of the United States, excluding agriculture" are held by 500 corporations, most of them management controlled. This knocked the private property underpinning out from under the system. In this book, he demonstrates (based on a private study for Nelson Rockefeller) that three-fifths of the "capital flowing into nonagricultural industry . . . is internally generated through profits and depreciation funds." This means (skipping over the complexities) that free enterprise based on individual initiative is no longer very free or very individual. What's left? Only the "capital" in capitalism—and there is even more of that under existing socialist systems (the basic purpose and horror of which derive from compulsory primitive accumulation of capital).

So if we are not capitalist, why are we not socialist? Primarily because the economic centers of power, while no longer based on private ownership of property, are still not co-equal with the state. Moreover, our national planning for social purpose—except in wartime—is minimal; indeed, inadequate. And, more important, both of these terms are based on ideas about property ownership which have become irrelevant—as much in Russia as in America—to the realities of industrial society. In this sense, no advanced or advancing industrial society can be either capitalist or socialist. It would be both and neither. The words are wrong, since they refer to ownership rather than control—or, as Mr. Berle has now decided to put it, to property rather than power. As the title suggests, in this book he seems to come close to dispensing with the independent idea of property altogether. I don't know whether he intends this as a rhetorical device to emphasize the primacy of power, or whether he is seriously suggesting that by removing the distinctiveness of the adjectives "private" and "public" one also dispenses with the need for the noun "property" itself.

The author's major impulse in this book—as in some other recent efforts—is to demonstrate that this great corporate power, being neither truly private nor public, is still not, or need not be, a disastrous contradiction of the ethos of our traditional liberal capitalist democracy. On the face of it, the corporate managers are not capitalists because they don't own anything important as individuals; and they are not part of a democracy because nobody elected them. Under traditional theory, all power is supposed to derive either from the electorate or from the ownership of property; now we find that the main power in our society derives from neither. On this premise, the line of thought Berle pursues begins with an analogy between the "Lords Spiritual" of medieval society and the better class of professors in our present universities; compares the corporate barons with the "Lords Temporal"; and ends with a concept of the "public consensus" which is uncomfortably mystical at times and is, in its philosophical roots, too close (for comfort) to the "will of the people" notion which has been used to justify a wide assortment of power systems, including Hitler's.

The author keeps insisting, as if it were the whole point, that there really is such a thing as a public consensus. I am sure there is, and I agree with him that it is undoubtedly an effective force; but he hasn't convinced me, and I rather doubt he has convinced himself, that it is the same thing as democracy. It is one thing to say that the holders of power are more or less responsive to the people over whom they exercise their power, and that a people always gets the leaders and the system it deserves because they can insist differently —and quite another thing to equate these facts of life with historical democracy. This is Pope's "What is, is right," which I have always thought of as the fallacy of misplaced tautology. In a double sense, there is no future in it. Mr. Berle rather sneaks a bit of future into his notion by pointing out that if the public consensus is sufficiently irritated or transgressed it will cause political intervention, and an aspect of the power system will then be changed. Right—but when and how much and by what means? And doesn't that say the system *could* be democratic rather than that it *is?*

We are left with the simple fact that the "Lords Temporal" are not elected. Like everyone familiar with business enterprise, the author curls his lip at the idea that corporate executives should be elected by people inexperienced in business management. That's an old story, and I don't think the Secretary of Defense—running one of the biggest business enterprises in the world—or even the Postmaster General, for that matter, should be elected by sassy democrats who never met a payroll and foolish women who insist on good looks. But, unlike "private" managers, they are accountable to elected officials, and that's not a bad idea. At least it is no worse than the idea of democracy itself. In fact, it's the same thing.

I have barely covered, in this space, some of the main points of these essays. It would be misleading not to say right out that the intellectual richness of the book is hardly indicated by the foregoing discussion. Moreover, certain broad subject categories have not even been mentioned—as, for instance, Mr. Berle's thesis concerning the future role of financial intermediaries, especially pension funds, in the system of industrial power. Another essay presents a structural comparison between the Soviet and American systems, and should be a startling eye-opener for many readers. Probably the best and most imaginative part of the book is the brief discussion of the role of planning in the immediate future of our system. And, again and again, Mr. Berle makes observations, presents information, or connects up points which may not be exceptional to specialized experts but, because of the author's *range*, can be startling to the general reader: e.g., the remark on bank credit at the top of page 160.

But let me give a better example: After stating that our economic system must be seen from the point of view of power rather than property, he says: "Power other than that derived from immediate capacity to apply brute force can be exercised only through organization." One thinks about this statement, and then connects it with the fact that our so-called capitalist system has survived at all only because of the extent of organization entailed by corporate concentration and government regulation; that the scientific and engineering capacity—the Sputnik superiority—of the Soviets was a triumph of organization; that the need for an increased measure of purposeful planning is daily becoming an issue of survival for America. . . . And slowly there emerges a dramatic image of the essence of the Soviet challenge, and America's potential responses to it. How much organization—meaning power—is enough? How much freedom is compatible with "enough"? Can our democracy create sufficient organization to meet the challenge, and at the same time nurture in the electorate adequate power over this organization? The ultimate issue, then, as the author states, is control over power—power over power. It certainly is *not* property.

❀ HOW HIGH UP IS, AND WHY

LEISURE, 1960

Not being a lawyer and on a payroll anymore, I wrote almost anything for anybody—meanwhile devoting myself to my lifetime career of trying to decide what to do next. So, having been a wiseguy Marxist corporate lawyer, I also wrote a stock-market column for a two-issue publishing venture inappropriately entitled Leisure. *(I had to sue to collect the fee for the second article, but that was fun: this particular entrepreneur had a*

*lawyer for a bail-out father, and my embarrassment in muscling
him for $85 was never equal to his embarrassment in trying to
get me to take $50 for his son's most recent millionairing.
When we settled, I wished instead he had adopted me.)*

*The real stock market frightens me—risk real money build-
ing stairways to the stars? you got to be crazy!—but that juve-
nile mental arena in which stock-market players actually play
the market is nothing but back-on-the-farm funsville. The
point, of course, is that they are playing with fun-money—
and I never had any, never having made enough real money to
get bored with spending it consumeristically.*

*Would you believe it, in the second article I puffed a par-
ticular stock, High Voltage Engineering, in order to describe
the parlay of engineering talent/government financing/business
savvy as a new road to greatness—and it became one of the
most gorgeous glamour stocks of the early Sixties! Now how
the hell could I have known that I was a jerk not to take my
own advice?*

When the Big Board started belching last August and had its biggest
day of indigestion in quite a while, I happened to be calling a broker
friend of mine to wangle another expense-account steak. I tried to
be polite before coming to the point, and in an appropriate tch-tch
tone asked him what had gone wrong down there in Money Gulch,
expecting to hear some depressed something about technical adjustments or the end of world. "Gee, I don't know," he answered
with boyish enthusiasm. "But isn't it exciting!"

Seven billion dollars' worth of paper values disappeared in the
course of a few hours, and this middle-aged enthusiast thought it
was exciting. Well, he should know—maybe it was. But it leads me
to wonder: What makes these market-people tick? How do they
figure it? My answer, for the moment, is that they look at it this
way: It isn't how you play the game, so long as you either win or
lose.

Besides, it's the only really hot crap-game in town.

The stock market used to be the private playground of the very
rich. Then came the Twenties when stocks were sold in barber shops
and beauty parlors, and Up was thought to be an American birthright. The "rolling readjustment" which started in 1929, and almost
rolled us all out to sea, substantially dampened popular enthusiasm
for the market. One of the long-term consequences of the blackest

of American Thursdays was that the postwar bull market had gotten well under way before the sons forgot their fathers' lessons and once again started to buy little pieces of the American future. So far it has all worked out very nicely: the sanguine sons have had a chance to patronize their gloomy fathers, and Up has clearly been reinstated as a Constitutional right.

As time goes on, and it does according to the New York Stock Exchange, playing the market is becoming less and less of a spectator sport. Every day more people are jumping out of the stands and taking a crack at the ball on their own. Some of them, as in the recent uranium bubble, have acted like those delinquent juveniles who used to interrupt the proceedings at Ebbets Field by racing onto the diamond and sliding wildly into second just for the hell of it. But a surprising number of investors have controlled that million-aire-itch and have decided to wait for a slower advent of wealth.

Playing the market is the most complex, exciting game ever invented by the complex, exciting mind of man. This game has had its full share of genius-champions—and perhaps more than its share of other types, including losers.

What is it, and why is it so complex? Well, I would say it is the hurricane center of our private property system, and just about everything we can think of is influenced by it: all our daydreams and reflections pour through this one sluice-gate of the Big Green. Anyone who has read newspaper reports of market action knows that all analysts and reporters assume it is the most natural thing in the world for the market to respond to news items—even minor, seemingly irrelevant rumors. Why? Because the people down there are all the time guessing. And everybody knows that guesses inevitably draw upon almost any little idea or half-thought that may pop into the context of the guess. For example, not only your own evaluation of a news event—say, the Khrushchev visit or the steel strike—is relevant to market action, but also your psychological notions as to how *other* particular minds are apt to respond to such events.

A bright young man in the security analysis department of one of the big brokerage or investment houses (he's from the Harvard Business School or the Wharton School of Finance) goes out to Keokuk to look over an electronic growth situation. He is peering behind the balance sheet and the P&L, but not just to see whether the machinery is shiny and the factory floor well swept. His main job is to penetrate the character façades of the key executives, to gauge their grasp of a booming industry and their personal resources for dealing with fast-moving events. Now, based in good part on his judgments, or guesses, the public will buy little pieces of paper with magical words printed on them—and at prices also determined by these judgments.

The key to this kind of activity is the future, because that is primarily what is being bought and sold on the Exchange. In the commodity markets, the actual name of the paper traded is "futures"—contracts at a set price for the delivery of unharvested or even unplanted crops. Stock certificates purport to be instruments of title, but in a bull market they are in fact largely "futures." That is, when you buy a share of IBM you are not paying just for your mite of title in $1.3 billion of assets, not even just for your share of a fabulous backlog of orders. You are also paying for a piece of the continuing revolution in office procedures: paper money for paper title to theoretical improvements in handling paper.

Let's take, as an example, last year's model of what can happen to a participant who buys a piece of future that never materializes. The market for automobiles, notorious for its glamorous ups and downs, was very good in 1955, 1957, and it is very good this year. Now, I have a friend Sam who, being in on the general affluence in 1957, decided to get in on the affluence of the market as well. Sam bought 50 shares of Chrysler at around 79. Note the shrewdness of his move: Chrysler was big enough, but not the biggest, consistently ranking third behind General Motors and Ford—so he wasn't being "conventional." Chrysler's sales and earnings tended to be somewhat more volatile than its bigger competitors, one reason being that it was not as highly integrated an operation.

Well, back there in 1957 Chrysler earned $13.75 a share, its best year since the top of the postwar car-buying boom. Most of this zoom came in the first two quarters, when the company earned $10.29 as compared to $2.14 in the comparable period in 1956. But the price range in 1956 was about 60 low and 87 high—so Sam figured the stock was a kind of a bargain, you might say, at 79.

The stock reached a high of 82½ in 1957—and a low of 44 in 1958. The company posted a deficit of $3.88 last year. At one point poor Sam had suffered about a 45 per cent paper loss. He wasn't pleased, either, that the dividend went from $4.00 to $1.50: that meant his yield dropped from 5 per cent to less than 2 per cent.

So Sam is waiting—he has to. He is waiting for the stock to go back to 79, so he can get out whole.

And that's how we come to know how high is Up. When too much future is included in the price of a share of stock—when everything has to work out perfectly over the next three to five years for you to get, say, 4.1 per cent annually on your investment—then Up is here, and Down is around the corner. (The median yield on Exchange stocks in 1958 was 4.1 per cent, as compared to 6.1 per cent the year previous.) A lot of people don't happen to be interested in yield, however. They want capital appreciation, for tax purposes and as a hedge against inflation. Indeed, these two reasons are supposed to account for most of the new money in the market over the past few years. So Up has to be redefined in terms of the huge sums of money that have no place else to go but the market in their search for an unearned dollar taxed at the benevolent capital gains rate of 25 per cent.

A clever and successful operator I know sold out his market holdings early last summer having defined Up as Right Now. He thought it was too good to last. His theory is that when a company is valued on the Exchange at, say, $50 million, and the men managing it would, as he puts it, "take twenty and run," it's time to fold up your tent. But I have the feeling he'll be back. Oh, he might wait until the market drops enough for him to make up the 25 per cent capital gains tax, or maybe just to prove to himself he was right. But he'll be back. After all, it's the only really hot crap-game in town.

❀ *PLUS ÇA CHANGE . . .*

PARTISAN REVIEW, 1967

Review of *The Limits of American Capitalism,*
by Robert L. Heilbroner

I wrote other reviews of a couple of Heilbroner's earlier books —one published in NYRB, the other written for Commentary *and not published. For a while, early in the Sixties, we were even a little friendly: along with a few other similarly interested types we had an occasional luncheon group we enthusiastically* called *The Deficit Club*—thinking in a positive way not of ours, but of the federal government's. A brief but pleasant comradeship of enlightenment, we all favored a greatly expanded federal deficit as the new beginning of American sanity. That was part of the exciting, even kind of happy, early Sixties. I would be shocked if any one of the economists or journalists who showed once or twice at our luncheons had now changed his view on this matter; and I would be equally nonplused if any one of them was now anything but bitter about the issue. A federal budget unbalanced for military purpose—but only for that purpose—is now the black core of American idiocy and ill will, and no longer anything to have pleasant luncheons about.

I admire Heilbroner's careful expositive talent and also appreciate the great difficulty of his undertaking—talking salable sense about economics to the largest pretty-good audience he can imagine. But what always fascinated me about him was that I saw he was even better than that and (second level of meaning) how did he ever manage to stick to that given role? Was it helplessness? (His first book was an immense success, a decade later still selling 50,000 copies a year around the world: that kind of success can be tyrannous.) Or did he know something—really, something else—about being smart and getting along that had escaped me? A substantial few people have fascinated me in the same way, over the years.

Robert Heilbroner writes a highly stylized book. He is like an abstract painter who executes a Real One for private consumption; and then hires himself out, so to speak, to translate it into a predigested version for a substantially less capable audience, offering just what—imagining the central drift of the *New York Times* for the coming period—is exactly necessary, no more and no less, for the deeper purposes of Good Citizenship. (He says he spent four years writing the thirty or forty thousand words comprising the present collection of two essays.) In this effort, equally interesting and misguided, no one can touch him.

I admire his talent as a rhetorician, although he is not of a size with J. K. Galbraith. But Heilbroner is the acknowledged Prince of Popularizers in that special field of awareness in which, it has been thought, the audience must be hog-tied in order even to be brought to sit still long enough to listen: *economics*. A fascinating fact that, in a country where the very souls of self, children, and predecessors are regularly sold at bargain prices for inadequate reasons, the Subject Itself must be presented in pidgin or pious English.

There are undoubtedly thousands of educated people in this country—perhaps tens of thousands—who could and should read this book with profit. If I was certain that I was talking to any one of them, I would not have the slightest hesitation in recommending it in a loud voice. But in one area after another, who knows what who knows? One either accepts the coerced presumptions of some professionalism or other (especially coerced as to language), or one confronts the very dark fact that the common language has suffered vast deterioration, and we are nearly become strangers mumbling incoherently each about his own non-professional past. (In 1959, Adolf Berle published a brilliant study of our altered political economy in which he allotted twenty-six of 158 pages to four prefaces, one each for Businessmen, American Liberals, Scholars, and the Uncommitted Public.)

I am suggesting that the audience has collapsed. This—and not the more widely remarked isolation of the artist or other communicator—is the central consequence of modern disruption. The modern "audience" is no longer even consistently prejudiced. The paradoxical result of this formulation, in place of the more conventionally romantic one, is that the writer and artist—if only he can, by leap of genius or benefit of accident or circumstance, find a live nerve among the animal debris of the audience—is immensely powerful: as powerful as that nerve. The deteriorated audience of disconnected nerves will buy anything: fashion is all. A second, not less important, result is that artificial simplicity with a fresh smell—what might be called beefed-up simplicity—is nearly irresistible: is now a primary form of modern herding.

What then, in this context, is the price of simplicity for the Prince of Popularizers in that one area of awareness (economics) where calculated miseducation takes its greatest toll? The price is personal depression running so deep that, self-deprived of poetry, it becomes rigidly willful and eventually fatuous. When a knowledgeable and talented writer strenuously and precisely limits himself to his own awful idea of the audience, the result is a success *only if a nerve is touched*. And that will be the result of luck or genius primarily—the hard, ugly work of simplifying is really secondary. Any willing talent can sneak into television; but only a Rod Serling can take and hold it by storm.

The nerve touched in *The Limits of Capitalism* is, unfortunately, the same one that was overmassaged in an earlier and rather more interesting book by Mr. Heilbroner, *The Future as History*. It is somehow very important to him to demonstrate that nothing very much is going to happen. I doubt that; but maybe. In any event, why the big effort to elevate this so-so sentiment to the level of Firm and Convincing Proof? Because if the future bites, the present may wiggle: it is, after all, the same animal. And a wiggling present does not simplify so readily.

The willed clarity which the author enforces on a very twitchy (in my opinion) present, requires large doses of old-fashioned nominalism dispensed in a heavily judicious manner. So the American system is called "capitalism"—which will not last forever, but is not apt to disappear overnight either. The supreme difficulty of getting anywhere while terming our system capitalist is overcome by equating "capitalism" and "business" and using the latter word to discuss whatever needs to be discussed, and the former to predict the future so as to ensure that the discussion amounts to as little as possible. Business is a facinating process which changes daily, while capitalism of course is an historical entity that can be displaced only by revolution. We can eat our cake while mushing it around in our plate. "It is certainly beyond the present limits of capitalism to replace the guiding principle of production for profit by that of production for use—which is to say, it is impossible to redirect the main flow of economic effort, away from the pull of market considerations to areas established by public policy considerations." But all production for consumption—whether consumption by welfare administrations, the military, the scientific academy, or ordinary suburbia—is for use as well as profit; and a market pulls differently according to whether it is free or managed—when the latter, the results are very much like those derived from "public policy considerations" even if not made by an officially constituted public government. If the alternative to the hoary capitalist presumption about the Profit Motive is thought to be the immediate construction of the humanist society of good will imagined by the classical socialists—then, sure, the old crap will continue. But if the question for the next several decades is, "Toward what and in consultation with whom will

American business busy itself?" then the old crap requires some new if-this, then-that kind of analysis, which in all likelihood would be both interesting and complicated. In any event, it would be political and psychological—as befits the front-running technological society in major, not to say convulsive, transition.

The Limits of American Capitalism consists of two brief essays, the first being a determinedly unimaginative depiction of the current corporate economy, refracted through traditional economic notions, and the second turning out to be a much more worthwhile effort to state—in strophes of careful hesitation—the cataclysmic conflict between the old business system and the new technological order. Now, please notice the problem of critically evaluating a book like this: many educated people do not know that the United States is a corporate society which is not the same thing as a capitalist society; and many more are not as deeply aware as they should be that business and technology, although they sleep together every night, are (like many such) mortal enemies. In the initial essay dealing with the first point, Mr. Heilbroner depicts our present order in a flattened-out manner that is useful only if it is news—and how am I to know? The second essay is very good no matter who is reading it: the data and insights, the narrative line on the subjects of poverty, the military and especially the new problems of employment created by technological success are all interesting and presented with expert brevity. Even the downbeat tone is expressed with more effect, as when he refers to "the temptations of luxury consumption, and the general lack of concern in a nation lulled by middle-class images of itself," in telling us why the so-called problem of poverty is not apt to be solved within the next generation, although he believes it to be the chief issue that can be resolved without a radical reordering of society.

Still, the depressive mood of the book is consistent, overwhelming, and self-inflicted by reason of the author's willful presumptions of clarity. But the author is better than this; and this result was unnecessary. Why popularize gloom in a reasonable tone of voice? With this method, even the Dark Forces are clarified to an unconscionable degree, and we are served up a future without potential disaster. What is presented here is history so well managed for purposes of clear exposition that conflict appears only as bits and pieces of nominalism. But the main point is not that some of us may personally prefer a frantic cry to reasonable gloom, but that the dynamism and variety of the present (whether or not destructive) are sacrificed to the idea of an audience that does not even exist in the absence of that idea. Clarity of this high order is useless, or worse. For example, at page 90 he writes: "An economic transformation of capitalism of such magnitude that its big businesses become, in effect, public agencies is not a serious possibility for the foreseeable American future. . . ." This is offered in disallowing the possibility of nationalization. But an accurately dynamic depiction of the present would require the writer to note the variety of ways in which the big corporations *are* public agencies—and treat themselves, and are treated, as such. And it might be added that nationalization, because of changes in the property system, is quite unnecessary; it was propounded by the socialists mostly because they were against traditional private property. (I have chosen to criticize Mr. Heilbroner's rhetoric, rather than what I divine to be his understanding. If I had been discussing the latter, I would suggest that his academic training has given him too much to unlearn concerning the centrality of free markets; and he has not learned as much as he could have from Adolf Berle with respect to the revolution in property forms which more fundamentally underlies the American corporate order.)

The two essays are united not only by mood and mistaken method, but by a theme as well, that as capitalism supplanted feudalism, the new technological order will supplant capitalism. "When" and "how" are the questions. When? Not for fifty years, says Mr. Heilbroner. How? By "a subversive process of historic change" in which the privileged groups of the old order are attracted, in spite of themselves, to the qualities of life of the new order. *Add:* as and when these are created, and made attractive and so on. Mr. Heilbroner finally says: "Veblen was too impatient for his engineers to take over; Schumpeter more realistic when he advised the intelligentsia to be prepared to wait in the wings for possibly a century. . . ." Nobody waits for a century. (For Veblen, the engineers were a metaphor; but that's another matter.) The intellectuals of the New Class are now gathering for a great national jamboree—under the expert auspices of an adventurous heir. In fifty years, all but a handful of Ancient Mariners from the present intellectual areas will be dead.

"Why do societies resist change? A full explanation of social inertia must reach deep into the psychological and technical underpinnings of the human community. But in the context of our present concern we need not delve to such depths." Oh?

❀ SOME DEDUCTIONS

COMMENTARY, 1964

Review of *The Great Treasury Raid,*
by Philip M. Stern; and
The Cold War and the Income Tax: A Protest,
by Edmund Wilson

Philip Stern is intimately related to the Stern Foundations, with which I have cohabited. I am tempted to say that he is the nicest rich man I know, except I don't remember if I know any others. Anyway, he's a very nice fellow, even if he is Julius Rosenwald's grandson.
  Our wealthy people—what they could have done! (Could they have done it?)

We have here two very strenuous efforts at clarification of the federal system of taxation, written by two upper-class purists who have been horrified unto death by their discovery (or rediscovery) of certain of the qualities of American social reality, especially as revealed in the Internal Revenue Code.

To begin with Mr. Stern: *The Great Treasury Raid* is probably the best popular survey of the federal tax system yet published. It is also easy to follow and substantially entertaining—largely because Mr. Stern includes so many of the choice anecdotes that are among the happier by-products of the Code. The best of them all, for me, is taken from the transcript of a 1946 case involving a man and his wife who claimed to be partners in a company along with their four children (ranging in age from seven years to three months). The wife was interrogated:

> Q. Now, do you participate in the management of the business of the LaSalle Livestock Company?
> A. Well, I have been producing partners.

Q. Beg pardon?
A. I have been too busy producing partners so far.

For those who are not in a position to produce partners, there is the more broadly based production of little $600 exemptions. A dynamic detail relevant to this production, which Mr. Stern did not find the space to fit in, is the swarm of expectant mothers who regularly enter maternity wards throughout the country for induced births on New Year's Eve. (The timeliness is worth $80 or more, and it's a shame to throw the money away.)

Mr. Stern, however, is not himself entertained by the Internal Revenue Code. At bottom, he is overwhelmed by its monumental irrationality and unfairness, and after describing the absurd inequities of the law, he proposes a return to a "pure" definition of income to which a graduated tax would be applied, with *no* exclusions or preferential rates. This means, among other things, doing away with the oil depletion allowance and abandoning the capital gains rate (in favor of an averaging device to account for the "bunched" income problem); it also means taxing Social Security payments. Mr. Stern calculates that all in all, under such a system, taxable income would be increased by $115 billion annually and the additional $40 billion the Treasury would collect thereon (at pre-1964 rates) would allow an across-the-board rate reduction of nearly half.

Thus, proceeding on the assumption that every time one citizen walks through a "loophole," all *other* citizens have to pay more to the gatekeeper, Mr. Stern manages to paint a vivid picture of the internal revenue mess. But that is not the same thing as painting a picture of the economic realities involved in the creation and operation of the law, or of the political realities to be faced in any possible reform of it.* Here, Mr. Stern has not done so well. The moralistic

---

* For example, the best functioning opportunity for reform during the past decade or so would have been the reduction of the top rate to 50 or 60 per cent. The immediate cost to the Treasury would not have exceeded $1 billion; the ritualistic cover would have been denied the high-income complainers; and the genuine unfairness to professionals, who have less room to maneuver in, would have been overcome. But even more interesting is that, beyond the obvious advantages, the lowering of rates would itself have "closed loopholes" and have been of distinct disadvantage to many upper-income types. Why? Because Uncle Sam would thereby have become a 60 per cent instead of a 91 per cent risk partner in numerous tax-tailored enterprises: many of the Code

tone of the book is heightened as it progresses, and finally becomes wearing, at least to this reader. Moreover, Mr. Stern knows better, as he indicates in the excellent chapter he calls "The Heavy Odds Against Reform." Why, then, did he succumb to the moralistic purism of his proposal for reform? Because the *only* alternative is to embrace the irrationality of the Code—and indeed of American life itself, which that exfoliation so ardently expresses—in an act of despairing love. To embrace the irrationality means to live with it, in and among it; it means pinpointing our anger, both for political effectiveness, and to keep from ending up consumed with hatred for the whole crazy system—as, indeed, Edmund Wilson has ended up.

What happened to Wilson was that he neglected, for one reason and another, to file any tax returns from 1946 through 1955. On one level, that's what happened to him. If we note what happened to him on another, more important level, however, his failure to file returns or pay taxes seems perfectly proper. He had departed from the contemporary American reality, and therefore could not be bothered to support it financially. What drew him back was that he made a bit too much money in the mid-Fifties (writing about the Dead Sea Scrolls) and was thus led to inquire of a lawyer-friend as to what this tax-return business was all about. The lawyer (who later died of a stroke while worrying about this and other matters) came up with only one positive suggestion—namely, that Mr. Wilson leave the United States in physical fact, and become a citizen of some other country.

The key to this book (and perhaps to Mr. Wilson's entire career) is that he did not accept this excellent advice. Charlie Chaplin left us owing close to a million dollars in unpaid taxes. But then Chaplin, born in England, was a make-believe American. Mr. Wilson is not a make-believe American: he is one of the realest Americans ever. If there is a written American language that honest men can admire, then no list of its creators and preservers could begin with any other name. But in the course of disclosing his discovery of the literary character of the Internal Revenue Code, he employs the phrase, "in the midst of all this pedantry." Oh, no, Mr. Wilson! In

---

preferences are useful only when played off against 91 per cent income. This is the kind of true economic and political complexity that one must deal with in reforming the tax system. (Yet imagine how the unions and the ADA would have screamed at any such proposal!)

America we do not use the term "pedantry" to describe any aspect of the system that permits an annual theft of $40 billion. That is not the term to use in referring to the brilliantly functional obscurity of the Code.

The Cold War and the Income Tax: A Protest is one of the zaniest books ever written, and absolutely fascinating. It is Edmund Wilson, one of the living glories of our literature, discovering present-day America—that place from which he has steadfastly refused to separate himself in a physical way while withdrawing from it spiritually and intellectually. This act of political discovery—ending with another and further spiritual withdrawal: "I have finally come to feel that this country, whether or not I continue to live in it, is no longer any place for me"—means that to the renewed interest in us recently evidenced by the Rockefellers and Stevensons and Clarks and Scrantons, we may now add the active and still Olympian contempt of our great native stylist. Why, it is almost like having Mencken back home again! And the fact that Wilson had to find out about the extent of federally financed research by reading a piece in an *English* magazine (the *New Statesman*) by an editorial writer for the Washington *Post* (Karl Meyer) is a minor matter. Just so he noticed at last.

Of course, he was dragged back by his tax delinquency—not, he wistfully avers, by any principle. And then it was not exactly in the best of taste to go on about the Cold War and the Bomb and the half-hidden horrors of CBR at just the moment when it became most useful to note that the taxes he didn't pay would have been spent on homicidal junk. And if he had to discover the bureaucratization of American society at IRS offices rather than at GM or the unemployment compensation office, so what? It is hard, however, to forgive his sentimental glorification of Major Eatherly, or his abysmal ignorance concerning the centrally American subject of money. He doesn't begin to understand that there is a society existing in which he makes the money on which the taxes are due *because* they are due . . . and paid . . . and spent . . . *even* on homicidal junk. Indeed, in his hysterical devotion to American Individualism (meaning *me, me, me*) come hell or high water, and whatever the historical facts of the matter may be, he is only a few ideological inches away from the right-wing amendment on the income tax—to preserve the integrity of the individual against the encroachments of an overweening federal bureaucracy, etc.

Still, he finally noticed. I'm grateful. And we can all be grateful to Philip Stern for his lucid and useful popularization of the Code. Although both books constitute all-out attacks on the Code, they are almost beyond comparison. Mr. Stern, enlightened heir to a great post-Civil War fortune, is in effect complaining that he has not had to pay enough tax. Mr. Wilson, honored heir to our pre–Civil War culture, couldn't be bothered paying any at all; when he got caught, he screamed. No, the books are beyond comparison.

❀ PRESCRIPTION AND PRICES

COMMENTARY, 1965

Review of *The Real Voice*, by Richard Harris

I met Kefauver when in 1952 he stopped by Yale to campaign, or catch his breath, or something. The main thing that impressed you was his size, and the quiet of him: and it turned out that he was, indeed, a big man determined to fit the small role history had assigned him. At Yale (he had a degree there) he dropped the cornpone, and then I realized: they still learn more from Lincoln than from Roosevelt, those that had to wait to start where the gun went off. (And believe me, friends, politicians of his kind are not in it for the loose change: if what you want is money, the traffic directions are now sufficiently clear.)

I knew him better than merely seeing him once, because myunclethejudge* got me a job with Rudy Halley, a summer between law school semesters, right after the great crime hearings. Rudy never heard anything but that gun going off (his mama said, "Run, baby, run!"). But Kefauver was a special Lincoln-nut—like Gene McCarthy is, a little bit—the last phony farmboy, the smartest Bryan ever, determined to ride any hobbyhorse at all to glory. They really believed: they thought purity was like penicillin—all you had to do was mass-produce it in a democratic way, and keep the price down. (Humphrey, too—dying of that disease.)

* Chief Judge David L. Bazelon, of the U.S. Court of Appeals in Washington, D.C.—known in the family, to distinguish him from me, as "Little Dave."

The late Senator Estes Kefauver did not become chairman of the Senate Subcommittee on Antitrust and Monopoly until January 1957. When he achieved this eminence, however, he made a real thing of it. He held a series of "administered price" hearings: steel, autos, finally drugs. The first two are monuments to economic fact-gathering—reputed to be the most impressive since the reports of the Temporary National Economic Committee at the tail-end of the New Deal. But the third, his extensive hearings on the drug industry (held shortly before he died a twice-defeated candidate for the Democratic Presidential nomination), was the one that got the most publicity. Unlike the others, the drug hearings resulted in an en-acted bill—a gold star on Capital Hill.

The Real Voice is a fascinating anecdotal narrative about the whole process by a very effective *New Yorker* writer with a good command of novelistic techniques. The villain of the drama described by Richard Harris here is the drug (that is, the prescription drug) industry—personalized somewhat by individual apologists and lobbyists, but mostly appearing straight as the huge profit-seeking mechanism it is. The drug industry has been zooming to financial glory by reason of a major technological bonanza. Like many such, the new drug technology seems to have had its origin in one of our war efforts: antibiotics as a big postwar item grew out of the demand for penicillin during World War II. Besides antibiotics, the big early sellers were cortisone and tranquilizers. But the drug industry is not merely fortunate, as some others are, in having been handed an opportunity to exploit technological advances; the drug industry is peculiar. This is not only because it has a very personal application to immediate matters of pain and death, or because it sells a new order of merchandise which might be called "necessitous luxuries." It is peculiar for two additional reasons.

First, the industry "sells" only to thousands of doctors, who in turn "sell" to millions of consumers. In this special distribution system, the doctor's profit has nothing to do with the industry's profit. Second, the industry seems to have been the special victim of the breakdown of our patent system as traditionally conceived. Briefly, it is too expensive to litigate-out a patent all the way; also, you can lose the patent altogether, since the courts are tougher than the Patent Office. According to Mr. Harris (who relies on the Kefauver staff work), what the drug firms have done has been to settle litigations among themselves whereby the patent is preserved and the take of the interested parties is apportioned out of court. This amounts to private administration of the patent privilege, also called "collusion."

The patent factor is not the main angle, however. The main thing is selling trade names and pharmaceutical variations to doctors. This is done by advertising and by salesmen. There is one salesman for every five workers in the drug industry—they are called "detail men." There is one detail man for every ten doctors in the country; they run their routes regularly, and give away tons of samples. Additional tons, along with elaborate brochures, arrive by mail. The industry indulged in 3.8 billion *pages* of journal advertising in 1959, sent out three-quarters of a billion "direct-mail impressions," and the detail men made nearly twenty million calls on doctors and pharmacists. In 1958, the 22 largest companies spent 24 per cent of gross on advertising and promotion. This ante keeps out more small fry than the patents ever could.

When the doctor, for instance, writes "Miltown" (a brand name) instead of "meprobamate" (its chemical name) on a prescription, the hundreds of millions of dollars of promotional expense are justified. To assist him in doing so, the drug companies—besides the great expenditure of money—concoct chemical names only a philologist could remember and spell ("clordizapoxide") to match the catchy trade names ("Librium"). And when a doctor prescribes Miltown or Librium, the druggist by law may not substitute the cheapest reliable meprobamate or clordizapoxide on the market. (The same applies to slight pharmaceutical variations and combination drugs.) Kleenex never had it so good.

Anybody who followed the boom market of the Fifties even casually knows how hot drug profits were. That was what Kefauver started after—in line with his antitrust and monopoly jurisdiction, his interest in non-market pricing, and his staff's initial probing of the industry. His first headline on the front page of the *New York Times* read: "Senate Panel Cites Markups on Drugs Ranging to 7,079%." The final headlines of the machine-of-concern which he had set in motion were, of course, those concerning thalidomide and the American woman who went to Sweden for an abortion rather than give birth to a child deformed by the drug. These headlines measure the shift of concentration in the hearings from pricing to side effects. The American people ended up more interested in occasional poison than in day-to-day prices. (This seems to me to offer some kind of poisonous food for thought.) In any event, the fact that the drug companies had cut some testing corners—had rushed with unseemly speed to make their wonder drugs available for the creation of their wonder profits—provided the decisive thrust for both the content and the passage of the final bill. This bill accomplishes something, it is said, regarding FDA supervision of testing and labeling as to side effects; but nothing much has been done about pricing and patent procedures. So be it: that is, I believe, the truth of American popular interest. There is not much real objection to the basic structure of corporate advertising power in this country.

The last word must be reserved for Senator Estes Kefauver. He was a bull of an intellectual from Tennessee—a graduate of the Yale Law School who campaigned in a coonskin hat. One of his chief assistants in the drug hearings viewed him as the last of the Populists, because of his antitrust tilting against vested urban windmills. Mr. Harris quotes a "veteran observer of affairs on Capitol Hill" to the effect that Kefauver was "The Shakespeare of Committee chairmen. . . . He takes the work of some Saxo Grammaticus on his staff and brings it to life for the man on the street." That language (the Library of Congress and the Shakespeare Folger Library are both situated on Capitol Hill) suggests that the Senator was exceptionally good at parlaying staff work, even of a decidedly intellectual or academic or expert nature, into headlines. With that talent for bridging the distance between his academic staff and the popular mind as he conceived it, no wonder he thought he could be President. He was an early, local Kennedy; a late, sophisticated Johnson.

But he was slow and careful, ponderous and profoundly calculated: his most frequently reported quality was "unruffled persistence." Kefauver was an even more withdrawn Wilson—*after the ball was over*. I had the occasion to stare at him for a half-hour or so, within a year or two of his death: I have hardly ever seen such a depressed individual outside of an asylum. In my opinion, he represents very meaningfully the Walpurgisnacht of American liberal *will*, relying on and appealing to native righteousness. I emphasize "will": the cultural sources had dried up before he did. As *The Real Voice* (the title is taken from Woodrow Wilson, incidentally) ends, Kefauver puts down a book—on the urging of his staff—to solicit an invitation to the signing ceremony of Public Law 87–781. He invited himself, but President Kennedy—who was uninterested in the drug

investigation but had taken over the action for headline reasons—
gave him the first cheap signing-pen. The book he had laid aside was
equal to the event—"a dog-eared copy of *How to Win Friends and
Influence People*."

9

▦ ON "THE NEW CLASS"

❀ THE NEW CLASS

COMMENTARY, 1966

This piece was adapted from my second book, Power in America: The Politics of the New Class, *published in 1967. That book was begun with one major question in mind, the question that emerged (for me) as central from my work in* The Paper Economy—*namely, What is power? As I mentioned, to a Marxist and a corporate lawyer, nothing could be more significant than the reduced critical importance of the concept of property and, consequently, the nature of power when not exclusively identified with that concept. I had an important conversation with Berle on this power-without-property theme that confirmed this direction of thought: I asked him what was the best writing on power viewed in this light, and he said there was nothing much. I was surprised, and took that as a signal to speculate further.*

At the beginning, I was convinced that the key was the characteristically negative attitude toward power in this moralistic nation, especially as expressed in and with respect to the House of Representatives—designed by the Constitution-makers as our major democratic opportunity, substantially abandoned as such, and then recently reconstituted, potentially, by the great apportionment decisions beginning with Baker v. Carr. *Secondly, I believed that power was now involved more with deception—especially including self-deception—than with straight-out force. Power had been misunderstood primarily because it was too often reduced to a matter of force or property (money) and too readily opposed in a wooden way to morality, whereas in fact there was a power-aspect as well as a moral-aspect to most acts, to most existence, and both*

370

power and morals very centrally involved the same kind of human subjectivity. So back to people and—on a social scale and to begin with—classes of people. Especially new classes.

If I had had the time and the strength to write the book twice, I would have organized it the second time around the idea of the New Class—which is the central surviving notion (for me) of Power in America, as power-without-property was of The Paper Economy.

PERHAPS THE profoundest event of this century in the United States has been the growth-to-dominance of corporations, which have become our chosen form for the social and political control of technology. Apart from the fact that this new system has worked so devastatingly well, the chief effect of the corporate order has been decisively to undermine the previously existing system of private property. In the process, the class of property-holders has been undercut, and a New Class of non-property-holding individuals has been created whose life conditions are determined by their position within, or relation to, the corporate order. They desire and they achieve a privileged standard of living; and while they do gather in some "property" for personal security, they do not look forward to the accumulation of capital for themselves. They are jobholders, not capitalists.

The propertyless New Class is thus most broadly defined as that group of people who gain status and income through organizational position. With some exceptions, they arrive at their positions—or at least are permitted to enter the race—mostly by virtue of academic qualification. This great change has so effectively sneaked up on us, we are so many of us so completely involved in it, that we do not recognize it for the major historical transformation it in fact is. Most of us thought we were just getting and holding "good jobs": actually, we were (for better or for worse) changing the whole world, albeit not necessarily in our intended direction.

To restate the proposition in other terms: Under the duress of modern technology, productive property has of necessity been organized in larger and larger aggregates. Hence the corporate revolution. Control of the major property held by the corporations is in the hands of non-owners. And, as technology gallops forward, its processes require more technologists, and ever more refined patternings of sophisticated men and sophisticated machines. As technology becomes more involved with accumulating know-how, and less dependent on the gross division of labor which characterized industrialism, the central factor in production again becomes people, their *particular* qualities and capacities: human beings thus once again become more important than machines (even though they may persist inordinately in "acting like" machines). The truly productive "property," then, is the skill of the person. Moreover, this skill is not merely individual, but is implicitly social and political in that it requires not only that the individual be able to do something, but that he be able to relate what he does to what others do. This is the entrée for a great deal of *purely* organizational or administrative effort, and consequently the opening for a great number of people who mostly organize and administer, and criticize and comment on, the activities of others. To begin with, then, we have technologists and administrative intellectuals as primary elements of the New Class.

How big is the New Class? Perhaps not yet as big as the small-property class or the still-uneducated working class, but these latter are declining in significance as well as quantity, while the New Class grows greatly both numerically and in strategic position. In 1960, some 2,000 institutions of higher learning cared for 3.2 million persons. The figure is rapidly increasing: various Bureau of the Census projections estimate that college enrollment will be two-to-three times as great by 1980. Persons twenty-five years of age or older in the 1960 population who had completed four years or more of college numbered 7.6 million; in 1980, the figure may well reach 14.4 million, nearly double. These people—two million college graduates a year—"capitalize" four years or more of their lives not for cultural adornment or use, but for reasons of career.

In attempting to appreciate the scope and character of this major phenomenon of the New Class, one may properly recollect the previous rise to power of the bourgeoisie, the property-owning class. That rise did not occur all at once: pockets of stagnation always existed alongside spurts of growth; at one time, a particular area might be the liveliest, then another; there were important national and geographic differences; and the people responsible for carrying out the change were not, while they were doing so, particularly easy to identify. The currently occurring changeover in emphasis from money-capital to education-capital—to be invested in the status play of organization life rather than directly and personally in the production of commodities for a market economy—is not apt to be simpler, clearer, or in any way less complicatedly "historical."

Surely, however, it has by now become fairly clear that the present scramble for educational advantage and the struggle to translate achieved educational status into organizational advantage have much in common with the fierce competition of early business growth. It is front-page news every spring when the letters are sent out from the admissions offices of the major Eastern colleges. Even the initial edge of family or propertied background is similar to the advantage enjoyed, say, by a seventeenth-century aristocrat in an earlier entrepreneurial age. The important fact here is that a particular old class-based advantage, to become fully effective, must be translated into terms appropriate to the *new* class: from aristocratic status and tenure to entrepreneurial use of property; and similarly, from a property edge to the educational and organizational use thereof. In the nineteenth century, the education of the upper classes was an occasional adornment; today it is a functional necessity. This being so, the capacity (often called "talent") to scramble forward in the environment of the elite academy is competitive with the wealth and family background which once almost exclusively governed admission. Writing in the *New York Times* on March 14, 1964, Robert Trumbull reported that Harvard, Yale, and Princeton were shifting, albeit glacially, from wealth to ability. He cited a study of the New York Social Register for 1963 by Gene R. Hawes to the effect that "while nearly two-thirds of the men listed went to Harvard, Yale, or Princeton, fewer than half of their sons" have done so.

Education, like capital in the past, is now a manipulable and alienable property. With capital alienated from the capitalist by the system of corporate ownership and investment out of retained earnings, the distinction between capitalist and *educated* proletarian fades into something less profound than it used to be. Indeed, the latter has the more significant and dynamic relation to the means of production in that the system cannot work without him; whereas the capital that *works*—machines and buildings rather than bank deposits and stock certificates—hardly needs the alienated capitalist at all. More and more he becomes a mere *rentier*, and his best defense is tradition.

In his thorough work on the New Deal, Arthur Schlesinger says that the idea of the "brain trust" had its beginnings in a conversation

that occurred in March 1932 between Sam Rosenman and candidate
Roosevelt concerning the general lack of ideas as to what to do
about the Depression—and especially the fact that the businessmen
and politicians did not have anything much to offer. Rosenman suggested going to the universities. The first ambassador from academia
to the future New Deal was Raymond Moley of Columbia. Moley
then recruited Tugwell, Berle, and some others. Thus began the revolutionary, non-priestly, and ultimately successful onslaught of the
New Class upon the heights of national power.

The breakthrough event, then, was the New Deal; but the New
Deal itself had roots. Roosevelt, for one thing, had been primed for
the event—as for much else—by his tour of duty under Woodrow
Wilson. In a speech in 1920 he said:

> Wilson's administration would not have been successful in the
> War if he had not adopted the policy of calling in the experts of
> the Nation, without regard to party affiliations, in order to create
> and send across the seas that great Army in record-breaking time.

Then, too, there was the precedent of the Progressive movement.
As Richard Hofstadter puts it:

> The development of regulative and humane legislation required
> the skills of lawyers and economists, sociologists and political
> scientists, in the writing of laws and in the staffing of adminis-
> trative and regulative bodies. . . . Reform brought with it the
> brain trust.

Hofstadter sees the Progressive movement as a revolt against organization, and especially against its spiritual consequences. The Progressives and the New Class—although in many social ways similar
—differ in this important respect: the New Class knows that it lives
in and through organizations. This much at least has been accomplished. Also fundamentally altered is the definition of a key term
for both, "opportunity": for the Progressives it meant "competition," but for the New Class it means "education," whether or not
competitive (and if so, then competitive inside organizations, not
between individuals outside organized life). On this difference, one
may reasonably base a new politics.

As an aspect of the New Class adventure, note that both Donald

Richberg and Raymond Moley, who were important early New Dealers, used that experience to go over to the big interests somewhat later. Walter Lippmann had done the same thing before them; John Dos Passos and others more recently. These intellectuals represent the rise of a class which, as it rises, makes necessary deals and so "amalgamates" with previously existing classes. There is really no good reason for this phenomenon to produce the general unease that it does. It is perfectly ordinary and, in the human scope of things, even desirable. What is unsettling, I think, is that these people are *intellectuals*. But that is exactly what is upsetting about the whole New Class phenomenon. This sort of thing, not a hero's lonely endeavor, is the pattern for the future of active thought in history. Can it ruin culture altogether?

If so, it is mainly because what we have known as "culture" was born as dry fruit, with a seed of genetic powerlessness. We may be in for an unpleasant time, while ideas and actions come into a better working relation by reason of the involvement of the intellectual in effective (not merely prescriptive) history. This means that the mode of lawyers—the intellectuals who were dealing with genuine issues of power in that long period when the rest of us were living in the academic desert—is likely to become a functional model for a large part of the cultural future.

But there are also social aspects of the New Class advance. Writing about FDR's tour of the European front during World War I, as Assistant Secretary of the Navy, Schlesinger mentions that Roosevelt "ran into" Robert A. Lovett, Fiorello H. LaGuardia, and Charles R. Merriam (and he informs us about the rank and service of each at that time). This social coziness is especially characteristic of Schlesinger's writing. It reveals a very clublike view of history: history almost as the conjoint action of talented classmates. Since historians do not merely collect facts but also dream the dream of a better story, I think Schlesinger here reveals *his* idea of a better story —namely, that America by now virtually has that ruling elite group, if not ruling class, that it has so noticeably lacked since the Civil War. And it is suggestive that Schlesinger should feel this way, for he more than anyone else is the historian of the New Class—of its great New Deal victory, and of the impressive return to Washington of its elite elements under the managerial style-baron, John F. Kennedy.

Following along with the basic cleavage in American society, the first great division noticeable among the members of the New Class is between those who work in private bureaucracies and those who work in public ones: perhaps, with more meaning, in profit and non-profit institutions. In each, the important matter for the New Class individual is his job, and the educational status which has afforded him his hold on the job. But most of the basic productive property in this country is under the control and direction of private corporations; apart from military considerations, the public governments—national, state, and local—are decidedly junior to the power of private bureaucracies. Accordingly, those members of the New Class who work in government partake of its inferior income and status while also suffering or benefiting (according to their particular natures) from the absence of the profit ideology as an organizing principle of purpose in their lives. On the other hand, the distinction between profit and non-profit is being reduced as time goes on: education, for instance, is becoming a big business; and the larger corporations take care of a great number of people who are not genuinely concerned with profitmaking.

The other great division among members of the New Class is between the technologists and the administrators who control and exploit them. (The New Class is the non-owning class: and they non-own everything important, eventually.) The technologist often prefers to concentrate on his work and mostly he needs only to be left alone in order to do so. But in bureaucratic life, this may be asking too much. The irascible Admiral Rickover, speaking some years ago before a professional group, declared:

> The work of professional persons in bureaucracies is severely hampered by administrative interference. We have such interference because we do not draw clear lines between the respective role of the professional man and the administrator and because, of the two, the administrator enjoys the higher prestige and position. He is in fact king.

Concentration on work—especially involving things and tools rather than people—in effect delivers the power of the organization to the people-oriented administrators. Sometimes this power is delivered ahead of schedule: writing about the New Deal experience,

Schlesinger refers to a certain Hugh Hammond Bennett, an early crusader against the evil of soil erosion. An important issue at the time was whether the problem was to be approached through the social and economic structure which induced soil erosion, or whether it was to be attacked directly in a physical way. "Bennett no doubt felt that one bureau could not do everything, and that the engineering approach, by avoiding the politically sensitive problem of rural poverty, could gain conservation a broader support." So everybody ends up playing politics, and it is not really the height of scientific insight to do so *after* surrendering power—and, incidentally, distorting the solution of the technical problem in favor of crudely imagined political obstacles. But this is typical, I fear, of the technical wing of the New Class. They are much too "rational" ever to become effective politicians—or, what is the same thing, non-concentrating administrators.

Finally, we can sense some of the quality of the New Class from its characteristic habitat—the suburbs.

What is a suburb? It is most obviously the new place where the new people live. The proliferation of suburbs constitutes the big postwar change in America: they are where the new money has been spent, where the much-discussed "income revolution" has erected its shopping-center barricades. One out of four Americans now resides, or at least sleeps, in a suburb: they grow three times as fast as central-city and rural areas. (Thus, for example, two suburban counties adjacent to Washington, D.C. are expected to increase by one-quarter during the four years ending in 1968.)

The suburbs are affluent frontier-towns, and as such they present an aspect of apparent homogeneity which is frightening even to many of the residents. An astute sociologist, William M. Dobriner, in *Class in Suburbia*, argues that this is a passing phase. The true and demonstrable differences between cities and suburbs he details as follows:

> To summarize, when compared with central cities, suburbs have higher fertility ratios, higher percentages of married persons, lower percentages separated, higher percentages in primary families, high socioeconomic status in the labor force, higher median income, lower median age, a higher percentage of mobile families, and a higher level of educational achievement.

Youthful people in youthful places.

Every town in America was at one time—and not so long ago—a frontier-town. The only thing new here is the upholstery and the purpose. But things change: even Chicago grew up a little bit. There is still a great deal of milling around and fumbling, as to location, for instance: in Nassau County, the average turnover on mortgages has been six-and-one-half years. The society and the culture of the New Class are being created: naturally, it takes time. First, the appeal of gadgets must be overcome; then, the true human scope of the job must be measured and accepted, without unalterable despair; finally, one actually reads some of the books he has bought. Meanwhile, there is PTA, flouridation, Nice Negroes, and in the end the really illicitly exciting thought of electing a councilman, or even a Congressman.

In 1964, the *Congressional Quarterly* identified fifty congressional districts as predominantly suburban. *CQ* has also predicted that with adequate arithmetical redistricting under the new Supreme Court rulings, the suburbs would gain something like twenty seats. Seventy Congressmen is a heavy swing-group: it almost equals the hard-core Southern contingent. And it is growing, while the latter is declining. James MacGregor Burns divides "political" issues into style-of-life and economic ones; and he suggests that the new swing-group of voters in the new suburbs can be appealed to, and given a political character, through style-of-life issues. Indeed—and probably through no others. Which indicates a very substantial change in American politics—based on the New Class, and involving matters that go somewhat deeper than ideological liberalism.

The new suburbs seemed to be all-out Republican at the beginning only because of their newness, the fact that the earlier suburbs were unrelentingly wealthy, and because of the Eisenhower magic. But President Johnson did just about as well in the suburbs as Eisenhower (except for the South), and the fifty suburban seats in the House were split almost evenly between Democrats and Republicans in 1964.

Political power to the suburbs will heighten the conflict, and induce adjustments, between the different and as yet undeveloped elements of the New Class who live there. Through political activity, they will come to know themselves better: their style will jell. With redistricting—state-legislative as well as congressional—the increased importance of the suburbs will provide an ideal atmosphere for the increased participation of New Class people in politics. And political participation, wherever and however it begins, is a learning process —not a rigid, standstill thing. Once they seriously begin to try, these people will learn how to operate their own society.

The regular "downstate" Republican leaders have been no fairer to the new people in the underrepresented suburbs than have the city Democratic bosses. In this sense, the suburbs are truly in the middle—and it is a question of which old-line force sends the most effective ambassadors, and does so first; or makes and accepts the surer alliance sooner with indigenous "style" representatives. Charles Percy in Illinois, for example, understands the necessity—and appears to have the capacity—to appeal to the Chicago suburbs. The old-guard Republicans do not and cannot accept the new order of doing business, and they seem to be splitting the party in an effort to hold on to the past. In Maryland, the Democratic bosses of Baltimore have allied themselves with the Southern-type ruralists of the Eastern Shore against the Washington suburban counties—and moderate Republicans in the area survived the Johnson sweep in 1964. And John Lindsay—despite the disaster of having been elected mayor of New York—is still the perfect suburban candidate (as well as the most adventurous scavenger among the ruins of the Republican party).

I find it of long-term significance that the Reform Democrats, even where they were weakest (in Chicago), did well in the once heavily Republican suburbs. In the suburbs, the Reformers are dealing with their own class even if not with their own liberal ideological grouping. And the class factor, the style factor, is the more important one.

Potentially the most significant contradiction or division in the New Class involves neither the job nor the dormitory, but specifically the "education" which is its historical entrée. To go at an understanding of this in a proper way, however, requires some subtlety. The advent of the New Class concerns not only a change in the property and power structure, but also brings about a considerable diffusion of what we may begin by calling "culture." Educational status does not function simply as a substitute for property, but also unavoidably provides a basis for awareness. In one sense or another, these new people *are* educated. With an excess neither of hope nor of despair, it would seem reasonable to explore the possibility that this increase in "culture" will itself amount to a political factor of independent significance.

In the basic sociological sense, of course, all classes develop their own culture—indeed, a class is finally defined by its culture (as in speaking of the "subculture" of the adolescent delinquent or the drug addict, and so on). The New Class naturally has and develops a culture of this kind. But it also becomes involved in realizing itself by means of culture in the non-sociological sense—which is to say, through serious reading of serious books. People whose passports to organizational position and class tenure were derived from education can be influenced by more than a few ideas on a narrow range, and they may more readily intellectualize their frustrations—and their ideals. If this is so, some great political battles of the future may well be fought over curricula in the schools—not simply repetitions of the current battles as to who gets into what schools, and how many places there are in all of them.

Education, moreover, induces ideals. It does so by making people read more than otherwise, and by delaying the process of gaining experience in the world. For these reasons and others, education produces frustration—a factor which has already led to a number of significant status-revolts and will undoubtedly lead to many more, both within and outside the ambit of the new student disruption (on the right-wing, Goldwater's appeal to New Class tension was patent). So far as the educated member of the New Class is concerned, his normal quotient of frustration is heightened by the manner in which he has been accepted into American society: he has been given a job. This is, of course, better than not being given a job, but when a person is trained to do something and then is either not allowed to do it or is encouraged to do it meaninglessly, additional frustration must inevitably result. This is the condition today of many educated individuals. Because more and more people have had to be educated—what else could be done with them?—there are more and more educated people around for whom jobs must be provided, and jobs are in fact provided. But "just jobs." In this sense, the ancient, trained irrelevance of the academic has become a model applied with great extension throughout society in dealing with a New Class for whom jobs must be provided, but whose irrelevance must meanwhile be maintained. This could not be clearer than it was in Washington, certainly before the 89th Congress, where thousands upon thousands of educated people occupied jobs in the federal bureaucracy in which they were supposed to analyze a wide range of social problems and provide programs to deal with these— which programs were almost never enacted by Congress. This is called staff policy research, and it is an infinitely frustrating way of life.*

Members of the New Class can be distinguished from one another by noting not only the extent of their frustration, but their manner of dealing with it. Some become utopians; others are compulsively realistic; almost all go through a more or less extended period of undertaking personal consumption as a form of idolatry; many create and live within a rigid aura of professionalism; most, at one time or another, retreat from their actual condition and over-identify with some more traditional grouping, as the right-wing intellectuals identify with small-property ownership, or the urban Jews with problems of social justice, and many serious Protestants with the Negroes.

As the former style of politics was based on patronage involving low-level jobs in big cities, there is now a new style of patronage based on the distribution of New Class jobs, in both the private and the public spheres. In the Fifties, professional and technical jobs grew by 2.4 million, from about 8 to about 11 per cent of the total labor force. Much of this growth was in defense; but there were also 796,000 new jobs in education, and 111,000 in welfare, religious, and other non-profit activities. The provision of such jobs constitutes a good deal of the story of the New Deal and the New Frontier—and apparently Modern Republicanism was not able or did not try too hard to slow down the process appreciably.

The growth of the New Class in England (to take only one foreign example) is both clearer and more disruptive than here. Because the old classes so thoroughly dominated education and the upper ranks of almost all major institutions, and because the education was not scientific or technical in emphasis, the New Class there

---

* At the spring meeting of the American Psychoanalytic Association in 1964, the incoming president disclosed the results of a survey of analysands. According to the report in the *New York Times* (May 2, 1964), 1,100 analysts with M.D.'s treat 11,000 patients a year: "Almost all are college-educated. Many have graduate degrees." This high education level was the main factor identifying these private patients. That, of course, and their frustrations.

has been made up of recognizably new people—with the wrong accents, for instance. Also, being a *mis*developed country for the modern world, England must change radically to survive—and the obvious direction is that taken some time ago by Sweden, toward high-quality technical performance. In this very special political conjunction, the Labour party has undertaken to represent the clamor for New Class jobs based, of course, on technical education both of a higher standard and to be made more generally available to the whole population. Harold Wilson's keynote speech to the party's annual conference in the fall of 1963 concentrated on this undertaking; and Richard Crossman, at that time, called for a "revolution against educational privilege." The revolution will be politely English, however; what is happening is that new schools are being built —Oxford and Cambridge are not being nationalized.

In America, by contrast, we are creating a culture, not overcoming one. But, still, in favor of the New Class.

My overriding point is that the "new men" are newer than they know. Meanwhile, we cannot answer the main question—what the effects will be when they achieve an awareness of themselves as a class. We cannot know just what the effects will be, but we know there will be some—and we cannot guess otherwise than that they will be important.

Yet in looking for understanding of the New Class phenomenon, one must not expect pure typologies; even if one found them, they might well be misleading as to the over-all course of events. No matter how serious and determinative one's propertied or propertyless relation to the means of production may be, man does not live by property alone—especially in periods of great change, and especially in America, with its raw national style, its inherent regionalism unto anarchy, its constituency-brokerage politics, and its conflicts between a national popular culture and the mature elite varieties.

All classes, moreover, have antecedents in history. The first of the bourgeoisie were not the first traders or property-accumulators, but rather the first to make trading and property-accumulation the dominant tone, and then the dominant activity, in their particular social orders. In doing so, they undoubtedly took in and assimilated previous existing social elements, items, and forms. Something like this is happening in the development of the New Class. Thus, doctors and lawyers and teachers, as well as technologists and other bureaucratic specialists, are incorporated into the ongoing (and eventually over-whelming) development. Indeed, lawyers, as has often been the case in the past, are probably the leading creative individuals in carrying the development forward.

The education of the New Class member—an electronics engi-neer or a systems-research analyst with a Ph.D. in sociology or a physicist working for the RAND Corporation or an economist deal-ing with manpower problems in the Department of Labor—consists of training *to think ahead*. These people administer and they plan—indeed, it is impossible to administer without becoming engaged in some form of gross plan, at least a "plan" for resolving the conflicts among the interests one is administering. Hence it is distinctly pos-sible that *all* the education of *all* the members of the New Class has a common denominator—namely, to plan something.

The whole theory of rule by property was that the accompanying competition dispensed with the need to plan, and thus dispensed as well with "planners" (intellectuals) and the state (the primary planning agency). This was never an accurate representation of the old trading order, since no matter how hard a businessman might try not to think ahead, and to cooperate with others in not doing so, he and they did in fact indulge. There was always communication be-yond the market, beyond that provided for by an Adam Smith mar-ket-model where communication was not so much refrained from on principle as it was considered to be impossible in fact. Where plan-ning is possible, it occurs. The more important planning begins with the business unit, in the application of technology. But it is not limited to that; the business unit is a political as well as a technologi-cal organization. Moreover, the relations *among* business units are exquisitely political, when they are not merely those of the imper-sonal market.

At the end of this brief analysis, then, we note that the New Class consists of the planners—the thinkers-ahead. This explains why they are so frustrated when they are members of the non-military public division and not nearly so much so when members of the private division: planning is encouraged in the latter, nearly forbidden in the former. But planning is inherent in the educated person's activ-ity. Conceptualizing and thinking ahead: this is planning and this is what education comes to. Indeed, what is this terribly feared politi-cal planning, really, but a kind of mutual consciousness, an awareness of what one is doing in relation to what others are up to at the same time? In any event, the fact that educated people have been placed in and around the centers of power (as this is or may become a fact of usefulness and not of mere adornment) indicates power's need for planning. It is a serious maladjustment of power in America which keeps this planning from going forward, and consequently frustrates the members of the New Class.

Their deeper sense of community *must* begin—however it may hopefully end—with the triumph of planning and its positive politics, as the dominant American style and purpose. It had better come peacefully: and any more exaggeration of adornment and redundancy—"just jobs"—may well lead at a not-so-later date to a convulsive reaction. So they must have their due. We have invited it: now we must satisfy it.

❀ SO THIS IS WASHINGTON?

UNPUBLISHED, 1963

I went to Washington in September of 1963 on a two-year fellowship at the Institute for Policy Studies (I had spent time there previously working with myunclethejudge). This pre-assassination letter-back-home was written for the New York Review of Books—it was early in the history of both NYRB and IPS, and we were experimenting with work in tandem; which didn't work.

I put it this way in the Acknowledgments section of Power in America:

And I wish to thank the city of Washington itself. The osmosis was nearly overwhelming. After one has tried to live there, what the professionals call Basic Research seems like nit-picking. I didn't pick many, but I did live there. And before I left, I had agreed with myself on the essence: *elevated sameness.* Of income, of education, of style, of hope, and even of despair. Washington is the one and true tour of duty, even the home or the asylum, of the New Class. Beginners properly come there to learn: learners cannot live there long enough. In that ultimate setting many propositions in this book might be nicely referenced-out. There, it is not the institutions of power, but the emotions of the people in and under them, that will tell the longer story—the one I have tried here only to begin to tell.

The two main points about the New Class are jobs and self-consciousness. If New Class people are not going to deploy intellectual culture in the comprehension of actual condition, who will? They are monopolists of that culture. But do they misuse it! They feel so put-upon (because they do not yet rule the world) that they have come to view self-criticism as a kind of betrayal to the Enemy—often understood as the Establishment they do not yet occupy. Since critical self-consciousness is my thing, I will never be popular with them. But I will be heard from. With intellectuals now a class, self-consciousness and class-consciousness join up for historical effectiveness. And cultural survival. (Karl Marx, spin some more in that busy grave of yours.)

I am suffering from cultural and other intellectual shock. From Manhattan to the District of Columbia (and assorted suburbs) is a few dollars and a few hours. No, not exactly.

What a pretty place. Every street is king-size, and all the trees uprooted in Manhattan were carted down here and replanted everywhere you look. The city is an historic adventure in architecture. The seriously residential group is aghast, etc., at both Federalese (the old mausoleum style) and the current fashionably packaged office-buildings and "high rises" (a word never heard in New York City, but ubiquitous elsewhere). I have been impressed, however, by the interest and variety of everything else—and by all means I don't mean just Georgetown, the local overpriced charmsville. The Negro slums are hard to notice because there is no wash on the fire-escapes, in fact no fire-escapes at all, and the streets through the slums (I have been assured ten times that they are, indeed, slums: "Just look inside one sometime") are all of a size and bushiness with Park Avenue, say. Parks everywhere—big ones, little ones, and Rock Creek, each with one or more national-hero statuariums. The city *looks* pretty good, no question.

Now to substance: Washington, D.C., is an intellectual ghetto. The shock of coming across the Real Thing is considerable after having presumed to live in one all my adult life; and having tarried a while as well in a half-dozen academic communities. The dominant tone of the town—you can pick it up on an unhurried but temporary visit, and I did previously—is of complete, nerve-shattering equality. Which is interesting and maybe even instructive, considering that it is a one-company town, and that particular company produces hierarchic bureaucracies only. If it hadn't been for some shopkeepers and one *Simchas Torah* get-together, I could actually say that I have not yet met an uneducated white man—and probably lady, too—in Washington, D.C., Ph.D.s abound, everybody is busily doing something in the head, it is impossible to make an uninteresting abstract remark, and everybody says he wants to know and actually listens when you try to tell him "what you're doing now." Advanced study seminars spring up like mushrooms—I conducted a three-drink one absolutely inadvertently one evening, which ended with two lifelong admirers and four deadly enemies. As I recall, the theme was that poetry is important—no, now I remember—that it is useful. I'm adjusting.

The second most harrowing thing about Washington is that so many people speak of President Kennedy with such cold contempt. As a political loudmouth from the sophisticated provinces, I have found this particularly unnerving. I had thought that it was rather advanced to accept, for the time being, the quiet Bostonian's rather gray but well-wrought managerial style, as refracted through the *New York Times*. But no, as one shrewdnik informed me, he is more or less numb inside and, on this emotional model, experiences occasional curiosity in relation to his supporters but much more genuine and responsive fear regarding his enemies, with the result that the better attention follows the stronger emotion. That's interesting. But it was downright fascinating to be told, and assured again and again by liberals in a position to know, that the whole White House/Congress operation, on which the future of gray managerialism in America depends, is thoroughly inept on the headquarters end. All that so-called shrewd Irish pressure on Congress—*pffft!* Apparently they are not even passable ward-heelers, where it might be useful to the nation. The renowned Irish Mafia is talented only in winning elections—as Representative and Senator, the President never accomplished very much, the implied reason being that he and his people never mastered the congressional operation. It's a bad thought, but the story is told with great conviction. So, back to the drawingboard on that one.

The New Frontier is like the New Deal in one essential only—lots of jobs for lots of educated people. But in this it has simply made a "thing" out of an irresistible trend that has not, in fact, been much resisted since the New Deal set it in motion. During the Depression, it was almost true that the best or only market for the services of the educated was in the District (I like that word, especially for this purpose). Joe McCarthy made it very unpleasant for educated people everywhere, particularly here in the neighborhood, and he left a profound effect on them: but I wonder if he managed to slow down the basic hiring process. I doubt it—although he certainly affected the selection/recruitment system. And since the War, there have been, let us say, oodles of openings for working intellectuals throughout: (a) the corporate order; (b) the so-called educational system; (c) the communications cobweb; (d) the lovely foundation establishment; (e) and so on and on. Outside of Washington, that is. But still many remain here; many newly come.

What is the selective principle? Which members of the New Class of educated consumers prefers the District? You can make more money on Madison Avenue. It's very comfortable and quite genteel in the universities, with three months altogether off every year. The corporations are bigger and more important than anything else. Ah, but if you "want to do something"—Washington, young man, Washington. Also, if you have studied the subject carefully and want to cuddle power intellectually, all the books say it's here. So they come here, for instance, from universities. Looking for power. After all, everybody knows that *the* problem of the twentieth century is that intellectuals have been powerless, while the people wielding power aren't smart enough. A simple solution to this problem has occurred to a large number of similarly situated intellectuals.

But this is the last place in the world, I assure you, "to do something." Nothing is being done here (except those jobs I mentioned as being desperately occupied). *The reek of frustration,* like musk issuing from a carved box of determined intellectuality, is overwhelming. All this monumental preparation "to do something," and nothing done or to be done! It brings me to tears, every cocktail hour on the cocktail hour (there are several, booze being 25 per cent cheaper than in New York City). A very charming fellow whose name shall be nameless (and who, as a matter of fact, is so good that he ought to be off writing at a university somewhere instead of making believe he is administering this and that) let me in on something good. He said that his particular department's regular message-and-bill has been sent down to Congress so often, and after benefit of so much talented rubdown, that its well-honed perfection was finally noticed by its machinists, and a number of them, seeing the light, quit forthwith. Some of the fellows, I suppose, are having more trouble whipping their term-papers into final perfect shape, and just hate to go home for Xmas before having done so. You can't blame them.

The elected officials are businessmen. In the business of getting elected, and making a living therefrom. You can't blame them, either.

Now who in the hell *are* you going to blame?

❀ ONLY THE PROS

UNPUBLISHED, 1966

Review of *Profiles in Power: A Washington Insight*, by Joseph Kraft

After I wrote this review for Commentary *(I think Norman Podhoretz did not want to publish it because of the tone of my remarks about the Kennedy Group: I was for Senator Robert, but also for critical understanding of what appeared to be a powerful government-in-exile soon to take power), Kraft referred to my "fascinating new book,* Power in America*" in one of his columns and has since utilized the idea of the new educated class quite effectively—especially in understanding the 1968 political year. So I am now particularly interested in this review for what I sensed about Kraft's view of "professionalism" (jobs-with-dignity). This re-demonstrates to me a major personal quality of New Class impingement, especially in the case of real talent distinctly aware of the New Class phenomenon. (For a nasty aspect of the same thing, see Christopher Lasch's writing and remarks thereon, below.) I am not much of a journalist, and Kraft is a very good one—they have a tremendous advantage in cozying up to fresh detail. When I sense something about the New Class, it is apt to come out as a theoretical suggestion; but when smart young journalists come up with something, it takes on the quality of current fact. High-class journalism is very likely the coming profession in*

our kind of country: it is both interdisciplinary and existential.
    (*As to the beginning remarks about "collections": I leave this
in as a potential criticism of myself, in the volume you are
now reading.*)

Not all collections are worth the effort. But, on careful reflection,
neither are all other books. Collections, at least, provide employment for collectors, and unearned increment for collectees. If you
happen to be fascinated by the fellow, collections are a marvelous
convenience. And those in paperback are a convenience as well for
the collectee, in that he does not have to fumble around in old car-
tons looking for tearsheets, but can inexpensively force the whole
corpus into the hands of historians among his acquaintance. Mostly,
however, the traditional view is persuasive, and collections should be
reserved for great writers and dead writers.

But with this collection of Joseph Kraft's political commentary
and characterization—mostly, I take it, from his Washington column in *Harper's*, but some also from *Esquire*, *Satevepost*, and *Commentary*—I have uncovered (perhaps it was hidden only from me)
another substantial reason for publishing magazine pieces by one
writer in a single book. Until I read *Profiles in Power*, it hadn't come
across to me what a really good writer Mr. Kraft is. Seeing him every
once in a while in magazines—and more recently in his newspaper
column—it was easy to slot him merely as another qualified comer in
the Kennedy entourage. If so, I feel now that somebody ought to
talk the Senator into running in '68, because it will be a shame to
have to wait for all the high-class fun-and-games that talent of this
calibre will provide in yet another Kennedy campaign. Also (though
senior readers may object), Walter Lippmann never came close to
writing this well, even a third of a century ago when he was forty-
two. We'll just have to face it, even if the fact cannot be fitted to
prevailing winds: as for the quality of political writing—there are
other examples—we have made great progress. (And just before
Everything Goes Under—*quel dommage!*)

The book consists of eighteen pieces of carefully worked-over re-
portage (no daily stuff here) averaging about ten printed pages or
thirty-five hundred to four thousand words each, arranged in three
bunches and bracketed by a freshly written Introduction and Epilogue attempting without major success to tie the package together
tighter than it would otherwise have been. The first part, "At the

Center," contains four pieces—pictures of Kennedy, Johnson, White House staff under the latter, and a brilliantly subtle essay called "The Hidden Change in Congress." His concise picture of Johnson is possibly the best to date, especially including the fact that, unlike so many others, Kraft is not squeamish about the President's style but makes it central: sees him not as helplessly vulgar but pointedly so, an extremely sophisticated as well as cyclonic serving of Texas cornpone. The brief piece on Congress is so good that it cannot be conveyed but should be studied, and I only urge you to read it: the key thought is that a new counter-coalition displaced the old conservative coalition by attrition and finally by dissolution of the civil rights cement that used to hold it together. "The spectacular record of 1964 was built on a shift of about fifteen House seats, mainly from Texas and Georgia." The change is so overwhelmingly important that, as he reports, the President himself is contemptuous of those who attribute it merely to Johnsonian magic.

Part II has an excessively clever title—"The Outside Insiders"—being six articles each concerned, in one way or another, with semi-independent intellectual seasoning in the Washington bouillabaisse. These include a piece on RAND, and another on the leading nuclear strategists, which are good backgrounding but otherwise embarrassingly thin (and dated, while barely revised). An essay, "Kennedy and the Intellectuals," is so slight that it should not have been included: merely adequate gossip—forced into an inadequate format —may not only fail to clarify, it can also distort a really serious subject. On Washington lawyers, however, the excellent gossip transcends itself, and the depiction is sharply informative. With one lawyer for every sixty persons—and new areas of practice regularly created by new activities of government—law managed by lawyers in Washington is a phenomenon apart. In a brief space, Mr. Kraft offers a compelling image of the Washington lawyer as the Democratic counterpart "of the well-known love affair between the Republican party and the Wall Street lawyers"—a counterpart, moreover, that has only fully matured, he suggests, under President Johnson. Besides noting that "the Washington lawyer works at the frontiers of his profession" and a number of other qualities of the breed, he observes perceptively the large extent to which major firms in the District "are the residue of past Administrations." ("Covington & Burling"—the largest one—"was put together by two attorneys who came to work for agencies set up during Woodrow Wilson's time." Mr. Justice Abe Fortas was a founding partner of the very distinguished New Deal firm, Arnold, Fortas & Porter.)

The balance of the articles—the remaining two from the middle section and the eight making up Part III, "The Bureaucratic Machinery"—are preponderantly portraits of individuals: James Reston, Robert McNamara, J. Edgar Hoover, Averell Harriman, Dean Acheson, McGeorge Bundy, and Dean Rusk. (The exceptions are excursions on a Pentagon faction, the Budget Bureau, and the Washington press corps.) With these portraits, the pattern of the book—and, so to speak, of the author—emerges (and one recalls that he did, after all, entitle the collection *Profiles*, etc.). The sketches are variously of career and personality and position and style of work: and they are unrelievedly good. The current Secretary of State, for instance, comes alive immediately (and permanently) once Kraft has noted that Mr. Rusk has an exceptional verbal gift and then states: "Rusk's true art . . . is to place a most uncommon gift at the service of the most common ideas." Now this is more than a Rusk or Washington insight: it has application elsewhere—indeed, plenty of elsewheres.

The portraiture is central and so good because Mr. Kraft has an underlying "generational" view of political life; and he is a young man probably still trying to figure out what kind of person to be (as who isn't, in America). So, except for Bundy, the named profiles are all of older men fully arrived or even over-ripe. Harriman is "The Old Crocodile"—a tough, scaly, unpleasant operative who both succeeds and survives (the former by virtue of the latter). Dean Acheson—"Gentleman of the Old School"—receives credit as the brilliant aristocratic amateur who contributed so much to the construction of American foreign policy, once Franklin D. Roosevelt decided the country needed one. And most engagingly, to this reader, the ominous J. Edgar Hoover is revealed as "The Compleat Bureaucrat" —not the independently awful nemesis of the liberals, as advertised, but merely an accomplished artist of survival in the center ring on the Potomac.

But Bundy is the bridge between the political generations—certainly if one characterizes these as Mr. Kraft does, as moving from the old-family Eastern Establishment (i.e., from the first Roosevelt to a *real* foreign policy in and since World War II) to the new group of intellectual experts whether or not with more-than-educational breeding. The point being that Bundy is, and has the profoundest connections with, both: he manages this exquisitely relevant feat of transition-politics by acting, according to Kraft, as a "manager of process" whose superb "mental apparatus is unclogged by general ideas." I fear that is correct. But when Kraft says the Establishment and the intellectuals "negate each other," I fear that is incorrect. The Establishment will not cease to be such simply because it is no longer exclusively WASP; and after a while, all families are quite "old" enough even though historical dust continues to overlay the final pecking order. (When Robert Kennedy presents himself as a noble Disestablishmentarian, advertising men and not social historians should step forward to judge the performance.)

If we connect this wrongo with Mr. Kraft's thin showing in "Kennedy and the Intellectuals," we come up with an important clue. In the earlier piece, stating the change from the New Deal to Kennedy days, he says: "In the process of policy formation"—read: crowded bureaucratic infighting—"there is more room than ever for the trained intellectual bureaucrat. But the kibbitzing intellectual celebrity has no place." And he honors Reston both for recruiting specially trained younger men—Anthony Lewis, Edwin Dale, Max Frankel—*and* for stepping aside as *Times* Washington bureau chief before that was necessary. In "Politics of the Washington Press Corps," while expertly debunking the conventional Principled Conflict between the President and the Press, he again elevates this idea of upgraded training, expertise, professionalization—the special province, of course, of the new generation. *But*, he notes as well that "news"—written by whomever—does not exist prior to being "shaped and put out for the eye of the beholder": indeed, he goes so far as to say that, the world having become so complex, commonsense will get you nowhere and "the stuff of public life eludes the grasp of the ordinary man. *Events have become professionalized.*" (Emphasis added.) The Presidency is then characterized as the No. 1 PR office in the nation, as follows: "For the White House, above all places, must translate into neutral, if not favorable, terms events that are too complicated for nonprofessional minds and that, *unless explained, appear to clash with traditional notions of morality and good government.*" (More emphasis added: and I further add that, without this particular clash, history would cease altogether to interfere with our preconceptions.)

My point is that there is nothing whatsoever new about this—*except* the justification. For example, the foreign policy Establishment whose death Mr. Kraft announces in the Epilogue to this book—the work of brilliant amateurs like Acheson and other non-specifically trained lawyers and military men and ordinary Porcellians—"was able, by publicity, honors, bits of hokum, and the collaboration of James Reston, to cast over the shoulders of a mediocre political hack the cloak of statesmanship. The reputation of Senator Arthur Vandenberg . . . was an Establishment invention" designed to entice primitive Republicans into the war-coalition. Not a bad piece of business, for old-fashioned amateurs: let us wait until the new fellows do as well.

The fact is, professionalism has become a raging epidemic, a social disease resulting from a purely commercial infection. Yes, intellectuals are now involved in affairs: so many of them, that they have had to be organized for this purpose: this organized involvement is the beginning of a genuine industrial division of labor among intellectuals—who, since their presumptions preclude the notion and they simply cannot bear the thought, call it "professionalism" and attempt to pull all remaining thought down with them, each into the cranny of his own job, meanwhile insisting that there is no other way of viewing or relating oneself to the world.

To practice and advertise professionalism in order to get and hold a job, certainly; but *believe* it? Why, that would be the same order of error the old property-owners made when, after getting some, they elevated the ownership of property into the sign of a special relation with God.

❀ THE INTELLECTUALS COME OF AGE

UNPUBLISHED, 1965

Review of *The New Radicalism in America,
1889–1963: The Intellectual as a Social Type,*
by Christopher Lasch

I was hot at work on my own ideas about the New Class when the New Republic *asked me to review Christopher Lasch's book. It turned out to be one of the most difficult books I ever tried to work with, especially as I felt that he was on my immediate track. Since then, he has attacked me at least twice.*

I will have something further to say about this fellow—but after you have read this review, written before I knew what was involved for me personally.

He is my idea of a prime current creative representative of the New Class, especially including his inept denial of the idea of the New Class, making him more representative than Michael Harrington or myself, for instance, who have each carefully explicated the idea while being deeply suspicious of the fact: Lasch "represents" the fact, in an advanced way, as well as any other literate American.

If a bright young historian turns foolish/dumb when he uncovers his own roots in the subject he is devoted to studying, outsiders may, viewing this event, savor the depth of the problem of self-understanding as I am trying to pose it. You see, what I am saying is that the Philosophes of the French Enlightenment and the Bolsheviks of the Russian Revolution were primary precursors of leave-home intellectuals who decided to be active in history, instead of becoming monks or priests or academics. And then, a fundamental change in the basic power-impetus of the Western world joined this zany development in elevating intellect above priestliness as no intellectual or priest in the history of the human race had ever conceived to be even potentially feasible. And it all happened all of a sudden.

The dominance of technology and the radical disengagement of numerous intellectuals both derived from bourgeois freedoms, and each has advanced the power-position of the intellectual as such. But now, the transformation of bourgeois forms of property—required by the first dynamic and insisted upon by the second—have joined the two groups of intellectuals as a new economic class created by and responsive to such changes in property. But each evidences a disastrous lack of self-consciousness, only that the one insists on submerging itself and the other in trumpeting its willful liberation. Each of these modes is a primitive and inadequate form of class-consciousness, especially for that Final Class which not only presumes to but does possess the historical monopolistic capacity to merge self-consciousness with class-consciousness and all the inherited human consciousness we have. (Internationally, this is even further complicated through the double-mirror vision of seeing the same phenomenon as a Westerner looking at the Communist East, a Communist looking at the

West; or, being the one but taking the other's point of view toward oneself.)

To begin with, this is a very good book. Almost of equal importance and interest, it is about *you*—the readers of the *New Republic*, for instance. It is a collection of biographical essays the figures in which serve as historical precedents in. an exposition of the social psychology of liberal/radical intellectuals in the United States. From Jane Addams to Norman Mailer, these precedents are selected on no principle other than Christopher Lasch's psychological interest—and the availability of autobiographical writing. Much of what he says, I am sure, is arguable; but almost all of it would find a snug place in any really good argument about the nature, function, and development of liberal intellectuals (were there any others?) in this country, in this century. Even the at-first-glance eccentric choice of persons to write about finally adds to the quality of the book: anyone might include Randolph Bourne and Lincoln Steffens, but who would have thought of doing a whole chapter on Mabel Dodge Luhan? It is, however, one of the most enjoyable in the collection. (Mrs. Luhan was psychoanalyzed three times and has written an interminable, multi-volume autobiography: her personal revolt had to do, she said, with sex.)

Mr. Lasch writes extremely well, which should go a long way toward helping the partisan reader overcome his resentment at seeing his heroes, or himself, reduced a notch or two. The author has a full repertory of fairly sharp notions about what's wrong with everybody. His model (and probably his teacher) is Richard Hofstadter, the admirable historian of Columbia, who has endorsed the book. Lasch is thirty-three years old, was born in Omaha, has an undergraduate degree from Harvard, a four-year-old Ph.D. from Columbia, and he now teaches at the State University of Iowa. He published a previous book, *The American Liberals and the Russian Revolution*, in 1962. So he stands fully armed between the new sit-in and the old crap-out generations, and he is raring to go.

Is it now the time to take a good look at our half-century-long selves, and add up the score? Or, more bluntly: Have we "arrived" sufficiently to chance it? I say, Yes: in a way, we are over-arrived; and, being prudent and resigned, it is going to happen anyway, because of the new activism of the students and the resulting conflict of generations, which is certain to be noisy. (The little monsters not only do not understand us older fellows but, I was horrified to discover, are barely interested in making up the deficiency.)

"The main argument of this book is that modern radicalism or liberalism can best be understood as a phase of the social history of the intellectuals." He means that the political ideas of American intellectuals were not merely or mostly political, but were something like a grandiose device for establishing the independent social position of intellectuals as a class. This process began around the turn of the century, and in all cases then and thereafter it consisted most deeply of a revolt of the American intellectual against his middle class family and culture; the intellectuals, he says, turned all aspects of personal relations into politics, and saw politics proper as an overriding and all-inclusive cultural endeavor. This was derived from their "pastlessness"—the rejection of family, and all it stood for. They were not intellectuals *of* the middle class, but in and by virtue of exodus *from* the middle class. So they concentrated on education and sex and other cultural concerns more than on politics as such. Seeing "society from the bottom up, or at least from the outside in," they identified with any and all perspectives outside the middle class, including immigrants, workers, children, Indians, Negroes, etc. This used to be referred to as the revolt against the Genteel Tradition; but Lasch places it deeper, at the very core of family-concern. Of course, the rejection of the family is an American phenomenon, and not limited to intellectuals; his point, however, is that it necessarily happened when the rebellion was intellectual, and that it in fact *did* happen then in the better, older families, not just between first- and second-generation immigrants.

It began with the women—with a rejection, by the female bearers of middle class culture, of the merely decorative role of "young ladies." So the first essay concerns Jane Addams, and the book proceeds from her through a number of confessional feminists to Randolph Bourne who is taken to be the purest culmination of the family-protest center of the New Radicalism, and therefore a connecting link with feminism. (In his early writing, Bourne counted heavily on the feminist movement as a social harbinger; being a hunchback, he considered that he could not marry.) While the earlier or purer feminists envied and desired for themselves what they thought to be the excitement and up-and-at-'em quality of the male role, Mrs. Luhan (his next subject, under the heading of "Sex as

Politics") pursued and collected numerous examples of what the male more pointedly has when he role-undresses. Having thus disclosed the will to power in the New Radicalism, it is detailed in the more extensive activities of the men in the next chapter, "Politics as Social Control." Here, the need to manipulate and control the environment is derived, again, from "pastlessness" and the rejection of one's sources. Then Herbert Croly, Walter Weyl, and Walter Lippmann, the original editors of the *New Republic*, come in for a drubbing by reason of their mixed cultural/political squirmings during World War I: also John Dewey. They represented, in the author's view, the desire of the liberal intellectuals to delude themselves, under the ideology of hard-boiled and pragmatic "realism," with the illusion that they were close to the government and that the government was in turn closely concerned with their ideal political illusions. The next chapter is a vivid one on "the politics of fantasy": it concerns the intimate revelations expressed in the relation of Colonel House and a journalist by the name of Lincoln Colcord, who was fed more and better by the Colonel than either Weyl or Lippmann. The social psychoanalysis of Colonel House, based on the death-wish, is fascinating. Following a loving portrait of Lincoln Steffens (he and Bourne, of those dealt with full-length, come off best of all), the book concludes with a "modern" chapter called "The Anti-Intellectualism of the Intellectuals" which begins with another drubbing of another set of *New Republic* editors (especially Edmund Wilson and George Soule), and proceeds from this sanguine beginning through uninteresting louse-ups of Niebuhr and Hook to inadequate portrayals of Dwight Macdonald and Norman Mailer. (Well, the one on Mailer isn't so bad.)

This final chapter is a splash of ice-water on the back of the neck. It is one thing to be entertained with stories about the foibles and failings of *les vieilles*, and quite another for some talented kid to come along and majestically squeeze you and yours into a history book. The author's method, even as an imaginative form of history maintaining some connection with fairness and accuracy, now falls apart. And then, like in a blinding flash, late but welcome, it is abundantly clear that the book—which has just dropped to the floor like a piece of dry ice—is not history at all. Or, to phrase the proposition more concisely: *That's history?* I like polemical cultural gossip as well as the next intellectual: sitting around comfortably listening to the latest stories from New York is my idea of an adequate way to kill an evening. But when you publish it (except in a novel), you have to stand up like everybody else and have rocks thrown at you.

First of all, does Lasch intend to get through life with the idea that "Marxism" is merely something you accuse Cold War liberals of not understanding because of their devil-theory of Communism? Sidney Hook may represent the dry season of pragmatism, but he read Marx, he profited thereby, and he wrote a great book relating Marx to Dewey—and *that* is why he acts like a brigadier-general when the slot-words "Soviet Union" are flashed on the screen.

Next point: Lasch talks about "class." If his book is really important, it is because by means of an imaginative leap he has divined and nicely backgrounded the emergence of "intellectuals" in America as a *New Class*—by the catalytic means of mixed cultural/political radicalism. I capitalize and italicize because of the importance of the phenomenon; to emphasize that it is the special American expression of exactly what Djilas was talking about when he used the term; and because I am referring to class in the true Marxist sense of a group of people defined by their relation to the means of production, and consequent command upon income; and because class does not consist merely of our classmates and colleagues and friends. You don't define and characterize a class by means of contemptuous moral strictures—these come afterward. And if it is a *class*, of course there will be a Croly-Weyl-Lippmann, a Schlesinger-Rovere, and many more to come, eagerly straying in and around the centers of power. That can be considered a betrayal only if you are talking about a moral position; if it is a class at issue, then their doings are as much of a triumph as Randolph Bourne's foresight or Benjamin Ginzburg's insight.

Maybe you don't like the class because you happen to belong to it. Tough. Also, the New Class, *being defined by its intellectual work*, would just naturally mix "culture" with its politics—just as the bourgeoisie mixed money-making with *its* politics, to say the least. So the New Radicals creating the New Class are not perfect: even if everything was going beautifully, how could they be—since they are so new? And, believe me, "they" are disappointed with themselves, too; they, too, expected more, each from his own middle class rebellion.

There is another "class" point Lasch misses, this one being one of the big reasons things did not go so beautifully—as a matter of fact, it underlies the whole New Class development, and more sharply in this country than anywhere else. *There was no cultured ruling class in this country after the Civil War.* What culture there was, as he noted, was a feminine adornment, having nothing much to do with the process of ruling. Such culture in the hands of the women was inevitably illusory and irrelevant, especially since all the practical experience of building and running a society was monopolized by businessmen who dutifully fell asleep once a week at recitals sponsored by their wives: sex was perhaps the least of what was sacrificed to this lack of "connection" between business and culture. So the new class of intellectuals was disastrously overextended by being compelled to think the thoughts of the non-existent ruling class, while at the same time securing its own class position. Quite a burden: no wonder they tended toward hysteria. But look what they've achieved in little more than half a century, and for Lasch's (and my own) benefit: it's *his* (our) inheritance.

Lincoln Steffens, after visiting revolutionary Russia in 1919, wrote: "I have seen the future, and it works"—and for him it continued to work until he died in 1936. "He saw, in short," says Mr. Lasch, "what others have discovered only in the 1950's or have yet to discover at all, that Communism represented a stage in the struggle of backward countries for economic development and national self-sufficiency." So *that's* what Communism represented! I see it now. It was only my typical confusion of culture and politics that misled me into being concerned about the Moscow Trials and all that horseshit.

One of the tenderest and truest insights in the book has to do with the characteristic *intensity of personal relationships* among intellectuals. He underscores this at a number of points, but presents it particularly in the chapter on poor Randolph Bourne—who had nothing much (not enough) besides his writing and his friendships, and of whom it can as a consequence be said that, thankfully, he died young: the Keats of Our Gang. But then in the concluding "modern" chapter Christopher Lasch reminds the reader that he has defined the intellectual no more seriously than "as people who derive pleasure and profit from playing with ideas." With a wishfully subjective definition like that, he undoes the real value of his work, as history or psychology or whatever it is. He can't get out from under "our problem" by putting all his carefully selected friends over here, and all those he wouldn't have to dinner over there. That's not the way to define "intellectual." I have been involved since the early Forties—both intimately and just passing through—in a number of highbrow gangs, and not one of them lacked its unqualified hangers-on. He cannot make a serious class or functional or even "social historical" distinction based on "better"—or a pseudonym like "playfulness."

This is the last line of the book: "Half a century after James delivered his first lecture on pragmatism, Norman Mailer forced himself into the thick of the Patterson-Liston fight—another Bostonian tourist in the guise of a 'Rocky Mountain tough.' " (The latter term is from James, in his "tough-minded" as against "tender-minded" metaphor, which has so overwhelmed later generations of American intellectuals.) In my opinion, William James was the first Hemingway—and I damn well hope and pray that Norman Mailer is the last. And I do not fail to understand the profound inevitability of sexual/cultural Hemingwayism in America. But enough is enough, it being nothing but an attempt of the intellectual to pre-empt business balls. The poor beleaguered American businessman—tough-minded, anti-cultured, even manly, and certainly with the symbolic male bank account—has his sexual holiday about two or three times a year, mostly in Chicago or Miami, and mostly prepaid. (I knew a fellow who lived in Greenwich Village who testified that desperately existential and otherwise effeminate intellectuals have done as well in one long afternoon.) If you can't like the businessman, at least feel some sympathy for him. He's an American, too—*even if he is your father.*

Postscript

Power in America was reviewed by Christopher Lasch in NYRB (Sept. 28, 1967). He begins by praising my first book inordinately and then gets down to business: "Power in America contains none

*of the virtues of the earlier book. . . ." He's new at the game:
"none" is a poorly chosen word since, read logically, the statement
proposes a patent impossibility—I did not contract paresis in the
few months between books. Having written scores of book reviews,
I know the gambit—the Second Book Tch-Tch Syndrome. But
manfully plowing through my verbiage, he uncovered "the main
thesis"—"Marx was wrong." (The hell it is.) Then he characterizes
my notion of the New Class, not badly at all: but by this time I am
bereft of all hope. And correctly, since I am shortly exposed as some
slimy kind of reformist: "As the new class becomes conscious of itself, it will make over the country in its own image—friendly, tolerant, noncompetitive," he says I said. But that I couldn't have said,
since I consider him and the NYRB prime bits of New Class dynamism in the United States. My notion of the New Class was largely
derived—after allowing for reports of the character of Comintern
bureaucrats as confirmed, for instance, by Djilas—from years and
years of unsuccessful avoidance of middlebrows, academic hustlers,
and even talented intellectual nasties, not more than one or two of
whom was ever "friendly, tolerant, or noncompetitive" on purpose
during a working day.*

*"Bazelon understands and sympathizes with some of the cultural
aspects of the student and Negro revolts, but he does not understand
the disaffection from which they spring." I don't understand disaffection as well as he does, he says. How is one to compare? Either
I don't for failure to agree with him, which says nothing; or I don't
because I have not myself experienced enough disaffection. For the
latter, I will compare drop-out points with him—and most of his
constituency—any day of the week, covering most of the years of
our lives.*

*Next, the profit motive: from careful reading, he found out I be-
lieve it is "obsolete." Sorry, but I never said that. I said the nineteenth century was a few years ago, but I never said the profit motive was obsolete—neither here nor in Russia. What I said was that
ownership is not the big bag it used to be—here, as well as in Russia.
That the major profit-making property is owned by organizations
which are not in turn owned, but merely controlled (and not mostly
by ownership). And I have been looking at the nature of this beyond-
owner control for ten-twenty years. And that's why I write about the
New Class—not because I love it or suffer "infatuation with managerialism." I have worked with the managers, and I can state that*

they offer few occasions for infatuation; but they are interesting, even when they are nothing (and I have known a few of them, too), because they run the system. Please excuse my lack of purity, but I thought the better New Class intellectuals might like some information and ideas from which leverage for their well-intentioned intelligence might be created—the leverage they desperately need, since intelligence only is supposed to be most of the muscle they got.

Next I am guilty of "the fallacy of technological indispensability, whereby the ascendancy of a class is inferred from the fact that it performs socially necessary work." From what was the ascendancy of the bourgeoisie inferred, may I ask? Not from its socially necessary work, but from its economically critical power, which has now shifted—and continues to shift—to the New Class. He continues: "By this kind of reasoning . . . the proletariat ought long ago to have succeeded to the power of the capitalists, and the slaves of the Old South should have dominated their masters." That is exactly what we expected; *a hundred years of effort was devoted to achieving exactly that; the reasoning—which was Marx's—was disproved only by the event; and in Russia it was not disproved at all, but displaced by the event of the non-owning New Class—which "succeeded to the power of the capitalists" in terms that even pure professors can understand, if they really try. And the New Class in America will finally displace rather than disprove, as it did in Russia—I hope not so badly, I hope not because of the inane doctrinal purities of our New Class loudmouths.* And the conclusion of this counter class-analysis: "In every society, the under class, being indispensable, should logically rule." Oh, boy.

Marx never spoke of an "under class" *—that is a modern term. And its primary meaning—*as distinct from the non-owning, exploited factory proletariat which Marx discussed and hoped would succeed "to the power of the capitalists"—is that it is not even a proletariat, but is quite dispensable: indeed, the horror of its potential—the very purport of its definition—is that it is superfluous. Uneducated black victims of the ghetto suffer incredible rates of unemployment and welfare dependency: they are not an "industrial reserve army."* It is a terrible disservice to them to indulge rhetoric—ours or theirs—*instead of firm analysis. They are the closest, most*

---

* The closest term of his, I think, was lumpen proletariat—which meant no-damn-good-at-all because *de*-classed.

essential emergence of the new genocidal problem (new with Hitler and Stalin). That is why it is so disgusting for intellectuals to reduce vital twentieth century issues to stale nineteenth century prejudices—like colonialism, "poverty" (what a horrible word for "not as good as the suburbs"), workers' revolt, and other sentimentalities of our parents.

Finally, we get down to the good rich stuff: I stink on Vietnam. The best way to understand this country, it turns out, is to take a good look at Vietnam—especially to recognize the striking similarity of yellow skin color and black skin color, as compared to white skin color. Understand this, and everything of significance with respect to classes follows easily enough. "Not only has the class struggle not subsided, it has been renewed with terrible intensity on an international scale," blah, blah, blah. (I didn't say it subsided, I said it changed—especially in calling upon a little realistic self-criticism on the part of analysts like Lasch and me and lots of others.)

Vietnam, he says, "shows once again . . . how helpless they [the Western empires] are in the face of revolutionary resistance." This is an idiot statement unless the Soviet Union and its nuclear weaponry are considered to be the fundament of "revolutionary resistance." (Lasch does not mention Russia once in his review.) So, if you like fine distinctions, he's not an idiot, he's something like a Stalinist ghost. (The Russian action toward Czechoslovakia re-allows figurative use of the term "Stalinist"—here, as well as in East Europe, where it certainly is used.)

And this final neo-anti-colonialist insight: "The consequences of America's impending defeat in the international class war are difficult to assess, because it is still not clear whether the economy is capable of adapting to peace or to the loss of its colonies." But a colony is a place you exploit: America has none it could conceivably have trouble adapting to the loss of—the main ones being advanced nations in Europe, Canada, and mineral areas elsewhere, the loss of the first leading to a reduction in the highest rate of return on capital and of the last to a rise in the price of oil and some metals, neither constituting a catastrophe. (And we have a lot to sell that the world wants to buy at a profit to us, even if not at political prices.) Peace —here less than almost anywhere else—will be very difficult to take, but for psychological and ideological reasons, not economic ones. Again, the immediate take may have to be reduced during a period of readjustment: but after many tears, 6 per cent guaranteed on rebuilding the nation (and all you can steal) will be palatable all around.

The power factor in the international class war still primarily concerns the relation between the United States and the Soviet Union. (Russia has powerless "colonies," too.)

In his review of my book, Christopher Lasch, within a few paragraphs of himself, says both that the New Class does not exist and that it is a failure.

To deal with our problems, we need something more than backward eighteenth century thinkers on the Right, and advanced nineteenth century ones on the Left.

In a later piece, reviewing books by Michael Harrington and Arnold Kaufman in NYRB (July 11, 1968), he does not kick me alone but stomps on the "Galbraith-Bazelon thesis" about the New Class (if you are going to walk the primrose path, better you should do it hand in handsome hand). And, shrewdly overcoming this treacherous reformism, he says: "The immediate constituency for a radical movement, it is clear, lies in the professions, in sections of suburbia, in the ghetto, and above all in the university, which more than any other institution has become a center of radicalism." (He works there.) That's not a bad definition of the New Class and its areas (including its most obvious ally)—and it certainly demonstrates that this high-minded professor is determined to insult me (and even bigger people, the courageous lad) in denying the existence of the New Class in order for him to manage that his ideas rather than anybody else's shall be established in leadership of the members thereof.

❀ THE IDEA OF "THE NEW CLASS"

THE URBAN REVIEW, 1969

I was upset enough by the reception given my exposition of the idea of the New Class to get this piece commissioned by the New York Times Magazine, intending it as a simplistic defense of the notion. They may have been right to turn it down: the issue is too big to presume upon a concise popular exposition, especially for jaded New Yorkers. But I am going to stay with the subject (I kept rewriting this piece, in fact, and peddled it in a briefer version after I put this collection together) because my issue is the responsible self-consciousness of the putatively superior Americans. And that is bigger and longer-lasting than fashionable items like Castro's wooden government of Cuba, the potential sainthood of Ho Chi Minh, thirdforce-here and thirdforce-there, TV hijinx here-and-there on the sad streets of this nation—and exciting new developments in costume and slogan-exchange as an excuse for not thinking, feeling, or bothering much with anything unpublic.

My own notion of the New Class (numerous other sources of the concept are mentioned in this essay) is in fact derived from a lifetime of difficult experience with the other intellectuals—those less acute, more academic, or merely less interesting than myself and my closer friends of the moment: the intellectual's Intellectual as the Other. When I was young, almost all of these unfortunate people had a name—Stalinoid middlebrow. Now, of course, they have had their names—as well as many elements of their circumstance—changed. I am very pleased for them. But my pleasure does not extend to indulging in any happy confusions: I knew them when. And when I knew them, you could have had them.

There is a way, however, of being an intellectual which is almost kind of supra-historical—apart from the confirming sentiments of your friends, even. (It is not, however, the mechanical Purism of a Lasch.) Indeed, the most reprehensible intellectual careerist experiences it now and again simply because he is (if he is) in fact an intellectual. What I want is to define, preserve, nurture, and even make recognizable to new people this supra-historical essence of intellectuality especially now when, having survived the failure of half-priests for several thousand years, it seems about to be overwhelmed by unaccustomed scientific success. How else to do this except by becoming very precise in distinguishing both the unaltered essence and the dangerous new circumstances? And especially in caring to distinguish them the one from the other.

"Intellectual," in this sense, may mean for the world a-coming what "Good Christian" meant on the American frontier.

Lasch's criticism of my book—and especially the idea of the New Class—was, I am sure, the impersonal result of his own New Class enthusiasms. I was an occasion, not a purpose. But the review by my friend, Lewis Coser—whom I met in the early days of Politics in 1944—is something all by itself. Only those thoroughly inside the literary life could even imagine where this kind of hatred might come from, all unknown to the recipient.

Coser reviewed Power in America *in Partisan Review (Summer 1967) as if he were reviewing* Mein Kampf, *on its original publication, for the Menorah Journal of Leipzig. He didn't waste the time Lasch did on compliments (a shorter review) —"Bazelon's The Paper Economy was not a very original book to be sure, but" and we are off. It is unpleasant to compare me to Burnham—"an injustice to the former" in my rehash of him —but: "C. Wright Mills"—I first met him over twenty years ago at Lew Coser's apartment in Queens*—"once called Burnham a Marx for the Managers; Bazelon sounds like a Lenin for Scarsdale." After thoroughly establishing what an unrelievedly lousy book it is—and such bad writing (he showed it to his students and they agreed)—and some resentment as to my statements about "the dangers of homosexuality" and the importance of getting "off the transatlantic ship" (Coser is a German refugee), we get this conclusion:*

As for the rest, dear reader, do not despair, you too are part of the cream that has separated from the curd, you can identify with the core-slice of the apple pie, obey the life-force and join the Reform Democrats in Scarsdale. By and by you will even elect a congressman who will help reorganize the House and aid in overcoming the confusions and contradictions in the American system. There is no need to get all worked up about the obscenity of LBJ, the lying of Dean Rusk, and the strutting of General Westmoreland. Just follow Bazelon, get off that transatlantic ship, join the suburban elite and know that you too can be among the New Samurai.

Somewhat later, in Dissent, *Lewis Coser wrote a piece entitled "How the Young Entered Politics in 1968—and Transformed It." This effort celebrated Senator Eugene McCarthy and his campaign against "those cynics and professional pessimists," etc. McCarthy, having studied Thomas More, was "a man for all seasons." The students were galvanized by McCarthy because he was "Mr. Clean" and embodied "certain funda-*

---

* That was the first time I went that far out in Queens. It was my first view of a suburb. I've never lived in one.

mental human virtues" which the students believe in. So McCarthy "is in the process of changing our political life." The students are active because of him: among other specifics, they "registered in the regular Minnesota Democratic party organization, turned out in force at party meetings, managed to outvote the regulars and to win the day for McCarthy, leaving Hubert Humphrey's hacks aghast. This is the way to proceed." (*My emphasis.*)

The candidate of the educated suburbs, enthusiastically supported by the children of the suburbs, utilizing the techniques of the Reform Democrats, will change "our political life."

So who is "a Lenin for Scarsdale" now?

The production of educated individuals is the major growth industry in the United States today. Being educated is now a way of making a better living, just as owning a business used to be—and remains—an avenue to financial advantage. Educated individuals who do in fact receive better incomes because of their education have something substantial in common. Equally important, each and all of them differ in a similar way from those who do not have these incomes, or do not have them because of educational status. This mixed cultural-and-economic development has been an accelerating one for decades —and, in the last decade or two, has taken on the character of a geometric progression. So, all in all, the question fairly arises, Do these people constitute a New Class in our society?

With our history of spatial and social mobility, the idea of class—and especially the accompanying (unnecessary) sense of rigid personal definition—has been anathema to most Americans. When sociologists have IBMed us for views of our own class position, overwhelming numbers of us have responded—"Middle Class." This indicates that we all tend to choose a safe non-definition; and that we are vaguely aware of Something-at-the-Bottom and Something-at-the-Top—where we fear to go, where we want to go. The essence of our view of ourselves is that we are forever *going.* And mobility between classes is, indeed, a strong feature of our system. Also, it is the main reason we persist in misunderstanding the idea of class.

It is nearly immoral in this country to remain in the same place; and to plan to do so is clearly corrupt. Conceived most broadly, Success is our major institution-*cum*-devotion. In addition, the most characteristic feature of American society—our immigrant variety—

has provided a very rich substitute-basis for class, in nevertheless distinguishing among people as to "type." Since our actual immigration occurred in specific ethnic waves—and, beginning with nothing, the longer here, the better we did, wherever we came from and whoever we used to be—the substitution of ethnic factors for those of economic class was not nearly so obtuse as it might otherwise have been.

While we do and inevitably will continue with our broad ethnic differentiations, the idea of economic class is a very useful one, not lightly to be denied. As a current and obvious example, the Negroes as a group are to be understood—at last—both as to race *and* poverty. The one without the other will be distorting. But even both together, of course, could achieve distortion in the image of an individual Negro. Neither economic class nor ethnic notions are an excuse for one's failure to comprehend an individual. We always have *that* job at hand.

There are two hundred million people in this country: not one should be ignored; they cannot all be comprehended individually. We do, we must, summarize others in broad categories. (And they will do it to us.) Historically, the primary one has been economic class.

Now, certain ideas we are almost literally *born* with: the English liberal arts people used to say that every baby was born a Platonist or an Aristotelian. Today, we are "born" with a built-in mechanism of class-analysis, namely, Some people are rich, some people are poor. Who will object to this simple idea? Only the shrewd, defensive person who sees clearly what is coming. What is coming is the sweetly naïve question, Daddy, *why* are some people rich, and some people poor?

In Europe, this nearly primeval rich/poor notion achieved a somewhat more sophisticated expression, as follows: Some people have enough property—own enough—to make a real difference, and the rest (an overwhelming majority) do not. In America, the simple version was further simplified: Some people are born lucky, and other people get lucky later. This peculiarly American interpretation is the source, for instance, of the puerile notion that nobody needs or deserves anything except "opportunity"—to be lucky, that is. Which is why the poverty program is built around our official determination to give clear losers a second chance to get lucky. And nothing else: certainly not the indulgence of clearly indicated hand-outs, like $5–10 billion to old people, or Any Job At All to young people who may need one.

In affluent America, where the majority is too well off to be called "poor," we have been limited too long to these simply inadequate views. On the downside, we have already developed—beyond Europe's imagining—the concept of the Underclass: not the poor or the merely unlucky, but the persistently ruined and rejected (and for No Good Reason). On the upside, we have accepted several million very rich Super-Consumers—and without bothering (an amazing fact!) to justify the manner in which individuals are chosen to participate in this National Wing-Ding of super-consumption. In other words, we *wanted* them to be chosen by unanalyzed chance. (In New York City banks alone, there are probably $100 billion or so in trust funds, constituting that much in unearned livings for the recipients. It is a major social feat to find out what good and bad is done with this very special money—which probably comes to as much, in annual interest, as the total expense account expenditure in any year.)

But without pursuing the exotic issues posed by the American Underclass, and our darling Overclass of Super-Consumers, we must recognize that the *New Class* of people from Anywhere who were lucky enough to get "A's" and "B's" and good jobs, are the center of the American "class" problem. *Get educated, get rich*—amounts to the profoundest possible change in the over-all system of American Expectations.

As to the more particular facts of the matter, the New Class in America is propertyless (in career-line, certainly), educated, mostly white, mostly mobile; it exists characteristically in suburbs and organizations—in and around the more advanced living and working areas of the new technological order. The most direct gross measurement of the size of the class would be, I suppose, the number of educated people in the total population. In 1960, there were 7.6 million people who had experienced four years or more of college; by 1985, the estimate is for 20.5 million. Meanwhile, the size of the higher education faculty has better than doubled since 1950, when 2.2 million students were in attendance. (Salaries are supposed to and probably will be doubled between 1957 and 1970.) In 1965, the enrollment was 5.7 million, and—if the early rate of increase persists —will be 11.6 million in 1985.

The New Class is different from other classes, even when individuals comprising it do not comprehend this, or deny it. The differences will be increasingly significant. Finally, the New Class, along with its special departures in value and style, will become dominant; or—just as likely—those who first and most effectively organize and control this class will become our rulers.

The central difference, for today, is that education supplements or supplants the ownership of property as the largest reason for a superior income. The major point in John Kenneth Galbraith's *The New Industrial State* is that the trained capacity of individuals has replaced capital as the primary factor of production.

> One should expect, from past experience, to find a new shift of power in the industrial enterprise, this one from capital to organized intelligence. And one would expect that this shift would be reflected in the deployment of power in the society at large.

In three little words—*Brains before money*. Please note that this monumental change is apt to be equally strange and disturbing to the losers-with-money *and* the winners-with-brains. Why? Because, as to winning and losing, this constitutes a serious reversal of roles in the United States.

For the class-analyst who has not progressed beyond the rich/poor idea he was born with, the significance of the change we are discussing can be obscure. For example, he may reflect: One fellow gets money because he has money, and another because he is educated. Both get money: so what else is new? Nothing else is new if we Americans again deny a discussion of cause, because of an obvious reflection on similarity of effect. (In this country, you win or you lose; winners are winners, and only losers discuss what happened along the way.)

The class of educated people differs within itself at least as much as the range of quality in American education (much more, in fact) —say, from a prize student in physics at Cal Tech to a recent squeak-through graduate of a local college in South Carolina. But, sticking to our basic economic definition, each is a member of the New Class. If this seems bizarre (and it certainly does to many of my snobbish intellectual acquaintances), please recall that in the past we somehow managed to become accustomed to lumping together Henry Fords and candy-store operators as "capitalists."

At one time, it was thought that if there was in fact a New Class, it consisted only of the top managers of basic industrial corporations —who clearly ran things, and just as clearly did not do so by virtue of ownership. Another view of this strange new phenomenon held that with the growth of modern industry, engineers and similarly hard-nosed technical types had been inadvertently (and perhaps temporarily) elevated to conditions of significance that entailed certain prima donna prerogatives. With the advent of Sputnik in 1957, this elevation became a well-advertised feature of Soviet society, and we began a strenuous—even excessive—imitation of it. All in all, however, what was being remarked was the fresh importance of highly trained persons in the central productive/power process. Even earlier, it was noticed that the essence of modern warfare had been turned over to people who talked in such a special language that even ordinary ex-G.I.s wondered how the generals from West Point could understand them (and maybe thereby experienced their first underdog sympathy for behind-the-lines brass). All this was early hysteria.

When technical people get into positions of power, they are required to do things they cannot really manage on their own while relying only on their prior technical training. They require, indeed, a large complement of additional faculty: they then and there find out that they have long been involved with, and even dependent upon, the liberal arts characters living across the street. Thank God. If educated people were to enter upon prominent roles in history with nothing but their salable technical competence to recommend them, they would be reduced immediately to interchangeable parts in the going machinery. Physicists need humanists currently (as people in show biz say) to "settle the audience," at the very least. And one day, when we finally arrive at the real point of what the New Class is all about, the humanists will need the physicists to remind the audience that intellectual rule was, after all, necessary.

Intellectuality is in fact indivisible: when you start thinking, only God or the FBI can stop you.

Since the New Class is new, and undeveloped as a class, I favor the broadest possible definition—anyone whose economic position is based on education, and any non-owner with a superior position within an organization, each receiving a better income thereby. The lack of precision in this approach is not inappropriate, in my view, to emergent historical phenomena. The fact that important corporate or military office, for example, may still be inhabited here and there by individuals without academic degrees—or *with* family money—should not be taken to negative the role of education or its union with organizational status not based on ownership. There are always exceptions of a kind: history is not a clear-cut logical process.

All education and *all* advantage-despite-non-ownership should be included in the definition, at the outset, because these constitute the primary departures from the previous social order. Neither was a major road to differential wealth and power, in the past. Today, joined, they are: ownership is much reduced in importance; knowing how to do something difficult is greatly elevated—wherever or however you learned it. This is an earthquake alteration in circumstance.

Classes appear in history not adventitiously, but because they have a function to perform. The function of this New Class is to deploy the entire human cultural heritage and capacity—consciously to think and plan about Anything and Everything—that may preserve and perfect the urban overpopulated dangerous technological order that has replaced traditional societies in the advanced areas, and threatens (with the greedy connivance of native populations) to do so everywhere upon the planet. The New Class is becoming the planetary leadership class, now that trained thought is becoming the value that commands other values. In the Communist countries it has displaced the propertied class and dominates the industrial and rural proletariat.

In other words, ideas—and the means of getting ideas—are being recruited and organized to serve an overriding power-function. Ultimate destruction itself is now a mere deduction from one intellectual exercise or another. Power today requires more and more highly trained intellect to achieve its purposes. And this is also the key to the noisy accelerating generational conflict we have been living through ever since a handful of kids demonstrated the weakness of the going racial system in the United States. This society now is so helplessly dependent on bright young people—their freshness and energy and available talent—*literally, their lack of old experience and capacity for the new*—that we are being compelled to treat the whole crowd as prima donnas.

When the systematic transmission of intellectuality from one generation to the other was not nearly so significant in power terms, it was entrusted to one captive priestly class or another. Intellectuals and similar entertainers—individuals better than others in dealing with symbols and images and ideas—were always important, spiritually. Now they are important in profoundly material terms as well. This has occasioned a shift in social power, both class and generational—the latter as a separate matter simply because the development has been too rapid for a nascent class to encompass the generational passage. The sons and fathers (some researchers say, *mothers*) of educated families are engaged in a conflict which is both *inter*-generational and *intra*-class: that is how rapid the pace of development of the New Class has been.

But note the extreme significance of placing the entire human heritage of consciousness in the hands of a self-interested economic class. When the bourgeoisie took power, they became a class controlling only the deployment of material wealth. Ideas, and the creators of ideas, were not then worth controlling; which is one source of our fabled Western freedoms. (The other source, equally significant for today, is that putative freedom for all was thought to be a condition for actual freedom of any putative member of a large and vaguely defined dominant class.) Now that ideas are more important than material wealth, the same avid desire to dominate may be expected to assert itself as to this factor of production, as it formerly did with the other. The danger in the past was substantial: the danger in the present is infinite.

The social dynamic of the New Class is clearly totalitarian; also, unfortunately, the personal impulse of some New Class intellectuals. Ideas are, in their essence, imperialist: nothing is to be unthought of.

Reaching somewhat, I will assert that the number one question-marks in our future are: (1) will the dominance of this New Class come about without unlivable disruption, and (2) will the quality-control of ideas it will exercise be superior to that of our present official governmentese and advertising culture, or substantially the same, but more thorough? (The chance that it might be genuinely similar to that of the Communist nations at their worst is, I think, behind us: wooden Stalinism was expensive and inefficient.)

The earlier forms of intellectualism—especially including the traditional professions—are readily assimilated to the New Class flow. These must relate their careerist intellectuality to that of the new people; and in addition, the traditional professions are themselves rapidly becoming organized and institutional, with a reduced free-lance individual quality. Even bohemians, the utter free lance, are being broadly welcomed out of their isolation—if only as television performers.

Most important, however, is the issue of models for the future: now that a great range of intellectuals in growing numbers are being invited to participate in operating the power mechanisms of the society, they must develop newly appropriate styles. When the academic sojourner bursts from the chrysalis of accumulated irrelevancy, he too often adopts a crude imitation of the established national style of the double-breasted, go-getter businessman. I much prefer the tweedy Walter Pidgeon lounger of years past; and for verbal style, I yearn for a running series of Oscar Wilde quotes in contrast to the current abracadabra of scientism.

For substantial content (and because of personal background), I recommend most of all the hard-earned and muscular style of the better lawyers. Practicing lawyers have been at it longer than other intellectuals—that is, out there in society, right next to the men of power. Indeed, under capitalism, the lawyer has been the prototypical intellectual active in affairs. He created and has been the chief caretaker of the formal property system. (In the United States, he created and staffed the machinery of government as well—almost as an afterthought.) Lawyers, over these active centuries, have developed a skeptical regard for the complex mix of ideas-and-acts that makes up the world of affairs; also, considerable white Stepin Fetchit sophistication in the role of intellectual servants of power. (Doctors do not make good models because, being swept along by the revolution in medicine, they precipitously have abandoned their cracker-barrels and are becoming imitation scientists; priests, of course, have been nearly destroyed by the practicality of the capitalist Zeitgeist.)

Since science applied as technology is the major force clearing the way for the New Class, the polysyllabic posturing of inappropriate scientism has already become its dominant style. So much so that, seeking any relief, the romantic primitivism of TV-educated youth, even with its show-biz language and dress, is readily welcomed.

A caveat: The utility of identifying a class of people in society—especially based on compelling similarities of condition—is that one can thereafter deduce compulsions of behavior and outlook. The continual danger in this form of deductive thinking, however, is that individuals, in all their wayward and awful variety, may be subjected to wooden reductionism. Whatever it was in the hungry past, this danger is augmented, certainly, by our very special affluence in the present: because affluence is a determining factor of immense (and unknown) magnitude; it is utterly new as such; any wild idea at all about it must be heard; and, *thus*, any breath of reductionism is utterly out-of-order.

The *idea* as distinct from the *fact* of the New Class is given us primarily by a wee, pained voice out of the socialist tradition. What this bitter voice said was: You intellectuals like Me, jumped from the Janus-head of the French Revolution, think that you are the only Free Spirits left active in history; and out of your exceptionally endowed Personal Freedom you now presume to awaken and lead your lesser brethren—*hear Me*, you want only one-up for yourselves on petty-bourgeois parentage, and will use any downtrodden human on the planet to achieve this exclusive group purpose of your own. You intellectuals are a New Class, exactly as Karl Marx defined old classes: and your self-justifying purity reminds me of John Locke.

Michael Harrington, somewhat more factually, has* traced back the idea of the New Class to a Polish anarchist by the name of Waclaw Machajski who, writing around the turn of the century, "saw the social democratic movement as the instrument, not of workers' emancipation, but of class power of messianic intellectuals." Milovan Djilas, the exceptional Yugoslavian revolutionary prisoner who provided the name that has stuck to the idea, conceived the fact quite differently from Machajski; Djilas meant to refer to the bureaucratic class in a socialist state, and excepted from that class only those party intellectuals who were sufficiently messianic to oppose it. Likewise, Leon Trotsky, the reclaimed Hegelian, who proposed to overcome history with his own Idea of History. In a series of editorials in *The Dial* immediately following World War I, Thorstein Veblen spoke vaguely of the engineers as a class; and just before America entered World War II, James Burnham popularized the idea in his bitter post-Marxist book, *The Managerial Revolution*. From outside the socialist tradition, the idea emerged as a consequence of scholarly property analysis, most particularly that of Adolf Berle.

So much for sources—except to mention that we have something loose in the world today that might be called Deadhead Marxism

* With the help of Max Nomad.

(or Pure Socialism). This attitude, whether derived from the new ignorance of the current generation or the established stupidity of the aging one, is a serious force to be contended with, in this country as well as elsewhere. It seems to have survived Stalinism as an ultimate intellectual disgrace. Marx was a major nineteenth century innovative thinker who lends himself all too well to the greedy reductionism of New Class intellectuals seeking quick community by means of the Best Ideas. (Unlike France or Italy, for instance, the Communists never had a serious working class base in the United States. Here, it was *all* New Class: some of the leaders were $250,000-a-year men in Hollywood.) It is the know-it-all simplicity of great ideas vulgarized that so appeals to those whose personal security is based on a bank account of current ideas rather than the other kind of currency—or a genuinely searching intellectuality. In truth, the surviving grandeur of Marx's thought concerns his approach to consciousness as part of the historical process, not the dogmatism of undifferentiated proletarian/bourgeois conflict.

The fact is that Marx's view of historical condition as creating distorted or prejudicial consciousness, when this view is utilized with something approaching Marx's own subtlety, is as useful today as it ever was, and ever will be. But his property-centered analysis has been superseded; the modern class system—and the modern historical dynamic—can no longer be comprehended in terms of ownership. Advantage, yes; ownership, no. Some New Class intellectuals who presume to speak for the dispossessed, however, insist upon the ownership dogma because it obscures their own special class position and interest. Under the Communist system, this is obvious. Obvious or not, it is just as true in the United States.

So I have urged the New Class idea in the American circumstance in order to induce consciousness of class upon intellectuals who all too readily assume romantic identity with other classes above or beneath them (not coalition, please note, but identity). The retort of the purest of these has been that I should read Marx more carefully in order to acquaint myself with owner/non-owner class warfare, instead of celebrating the education of the residents of Scarsdale.

If there is a New Class as described, then clearly we are dealing with a major phenomenon with a multitude of ramifications, not the least difficult of which is that the members of the class must themselves explicate its own conditions of consciousness. The pursuit of such critical self-consciousness—which will then jell into class-consciousness—strikes me as far and away more urgent and important than whether one initially assumes a hopeful or despairing outlook on the phenomenon (another critical assault upon my views). The New Class in the United States may very well end up as an overwhelming disaster: it did in Russia, constituting self-protective bureaucracy instead of revolution. But what all-hating impulse commands that one assume this at the outset (especially since there is no alternative)? It would be both black-hearted and presumptuous; and, on the part of university professors at the center of the New Class development, it also misses the *class* point altogether. Are these pure ones members of no class at all, no matter who pays their salary or otherwise simulates affection on their behalf? I suggest that their insistence on worker/capitalist conflict is merely a device, derived from their own class position, to take us back to pre-Marxist romanticism.

The class-consciousness of the heterogeneous New Class is contradictory and primitive. These people, who know the economic value of their education, will most often not extend that meaning ideologically, but will continue to identify with their class sources or aspirations: that is, rather than class condition. Even many of the radical ones who ally themselves with the colored Underclass presume to do so romantically, as individuals, rather than as a matter of political coalition (with retained awareness of differences in interest). Right-wing organization men often hold on to small-property ideology with what an outsider can only call desperation. The careful centrist types simply identify with Establishment style, thinking it is that of the Protestant upper crust. Currently, the main point about the relations to other classes is that these are confused and confusing, self-deceptive and *fashionable*—very much in the process of rapid development. The distinct and separate class identity of this new formation is yet to be created. And that would be one of the more important benefits of recognizing the existence of the class *now*—to participate in the creation of that identity and style, rather than merely suffering it in imitation after others establish it.

The alternative to the New Class idea would be to view the various departments of a university as so many trade schools, and their graduates as skilled workers. Non-owning top management, whether or not educated, would then be understood simply as hired hands of the plutocratic rich. The observable differences in our social order could be stated as a general upgrading of the working force; the numerical growth and augmented assertiveness of the non-owning proprietors of the university trade schools; and an increased number of "junior partnerships" bestowed upon deserving proletarians. In this way, neither education and intellectual status nor organizational position would have independent significance, and the property idea would still reign supreme. After a while, someone might come up with the idea, once again, that doing away with private property would solve all of our problems by bringing about a classless society.

▌EPILOGUE

The Luddite Rebellion on Channel Four

SO THE issue is "community," and the youth have already decided for it. Nothing, not even sanity, is to stand in the way of groupishness.*

What remains for the fading generation? I think, to convey the relevance of the past, such as it was, and especially as it was impinging on the issue of *re*constituted individuality in the newly overorganized world. The new crowd will create the groups; we will remind them of their potential selfhood. That is, to be a parent. A good, *modern* parent.

With the advanced portion of mankind now living so much longer, we must soon undergo, also, a revolution in the uses of age. This will have to be in the direction of some kind of persisting parenthood: service to the next generation, according to individual inclination and capacity and circumstance. Which implies a highly extended notion of parenthood for a much longer period of life (for many, it will be second-chance or atonement parenthood). But there must be some human use and dignity for age that is not simply the coerced result of waiting-for-the-estate and similar traditional ploys and tyrannies of the aged.

As to youth and age, we will adjust—that is, walk out of the jungle like men—by (1) honoring the vitality and desire of youth, without the diseased fawning upon it that is demanded by the media culture of affluence and eternal-youth females; and (2) by an early accep-

---

* When I first heard about LSD, I thought they were kidding: Who needs a drug to go crazy, I exclaimed to myself. Now I understand: like with pot, it's the togetherness that counts. I suspect there are few solo drinkers in this new group.

tance of everyone's future—that is, age—by true judgment and use of the living witnesses thereof, rather than by reduction to fantasies of life after death, or Alka-Seltzer age after Pepsi-Cola youth. This, and not—as traditionally—the treatment accorded females, shall become the new and true measure of the level of civilization achieved by a particular social order. The age difference is now perhaps greater than the sex difference (the one lengthening while the other narrows).

One of the bigger problems on the agenda of any old-fashioned intellectual is imagining the youthful individual who, say, accepts the essence but not any particular accoutrement of fashion of the New Politics and the New Style, a well-to-do product of the New Class born of and into suburbs and organizations, a nice kid with a foul mouth—half-educated and also only half-interested in his elders. You know what I mean, our sons and our students: the new audience.

Take it this way: Assume that the New Class exists and is as important as I have suggested, that both father and son are members of it, and that we want a logical category to present the proposition. Let's take form-and-content: form* is the occasional wisdom of parenthood, while content is the so-so animal vitality of youth. Why are we now so formless? Why is it that content/youth is so raised, and form/parenthood so reduced?

Because of affluence. Poor people, young and old, have for ages been given form by their poverty, that is, the myriad iron necessities of difficult physical existence that both induced and limited their doings. Indeed, poverty is the truest primitive *form* of human existence (bigger even than sex, which became popular in order to make poverty bearable, and to while away the time of the idle rich). The well-to-do, however, are required to create form beyond that dictated by simple poverty. The form-beyond-poverty appearing among the affluent in this country, to date, is more a disease of fantasy than a design of imagination. And the *nouveau riche* greed that is not used up in Consumerism and similar celebrations of self is still available for spiritual aggrandizement—both narrowly egotistic and broadly ideological.

---

* "Form" is the noticeable outline of any particular conjoined interest-against-circumstance working themselves out into experience.

We may surmount poverty, but never form; form is the fundament of inter-expectation, the literal stuff of language itself. Without form believed in at least enough to be practiced as openers, the most civilized man must devote the truest energy of his life to forestalling an immediate return to the jungle *later today*: at best, tomorrow morning *if hope fails early*. (The return will be incompetent: the jungle will not welcome: but that is beside the point.)

If *they* are just young, and *we* are just old, another incompetent return to the jungle may be near. Things are changed that much. The disjunction between generations, planned and deeply desired by totalitarian regimes, turns out to be also a seemingly irresistible effect of all that is most modern—without any such stated intention at all.

In *Target Zero* (1955), an ordinary combat movie set in Korea, the American soldiers face an imminent attack, their defense is hopeless, etc. (they are in the end saved, as usual, by superior firepower). The American-Italian lieutenant speaks to the American-Apache signalman: "What do you say, Injun?" "Now I know how Custer felt," is what he says. How about that! A million dollars' worth of Regular Guy wampum thus bestowed by the media in reparations to the American Indian. *How hard we have tried for community!* And what means we have used and are still using to get it.

The public schools were half-a-parent to the sons of the immigrants—*Aquí se habla inglés*, the sign read. And for the sons of the English-speaking generations, movies and television and other commercial media are, again, half-a-parent (at least). And much more than language and the pledge of allegiance is taught there. As McLuhan has suggested (I guess), groupishness—which he calls tribalism—is a large part of the curriculum. I see it also from the other way around: when I watch television (and this is mostly *why* I watch it) I have noticed that my personality dissolves into that demon eye, and all that remains of my sometime sense-of-myself is a little *tinkle* here and there (mostly of might-have-been) whenever I dissolve too enthusiastically into a particular image or other bit of electronic business. *Some parent!* I'll take the lousy P.S. 41's of my youth any day. It's just a baby-sitter, and that's just what I use it for—me, the aging baby. (I am beginning to think that television is a Jewish mother.)

An anecdote: I helped give a seminar on corporations and other monsters at the Institute for Policy Studies during the non-academic year 1967–68. Our modus was to invite in guest conductors. One of these, a former SDSer, was a nice, energetic, serious-minded young man who was trying to organize lower middle class whites in Chicago. As a measure of his difficulty therein, and also to indicate imaginative scope, he pointed to the matter of trade name vs. generic drugs, for use as a political ploy. Illustrating his point, he described the process from doctor to druggist whereby he purchased an expensive brand-name penicillin for himself following some kind of oral surgery.* I asked why—since it was clear that he knew the difference between trade name and generic drugs at the time, that is, had already educated himself politically as he was now attempting to do with others. His answer was that he would have been "embarrassed" to (1) ask his doctor to write a generic prescription or (2) insist that the druggist fill the prescription generically. Why? I asked again (I'm clever that way). He was in pain, he said; and embarrassed.

Note that *he* chose the drug issue as a proper one exampling "consumer revolt"—*his* term. And he just naturally assumed that his personal effort in relation to this revolt did not include his questioning his own doctor or druggist, to each of whom he was actually transferring money in a classic act of command: *but the modern consumer does not buy, he "joins in."* This young man just naturally joined in; but his "revolt"—as a Leader, yet—was limited to an explicitly marked-out area of ideology that was there to be sold to others. The reason he did not question his own doctor or druggist was that any such action would have been irrelevant to the ideological point: *he knew that his own vote on generic drugs was secure.* So, besides that, he joined in: he was in pain, which has nothing to do with politics. (Throughout the entire exchange with him, I was treated as if I simply had not comprehended the actual subject under discussion.)

The New Left does not want to act individually—or to see any problems as properly those of the individual, in any serious quantum or aspect. Their deep confusion of morality and politics, in public action, is accompanied by a non-moral approach to anything that is not seen as political, in private action.

* As Trotsky once remarked nastily, the typical example of pain used by bourgeois thinkers was a visit to the dentist.

The discussion continued, with emphasis (his) on even more imaginative devices furthering consumer revolt. They all consisted of on-location network programming suggestions. For instance, "when the time was ripe" (we used to say, "in the next period"), he was thinking, along the lines of "Supermarket Sweepstakes," of organizing a "cook-in" (I guess). He thought maybe some guerrillas with Sterno-stoves could fry overpriced cuts of meat right there in the supermarket. What would the Bosses do about *that?* I liked the idea, but offered what I thought was an even better one: collect a cadre of former campfire types, and organize a piss-in directed at the frozen food bin. My argument was that a lot of that frozen food was not only overpriced but wasn't really edible anyway—and by pissing on it, we could score twice.

Little did I suspect that a few months later they would throw beer cans filled with urine at the Irish and Polish cops I went to grade school with in Chicago, as one more imaginative political effort on behalf of the New Class. Maybe I should have kept my big mouth shut.

Maybe I should *always* have kept my big mouth shut. I have a friend who did, and believes I should have. But he's a hard-pressed psychoanalyst, and they're peculiar—from all that strenuous listening. I didn't listen that hard, so my mouth kept working overtime. Now, of course, it's just a bad habit (but so is his listening).

The three greatest killers in America are cancer, heart disease, and awareness. I tried for twenty-five years to get intellectuals to recognize that the very *environment* included media culture and that, unanalyzed and snobbishly ignored, its insane potential was incalculable. But they weren't listening. Now a mutant generation, teaching the teacher, confronts them with the ripening fact, and Dwight Macdonald (for instance)—who first taught me the outlines of popular culture criticism—is hoisted to the third floor of a Columbia building in one of their baskets and lowers himself to report: "I have seen the future, and it works."

The closest clue is that *the youth have no notion of reality itself—* not for means or ends or structure—that truly excludes the media. The Battle of Chicago, their greatest achievement, was specifically a volunteer acting/programming effort made possible through a coalition of SDS and the Yippies: New Left *and* New Style.

Through television—that bullhorn of affluence—politics and entertainment are beginning to merge: the overlap is that substantial. Television is the culmination of the culture that industrialism has been giving the masses ever since the advent of newspapers in the eighteenth century and general literacy in the nineteenth. (The photography et al, of the last hundred years has meant more than the printing press, of course, in displacing experienced reality with manufactured images thereof, since it bypasses literacy.) Prior to these great developments, lately ending in the endless and overwhelming visualism of television, the culture of the masses consisted exclusively of religion, fragments of folklore, and work-knowledge (both male and female). This *new* popular culture introduced over the past two centuries has had two major effects: it has broadened the audience—now joined in this by modern mass education for the uses of technology—of those subject to the influence of culture, whatever that may be; and it has established (or immeasurably broadened) a new historical or metaphysical category—*the media event.*

Since Chicago '68, one can merely point, and need not strain to define this term—even though it occurred in newspapers more than a century ago (and in churches since time began). My point is that the media event has grown geometrically with urban concentration and electronic sophistication. The critical capacity to recognize and analyze this sort of thing, unfortunately, has not. The consequence is that media influence is far more extensive than it need be, even among our most educated citizens; and the ability to imagine non-media reality is far more atrophied than it need have become, especially among their children. The inherent anti-intellectualism of the media is taken over even by the intellectuals among the youth, and they don't even seem to know where they got it from. I wouldn't be surprised if it turns out that they drop out of college so much because they are still enrolled in television, so what's the loss; a year or two of college is enough to convince them that it is only somewhat different from television and Pepsi activism, not better. Their notions of direct and immediate justice they had to get from "Gunsmoke" et al because that's the only place anybody can get that stuff anymore. (I have an occasional nightmare that they read books as if they were props borrowed from a Susskind discussion show.)

The hugely successful comedy-patch called "Laugh-In" seems the farthest achievement yet of their kind of acted-out criticism of and contribution to network programming. On the surface, it is all New

Style; but in form, it derives entirely from a clever wedding of the new techniques of TV commercials and old Bob Hope one-liners. In my day, we had lines from radio shows that were repeated endlessly by everyone—e.g., Joe Penner's "Wanna buy a duck?" But the "Laugh-In" lines are more broadly effective. I don't recall that the sit-down strikers in Lansing yelled "Wanna buy a duck?" at the Pinkertons surrounding the plant. But in the spring of 1968, I did see (on television, of course) placards of CWA strikers picketing a Bell Telephone installation with the legend "Ma Bell, here come de judge."

And it is very much also my point that here-come-de-judge is an ancient one-liner from *vaudeville* days. (Also, of course, that the influence of the media is not limited to devastation of the New Youth.)

Are they mutants? *Maybe they are*. That is the favored hypothesis as far as I am concerned—which I will be overjoyed to abandon at the earliest real opportunity. If so, then there must have been some changes—real big and brand new—in the world they were born into and grew up in, as compared to ours. I suggest four: (1) The Bomb; (2) television; (3) affluence; (4) pills.

All of these, you will notice, have a common denominator: they are the superior effects of advanced technology upon what remains of the human.

Translating from their generation to ours (we have to, they won't):

The Bomb: The ultimate power that formerly belonged to God or Nature is now held by Man: is omnipresent, is suicidal.

Television: Thoroughly off-camera reality is probably unnecessary, certainly as basically unimportant as it is obviously uninteresting.

Affluence: Life is a challenge to have Meaningful Fun all the time: sex is a rather important way of having Meaningful Fun—but only if you cool it about the male/female hang-up.

Pills: Pain and death and boredom are nearly manageable.

Affluence is the key "blessing" of technology (if you grant the apposite diabolism of The Bomb). But first a word or two about pills, to get us straightened away:

By "pills" I mean to include the whole cornucopia of medical technology, all the new chemical/physical devices for manipulating the body (including the mind and the emotions): organ-transplants, antibiotics, tranquilizers and pep-pills, dumb answers from experts, word-pills from psychiatrists, modern hospital chromium-plated machines and personalities, and any other relevant science-fiction. Everything except aspirin—I was born during the Aspirin Age—and early stuff like morphine, hashish, X-rays, and adrenalin. As I understand it, almost everything else of significance is postwar. Antibiotics and mood-pills and acted-out science-fiction are the main things. (Alcohol and tobacco are as profoundly American—and historical— as Valley Forge, the Second Battle of Bull Run, and every new salesman's-territory from Plymouth to San Diego.)

But the surviving point is that "pills" do not yet dispense with the human effort to deal with the human condition. Not really.

Meanwhile, this country has been traumatized by its achieved wealth and the mad dash to accumulate it—also known, on state occasions, as American History.

Now that is the simple fact of the matter. The difficulty in appreciating this fact derives entirely from our unshakable conviction that wealth was supposed to mean something else.

America is a mess—of this there is no more question today than there ever was. But, in the past, it had been clear enough to me that, by and large, America was an open-hearted mess. On this point, today, I am afraid that some serious research is required.

I did not expect this cultural nihilism, and fervent anti-intellectualism, of our most favored sons. With hindsight, knowing what I know about middlebrowism, I should have; but I didn't. (Where is that slim but noble minority of highbrows among the youth?) Standing on the rubble of my American experience, I acknowledge the truth to my Jewish forebears: Jesus Christ was not the Messiah —*and neither is this country*. Believe me, Bubba.

I concluded a piece in *Esquire*—not republished here—by saying: "No one can become rich without changing himself in other ways as well." And that's for sure.

We Americans absolutely have to discover some reasonable, feasible way of getting together without becoming Successful all over each other. Further commitment to that institution will only create more affluence, without creating any more capacity to deal with it, live with it, or make something out of it. And becoming Successful is gloved-in with our malignant commitment to being fashionable: fashion is now our pseudo-form of love—the simple absolute confounding of self and other—since fashion is a way of identifying yourself to others who could not otherwise be bothered to know you by any other names or means. The price is that you become the means you have chosen of identifying yourself to others. (Who then takes care of the unidentified you?)

It's all right if you come from Nowhere off some ship or farm or other, and devote yourself to play-acting Success: but *born* to it? That is silly on the face of it. How can you live your life in a darkened theater? The empty seats themselves stand up and shout, *It's all over, go home!*

Affluence, our success, could destroy this nation, the whole incredible experiment—*pfft!* Either we use this wealth better—each one his own dollar *and* substantial social re-investment (serious redistribution of income)—or it will ruin us. Whether or not we blow up the world, no one will recognize anyone on the streets or in the homes—not the husbands the wives, the sons the fathers, the mothers the daughters. And all the Bosses will be self-anointed, uneasily mumbling to themselves in freshly padded closets. We have broken through the poverty-barrier: all the rules of living are changed. Get with it, America—or go under.

The true mutation is affluence: our young sons are merely the first complete victims. All their demonstrations and creative costuming and chemical adventures and upper-class window-smashing and flamboyant refusal of soap and scissors and crude disbeliefs are nothing but the first loud scream of pain: *Daddy, why did you make me rich, just rich? Why not one word what to do with it? Why did you leave me to learn everything important from horse operas?*

Their problem, not mine: my daddy didn't make me rich. But my problem is no longer significant, except to me. And what did the Real Daddies do? They offered only a tightly scripted private life (or acquiesced in the one provided by the female), thus all unknowingly to invite a public life allowing the fullest, freest, most irresponsible fantasy—images derived from the warmed-over spontaneity of all the dead decades since Romanticism ceased to be an earnest error. Raised on TV-dinners, their sons were then sent out into the world of fancy restaurants with nothing but a piece of Carte Blanche plastic to guide them. No map to the Indies that.

And now, in the midst of a Grand Reversal of mood—with private life bursting into public scripting—we even have a whole new category of person, the fashionable psychopath called the Weirdo. He is the putatively imaginative public actor, born of television. So it naturally cannot resist him. But I can. Because I do not need him as the Weirdo he is—that is too destructive, of all the remaining fragile distinctions between indulged dream and the trembling reality of remaining social form. I can't make do with the idiot formlessness the Weirdo-admirers, in youthful ignorance, take as romantic freedom. (In the end, neither will they be able to take it that way.)

We need form, because form is part of language. Not the picture-language of television, but the real old language of the historical/human heritage. If this ancient language is in fact to be transcended by electronics, etc. (meanwhile the latter gobbling up all of the former's product), I assert forcefully that the current technique of transcendence is inadequate, so I ain't going along just yet. I will not abandon it, and the form underlying it, until it is made clear to me that the new electronic transcendence has not merely outshouted the past. Until then, I will remain—and urge others to remain—a two-language immigrant, as it ever was on these evergreen shores. (Who knows, for someone like myself a couple of generations from now, real English may serve him as *Yiddishkeit* did me.)

So I cannot allow myself to be led by the New Youth: they exhibit so much of the Old Crap along with their unarguable Newness. For one important particularity: they quite ignore their own primary representation of the rampant elitism in our society. The basic issue in our kind of society—about to replace even the primitive American Success drive, or substantially redirect it—is very simply who is qualified to do this, that, and the other rather complicated technological-administrative type thing. The affluent youth are born into these considerations, pursue them avidly along with their basic groupishness, while denying elitism by identifying with every which other available primitive person-or-thing on the face of the planet. Their careerism is so much a part of their chic radicalism, that they do not even bother to discuss them separately.*

They are working toward a New Individualism in the Organized Environment, let us hope. So once again, what is the possible relevance of the Old Individualism that they reject so devastatingly? I

---

* Note the superior organizational capacity of the white disruptionists as compared to the ghetto youth, as well as the differences in style and object; but notice also the true organizational force of skin-color togetherness, whether or not joined with white-type capacities.

think, to serve as models, indeed as a storehouse of suggestive ideas, once the inadequacies of merely comprehensive groupishness begin to appear to them. They will not so much imitate full patterns of the Old Individualism, and certainly they will not abandon the basic imagined collectivism, as they will adapt and trim and cut old cloth to new use; not hand-me-downs, but patchwork costume, so that new quasi-individualisms will emerge from the strongest needs produced by overindulged groupishness. Look first, for harbingers, to the styles of reform adopted or sewn together by the deepest damaged hippies and half-assed revolutionaries when those of them who still can, do finally make the all-out effort to save themselves.

So we veterans in the regiments of irrelevance should not attempt to sell whole uniforms, but only choice bits of attractive haberdashery. And, sadly, no business at all . . . until winter comes.

So this is the box: Affluence and Consumerism and Success and All That will not do it for us—only doing for each other, *enacting off-camera realizations of relation that are expressive even if substantially less than ultimate,* will do it. The frontier of need is now personal relation: no wonder we are all so overwhelmed with despair —and the even more desperate (and costly) avoidance of despair. So much so that neurosis is no longer even interesting: have you noticed that no one talks much about it anymore? That was private; now we have public psychosis to keep us busy. (Do you remember when identity-crisis replaced anxiety-state as the name for after-midnight phone calls?)

As we all become increasingly powerless, not because of Vietnam or any such thing, but because we can neither do with nor without each other, in newer and more important ways—again, because affluence and success are no longer a substitute for as much of life as once we dreamed—each of us feels, against this encroaching powerlessness, that *he* particularly is entitled to just a little bit more command, before he signs on to deal-making reasonableness (the only form of our salvation). Because it's so hard for him; because he took such a beating in the past; because he is, comparatively, so good and tried so hard; and even because he recognized just this newness of our condition—a sure sign of superiority. Thus the terrible urgency of our need to cooperate keeps us from doing so except on brutal levels of dominance/submission: *retrieved primitivism.* That is why

Fashion has been chosen as temporary mediating czar in the People Business.

Our powerlessness thus elevates the problem of power—of will, command, insistence. This problem of power is *not* one of physical force, and should not be reduced to that. Modern power most particularly involves deception (especially self-deception: finally self-deception). *We march to our doom in an endless parade of mutually self-deceptive willfulness.* So now, to save ourselves, we must negotiate deals. Which requires that we be honest on occasion even about necessary falsehoods—that is, develop taste and sophistication and even apply some other human qualities to the choice and use of falsehoods. That is the new touchstone, as formerly the most difficult and heroic act was for the physically weaker person to say, to the face of the physically stronger one, that the latter prevailed in this or that because of his *physical* strength, not for any superior quality of what he said. *That* poetic honesty (on choice occasions). We must put an end to the extension-and-celebration of our worst qualities.

To hell with the Big Stuff like love and success and winning and losing: let's make existential deals. There is no other way out of this post-affluence mess. All else is survival only: and deeper and deeper and ever more hopeless fantasies of life, instead of the real thing. And if this current over-full trend continues unchecked, finally there will be, both in personal and public life, only two kinds of people—those who write scripts for group living, and those who act roles in scripts they never wrote. (And the scripts will all be culled mostly from B-movies.)

Now, finally, I would like to sum up this autobiographical/intergenerational effort to review my intellectual career as I have attempted it in this book.

The final truth of my feeling about the New Youth is this: *If* I believed in the searching validity of their sexuality in and for this weird modern environment we gave them, I would accept acres and acres of *their* nonsense and *my* disgust and *our* fear-for-their-future, and, in general, the unspeakable ineptitude of this damned generational passage. But I don't see or imagine it. I don't think they are interested in sex, as Lawrence, for instance, taught my generation to try to believe in it. I think they are interested in fun-and-games and instant individuality, and sex has something to do with that—but they just haven't told us what, even if they do in fact have some notion of it for themselves.

If they are modern Romantics and have chosen animal vitality and what Lawrence called the blood-connection, rejecting the preservation of dying forms as in the quiet classicism of an Eliot, then they must be measured and judged against our greatest such spirit—Lawrence himself. Lawrence was anti-intellectual, too; he urged the English miners to wear red pants on weekends; he searched the world over for primitivisms with which to deny the forms of industrial society: he even wore a beard. Sex, however, was for him the center of a whole animal life continuous with it: a private sacrament. But the New Youth merge male and female styles, whereas Lawrence detested even the effort to merge the beyond-sex personal individualities of a man and a woman. He would not have been able to tolerate their sloppy togetherness, and might well have seen them as an indiscriminate bunch of Miriams*—both male and female, with trust funds. No, I cannot take them as even approaching Lawrence's ideal of animal rebirth. If they are Lawrence's heirs, it is clear to me that the estate is much depleted by modern taxes on Romanticism.

The best I see in them sexually is that they are trying frantically to get rid of their hatred of parent-adults enough to free themselves to maybe try to begin to like each other in a grown-up way. If this is their project, they are not yet doing very well with it. In my day, youth was a substitute for chemicals and other special arrangements; not so, for them. I accuse them of not believing in their own youthful vitality enough to use it well. And I deny my supposed responsibility for this silliness of theirs. Even being young—and up-to-here with Orange Juice—they chose nastiness and hostility and disruption. And they did not discuss this with me adequately before making their decision. That was a jerk-middlebrow thing to do. They remind me of a jerk-middlebrow from my day—very commercial, very successful—Philip Wylie. Wylie was all by himself, genuinely unique, in pre-Sixties popular culture. He was a fabulous parody of the intellectual writing for a mass audience. No question, he broke paths: both Vance Packard and Joe Pyne owe him a generational debt. He may have been the first to demonstrate to the Bosses the

* The gluey ingénue of Sons and Lovers, his first love along the route of bursting free of mother love and the overwhelming weight of the family.

commercial utility of wild hostility and contempt and other rampant negativism. Oh, if we had only known then how far we could go with the simple expedient of dramatizing our worst faults—that is, *"selling out" for and with something much more reprehensible than money*.

Like most Americans who don't quite manage to dig the American situation, these kids—with more resource at their disposal than any previous generation in this country or anywhere else—see and imagine no farther than instant idealism; and then, very quickly upon discouragement, they indulge panty-raid Luddite rebellion. I don't think they are serious—*not about enough of anything*. And this seems true to me whether or not my generation "created" them (by inadvertence).

I will finally put it this way: Revolutions and other historic mutations are no golden road to anywhere. The loss of form is decisive. If not enough form survives to continue the probability of communication among the survivors, then the relation among survivors will be beneath language, therefore unbearably exploitative—most likely even worse than before. *Free the slaves. (But beware of freed slaves.)* Our basic human problems must be solved *within* the confines of human communication—one-shot departures outside these confines are delusional shots-in-the-dark.

Free the slaves. (But beware of freed slaves.) This prescription applies to women, Negroes, the poor generally, and our own sons—the New Youth. This is the burden of the twenty-first century. Freed slaves lack identity, and are infinitely dangerous thereby—to themselves and others. Freed slaves know only slaves and masters, and that they were once the one and now ought to be the other. That is not enough with which to become truly human. The further knowledge they need they in fact regularly refuse when it is offered by former masters (or those identified as such); and they are not yet able to generate it for themselves. *This is the burden of the twenty-first century*.

A slave conceives the master as all-powerful. He therefore conceives freedom as an endowment of all necessary power—exactly that power which made and kept him a slave. He thus misconceives freedom, with disastrous consequences for everyone. This is the burden of affluence that may truly emancipate: *therefore, of the twenty-first century*.

Let these New Ones of ours go to school with the desperate youth of the Communist world. *There* lies the realest struggle of youth against authoritarianism—where the rebels do not have to divert their energies by imagining adequately monstrous tyrannies. These simply exist. As also material deprivation. But not for us. *That* is the American problem. Which our most advantaged American youth refuse to recognize—*even* to recognize. When the youth of the Eastern world are forced to deal with our kind of advantage, they are apt to do better with it: They will understand relevant authority, rather than merely attacking any existing authority. By the time they get rich, they may well know more—maybe even enough.

I am afraid that they will get to the far side of that big moon before we do.

It's been fun, and I could go on forever—because I would like to write a full autobiography one day about this intellectual American life of mine, but "time waits for no publisher/The years print a book of their own."

Just a final note on the song "Bill Bailey, Won't You Please Come Home?" According to George Avakian, writing album copy for a Turk Murphy collection—recorded, incidentally, at the home of Leslie Farber—the song did not become famous only as a Clayton, Jackson & Durante winner in vaudeville or because it was played by Kid Ory. Shortly after its initial popularity in this country, it was sung by a choir of angels in a 1905 one-act play by George Bernard Shaw called *Passion, Poison and Petrifaction, or The Fatal Gazogene.** Hughie Cannon wrote the song in 1902 supposedly "to avenge the mistreatment of a real-life William Bailey, a Negro laborer whose wife gave him an unholy pushing-around." It seems the real Bill Bailey never shook loose.

---

* THE LADY: Strange! As I sat there methought I heard angels singing, Oh, won't you come home, Bill Bailey? Why should angels call me Bill Bailey? My name is Magnesia Fitztollemache.

INDEX